Children's Fiction Series,
1850–1950

Children's Fiction Series

Series

A Bibliography, 1850–1950

by PHILIP H. YOUNG

McFarland & Company, Inc., Publishers
Jefferson, North Carolina, and London

British Library Cataloguing-in-Publication data are available

Library of Congress Cataloguing-in-Publication Data

Young, Philip H., 1953–
     Children's fiction series : a bibliography, 1850-1950 / by Phillip
H. Young
          p.   cm.
     Includes bibliographical references and index.
     ISBN 0-7864-0321-7 (library binding : 50# alkaline paper) ∞
     1. Children's stories, American — Bibliography.   2. Children's
literature in series — Bibliography.   3. American fiction —19th
century — Bibliography.   4. American fiction — 20th century —
Bibliography.   I. Title.
Z1232.Y68   1997
[PS374.C454]
016.813008'09282 — dc21   96-45311
                                                                CIP

Manufactured in the United States of America

McFarland & Company, Inc., Publishers
  Box 611, Jefferson, North Carolina 28640

To my dear wife, Nancy

CONTENTS

PREFACE

I suppose it is not surprising that a librarian by profession and a book collector by avocation would become interested in organizing the myriad series of old children's books. It seems that every antique or used book shop that I visit has at least a sampling of this genre, which became popular before the turn of the century and flourished through the pretelevision age when children read books for entertainment. Unfortunately, these popular series have been purposely overlooked by students of juvenile literature and have received only some notice from social historians. However, these fiction series provide important insights about American popular culture before, during, and after the world wars, a significant turning point in American history.

I have prepared this bibliography as a resource for book collectors and dealers, librarians, and researchers. A variety of methods were used to obtain the bibliographical information, including searching used book and antique stores, accessing electronic databases (especially the Online Computer Library Center), researching the printed National Union Catalog, and consulting other bibliographies. Despite much cross-checking, I have no doubt that errors have crept into this work, which is so data intensive, and I also am sure that I have missed some series which should have been included. I am pleased, however, to present the most comprehensive listing available for these books.

For this bibliography I have concentrated on series published in America from the 1890s to the 1950s, sometimes accepting titles outside this scope if part of the series fits into it.

Researching the children's fiction series is not a simple task. Series conceived as such and published in sequence without title variations and not used as parts of other series were few and far between. Frequently, books from a series were republished under variant titles or combined with ones from other series to create new series. Many of the early series grew out of so-called "nickel" or "dime" novels. These series, such as "Log Cabin Library" and "New York Five Cent Library" often ran into the several hundreds of titles, but because they were not full-length books I have omitted them from this bibliography. Some series such as the "Peerless Series" were originally published in the earlier format but made a successful transmigration to the book format.

Sometimes, when a lone novel was very successful, the author would write sequels continuing characters, settings, etc., such as Louisa May Alcott's *Little Women*, which was followed by other titles using the same characters. I have included some of these "de facto" series, even though they were never given a true series name. Many authors, such as James Otis Kaler, Oliver Optic and Horatio Alger, were quite prolific, and it is very difficult to tell which books belong to a series and which were meant to be independent novels.

I have discovered references to a number of series for which I could only find one title. Although it is possible that a publisher might have launched a new series which was immediately cancelled after the first title flopped, I think it more likely that other titles simply remain undiscovered.

Series titles are listed alphabetically except that initial articles are omitted for ease of alphabetization. Names as series titles are not inverted, e.g. "Ruth Fielding" will be found under "R" not "F." I have omitted the words "series" or "books" except where they do not seem redundant. Subtitles are separated from titles by semicolons and, if present, the conjoining "or" is set off by a comma. In most entries herein that lack subtitles, the books were published without them, but some of these instances result from my inability to identify a subtitle. Book titles within each series are given in chronological order of initial publication date. Wherever known I have used the original numbers for titles in a series, but frequently they are unavailable.

Dates of publication are given where known and are intended to represent the first appearance of each title in the series. Publishers given are also those of the original appearance of the books in the series; where more than one is listed it appears to be a case of virtually joint publication by a second firm. It should be noted that publication dates and details of publishing house origins are frequently difficult to discover and should not be considered absolute.

Multiple series with the same title are distinguished using Roman numerals, e.g. "Boy Scouts I," "Boy Scouts II." In most of these cases, the sequence of presentation in this work is arbitrary and has no significance, but when the duplicate names are numerous I have ordered them alphabetically by author. Some series have variations in name; in such cases I have selected one name and used a "see" reference from the variants. Occasionally, books have appeared in several different series. Where I have observed such situations I have used "see also" references to alert the reader to the duplications.

For assistance in bringing this project to fruition I acknowledge primarily the tolerance of my dear wife Nancy who, although threats have been uttered, has never really prevented me from perusing just one more antique shop or picking up just one more old book. I also appreciate the work done by my secretary, Lynn Berry, who waded through my voluminous notebook of handwritten lists to enter a first draft into the computer.

RESOURCES

Billman, Carol. *The Secret of the Stratemeyer Syndicate.* New York: Ungar Publishing, 1986.

Deane, Paul. *Mirrors of American Culture; Children's Fiction in the Twentieth Century.* Metuchen, N.J.: Scarecrow Press, 1991.

Ditky, Alan S. *The American Boy's Book Series Bibliography 1895–1935.* San Bernardino, CA: The Borgo Press, 1984.

Drew, Bernard A. *Heroines; A Bibliography of Women Series Characters in Mystery, Espionage, Action, Science Fiction, Fantasy, Horror, Western, Romance and Juvenile Novels.* New York: Garland Publishing, 1989.

_____. *Western Series and Sequels; A Reference Guide.* New York: Garland Publishing, 1986.

Girls Series Books; A Checklist of Hardback Books Published 1900–1975. Minneapolis: University of Minnesota Libraries, Children's Literature Research Collections, 1978.

Hudson, Harry K. *A Bibliography of Hard-Cover Boy's Books.* Rev. ed. Tampa: Data Print, 1977.

Husband, Janet. *Sequels; An Annotated Guide to Novels in Series; An Annotated Checklist of Stratemeyer and Stratemeyer Syndicate Publications.* Chicago: American Library Association, 1982.

Johnson, Deidre. *Stratemeyer Pseudonyms and Series Books.* Westport, Conn.: Greenwood Press, 1982.

Jones, Dolores Blythe. *An "Oliver Optic" Checklist; An Annotated Catalog-Index to the Series, Nonseries Stories, and Magazine Publications of William Taylor Adams.* (Bibliographies and Indexes in American Literature, 4.) Westport, Conn.: Greenwood Press, 1985.

_____. *Bibliography of the Little Golden Books.* New York: Greenwood Press, 1987.

Kensinger, Faye Riter. *Children of the Series and How They Grew; or, A Century of Heroines and Heroes, Romantic, Comic, Moral.* Bowling Green, Ohio: Bowling Green State University Popular Press, 1987.

Roman, Susan. *Sequences; An Annotated Guide to Children's Fiction in Series.* Chicago: American Library Association, 1985.

Rosenberg, Judith K. *Young People's Books in Series; Fiction and Non-Fiction, 1975–1991.* Englewood, Colo.: Libraries Unlimited, 1992.

_____. *Young People's Literature in Series: Fiction; An Annotated Bibliographical Guide.* Littleton, Colo.: Libraries Unlimited, 1972.

_____. *Young People's Literature in Series; Fiction, Non-Fiction and Publishers' Series 1973-1975.* Littleton, Colo.: Libraries Unlimited, 1977.

_____, and Kenyon C. Rosenberg. *Young People's Literature in Series: Publisher's and Non-Fiction Series; An Annotated Bibliographical Guide.* Littleton, Colo.: Libraries Unlimited, 1973.

Smith, Dora. *Fifty Years of Children's Books 1910–1960.* National Council of Teachers of English, 1963.

INTRODUCTION

Prior to the mid-nineteenth century, books for children were mostly religious in nature or moral tracts and stories, but during the second half of the century fiction primarily for children's entertainment began to be written and published. This genre burgeoned rapidly in softbound magazines, "dime novels" and the hardback book format. Often, stories which originally appeared in the popular children's magazines were later published as hardback books, and many prolific writers of juvenile literature made this transition. Just as stories were serialized in children's magazines, books based on continuing characters began to be issued as named series. Topics of these series ranged from home and family to adventure, travel, historical fiction, and science fiction. Publishers quickly realized the promotional appeal of following up a "hit" book with other books using the same characters or concepts to make a series. Other series were created by grouping unrelated titles around a general theme.

Juvenile fiction series were becoming very popular by the turn of the century and continued to grow in volume and popularity through the Second World War. Children were portrayed as participants in the glorious military victories that propelled the United States into its role of world leadership. The series played an important role as entertainment for children and as a psychological tool for expanding their imagination beyond their limited local environment. In this function they were challenged only by radio shows which, though limited in number, appealed to similar entertainment interest. By mid-century, however, a new and all-pervasive medium called television appeared, significantly changing the lives of the "baby boom" children. Their free time became increasingly devoted to watching entertainment on the small screen rather than reading, a trend which continues today. Children's fiction in series continued to be produced after 1950 (and to today), but its heyday was over. Although there were series before and after, the *floruit* of this phenomenon can be seen to have been in the decades before and after 1900.

Probably the first children's series were the Rollo books, which were originally written in the 1830s. By the end of the century, several publishers were producing juvenile series and beginning to realize the profit potential in these works written for entertainment and not moral exhortation. Current events of political and technological interest were incorporated into titles, even if the stories themselves often were rather generalized. These themes appealed to the target audience of readers eight to twelve years old, a time when children are physical, adventurous, independent, imaginative, and engaged in building groups (Deane). The characters of the series are "exaggerated types, not perfect but indisputedly extraordinary adolescents ... skilled at everything that comes their way, be the challenge a matter of commerce, science, the arts, or sports" (Billman, p.29).

The books were printed in a typeface and written in a style to make them easily and quickly readable, and they included artwork (especially dust-jackets and frontispieces) designed to pique a child's interest. Authors focussed on plot, not characterization or description. For example, publishers' intentions are clearly evident in the following advertising description of the "Airship Boys Series":

> Fascinating stories of that wonderful region where imagination and reality so nearly meet. There is no more interesting field for stories for wide-awake boys. Mr. Sayler combines a knowledge that makes these books correct in all airship details. Full of adventure without being sensational. The make-up of these books is strictly up-to-date and fetching. The covers are emblematic, and the jackets are showy and in colors. The illustrations are full of dash and vim.

A similar notice for the "Girl Aviators Series" helps identify the intended audience: "Just the type of books that delight and fascinate the wide awake girls of the present day who are between the ages of eight and fourteen years."

The general subjects or themes of the children's fiction series which tie the titles together can be divided into twelve types:

1. **Fictional personalities, single or groups** (e.g., "The Adele Doring Series"; "The Adventure Boys Series"; "Aunt Jane's Nieces Series")

2. **Mysteries** (e.g., "Bob Dexter Mystery Series"; "Jerry Todd Series"; "Kenneth Carlisle Detective Stories")

3. **Technological novelties** (e.g., "The Aeroplane Boys Series"; "The Motion Picture Boys Series"; "The Tom Swift Series")

4. **Education institutions** (e.g., "The Boys of Columbia High Series"; "Andover Series"; "Co-Ed Series")

5. **Moral Correctness, self-improvement, setting affairs right** (e.g., The Alger Series"; "The Bound to Succeed Series"; "The Go-Ahead Series")

6. **Historical, events or personalities** (e.g., "The Buffalo Bill Series"; "The Civil War Series"; "The Conquest of the United States Series")

7. **Exotic location adventure** (e.g., "Bomba the Jungle Boy Series"; "The Camp and Trail Series"; "The Deep Sea Series")

8. **Sports** (e.g., "The Baseball Joe Series"; "The Boys Big Game Series"; "Champion Sports Series")

9. **Military** (e.g., "The Army Boys Series"; "The Battleship Boys Series"; "The Big War Series")

10. **Nursery Rhymes, Fairy Tales, Fables** (e.g., "Aunt Mavor's Nursery Rhymes Series"; "The Christmas Stocking Series"; "Little Folk's Series")

11. **Publisher's Collections** (e.g., "Appleton's Boys Library"; "Boy's Prize Library"; "The Henty Series")

12. **Topical** (e.g., "Little Cousin Series"; "Bedtime Stories"; "Make Believe Stories")

Of course, frequently series fall under more than one type, e.g. ,"The Beverly Gray College Mystery Series"; "The Boy Scouts of the Air Series"; or "The College Sports Series."

Adventure, daring, and growing up are the real subjects of these books, and characterization and realistic plot are secondary. Frequently, the action takes place in exotic locations, such as jungles, rivers, or mountains. An important subset of these action/adventure novels are ones with a military theme, reflecting the historical realities of the Spanish-American War and two world wars but injecting unrealistic juvenile participation into their action. The earlier themes of family, friends, and innocent fun turned to patriotism and military participation during these war years. Another type of juvenile series novel focussed not so much on action and adventure but on the central characters themselves. Often, the name of the central character was also the actual or *de facto* series title, such as the Honey Bunch, Nancy Drew, and Pee-Wee Harris series. Sometimes, these personality oriented series were meant to be read in sequence as the character grew up or otherwise developed, but frequently the character did not evolve and the reading sequence was unimportant. Several series were simply collections of classic fables and fairy tales or nursery rhymes with no pretense to originality, and some were simply collections of previously successful children's literature.

More often than not the adventure books were geared towards boys and the personality books towards girls, although there are many exceptions to this broad generalization, e.g. "The Motor Maids," "The Outdoor Girls," and "The Airplane Girls." Most of the juvenile series books were clearly directed to one sex or the other, either overtly in the series title (e.g., The Mountain Boys, The Campfire Girls) or less obviously by the name of the central character (e.g., Dave Hamilton, Molly Brown). Authors' names, whether real or pseudonym, reinforced this trend so that books directed to boys were written by male authors and ones for girls by female authors. This tendency is not surprising, given the juvenile audience and children's basic tendency to stick together with members of their own sex. It also reflects the guiltless, sex-role typing which was a typical aspect of American culture until recently.

Often, the juvenile series books were overtly aimed at self-improvement for their readers. Qualities such as "pluck," "winning," "making good," etc., appear frequently in titles, and books were advertised for readers who are "heads up" and "aware." Of course, the epitome of this attitude is exemplified in the well-known Horatio Alger books and similar stories in which the only series linkage of one to one another is the general theme of pulling oneself up by the bootstraps. Other titles deal with honor and finding the proper level or "place" in society. The overt nature of these messages seems somehow quaint and far away today!

It is interesting to observe the subtle advertising intent in the wording of titles and in the books' settings for the purpose of piquing the interest of potential readers. Words such as "secret," "treasure," "adventure" and "mystery" occur frequently and have obvious allure to children. Many other words in the book titles and series titles were carefully chosen for their appeal to their young audience. Several series used familial terms, such as "aunt" or "uncle," and many series had in their titles the terms "boys," "girls" or "young." A word that frequently appears in book titles is "afloat," water typically being especially alluring to young children. Often, the titles used a present tense verb or a present participle to reinforce a potential reader's feeling of "being there" during the action, as in "The Corner House Girls Facing the World," "Winning the Merit Badge," and "Mary Louise Stands the Test." There is a clear seductiveness for children in the series settings and themes, which focus on excitement, fun, and intrigue such as driving cars or motorcycles, camping outdoors with friends, flying early airplanes, and using personal skills to rescue someone in trouble or otherwise to "save the day." The popularity of scouting series is notable as evidenced by the great numbers of Boy Scout, Girl Scout, and Campfire Girls series.

If the popular fiction series were extremely successful in appealing to children, they were not with literary critics. Librarians and teachers spoke out vehemently against the series books, criticizing their cheapness, mediocrity of style, crude language, poor grammar, impossible plots, and especially the fact that their popularity kept children from reading "good" books. The popular series caused a special dilemma for librarians who were torn between the cultural goal of uplifting children and providing anything children wanted. One librarian wondered: "Shall the libraries resist the flood and stand for a better and purer literature and art for children, or shall they meet the demands of the people by gratifying a low and lowering taste?" (*Library Journal*, Dec. 1905). As recently as 1972, a publication (Rosenberg) noted: "Because of this bibliography's proposed use as a book selection aid, series of consistently low quality have been omitted. Best-known of these are the Hardy Boys, Tom Swift, Nancy Drew, Cherry Ames, the Bobbsey Twins, the Oz books, and the Five Little Peppers." However, although snubbed by contemporary critics and even today by historians of children's literature, these series attained the status of popular classics in their day and beyond. Tom Swift, Nancy Drew, the Hardy Boys, and other heroes of the series became household names. Some of the characters whose origin was in this genre survived into the television medium, and some of their books continue as reprints or foundations for modern book series.

For today's book collector or librarian the early juvenile novels in series pose interesting challenges to discover or acquire all the published books in the series. Typically, the titles of the juvenile series books followed a standard formula: book title including the series name; the word "or"; and a subtitle with extra wording about the content to entice the reader/buyer, for example, *The Moving Picture Girls Under the Palms; or, Lost in the Wilds of Florida*. Frequently, the fact that a book belonged to a series is evident only from its title or from advertising notes within the book itself. A title like *The Motor Boys Afloat* implies other stories about "The Motor Boys," but the existence of a series is not immediately apparent from a title like *Dick Hamilton's Airship* which would seem to be an independent novel. The book sleuth frequently must search for publishers' clues indicating the existence of other books in a series. Often, after the author's name on the title page there are identifying credits listing other books clearly in the same series. Sometimes, other whole series by him/her also become apparent in these credits. Publishers frequently used the last pages of popular books to advertise other books in the same series and other series also published by them. Sometimes, the series name was printed on the book's cover or spine and at the top of the title page, or as a running header or footer throughout the book.

The convoluted publication histories of many of these juvenile novel series frequently impede collectors and researchers. Many of these books were published simultaneously by different firms and, then, reprinted from time to time depending on their popularity. Sometimes, advance notices advertised titles which, for various reasons, did not ever get published. Occasionally, a book was used in two different series, usually with a variant or completely altered title. Books in a series normally were given decorated bindings and dustjackets of a uniform style so that they formed a set visually, but sometimes variant bindings or dustjackets broke the visual symmetry of a true series. In several cases, such as the Nancy Drew or Tom Swift books, older series were resurrected and begun again at a much later date, bearing only tangential relationships to the earlier ones. Successful series often spawned new ones on related themes. The relationship could be topical, such as "The Motorcycle Boys" being followed by "The Motorcycle Girls," or a continuation of a character, such as Larry Dexter in "The Great Newspaper Series," "The Young Reporter Series," "The Grammar School Boys," and "High School Boys" or the several series based on the character Grace Harlowe.

Tracking authorship of the juvenile series novels can be tricky. Frequently, the stated name on the title page is a pseudonym for one or, occasionally, several real people. This is the case especially in series published by the so-called Stratemeyer Syndicate, which produced many books in this genre with an almost assembly-line efficiency. Some series were authored by two or more people during the life of the series. In some cases, such as "The Campfire Girls" and "The Boy Scouts," there are actually several series with the same names which can only be distinguished by variant authors or publishers.

Despite certain difficulties of collecting and studying these series novels, working with them is extremely rewarding, and their common presence in antique and used book shops even today underscores their importance for revealing the popular culture of a bygone era. Although these books are generally ignored in textbook presentations of juvenile literature, which tend to discuss only books of "literary merit," names like the Hardy Boys, the Little Colonel, and the Happy Hollisters, familiar to almost anyone who was a child at the appropriate time, are an important part of the popular culture of their day. Fortunately, more specialized studies have appeared to remedy this situation. An excellent introduction to these sources can be found in chapter two of the 1978 edition of the *Handbook of American Popular Culture,* and an important in-depth study has appeared recently in Paul Deane's *Mirrors of American Culture; Children's Fiction in the Twentieth Century.*

THE BIBLIOGRAPHY

1. ABBEY GIRLS
author: Elsie Oxenham [pseudonym of Elsie Jeanette Dunkerley]
publishers: Collins [1–18, 20, 23–24, 26–30]; Muller [19, 21–22, 25]
1. The Abbey Girls (1920)
2. The Girls of Abbey School (1921)
3. The Abbey Girls Go Back to School (1922)
4. The New Abbey Girls (1923)
5. The Abbey Girls Again (1924)
6. The Abbey Girls in Town (1925)
7. Queen of the Abbey Girls (1926)
8. Jen of the Abbey School (1927)
9. The Abbey Girls Win Through (1928)
10. The Abbey School (1928)
11. The Abbey Girls at Home (1929)
12. The Abbey Girls Play Up (1930)
13. The Abbey Girls on Trial (1931)
14. Schooldays at the Abbey (1938)
15. Secrets of the Abbey (1939)
16. Stowaways in the Abbey (1940)
17. Maid of the Abbey (1943)
18. Two Joans at the Abbey (1945)
19. The Abbey Champion (1946)
20. Robins in the Abbey (1947)
21. A Fiddler for the Abbey (1948)
22. Guardians of the Abbey (1950)
23. Schoolgirl Jen at the Abbey (1950)
24. Selma at the Abbey (1952)
25. Rachel in the Abbey (1952)
26. A Dancer from the Abbey (1953)
27. The Song of the Abbey (1954)
28. Tomboys at the Abbey (1957)
29. Two Queens at the Abbey (1959)
30. Strangers at the Abbey (1963)

2. ACE
author: George Earnest Rochester
illustrator: Stanley Bradshaw
publisher: John Hamilton
1. The Black Squadron (1935)
2. Lynx, V.C. (1936)
3. The Black Hawk (1936)
4. Pirates of the Air (1936)
5. The Despot of the World (1936)
6. The Secret Squadron in Germany

3. ADELE DORING
author: Grace May North [pseudonym of Carol Norton]
publisher: Lothrop, Lee & Shepard
1. Adele Doring of the Sunnyside Club (1919)
2. Adele Doring on a Ranch (1920)
3. Adele Doring at Boarding-School (1921)
4. Adele Doring in Camp (1922)
5. Adele Doring at Vineyard Valley (1923)

4. ADMIRAL'S GRANDDAUGHTER
author: Elizabeth Lincoln Gould
publisher: Penn
1. The Admiral's Granddaughter (1907)
2. The Admiral's Little Housekeeper (1910)
3. The Admiral's Little Secretary (1911)
4. The Admiral's Little Companion (1912)

5. ADVENTURE
authors: Fergus Hume [132]; William Ward [5, 30, 44, 65, 73, 110]; Richard Marsh [129]
publisher: Arthur Westbrook
5. The Passenger from Scotland Yard: A Story of Mystery (1912)
30. Jesse James' Ruse; or, The Mystery of the Two Highwaymen
44. Jeff Clayton's Lost Clue; or, The Mystery of the Wireless Murder (1910)
65. Jeff Clayton's Red Mystery; or, The Nihilist Conspiracy (1910)

11

68. Old Sleuth's Triumph; or, The Great Bronx Mystery (1909)
73. Jeff Clayton's Fatal Shot; or, Solving the Great Chinatown Mystery (1911)
87. The Great River Mystery; or, In the Clutches of a Beautiful Blackmailer (1909)
110. Jeff Clayton at Bay; or, The Mystery of the Great Ruby (1911)
129. The Mystery of the Beetle; or, The House with the Open Window [alternate title: The Beetle, a Mystery] (1912)
132. Secret of the Chinese Jar; or, The Loot of the Summer Palace (1912)
135. The Dagger of Fate; or, The House of Mystery (1912)
192. The Lone House by the Sea; or, The Mystery of the Unknown Man (1908)

6. ADVENTURE AND JUNGLE
author: Oliver Optic [pseudonym of William Taylor Adams]
publisher: M. A. Donohue
1. The Casket of Diamonds

7. ADVENTURE AND MYSTERY [see also BLACK RIDER; BOYS ADVENTURE I; BOYS' MYSTERY; EAGLE LAKE]
authors: Capwell Wyckoff [7, 10 ,22]; Philip Hart [12, 13, 20, 21, 23]; DeWitt Hanes [19]
publisher: Saalfield
7. The Secret of the Armor Room (1930)
10. In the Camp of the Black Rider (1931)
12. The Strange Teepee (1931)
13. The Mystery of Eagle Lake (1931)
19. The Big Opportunity (1934)
20. The Midnight Canyon Mystery (1935)
21. The Mystic Owls in Mystery (1935)
22. The Sea Runners' Cache (1935)
23. The Forgotten Island (1935)

8. ADVENTURE BOYS [alternate title: JEWEL]
author: Ames Thompson [pseudonym of Josephine Chase]
publisher: Cupples & Leon
1. The Adventure Boys and the Valley of Diamonds (1927)
2. The Adventure Boys and the River of Emeralds

3. The Adventure Boys and the Lagoon of Pearls
4. The Adventure Boys and the Temple of Rubies
5. The Adventure Boys and the Island of Sapphires (1929)

9. ADVENTURE CLUB
author: Ralph Henry Barbour
publisher: Dodd, Meade
1. The Adventure Club Afloat (1917)
2. The Adventure Club with the Fleet (1918)

10. ADVENTURE GIRLS
author: Clair Blank
publisher: A. L. Burt
1. The Adventure Girls at Happiness House (1936)
2. The Adventure Girls at K Bar O (1936)
3. The Adventure Girls in the Air (1936)

11. ADVENTUROUS ALLENS
author: Harriet Pyne Grove
publisher: A. L. Burt
1. The Adventurous Allens (1932)
2. The Adventurous Allens Afloat (1932)
3. The Adventurous Allens Find Mystery (1932)
4. The Adventurous Allens Marooned (1932)
5. The Adventurous Allens' Treasure Hunt (1933)

AEROPLANE see BIRD BOYS

12. AEROPLANE BOYS I [see also YANKEE FLYER]
author: Ashton Lamar [pseudonym of Harry Lincoln Sayler]
illustrators: S. H. Riesenberg [1, 3–5, 7]; Joseph Pierre Nuyttens [6]; Norman P. Hall [8]; M. G. Gunn [2]
publisher: Reilly & Britton
1. In the Clouds for Uncle Sam; or, Morey Marshall of the Signal Corps (1910)
2. The Stolen Aeroplane; or, How Bud Wilson Made Good (1910)
3. The Aeroplane Express; or, The Boy Aeronaut's Grit (1910)
4. The Boy Aeronauts' Club; or, Flying for Fun (1910)

5. A Cruise in the Sky; or, The Legend of the Great Pink Pearl (1911)
6. Battling the Bighorn; or, The Aeroplane in the Rockies (1911)
7. When Scout Meets Scout; or, The Aeroplane Spy (1912)
8. On the Edge of the Arctic; or, An Aeroplane in Snowland (1913)

AEROPLANE BOYS II see AVIATOR I

AEROPLANE BOYS III see BIRD BOYS

13. AGENT NINE
author: Graham M. Dean
publisher: Goldsmith
1. Agent Nine Solves His First Big Case; A Story of the Daring Exploits of the "G" Men (1935)
2. Agent Nine and the Jewel Mystery (1935)

14. AIMWELL
author: Walter Aimwell
publishers: Worthington; Gould & Lincoln
1-6. [titles unknown]
7. Jerry; or, The Sailor Boy Ashore (1864)

15. AIR ADVENTURE
author: Hugh McAlister
publisher: Saalfield
1. A Viking of the Sky; A Story of a Boy Who Gained Success in Aeronautics (1930)
2. The Flight of the Silver Ship; Around the World Aboard a Giant Dirigible (1930)

16. AIR COMBAT STORIES
authors: Thompson Burtis [1-4]; Eustace Adams [5-6]; A. Avery [7]
publisher: Grosset & Dunlap
1. Daredevils of the Air (1932)
2. Four Aces
3. Wing to Wing
4. Flying Blackbirds
5. Doomed Demons
6. Wings of the Navy
7. War Wings
8. A Yankee Flyer in the RAF (1941)

17. AIR MAIL
author: Lewis Edwin Theiss
publisher: Wilcox & Follett
1. Piloting the U.S. Air Mail (1927)
2. The Search for the Lost Mail Plane (1928)
3. Trailing the Air Mail Bandit (1929)
4. [title unknown]
5. The Pursuit of the Flying Smugglers (1946)

18. AIR MYSTERY [see also SKY SCOUTS]
author: Van Powell
publisher: Saalfield
1. The Mystery Crash
2. The Haunted Hanger
3. The Vanishing Airliner

19. AIR PILOT
author: Philip Lee Wright
publisher: Barse
1. The East Bound Air Mail; or, Fighting Fog, Storm and Hard Luck (1930)
2. An Air Express Holdup; or, How Pilot George Selkirk Carried Through (1930)
3. The Mail Pilot's Hunch; or, A Crash in Death Valley (1931)

20. AIR SERVICE BOYS
author: Charles Amory Beach [pseudonym of the Stratemeyer Syndicate]
illustrators: Robert Gaston Herbert [1-3]; Clare Angell [4]; Walter S. Rogers [5]; Cress [6]
publishers: George Sully; World
1. Air Service Boys Flying for France; or, The Young Heroes of the Lafayette Escadrille (1918)
2. Air Service Boys Over the Enemy's Lines; or, The German Spy's Secret (1918)
3. Air Service Boys in the Big Battle; or, Silencing the Big Guns (1919)
4. Air Service Boys Over the Rhine; or, Fighting Above the Clouds (1919)
5. Air Service Boys Flying for Victory; or, Bombing the Last German Stronghold (1919)
6. Air Service Boys Over the Atlantic; or, the Longest Flight on Record (1920)

21. AIRPLANE BOYS

authors: Edith Janice Craine; Latharo
  Hoover; John Luther Langworthy
publisher: World Syndicate
  1. Airplane Boys on the Border Line
     (1930)
  2. Airplane Boys; or, The Young Sky
     Pilot's First Air Voyage (1929)
  3. Airplane Boys at Cap Rock (1930)
  4. Airplane Boys Flying to Amy-Ran
     Fastness (1930)
  5. Airplane Boys at Platinum River
     (1931)
  6. Airplane Boys with the Revolutionists
     in Bolivia (1931)
  7. Airplane Boys in the Black Woods
     (1932)
  8. Airplane Boys at Belize (1932)
  9. Airplane Boys and the Phantom Air-
     craft (1930)
  10. Airplane Boys Discover the Secrets of
     Cuzco (1930)
  11. Airplane Boys Flight; or, A
     Hydroplane Roundup

22. AIRPLANE GIRL

author: Harrison Bardwell [pseudonym of
  Edith Janice Craine]
publisher: World Syndicate
1. Roberta's Flying Courage (1930)
2. The Lurtiss Field Mystery (1930)
3. The Airplane Girl and the Mystery of
   Seal Islands (1931)
4. The Airplane Girl and the Mystery
   Ship (1931)

23. AIRSHIP BOYS

authors: Harry Lincoln Sayler; De Lysle F.
  Cass
illustrators: J.O. Smith [2]; S. H. Riesenberg [3–6]; F. R. Harper [1]; Harry
  Kennedy [8]
publisher: Reilly & Britton
1. The Airship Boys; or, The Quest of the
   Aztec Treasure (1909)
2. The Airship Boys Adrift; or, Saved by
   an Aeroplane (1909)
3. The Airship Boys Due North; or, By
   Balloon to the Pole (1910)
4. The Airship Boys in the Barren Lands;
   or, The Secret of the White Eskimos
   (1910)

5. The Airship Boys in Finance; or, The
   Flight of the Flying Cow (1911)
6. The Airship Boys' Ocean Flyer; or,
   New York to London in Twelve Hours
   (1911)
7. The Airship Boys as Detectives; or, On
   Secret Service in Cloudland (1913)
8. The Airship Boys in the Great War; or,
   The Rescue of Bob Russell (1915)
   [The Airship Boys in Africa by
   Turner Cassity, Broadside Press 1970
   The Airship Boys in Africa; A Dra-
   matic Narrative in Twelve Parts by
   Turner Cassity, Hentricks 1984]

24. ALGER

authors: Horatio Alger [1–97, 168–174,
   197]; Oliver Optic [pseudonym of
   William Taylor Adams] [124–167];
   Edward Stratemeyer [98–123]; Roy
   Franklin [175, 178, 181, 184, 187, 189,
   191, 193, 199, 201]; Frederick Gibson
   [188, 194, 200]; Matt Royal [196];
   Donald Grayson [179, 182, 185]; Emerson Baker [202]; Remson Douglas
   [186, 192]; Edward Sylvester Ellis [198];
   Frank H. MacDougal [176, 190]; Allan
   Montgomery [180, 183]; Gale Richards
   [177]
publisher: Street & Smith
  1. Driven from Home; or, Carl Craw-
     ford's Experience (1915)
  2. A Cousin's Conspiracy; or, A Boy's
     Struggle for an Inheritance (1915)
  3. New Newton; or, The Fortunes of a
     New York Bootblack (1915)
  4. Andy Gordon; or, The Fortunes of a
     Young Janitor (1905)
  5. Tony, the Tramp; or, Right Is Might
     (1915)
  6. The Five Hundred Dollar Check
     (1915)
  7. Helping Himself; or, Grant Thorn-
     ton's Ambition (1880)
  8. Making His Way; or, Frank Court-
     ney's Struggle Upward (1915)
  9. Try and Trust; or, Abner Holden's
     Bound Boy (1915)
  10. Only an Irish Boy; or, Andy Burke's
      Fortune (1915)
  11. Jed, the Poorhouse Boy; or, Alone in
      New York (1915)

12. Chester Rand; or, The New Path to Fortune (1915)
13. Grit; or, The Young Boatman of Pine Point (1916)
14. Joe's Luck; or, Always Wide Awake (1916)
15. From Farm Boy to Senator; Being the History of the Boyhood and Manhood of Daniel Webster (1900)
16. The Young Outlaw; or, Adrift in the Streets (1916)
17. Jack Ward; or, The Boy Guardian (1916)
18. Dean Dunham; or, The Waterford Mystery (1891)
19. In a New World; or, Among the Goldfields of Australia (1916)
20. Both Sides of the Continent; or, Mark Stanton (1890)
21. The Store Boy; or, The Fortunes of Ben Barclay (1916)
22. Brave and Bold; or, The Fortunes of Robert Rushton (1916)
23. A New York Boy (1891)
24. Bob Benton, the Young Ranchman of Missouri (1916)
25. The Young Adventurer; or, Tom's Trip Across the Plain (1916)
26. Julius, the Street Boy; or, Out West (1916)
27. Adrift in New York; or, Tom and Florence Braving the World (1916)
28. Tom Brace; or, Who He Was and How He Fared (1901)
29. Struggling Upward; or, Luke Larkin's Luck (1916)
30. The Adventures of a New York Telegraph Boy; or, "Number 91" (1900)
31. Tom Tracy; or, The Trials of a New York Newsboy (1900)
32. The Young Acrobat of the Great North American Circus (1900)
33. Bound to Rise; or, Up the Ladder (1917)
34. Hector's Inheritance; or, The Boys of Smith Institute (1917)
35. Do and Dare; or, A Brave Boy's Fight for Fortune (1917)
36. The Tin Box and What It Contained (1917)
37. Tom the Bootblack; or, A Western Boy's Success (1917)
38. Risen From the Ranks; or, Harry Walton's Success (1917)
39. Shifting for Himself; or, Gilbert Grayson's Fortunes (1917)
40. Wait and Hope; or, A Plucky Boy's Luck (1917)
41. Sam's Chance and How He Improved It (1917)
42. Striving for Fortune; or, Walter Griffith's Trials and Successes (1901)
43. Phil, the Fiddler; or, The Story of a Young Street Musician (1917)
44. Slow and Sure; or, From the Street to the Shop (1917)
45. Walter Sherwood's Probation; or, Cool Head and Warm Heart (1917)
46. The Trials and Triumphs of Mark Mason (1917)
47. The Young Salesman (1917)
48. Andy Grant's Pluck (1917)
49. Facing the World; or, The Haps and Mishaps of Harry Vane (1917)
50. Luke Walton; or, The Chicago Newsboy (1900)
51. Strive and Succeed; or, The Progress of Walter Conrad (1917)
52. From Canal Boy to President; The Boyhood and Manhood of James A. Garfield (1901)
53. The Erie Train Boy (1900)
54. Paul the Peddler; or, The Fortunes of a Young Street Merchant (1900)
55. The Young Miner; or, Tom Nelson Out West (1900)
56. Charlie Codman's Cruise; or, A Young Sailor's Pluck (1918)
57. A Debt of Honor; or, On His Own Merit (1900)
58. The Young Explorer; or, Claiming His Fortune (1918)
59. Ben's Nugget; or, A Triumph of the Right (1918)
60. The Errand Boy; A Story for Boys (1886)
61. Frank and Fearless; or, Won by Pluck (1897)
62. Frank Hunter's Peril; or, A Struggle for the Right (1896)
63. Adrift in the City; or, Won by Grit (1918)
64. Tom Thatcher's Fortune; or, The Secret of a Letter (1888)

65. Tom Turner's Legacy; and How He Secured It (1902)
66. Dan the Newsboy; or, Winning Success (1893)
67. [title unknown]
68. Lester's Luck; or, Won by Courage (1901)
69. [title unknown]
70. Frank's Campaign; or, The Farm and the Camp (1918)
71. Bernard Brook's Adventures; or, Working His Way Upward (1903)
72. Robert Coverdale's Struggles; or, On the Wave of Success (1918)
73. Paul Prescott's Charge; or, On Fortune's Wheel (1910)
74. Mark Manning's Mission; or, Making His Own Fortune (1905)
75. Rupert's Ambition; or, A Struggle for Success (1899)
76. Sink or Swim; or, Pluck Always Succeeds (1918)
77. The Backwoods Boy; or, The Story of Abraham Lincoln (1883)
78. Tom Temple's Career; or, A Struggle for Fame and Fortune (1888)
79. Ben Bruce; or, Only a Bowery Newsboy (1901)
80. The Young Musician; or, Fighting His Way (1919)
81. The Telegraph Boy; or, Making His Way in New York (1919)
82. Work and Win; or, A Hard Earned Reward (1919)
83. The Train Boy; or, Up the Ladder (1919)
84. The Cash Boy (1919)
85. Herbert Carter's Legacy; or, The Inventor's Son (1919)
86. Strong and Steady; or, Paddle Your Own Canoe (1919)
87. Lost at Sea; or, Robert Roscoe's Strange Cruise (1904)
88. From Farm to Fortune; or, Nat Nason's Strange Experience (1905)
89. Young Captain Jack; or The Son of a Soldier (1901)
90. Joe, the Hotel Boy; or, Winning Out by Pluck (1906)
91. Out for Business; or, Robert Frost's Strange Career (1900)
92. Falling in with Fortune; or The Experiences of a Young Secretary (1900)
93. Nelson the Newsboy; or, Afloat in New York (1901)
94. Randy of the River; or, The Adventures of a Young Deckhand (1906)
95. Jerry, the Backwoods Boy; or, The Parkhurst Treasure (1904)
96. Ben Logan's Triumph; or, The Boy of Boxwood Academy (1908)
97. The Young Book Agent; or, Frank Hardy's Road to Success (1906)
98. The Last Cruise of the Spitfire; or, Luke Foster's Strange Voyage (1900)
99. Reuben Stone's Discovery; or, The Young Miller of Torrent Bend (1906)
100. True to Himself; or, Roger Strong's Struggle for Place (1900)
101. Richard Dare's Venture; or, Striking Out for Himself (1899)
102. Oliver Bright's Search; or, The Mystery of a Mine (1899)
103. [title unknown]
104. The Young Auctioneer; or, The Polishing of a Rolling Stone (1903)
105. Bound to Be an Electrician; or, Franklin Bell's Success (1903)
106. Shorthand Tom; or, The Exploits of a Bright Boy (1903)
107. Fighting for His Own; or, The Fortunes of a Young Artist (1903)
108. Joe the Surveyor; or, The Value of a Lost Claim (1903)
109. Larry the Wanderer; or, The Rise of a Nobody (1904)
110. The Young Ranchman; or, Between Boer and Briton (1900)
111. The Young Lumbermen; or, Out for Fortune (1903)
112. The Young Explorers; or, Adventures Above the Arctic Circle (1909)
113. Boys of the Wilderness; or, Down in Old Kentucky (1903)
114. Boys of the Great Northwest; or, Across the Rockies (1904)
115. Boys of the Gold Fields; or, The Nugget Hunters (1906)
116. For His Country; or, The Adventures of Two Chums (1899)
117. Comrades in Peril; or, Afloat on a Battleship (1899)
118. The Young Pearl Hunters; or, In Hawaiian Waters (1899)

119. The Young Bandmaster; or, Against Big Odds (1900)
120. Boys of the Fort; or, True Courage Wins (1901)
121. On Fortune's Trail; or, The Heroes of the Black Hills (1902)
122. Lost in the Land of Ice; or, Under the Northern Lights (1902)
123. Bob, the Photographer; or, Strictly on the Job (1902)
124. Among the Missing; or, The Boy They Could Not Beat (1890)
125. His Own Helper; or, By Sheer Pluck (1913)
126. Honest Kit Dunstable; or, The Boy Who Earned Money (1887)
127. Every Inch a Boy; or, Fighting for a Hold (1884)
128. The Young Pilot; or, His Own Best Protector (1887)
129. Always in Luck; or, Working for a Living (1887)
130. Rich and Humble; or, Life's Best Gift (1925)
131. In School and Out; or, Happy Days (1925)
132. Watch and Wait; or, The Building of a Man (1892)
133. Work and Win; or, The Best Way to Succeed (1893)
134. Hope and Have; or, On His Own Resources (1894)
135. Haste and Waste; or, The Result of Indifference (1894)
136. Royal Tarr's Pluck; or, The Boy Who Fought Fair (1883)
137. The Prisoners of the Cave; or, By Sheer Will Power (1888)
138. Louis Chiswick's Mission; or, Up the Ladder of Success (1883)
139. The Professor's Son; or, Against All Odds (1884)
140. The Young Hermit; or, What Life Gave Him (1888)
141. The Cruise of "The Dandy"; or, Doing His Best (1888)
142. Building Himself Up; or, A Fight for Right (1881)
143. Lyon Hart's Heroism; or, Courage Wins (1883)
144. Three Young Silver Kings; or, In Search of Treasure (1887)

145. Making a Man of Himself; or, His Single-Handed Victory (1884)
146. Striving for His Own; or, Working Toward Success (1865)
147. Through by Daylight; or, King of the Rails (1869)
148. Lightning Express; or, Sure Hand and Keen Eye (1869)
149. On Time; or, Bound to Get There (1869)
150. Switch Off; or, When Danger Threatens (1869)
151. Brake Up; or, A Roving Commission (1870)
152. Bear and Forbear; or, On His Mettle (1870)
153. The "Starry Flag"; or, A Splendid Adventure (1867)
154. Breaking Away; or, Pluck Brings Luck (1867)
155. Seek and Find; or, The Mystery Boy (1867)
156. Freaks of Fortune; or Saved from Himself (1896)
157. Make or Break; or, The Way to Succeed (1896)
158. [title unknown]
159. The Boat Club; or, Good Fellows All (1926)
160. All Aboard; or, A Cruise for Fun (1926)
161. Now or Never; or, The Reward of Friendship (1925)
162. Try Again; or, The Boy Who Did Right (1926)
163. Poor and Proud; or, Something to Live For (1899)
164. Little by Little; or, When Success Beckons (1888)
165. The Sailor Boy; or, On Fortune's Trail (1865)
166. The Yankee Middy; or, True to His Colors (1865)
167. Brave Old Salt; or, The Boy They Could Not Down (1894)
168. Luck and Pluck; or, John Oakley's Inheritance (1926)
169. Ragged Dick; or, Street Life in New York (1926)
170. Fame and Fortune; or, The Progress of Richard Hunter (1926)

171. Mark, the Match Boy; or, Richard Hunter's Ward (1926)
172. Rough and Ready; or, Life Among the New York Newsboys (1869)
173. Ben, the Luggage Boy; or, Among the Wharves (1926)
174. Rufus and Rose; or, The Fortunes of Rough and Ready (1926)
175. Fighting for Fortune; or, Making a Place for Himself (1909)
176. The Young Steelworker; or, Up the Ladder (1896)
177. The Go-Ahead Boys; or, Out for Fun (1904)
178. For the Right; or, Winning Life's Battles (1909)
179. The Motor Cycle Boys; or, Full Speed Ahead (1909)
180. The Wall Street Boy; or, High Finance (1911)
181. Stemming the Tide; or, The Making of a Man (1909)
182. On High Gear; or, The Motor Boys on Top (1909)
183. A Wall Street Fortune; or, A Fight for Right (1911)
184. Winning by Courage; or, Never Say Fail (1910)
185. From Auto to Airship; or, Among the Clouds (1909)
186. Camp and Canoe; or, The Way to Succeed (1911)
187. Winning Against Odds; or, On His Own (1910)
188. The Luck of Vance Sevier; or, Rewarded by Fate (1912)
189. The Island Castaway; or, A Plucky Flight (1911)
190. The Boy Marvel; or, The Way to Success (1913)
191. A Boy with a Purpose; or, Climbing Upward (1911)
192. The River Fugitives; or, The Boys Who Played Fair (1911)
193. Out for a Fortune; or, By Sheer Merit (1911)
194. The Boy Horse Owner; or, On His Own (1913)
195. [title unknown]
196. Paul Hassard's Peril; or, Out of the Jaws of Death (1908)
197. His Own Master; or, Adrift on Life's Tide (1910)
198. When Courage Wins; or, On Top of the World (1915)
199. Bound to Get There; or, A Boy Who Could Not Be Downed (1910)
200. Who Was Milton Marr?; or, Solving a Life's Mystery (1912)
201. The Lost Mine; or, A Perilous Treasure Hunt (1911)
202. Larry Borden's Redemption; or, The Boy Who Made Good (1913)
[numbers unknown:
Jacob Marlowe's Secret (1899)
Mark Mason's Victory; or, The Trials and Triumphs of a Telegraph Boy (1900)]

25. ALGER SERIES FOR BOYS [see also ALGER]

authors: James Franklin Fitts; Horatio Alger, Jr.
publishers: A. L. Burt; M. A. Donohue
[only some of the following are the correct series numbers]

1. Captain Kidd's Gold; the True Story of an Adventurous Sailor Boy (1888)
2. Andy Gordon; or, The Fortunes of a Young Janitor (1900)
3. Making His Way; or, Frank Courtney's Struggle Upward (1900)
4. The Young Salesman (1875)
5. Tom the Bootblack; or, A Western Boy's Success (1880)
6. The Island Treasure; or, Harry Darrel's Fortunes (1888)
7. Bound to Rise; or, Up the Ladder (1920)
8. Brave and Bold (1920)
9. Walter Sherwood's Probation; or, Cool Head and Warm Heart (1909)
10. Five Hundred Dollars (1890)
11. The Young Outlaw; or, Adrift in the Streets (1900)
12. Strive and Succeed; or, The Progress of Walter Conrad (1912)
13. The Telegraph Boy; or, Making His Way in New York (1909)
14. Julius, the Street Boy; or, Out West (1900)
15. Sam's Chance; or, How He Improved It (1913)

16. Facing the World; or, The Haps and Mishaps of Harry Vane (1894)
17. Herbert Carter's Legacy; or, The Inventor's Son (1899)
18. Wait and Hope; or, A Plucky Boy's Luck (1899)
19. Grit; or, The Young Boatman of Pine Point (1900)
20. Jack's Ward; or, The Boy Guardian (1910)
21. The Young Miner; or, Tom Nelson Out West (1910)
22. Frank's Campaign; or, The Farm and the Camp (1890)
23. Try and Trust; or Abner Holden's Bound Boy (1890)
24. Sink or Swim; or, Harry Raymond's Resolve (1900)
25. Tony the Tramp; or, Right Is Might (1910)
26. The Store Boy; or, The Fortune of Ben Barclay (1899)
27. Paul Prescott's Charge; A Story for Boys (1908)
28. Helping Himself (1905)
29. Only an Irish Boy; or, Andy Burke's Fortunes (1900)
30. A Cousin's Conspiracy; A Boy's Struggle for an Inheritance (1907)
31. Hector's Inheritance; or, The Boys of Smith Institute (1900)
32. Strong and Steady (1900)
33. Wait and Hope (1900)
34. Joe's Luck (1900)
35. In a New World; or, Among the Gold Fields of Australia (1900)
36. Shifting for Himself (1900)
37. Helen Ford (1866)
38. Slow and Sure; or, From the Street to the Shop (1900)
39. Frank Fowler, the Cash Boy (1887)
40. Strive and Succeed (1900)
41. Brave and Bold; or, The Fortunes of Robert Rushton (1900)
42. The Last Cruise of the Spitfire; or, Luke Foster's Strange Voyage (1894)
43. Shifting for Himself; or, Gilbert Greyson's Fortune (1899)
44. Helping Himself (1900)
45. Chester Rand; or, The New Path to Fortune (1899)

46. Struggling Upward; or, Luke Larkin's Luck (1900)
47. The Young Musician; or, Fighting His Way (1900)
48. The Young Adventurer (1912)
49. The Young Explorer; or, Claiming His Fortune (1900)
50. The Young Acrobat (1900)
51. Risen from the Ranks; or, Harry Walton's Success (1899)
52. Mark Mason; His Trials and Triumphs (1900)
53. Bob Burton, the Young Ranchman of Missouri (1900)
[there are probably quite a few more titles unknown here]

26. ALL ABOUT
author: [none]
publisher: Cupples & Leon
1. All About the Small Red Hen (1917)
15. All About Kitty Cat (1927)

27. ALL AMERICAN SPORTS [also called COLLEGE SPORTS SERIES]
author: Harold Sherman
publisher: Gold
1. Interference (1929)
2. It's a Pass
3. Over the Line
4. Under the Basket
5. Down the Ice
6. Strike Him Out
7. The Tennis Terror
8. Captain of the Eleven

28. ALL-OVER-THE-WORLD
author: Oliver Optic [pseudonym of William Taylor Adams]
publisher: Lee & Shepard
series 1: 1. A Missing Million; or, The Adventures of Louis Belgrave (1891)
2. [title unknown]
3. A Young Knight-Errant; or, Cruising in the West Indies (1893)
series 2: 1. [title unknown]
2. The Young Navigators; or, The Foreign Cruise of The Maud (1893)

3. Up and Down the Nile; or,
   Young Adventurers in
   Africa (1894)

series 3: 1. Across India; or, Live Boys in
   the Far East (1895)
2. Half Round the World; or,
   Among the Uncivilized (1896)
3. [title unknown]
4. Pacific Shores; or, Adventures
   in Eastern Seas (1898)

unknown #: American Boys Afloat; or,
   Cruising in the Orient (1893)
   Strange Sights Abroad; or, A
   Voyage in European
   Water (1893)

29. ALLEN CHAPMAN [*see also* BOYS OF BUSINESS]

author: Allen Chapman [pseudonym of
Edward Stratemeyer]
publisher: Goldsmith
1. Bart Stirling's Road to Success; or, The
   Young Express Agent
2. Working Hard to Win; or, The Adventures of the Two Boy Publishers
3. Bound to Succeed; or, Mail-Order
   Frank's Chances
4. The Young Storekeeper; or, A Business
   Boy's Pluck
5. Nat Borden's Find; or, The Young
   Land Agent (1911)

30. ALMA

author: Louise M. Breitenbach [Louise
Marks Breitenbach Clancy]
publisher: L. C. Page
1. Alma at Hadley Hall (1912)
2. Alma's Sophomore Year (1913)
3. Alma's Junior Year (1914)
4. Alma's Senior Year (1915)

31. ALONG THE COAST

author: Hugh Pendexter
publisher: Small, Maynard
1. The Young Fisherman; or, The King of
   Smugglers' Island (1912)
2. Young Sea-Merchants; or, After Hidden Treasure (1913)

32. ALTEMUS' ANNAPOLIS SERIES [*see also* DAVE DARRIN]

author: Harrie Irving Hancock

publisher: Henry Altemus
1. Dave Darrin's First Year at Annapolis;
   or, Two Plebe Midshipmen at the
   United States Naval Academy (1910)
2. Dave Darrin's Second Year at Annapolis; or, Two Midshipmen as Naval
   Academy "Youngsters" (1911)
3. Dave Darrin's Third Year at Annapolis;
   or, Leaders of the Second Class Midshipmen (1911)
4. Dave Darrin's Fourth Year at Annapolis; or, Headed for Graduation and the
   Big Cruise (1911)

33. ALTEMUS' DAINTY SERIES

authors: M. Nataline Crumpton [1]; G.
Manville Fenn [4,10,11, 20,23]; Mary
C. Rowsell [5]; Frances E. Crompton
[6,16,18]; L.T. Meade [7,21]; Ruth
Ogden [8]; Mary D. Brine [9,15,17];
John Strange Winter [13,22]; Harriet T.
Comstock [14]; Evelyn Everett Green
[19]; Tudor Jenks [24]; Amanda M.
Douglas [25]
publisher: Henry Altemus
1. The Silver Buckle
2. Charles Dickens' Children Stories
3. The Children's Shakespeare
4. Young Robin Hood
5. Honor Bright
6. The Voyage of the Mary Adair
7. The Kingfisher's Egg
8. Tattine
9. The Doings of a Dear Little Couple
10. Our Soldier Boy
11. The Little Skipper
12. Little Gervaise and Other Stories
13. The Christmas Fairy
14. Molly, the Drummer Boy
15. How "A Dear Little Couple" Went
    Abroad
16. The Rose-Carnation
17. Mother's Little Man
18. Little Swan Maidens
19. Little Lady Val
20. A Young Hero
21. Queen of the Day
22. That Little French Baby
23. The Powder Monkey
24. The Doll That Talked
25. What Charlie Found to Do

ALTEMUS' ROSE CARNATION *see*
ROSE CARNATION

34. ALTEMUS' YOUNG PEOPLE'S LIBRARY
authors: Hartwell James [1]; Dinah Maria Mulock Craik [2]
publishers: Henry Altemus
1. Animal Stories for Young People (1902)
2. The Little Lame Prince and His Traveling-Cloak; a Parable for Old and Young (1900)

35. AMELIARANNE
author: Eleanor Farjean
publishers: David McKay [1,3]; Harrap [2–3]
1. Ameliaranne and the Magic Ring (1933)
2. Ameliaranne's Prize Packet (1933)
3. Ameliaranne's Washing Day (1934)

36. AMERICAN BOYS I
author: Edward Stratemeyer
publisher: Lee & Shepard
1. Lost on the Orinoco; or, American Boys in Venezuela (1902)
2. The Young Volcano Explorers; or, American Boys in the West Indies (1902)
3. Young Explorers of the Isthmus; or, American Boys in Central America (1903)
4. Young Explorers of the Amazon; or, American Boys in Brazil (1904)
5. Treasure Seekers of the Andes; or, American Boys in Peru (1907)
6. Chased Across the Pampas; or, American Boys in Argentina and Homeward Bound (1911)

37. AMERICAN BOYS II
author: Oliver Optic [pseudonym of William Taylor Adams]
publishers: Lee & Shepard; Lothrop, Lee & Shepard
2. All Aboard; or, Life on the Lake (1883)
5. The Boat Club
21. Haste and Waste; or, The Young Pilot of Lake Champlain (1894)
22. Hope and Have; or, Fanny Grant Among the Indians: A Story for Young People (1894)
23. In School and Out
25. Just His Luck (1877)
27. Little by Little; or, The Cruise of the Flyaway (1888)
31. Now or Never
32. Poor and Proud; or, The Fortunes of Katy Redburn: A Story for Young Girls (1886)
33. Rich and Humble
40. Try Again; or, The Trials and Triumphs of Harry West: A Story for Young Folks (1885)
43. Watch and Wait; or, The Young Fugitives: A Story for Young People (1899)
47. Work and Win
51. Field and Forest
52. Outward Bound
53. The Soldier Boy
54. The Starry Flag
55. Through by Daylight
62. A Missing Million
63. A Millionaire at Sixteen
64. A Young Knight-Errant
65. Strange Sights Abroad
89. Going West
90. Little Bobtail
95. All Adrift
100. Up the Baltic

38. AMERICAN BOY'S BIO-GRAPHICAL SERIES
author: Edward Stratemeyer
publisher: Lee & Shepard
1. The American Boy's Life of William McKinley (1901)
2. The American Boy's Life of Theodore Roosevelt (1901)

AMERICAN BOYS' SPORTS *see* JACK WINTER

39. AMERICAN GIRLS
authors: Virginian Frances Townsend [1]; Ednah Dow Littlehale Cheney [2]
publisher: Lothrop, Lee & Shepard
1. The Hollands (1897)
2. Sally Williams the Mountain Girl (1900)
3. Into the Light; or, The Jewess (1899)

40. AMERICAN GIRL'S SERIES

authors: [various: see each title]
publisher: Lothrop, Lee & Shepard
  6. The Hollands (1897) [au: Virginia
      Frances Townsend]
 15. Pretty Lucy Merwyn (1894) [au: Mary
      Lakeman]
 16. Rhoda Thornton's Girlhood (1873)
      [au: Mary Elizabeth Smith Pratt]
 28. Hester Strong's Life Work; or, The
      Mystery Solved (1900) [au: S.A.
      Southworth]
 29. Hillsboro Farms (1900) [au: Sophia
      Dickinson Cobb]
 34. Katherine Earle (1902) [au: Adeline
      Trafton Knox]
unknown numbers:
Six in All (1872) [au: Virginia Frances
   Townsend]
Ruth Eliot's Dream; a Story for Girls
   (1882) [au: Mary Lakeman]
Her Friend's Lover (1887) [au: Rebecca
   Sopia Clarke]
In Trust; or, Dr. Bertrand's Household
   (1894) [au: Amanda Minnie Douglas]
Into the Light; or, The Jewess (1899) [au:
   C.A.O.]
An American Girl Abroad (1900) [au:
   Ednah Dow Littlehale Cheney]

41. AMERICAN LIFE

author: George Philip Krapp
publisher: Rand McNally
 1. Tongo; A Tale of the Great
    Plains (1927)
 2. Kipwillie; A Story of City Life (1927)
 3. Fanton Farm; A Story of Country Life
    (1927)
 4. Inland Oceans; A Tale of the Great
    Lakes (1927)
 5. Sixty Years Ago; A Tale of the Civil
    War (1927)

42. AMERICAN SCOUTING

author: Everett Titsworth Tomlinson
publisher: David Appleton
 1. The Pursuit of the Apache Chief; A
    Story of the Campaign Against Geron-
    imo (1920)
 2. Scouting on the Border; A Story of
    American Boys and the Mexican
    Raiders (1920)

 3. The Mysterious Rifleman; A Story of
    the American Revolution (1921)
 4. Scouting with Mad Anthony; A Story
    of the Indian Wars (1922)
 5. Scouting on the Old Frontier with
    Flintlock and Fife (1923)
 6. Scouting in the Wilderness; The Fort
    in the Forest (1924)
 7. Pioneer Scouts on the Ohio
 8. Scouting on Lake Champlain; The
    Young Rangers (1925)
 9. Scouting on the Mohawk
 10. Washington's Young Scouts; In the
     Camp of Cornwallis (1926)
 11. Scouting in the Desert; Scouting with
     General Funston (1927)
 12. The Spy of Saratoga (1928)

AMERICAN TRAIL BLAZERS *see*
   TRAIL BLAZERS

43. AMONG THE SIOUX

author: Joseph Mills Hanson
publisher: A. C. McClurg
 1. With Sully into the Sioux Land (1910)
 2. With Carrington on the Bozeman
    Road (1912)

44. ANDOVER

author: Claude Moore Fuess
publisher: Lothrop, Lee & Shepard
 1. All for Andover; the School Life of
    Steve Fisher and His Friends (1925)
 2. The Andover Way (1926)

45. ANDY BLAKE

author: Leo Edwards [pseudonym of
   Edward Edson Lee]
illustrator: Bert Salg
publishers: Grosset & Dunlap; David
   Appleton
 1. Andy Blake (1921)
 2. Andy Blake in Advertising (1922)
 3. Andy Blake's Comet Coaster (1928)
 4. Andy Blake's Secret Service (1929)
 5. Andy Blake and the Pot of Gold (1930)
 6. Andy Blake: Boy Builder (1931)

46. ANDY LANE FLYING STO-RIES

author: Eustace Lane Adams
publisher: Grosset & Dunlap

1. Fifteen Days in the Air (1928)
2. Over the Polar Ice (1928)
3. Racing Around the World (1928)
4. The Runaway Airship (1929)
5. Pirates of the Air (1929)
6. On Wings of Flame (1929)
7. The Mysterious Monoplane (1930)
8. The Flying Windmill (1930)
9. The Plane Without a Pilot (1930)
10. Wings of Adventure (1931)
11. Across the Top of the World (1931)
12. Prisoners of the Clouds (1932)

47. ANIMAL LAND
author: [unknown]
publisher: Charles E. Graham
1. A Visit to the Farm (1900)

48. ANN BARTLETT
author: Martha Johnson [pseudonym of Elizabeth Lansing]
publisher: Thomas Y. Crowell
1. Ann Bartlett, Navy Nurse (1941)
2. Ann Bartlett at Bataan (1943)
3. Ann Bartlett in the South Pacific (1944)
4. Ann Bartlett Returns to the Philippines (1945)
5. Ann Bartlett on Stateside Duty (1946)

49. ANN STERLING
author: Harriet Pyne Grove
publisher: A. L. Burt
1. Ann Sterling (1926)
2. Ann and the Jolly Six (1926)
3. Ann Crosses a Secret Trail (1926)
4. Ann's Search Rewarded (1926)
5. The Courage of Ann (1926)
6. Ann's Ambitions (1927)
7. Ann's Sterling Heart (1928)

50. ANNAPOLIS I
author: Edward Latimer Beach
publisher: Penn
1. An Annapolis Plebe (1907)
2. An Annapolis Youngster (1908)
3. An Annapolis Second Classman (1909)
4. An Annapolis First Classman (1910)

51. ANNAPOLIS II
author: Clark Fitch [pseudonym of Upton Sinclair]
publisher: David McKay

1. Bound for Annapolis; or, The Trials of a Sailor Boy (1903)
2. Clif, The Naval Cadet; or, Exciting Days at Annapolis (1903)
3. The Cruise of the Training Ship; or, Clif Faraday's Pluck (1903)
4. From Port to Port; or, Clif Faraday in Many Waters (1903)
5. A Strange Cruise; or, Clif Faraday's Yacht Cruise (1903)

52. ANNAPOLIS III
author: William Oliver Stevens
publisher: J. B. Lippincott
1. "Pewee" Clinton, Plebe (1912)

ANNAPOLIS IV *see* **DAVE DARRIN**

53. ANNE CARTER
author: Isla May Mullins
publisher: L. C. Page
1. The Blossom Shop: A Story of the South (1913)
2. Anne of the Blossom Shop; or, The Growing Up of Anne Carter (1914)
3. Anne's Wedding: A Blossom Shop Romance (1916)
4. The Mt. Blossom Girls; or, New Paths from the Blossom Shop (1918)
5. Tweedie (1919)
6. Uncle Mary (1922)

54. ANNE OF GREEN GABLES
author: Lucy Maud Montgomery
publishers: L. C. Page [1–4, 10]; Stokes [5–9]; Oxford University Press [11]
1. Anne of Green Gables (1908)
2. Anne of Avonlea (1909)
3. Chronicles of Avonlea (1912)
4. Anne of the Island (1915)
5. Anne's House of Dreams (1917)
6. Rainbow Valley (1919)
7. Rilla of Ingleside (1921)
8. Anne of Windy Poplars (1936) [alt. title: Anne of Windy Willows]
9. Anne of Ingleside (1939)
10. Further Chronicles of Avonlea (1953)
11. The Anne of Green Gables Cookbook by Kate Macdonald (1985)

55. ANNE THORNTON
author: Lotta Rowe Anthony

publisher: Penn
1. Anne Thornton, Wetamoo (1922)
2. Anne Thornton, Junior Guide (1924)
3. Anne Thornton (1925)

56. APPLE MARKET STREET
author: Mabel Betsy Hill
publisher: Stokes
1. Down-Along Apple Market Street (1934)
2. Summer Comes to Apple Market Street (1937)
3. Surprise for Judy Jo; an Apple Market Story (1939)
4. Jack O'Lantern for Judy Jo; an Apple Market Street Story (1940)
5. Along Comes Judy Jo (1943)
6. The Snowed-in-Family; a Judy Jo Story (1951)
7. Judy Jo's Magic Island (1953)

57. APPLETON'S BOYS' LIBRARY
author: Ralph Henry Barbour
publisher: David Appleton
1. Four in Camp; A Story of Summer Adventures in the New Hampshire Woods (1905)
2. Four Afloat; Being the Adventures of the Big Four on the Water (1907)

58. ARDEN BLAKE MYSTERY SERIES
author: Cleo F. Garis
publisher: A. L. Burt
1. Missing at Marshlands (1934)
2. Mystery of Jockey Hollow (1934)
3. The Orchard Secret (1934)

59. ARGYLE
author: Oliver Optic [pseudonym of William Taylor Adams]
publisher: Hurst
1. Little by Little

60. ARMY [see also UNCLE SAM'S BOYS]
author: Andrew S. Burley
publisher: M. A. Donohue
1. Uncle Sam's Army Boys in Italy; or, Bob Hamilton Under Fire in the Piave District (1919)
2. Uncle Sam's Army Boys in Khaki Under Canvas; or, Bob Hamilton and the Munition Plant Plot (1919)
3. Uncle Sam's Army Boys on the Rhine; or, Bob Hamilton in the Argonne Death Trap (1919)
4. Uncle Sam's Army Boys with Old Glory in Mexico; or, Bob Hamilton Along Pershing's Trail (1919)

61. ARMY AND NAVY
author: Oliver Optic [pseudonym of William Taylor Adams]
publisher: Hurst
1. The Yankee Middy; or, The Adventures of a Naval Officer: A Story of the Great Rebellion (1863)
2. The Soldier Boy; or, Tom Somers in the Army: A Story of The Great Rebellion (1893)
3. The Young Lieutenant; or, The Adventures of an Army Officer: A Story of the Great Rebellion (1893)
4. Brave Old Salt; or, Life on the Quarter Deck: A Story of the Great Rebellion (1894)

62. ARMY BOY
author: Charles Evans Kilbourne
publisher: Penn
1. An Army Boy in Peking (1912)
2. An Army Boy in the Philippines (1913)
3. An Army Boy in Mexico (1914)
4. An Army Boy in Alaska (1915)

63. ARMY BOYS [see also UNCLE SAM'S ARMY BOYS]
author: Homer Randall
illustrator: Robert Gaston Herbert
publishers: World Syndicate; Sully
1. Army Boys in France; or, From Training Camp to Trenches (1918)
2. Army Boys in the French Trenches; or, Hand to Hand Fighting with the Enemy (1918)
3. Army Boys on the Firing Line; or, Holding Back the German Drive (1919)
4. Army Boys in the Big Drive; or, Smashing Forward to Victory (1919)
5. Army Boys Marching into Germany; or, Over the Rhine with the Stars and Stripes (1919)
6. Army Boys on German Soil; Our

Doughboys Quelling the Mobs (1920)

64. ARNOLD ADAIR
author: Laurence La Tourette Driggs
publisher: Little, Brown
1. The Adventures of Arnold Adair, American Ace (1918)
2. Arnold Adair with the French Aces (1920)
3. Arnold Adair with the English Aces (1922)

65. ASHTON KIRK
author: John T. McIntyre
publisher: Penn
1. Ashton Kirk, Investigator (1914)
2. Ashton Kirk, Secret Agent
3. Ashton Kirk, Special Detective
4. Ashton Kirk, Criminologist

66. AUGUSTUS
author: Le Grand Henderson
publisher: Bobbs-Merrill; Grosset & Dunlap
1. Augustus and the River (1939)
2. Augustus Goes South (1940)
3. Augustus and the Mountains (1941)
4. Augustus Helps the Navy (1942)
5. Augustus Helps the Army (1943)
6. Augustus Helps the Marines (1943)
7. Augustus Drives a Jeep (1944)
8. Augustus Flies (1944)
9. Augustus Saves a Ship (1945)
10. Augustus Hits the Road (1946)
11. Augustus Rides the Border (1947)
12. Augustus and the Desert (1948)

67. AUNT HATTIE'S LIBRARY FOR BOYS
author: Madeline Leslie
publisher: Henry A. Young
1. The Apple Boys (1867)

68. AUNT HATTIE'S LIBRARY FOR GIRLS
author: Madeline Leslie
publisher: Henry A. Young
2. Little Miss Fret (1867)

69. AUNT HATTIE'S LIBRARY FOR HER LITTLE FRIENDS
author: Madeline Leslie
publisher: Graves & Young
1. Lily's Birthday (1867)

70. AUNT JANE'S NIECES
author: Edith Van Dyne [pseudonym of Lyman Frank Baum]
publisher: Reilly & Britton
1. Aunt Jane's Nieces (1906)
2. Aunt Jane's Nieces Abroad (1907)
3. Aunt Jane's Nieces at Millville (1908)
4. Aunt Jane's Nieces at Work (1909)
5. Aunt Jane's Nieces in Society (1910)
6. Aunt Jane's Nieces and Uncle John (1911)
7. Aunt Jane's Nieces on Vacation (1912)
8. Aunt Jane's Nieces on the Ranch (1913)
9. Aunt Jane's Nieces Out West (1914)
10. Aunt Jane's Nieces in the Red Cross (1915)

71. AUNT JENNY'S MUSICAL SERIES
author: [unknown]
publisher: McLoughlin Brothers
1. The Marriage of the 3 Little Kittens (1860)
2. Little Tom Tucker (1880)
3. Jack Spratt (1880)
4. Pussies Party (1864)
5. Little Bo Peep (1860)
6. The Three Blind Mice (1899)

72. AUNT LAURA'S SERIES
author: Sarah Catherine Martin
publisher: P. G. Thomson
1. Old Mother Hubbard and Her Wonderful Dog (1900)

73. AUNT LOUISA'S BIG PICTURE
authors: Marie-Catherine, Madam d'Aulnoy [3]; C. C. Moore; Laura Valentine [25]
publisher: McLoughlin Bros.
1. Robinson Crusoe (1870)
2. Hare and the Tortoise (1880)
3. The White Cat (1877)
4. Puss in Boots (1880)
5. Cock Robin (1869)
6. Mother Hubbard's Dog (1870)
7. The 3 Little Kittens (1874)

8. Jack and the Bean Stalk (1879)
9. [title unknown]
10. Domestic Animals (1880)
11. Home Games for Little Girls(1870)
12. The Three Good Friends: Lillie, Carrie and Floss (1880)
13. Nursery Rhymes (1880)
14. Nonsense for Girls (1880)
15. Wild Animals for Children (1879)
16–20. [titles unknown]
21. Visit to the Menagerie (1899)
22. Four-Footed Friends and Favorites
23. The History of Tom Thumb (1889)
24. The Ten Little Niggers (1889)
25. The Story of the 3 Bears (1870)
26. House that Jack Built (1880)
27. Santa Claus and His Works (1870)
28. Kindness to Animals; A Picture Book for the Young (1890)
29. Yankee Doodle (1879)
30. Hey Diddle Diddle (1872)
unknown numbers:
1. Visit of St. Nicholas (1869)
2. The Three White Kittens; or, Tit, Tiny and Tittens (1869)
3. Rip Van Winkle (1869)
4. Baby (1869)
5. Be Kind to Thy Father; and Other Poems (1869)

74. AUNT MARY'S LITTLE SERIES
author: [unknown]
illustrator: E. P. Cogger
publisher: McLoughlin Bros.
1. Mischievous Boy (1851)
2. Little Sailor Boy (1856)
3. Old Mother Hubbard (1879)

75. AUNT MAVOR'S EVERLAST-ING SERIES
author: [unknown]
publishers: Routledge; Warne & Routledge
1. The House That Jack Built (1860)
7. Little Totty (1860)
8. The Cherry Orchard (1860)
15. The Babes in the Woods (1860)
21. British Sailors (1866)
27. Little Dog Trusty(1858)
28. Jack and the Bean Stalk (1865)

76. AUNT MAVOR'S EVERLAST-ING TOY BOOKS
author: [unknown]
publishers: Routledge, Warne & Routledge; G. Routledge; Edmund Evans; Vincent Brooks
1. [title unknown]
2. Baby's Birthday (1870)
3. The Railroad Alphabet (1889)
4. The Children in the Wood(1865)
5. Punch and Judy (1860)
6. Pictures From the Street (1860)
7. [title unknown]
8. [title unknown]
9. The Cat's Tea Party (1860)
10. Tom Thumb's Alphabet (1860)
11. The Three Bears (1860)
12. Little Red Riding Hood (1860)
13. Happy Days of Childhood (1880)
14. The Farmyard (1860)
15. The Babes in the Woods (1860)
16. The House That Jack Built (1880)
17. Hop O' My Thumb (1880)
18. History of Bluebeard (1880)
19. The Good Boys' and Girls' Alphabet (1880)
20. The Butterfly's Ball (1880)
21. British Sailors (1866)
22. The History of A Apple Pie (1839)
23. Aladdin; or, The Wonderful Lamp (1859)
24. Our Puss and Her Kittens
25. The History of John Gilpen (1858)
26. Sinbad the Sailor (1858)
27. The History of Tom Thumb (1860)
28. Jack and the Bean Stalk (1865)
29. Grammar in Rhyme (1868)
30. The Frog He Would A-Wooing Go (1860)
31. The History of the White Cat (1870)

77. AUNT MAVOR'S LITTLE LIBRARY
author: [unknown]
publishers: Routledge; Warne & Routledge
1. The Alphabet of Animals (1899)
2. The History of the Little Old Woman Who Lived in a Shoe (1855)
3. Aunt Mavor's Pretty Name Alphabet (1856)
4. Aunt Mavor's First Book; Being an

Illustrated Alphabet with Easy Words (1859)
5. The Multiplication Table (1860)
6. Aunt Mavor's Alphabet of Trades and Occupations (1859)
7. The History of Little Bo-Peep the Shepherdess: Shewing How She Lost Her Sheep and Couldn't Tell Where to Find Them (1858)
8. Our Kings and Queens; or, The History of England in Miniature: For the Use of Little Children (1864)

78. AUNT MAVOR'S NURSERY RHYMES

author: [unknown]
publisher: McLoughlin Bros.
1. Old King Cole and Other Rhymes
2. The Tailor and Carrion Crow and Other Rhymes
3. Aunt Mavor's Second Book of Nursery Rhymes (1857)
4. The Frog He Would A-Wooing Go and Other Rhymes (1855)

79. AUNT MAVOR'S PICTURE BOOKS FOR LITTLE READERS

author: [unknown]
publisher: George Routledge
1. The Old Cornish Woman (1850)
3. Aladdin (1850)
6. Alphabet of the Exhibition (1856)
7. Uncle Hugh's Country
8. Alphabet of Foreign Things (1856)
9. Dogs' Dinner Party (1854)
10. The Exhibition and Grand London Sights (1850)
11. Hop O' My Thumb (1858)

80. AUNT MAVOR'S SERIES

author: [unknown]
publisher: McLoughlin Bros.
1. Little Boy Blue and Other Tales (1899)
2. Ding Dong Bell and Other Tales (1889)
3. Goosey, Goosey Gander and Other Tales (1890)

AUNT MAVOR'S TOY BOOKS *see* **AUNT MAVOR'S EVERLASTING TOY BOOKS**

81. AUTO BOYS

author: James Andrew Braden
publisher: Saalfield
1. The Auto Boys (1908)
2. The Auto Boys' Adventure (1908)
3. The Auto Boys' Outing (1909)
4. The Auto Boys' Quest (1910)
5. The Auto Boys on the Road
6. The Auto Boys' Camp (1912)
7. The Auto Boys' Big Six (1912)

82. AUTOMOBILE GIRLS

author: Laura Dent Crane
publisher: Henry Altemus
1. The Automobile Girls at Newport; or, Watching the Summer Parade (1910)
2. The Automobile Girls in the Berkshires; or, The Ghost of Lost Man's Trail (1910)
3. The Automobile Girls Along the Hudson; or, Fighting Fire in Sleepy Hollow (1910)
4. The Automobile Girls at Chicago; or, Winning Out Against Heavy Odds (1912)
5. The Automobile Girls at Palm Beach; or, Proving Their Mettle Under Southern Skies (1912)
6. The Automobile Girls at Washington; or, Checkmating the Plots of Foreign Spies (1913)

83. AVIATION

author: John Prentice Langley
publisher: Barse & Hopkins
1. Trail Blazers of the Skies; or, Across to Paris and Back (1927)
2. Spanning the Pacific; or, A Non-Stop Hop to Japan (1927)
3. Masters of the Airlanes; or, Around the World in 14 Days
4. The "Pathfinder's" Great Flight; or, Cloud Chasers Over Amazon Jungles (1928)
5. Air Voyagers of the Arctic; or, Sky Pilots' Dash Across the Pole (1929)
6. Desert Hawks on the Wing; or, Headed South — Algiers to Capetown (1929)
7. Chasing the Setting Sun; or, A Hop, Skip and Jump to Australia (1930)
8. Bridging the Seven Seas; or, On the Air-Lane to Singapore (1930)

9. The Staircase of the Wind; or, Over
   the Himalayas to Calcutta (1931)

84. AVIATOR I [*also called* AERO-PLANE BOYS II]
author: Frank Cobb
publisher: Saalfield
1. Battling the Clouds; or, For a Comrade's Honor (1927)
2. An Aviator's Luck; or, The Camp Knox Plot (1927)
3. Dangerous Deeds; or, The Flight in the Dirigible (1927)

85. AVIATOR II
author: Henry Harley Arnold
publisher: A. L. Burt
1. Bill Bruce and the Pioneer Aviators (1928)
2. Bill Bruce, the Flying Cadet (1928)
3. Bill Bruce Becomes an Ace (1928)
4. Bill Bruce on Border Patrol (1928)
5. Bill Bruce in the Trans-Continental Race (1928)
6. Bill Bruce on Forest Patrol (1928)

86. BABS
author: Alice Ross Colver
publisher: Penn
1. Babs (1917)
2. Babs at Birchwood (1919)
3. Babs at College (1920)
4. Babs at Home (1921)

87. BACK TO THE SOIL
author: Ed Ward [pseudonym of the Stratemeyer Syndicate] [another source lists the author as Burbank L. Todd]
illustrator: H. Richard Boehm
publisher: Sully & Kleinteich
1. Hiram, the Young Farmer; or, Making the Soil Pay (1914)
2. Hiram in the Middle West; or, A Young Farmer's Upward Struggle (1915)

88. BAILEY TWINS
author: Claude A. LaBelle
publisher: A. L. Burt
1. The Bailey Twins at Farnham Hall (1930)
2. The Bailey Twins and the Farnham Hall Cadets [alternate: title: The Bailey Twins and the Farnham Cadet Corps] (1930)
3. The Bailey Twins at Summer Camp (1930)
4. The Bailey Twins in the Philippines (1930)
5. The Bailey Twins and the Secret Code (1930)

89. BANNER BOY SCOUTS
author: George A. Warren
publishers: Cupples & Leon; Saalfield; World
1. The Banner Boy Scouts; or, The Struggle for Leadership (1912)
2. The Banner Boy Scouts on a Tour; or, The Mystery of Rattlesnake Mountain (1912)
3. The Banner Boy Scouts Afloat; or, The Secret of Cedar Island (1913)
4. The Banner Boy Scouts Snowbound; or, A Tour on Skates and Iceboat (1916)
5. The Banner Boy Scouts Mystery (1937)
6. The Banner Boy Scouts in the Air (1937)

BANNER CAMPFIRE GIRLS *see* CAMPFIRE GIRLS II

90. BAR B
author: Edwin Legrand Sabin
publisher: Thomas Y. Crowell
1. The Bar B Boys; or, The Young Cow-Punchers (1909)
2. Range and Trail; or, The Bar B's Great Drive (1910)
3. Circle K; or, Fighting for the Flock (1911)
4. Old Four-Toes; or, Hunters of the Peaks (1912)
5. Treasure Mountain; or, The Young Prospectors (1913)
6. Scarface Ranch; or, The Young Homesteaders (1914)

91. BARBARA HALE [*see also* LILIAN GARIS BOOKS]
author: Lilian C. McNamara Garis
publisher: Grosset & Dunlap
1. Barbara Hale: A Doctor's Daughter (1926)
2. Barbara Hale and Cozette (1926)

3. Barbara Hale's Mysterious Friend (1926)

92. BARBARA WINTHROP
author: Helen Katherine Broughall
publisher: L. C. Page
1. Barbara Winthrop at Boarding School (1925)
2. Barbara Winthrop at Camp (1926)
3. Barbara Winthrop Graduate (1927)
4. Barbara Winthrop Abroad (1929)

93. BASEBALL
author: Christy Mathewson
publishers: Dodd, Meade; Grosset & Dunlap; New York Book
1. Pitching in a Pinch (1917)
2. Pitcher Pollock (1914)
3. Catcher Craig (1915)
4. First-Base Faulkner (1916)
5. Second-Base Sloan (1917)
6. Third Base Thatcher (1923)
7. Won in the Ninth (1916)

94. BASEBALL JOE
author: Lester Chadwick [pseudonym of the Stratemeyer Syndicate]
publisher: Cupples & Leon
1. Baseball Joe of the Silver Stars; or, The Rivals of Riverside (1912)
2. Baseball Joe on the School Nine; or, Pitching for the Blue Banner (1912)
3. Baseball Joe at Yale; or, Pitching for the College Championship (1913)
4. Baseball Joe in the Central League; or, Making Good as a Professional Pitcher (1914)
5. Baseball Joe in the Big League; or, A Young Pitcher's Hardest Struggles (1915)
6. Baseball Joe on the Giants; or, Making Good as a Ball Twirler in the Metropolis (1916)
7. Baseball Joe in the World Series; or, Pitching for the Championship (1917)
8. Baseball Joe Around the World; or, Pitching on a Grand Tour (1918)
9. Baseball Joe, Home Run King; or, The Greatest Pitcher and Batter on Record (1922)
10. Baseball Joe Saving the League; or, Breaking Up a Great Conspiracy (1923)
11. Baseball Joe, Captain of the Team; or, Bitter Struggles on the Diamond (1924)
12. Baseball Joe, Champion of the League; or, The Record That Was Worth While (1925)
13. Baseball Joe, Club Owner; Putting the Home Town on the Map (1926)
14. Baseball Joe, Pitching Wizard; or, Triumphs Off and On the Diamond (1928)

95. BASKETBALL
author: Harold M. Sherman
publisher: [unknown]
1. Mayfield's Fighting Five
2. Get 'Em, Mayfield
3. Shoot That Ball

96. BATTLESHIP BOYS
author: Frank Gee Patchin = Frank Glines Patchin
publishers: Saalfield; Henry Altemus
1. The Battleship Boys at Sea; or, Two Apprentices in Uncle Sam's Navy (1910)
2. The Battleship Boys' First Step Upward; or, Winning Their Grades as Petty Officers (1911)
3. The Battleship Boys in Foreign Service; or, Earning New Ratings in European Seas (1911)
4. The Battleship Boys in the Tropics; or, Upholding the American Flag in a Honduras Revolution (1912)
5. The Battleship Boys Under Fire; or, The Dash for the Besieged Kam Shau Mission (1916)
6. The Battleship Boys in the Wardroom; or, Winning Their Commissions as Line Officers on the Eve of the Great War (1918)
7. The Battleship Boys with the Adriatic Chasers; or, Blocking the Trail of the Undersea Raiders (1918) [alternate subtitle: Blocking the Paths of the Undersea Raiders]
8. The Battleship Boys on Sky Patrol; or, Fighting the Hun from Above the Clouds (1918)

97. BEANY MALONE
author: Lenora Mattingly Weber
publisher: Thomas Y. Crowell
1. Meet the Malones (1943)

2. Beany Malone (1948)
3. Leave It to Beany (1950)
4. Beany and the Beckoning Road (1952)
5. Beany Has a Secret Life (1955)
6. Make a Wish for Me (1956)
7. Happy Birthday, Dear Beany (1957)
8. The More the Merrier (1958)
9. A Bright Star Falls (1959)
10. Welcome, Stranger (1960)
11. Pick a New Dream (1961)
12. Tarry Awhile (1962)
13. Something Borrowed, Something Blue (1963)
14. Come Back, Wherever You Are (1969)

98. BECKY BRYAN
author: Betty Baxter
publisher: Goldsmith
1. Becky Bryan's Secret (1937)
2. The Unseen Enemy (1938)
3. Daughter of the Coast Guard (1938)

BEDTIME ANIMAL STORIES *see*
   BEDTIME STORIES

99. BEDTIME STORIES [*see also* UNCLE WIGGILY]
author: Howard Roger Garis
illustrator: Louis Wisa
publishers: A. L. Burt; R. F. Fenno
1. Johnnie and Billie Bushytail (1910)
2. Lulu, Alice and Jimmie Wibblewobble (1912)
3. Jackie and Peetie Bow Wow [alternate title: Uncle Wiggily and Jackie and Peetie Bow Wow](1912)
4. Buddy and Brighteyes Pigg (1913)
5. Bully and Bawly No-Tail (The Jumping Frogs) [alternate title: Uncle Wiggily and Bully and Bawly No-Tail] (1915)
6. Nannie and Billy Wagtail: The Goat Children
7. Jacko and Jumpo Kinkytail: The Funny Monkey Boys (1917)
8. Toodle and Noodle Flat-Tail, The Jolly Beaver Boys (1919)
9. Woodie and Waddie Chuck: the Jolly Groundhog Boys (1922)
10. Uncle Wiggily's Fortune (1913)
11. Dottie and Willie Flufftail: the Funny Lamb Children (1920)
12. Neddie and Beckie Stubtail (Two Nice Bears) [alternate title: Uncle Wiggily and Neddie and Beckie Stubtail] (1913)
13. Charlie and Arabella Chick (1914)
14. Jollie and Jillie Longtail (1900)
15. Uncle Wiggily's Automobile (1913)
16. Dickie and Nellie Fliptail: the Jolly Sparrow Children (1921)
17. Sammie and Susie Littletail (1910)
18. Uncle Wiggily's Airship (1915)
19. Uncle Wiggily's Puzzle Book (1928)
20. Uncle Wiggily in Wonderland (1921)

100. BEDTIME STORY-BOOKS
author: Thornton W. Burgess
publisher: Little, Brown
1. The Adventures of Reddy Fox
2. The Adventures of Johnny Chuck
3. The Adventures of Petter Cottontail
4. The Adventures of Unc' Billy Possum
5. The Adventures of Mr. Mocker
6. The Adventures of Jerry Muskrat (1922)
7. The Adventures of Danny Meadow Mouse
8. The Adventures of Grandfather Frog
9. The Adventures of Chatterer, the Red Squirrel
10. The Adventures of Sammy Jay
11. The Adventures of Buster Bear
12. The Adventures of Old Mr. Toad
13. The Adventures of Prickly Porky
14. The Adventures of Old Man Coyote
15. The Adventures of Paddy the Beaver
16. The Adventures of Poor Mrs. Quack
17. The Adventures of Bobby Coon
18. The Adventures of Jimmy Skunk
19. The Adventures of Bob White
20. The Adventures of Ol' Mistah Buzzard

101. BEETON'S JUVENILE SERIES
author: Elizabeth Stuart Phelps
publisher: Ward, Lock & Tyler
1. Trotty's Book; the Story of a Little Boy (1872)

102. BELL HAVEN
author: George Barton
publisher: J. C. Winston

1. The Bell Haven Nine (1914)
2. The Bell Haven Eight (1914)
3. The Bell Haven Eleven (1915)
4. The Bell Haven Five (1915)

103. BEN LIGHTBODY
author: Walter Benham
publisher: Henry Altemus
1. Ben Lightbody, Special Agent; or, Seizing the First Chance to Make Good (1910)
2. Ben Lightbody's Biggest Puzzle; or, Running the Double Ghost to Earth (1910)

104. BENZIGER'S JUVENILE SERIES
author: Mary Greene Bonesteel
publisher: Benziger Brothers
1. The Young Color Guard; or, Tommy Collins at Santiago (1902)

105. BERKELEY
author: Oliver Optic [pseudonym of William Taylor Adams]
publisher: American Publishers
1. The Casket of Diamonds; or, Hope Everton's Inheritance (1892)

106. BERT WILSON
author: J. W. Duffield
publisher: Sully & Kleinteich
1. Bert Wilson at the Wheel (1913)
2. Bert Wilson's Fadeaway Ball (1913)
3. Bert Wilson, Wireless Operator (1913)
4. Bert Wilson, Marathon Runner (1914)
5. Bert Wilson at Panama (1914)
6. Bert Wilson's Twin Cylinder Racer (1914)
7. Bert Wilson on the Gridiron (1914)
8. Bert Wilson in the Rockies (1915)

107. BEST BOOKS FOR BOYS
author: Oliver Optic [pseudonym of William Taylor Adams]
publisher: Caldwell
1. Outward Bound
4. All Aboard
8. The Boat Club
36. Now or Never

108. BETH
author: Marion Ames Taggart
publisher: W. A. Wilde

1. Beth's Wonder-Winter (1914)
2. Beth's Old Home (1915)
3. Beth of Old Chilton (1916)

109. BETH ANNE
author: Mary Pemberton Ginther
publisher: Penn
1. Beth Anne Herself (1915)
2. Beth Anne, Really-for-Truly (1916)
3. Beth Anne's New Cousin (1917)
4. Beth Anne Goes to School (1919)

110. BETH DEAN
author: Margaret Hill
publisher: Little, Brown
1. Goal in the Sky (1953)
2. Hostess in the Sky (1955)
3. Senior Hostess (1958)

111. BETSY
author: Carolyn Haywood
publisher: Harcourt [1–4]; Morrow [5–24]
1. "B" Is for Betsy (1939)
2. Betsy and Billy (1941)
3. Back to School with Betsy (1943)
4. Betsy and the Boys (1945)
5. Little Eddie (1947)
6. Eddie and the Fire Engine (1949)
7. Betsy's Little Star (1950)
8. Eddie and Gardenia (1951)
9. Eddie's Pay Dirt (1953)
10. Betsy and the Circus (1954)
11. Betsy's Busy Summer (1956)
12. Eddie Makes Music (1957)
13. Betsy's Winterhouse (1958)
14. Eddie and Lovella (1959)
15. Annie Pat and Eddie (1960)
16. Snowbound with Betsy (1962)
17. Eddie's Green Thumb (1964)
18. Eddie the Dog Holder (1966)
19. Betsy and Mr. Kilpatrick (1967)
20. Merry Christmas from Betsy (1970)
21. Eddie's Happenings (1971)
22. Eddie's Valuable Property (1975)
23. Betsy's Play School (1977)
24. Eddie's Menagerie (1978)

112. BETSY HALE
author: Mary Pemberton Ginther
publisher: Winston
1. Betsy Hale (1923)
2. Betsy Hale Succeeds (1923)
3. Betsy Hale Tries (1923)

113. BETSY-TACY

author: Maud Hart Lovelace
publishers: Thomas Y. Crowell (1–10);
Harper (3–4)
1. Betsy-Tacy (1940)
2. Betsy-Tacy and Tib (1941)
3. Over the Big Hill (1945) [alternate title: Betsy and Tacy Over the Big Hill]
4. Downtown (1943) [alternate title: Betsy and Tacy Go Downtown]
5. Heaven to Betsy (1945)
6. Betsy, in Spite of Herself (1946)
7. Betsy Was a Junior (1947)
8. Betsy and Joe (1948)
9. Betsy and the Great World (1952)
10. Betsy's Wedding (1955)

114. BETTY BAIRD

author: Anna Hamline Weikel
publisher: Little, Brown
1. Betty Baird (1906)
2. Betty Baird's Ventures (1907)
3. Betty Baird's Golden Year (1909)

115. BETTY GORDAN

author: Alice B. Emerson [pseudonym of the Stratemeyer Syndicate]
illustrators: Thelma Gooch [1–6]; Walter S. Rogers [7]; Ernest Townsend [8,11]; Bess Goc Willis [9]; Russel H. Tandy [12–13]; A. Suk [14]
publisher: Cupples & Leon
1. Betty Gordan at Bramble Farm; or, The Mystery of a Nobody (1920)
2. Betty Gordan in Washington; or, Strange Adventures in a Great City (1920)
3. Betty Gordan in the Land of Oil; or, The Farm That Was Worth a Fortune (1920)
4. Betty Gordan at Boarding School; or, The Treasure of Indiana Chasm (1921)
5. Betty Gordan at Mountain Camp; or, The Mystery of Ida Bellethorne (1922)
6. Betty Gordan at Ocean Park; or, Gay Days on the Boardwalk (1923) [alternate subtitle: School Chums on the Boardwalk]
7. Betty Gordan and Her School Chums; or, Bringing the Rebels to Terms (1924)
8. Betty Gordan at Rainbow-Ranch; or, Cowboy Joe's Secret (1925)
9. Betty Gordan in Mexican Wilds; or, The Secret of the Mountains (1926)
10. Betty Gordan and the Lost Pearls; or, A Mystery of the Seaside (1927)
11. Betty Gordan on the Campus; or, The Secret of the Trunk Room (1928)
12. Betty Gordan and the Hale Twins; or, An Exciting Vacation (1929)
13. Betty Gordan at Mystery Farm; or, Strange Doings at Rocky Ridge (1930)
14. Betty Gordan on No-Trail Island; or, Uncovering a Queer Secret (1931)
15. Betty Gordan and the Mystery Girl; or, The Secret at Sundown Hall (1932)

116. BETTY LEE

author: Harriet Pyne Grove
publisher: A. L. Burt
1. Betty Lee, Freshman (1931)
2. Betty Lee, Sophomore (1931)
3. Betty Lee, Junior (1931)
4. Betty Lee, Senior (1931)

117. BETTY WALES

author: Margaret Warde [pseudonym of Edith Kellogg Dunton]
illustrators: Eva M. Nagel [1–10]; Elizabeth Pilsby [8]
publishers: Grosset & Dunlap; Penn
1. Betty Wales, Freshman; A Story for Girls (1904)
2. Betty Wales, Sophomore; A Story for Girls (1905)
3. Betty Wales, Junior; A Story for Girls (1906)
4. Betty Wales, Senior; A Story for Girls (1907)
5. Betty Wales, B. A.; A Story for Girls (1908)
6. Betty Wales & Co.; A Story for Girls (1909)
7. Betty Wales on the Campus; A Story for Girls (1910)
8. Betty Wales Decides; A Story for Girls (1911)
9. The Betty Wales Girls and Mr. Kidd [A play in three acts based on her Betty Wales books] (1912)
10. Betty Wales, Business Woman (1917)

118. BEVERLY GRAY COLLEGE MYSTERY

author: Clair Blank
publisher: Grosset & Dunlap
1. Beverly Gray, Freshman (1934)
2. Beverly Gray, Sophomore (1934)
3. Beverly Gray, Junior (1934)
4. Beverly Gray, Senior (1934)
5. Beverly Gray's Career (1935)
6. Beverly Gray at the World's Fair (1935)
7. Beverly Gray on a World Cruise (1936)
8. Beverly Gray in the Orient (1937)
9. Beverly Gray on a Treasure Hunt (1938)
10. Beverly Gray's Return (1939)
11. Beverly Gray, Reporter (1940)
12. Beverly Gray's Romance (1941)
13. Beverly Gray's Quest (1942)
14. Beverly Gray's Problem (1943)
15. Beverly Gray's Adventure (1944)
16. Beverly Gray's Challenge (1945)
17. Beverly Gray's Journey (1946)
18. Beverly Gray's Assignment (1947)
19. Beverly Gray's Mystery (1948)
20. Beverly Gray's Vacation (1949)
21. Beverly Gray's Fortune (1950)
22. Beverly Gray's Secret (1951)
23. Beverly Gray's Island Mystery (1952)
24. Beverly Gray's Discovery (1953)
25. Beverly Gray's Scoop (1954)
26. Beverly Gray's Surprise (1955)

BIBLE PEARLS *see* **PEARL**

119. BIG BROTHER

author: George Carey Eggleston
publisher: [unknown]
1. The Big Brother (1876)
2. Captain Sam; or, The Boy Scout of 1814
3. The Signal Boys; or, Captain Sam's Company (1877)

120. BIG FIVE MOTORCYCLE BOYS

author: Ralph Marlow
publisher: A. L. Burt
1. The Big Five Motorcycle Boys' Swift Road Chase; or, Surprising the Bank Robbers (1914)
2. The Big Five Motorcycle Boys in the Tennessee Wilds; or, The Secret of Walnut Ridge (1914)
3. The Big Five Motorcycle Boys Through by Wireless; or, A Strange Message from the Air (1914)
4. The Big Five Motorcycle Boys on Florida Trails; or, Adventures Among the Saw Palmetto Crackers (1914)
5. The Big Five Motorcycle Boys Under Fire; or, With the Allies in the War Zone (1915)
6. The Big Five Motorcycle Boys at the Front; or, Carrying Dispatches Through Belgium (1915)
7. The Big Five Motorcycle Boys on the Battle Line; or, With the Allies in France (1916)

121. BIG FOUR

author: Ralph Henry Barbour
publisher: David Appleton
1. Four in Camp (1905)
2. Four Afloat (1905)
3. Four Afoot (1906)

122. BIG GAME

author: Elliot Whitney [pseudonym of H.L. Saylor, G.N. Madison, and H. Bedford Jones]
publisher: Reilly & Britton
1. The Giant Moose (1912)
2. The King Bear of Kodiak Island
3. The White Tiger of Nepal
4. The Rogue Elephant
5. The Blind Lion of the Congo
6. The Pirate Shark
7. The King Condor of the Andes
8. The Black Fox of the Yukon
9. The Bobcat of Jump Mountain
10. The Crazy Elk of Terrapin Swamp
11. The Boss of the Bighorns (1924)

123. BIG LEAGUE

author: Burt L. Standish [pseudonym of Gilbert Patten]
illustrators: Charles L. Wrenn, T. S. Tousey, Howard L. Hastings, R. Emmett Owen
publishers: Barse & Hopkins; Grosset & Dunlap
1. Lefty o' the Bush (1914)

2. Lefty o' the Big League (1914)
3. Lefty o' the Blue Stockings (1914)
4. Lefty o' the Training Camp (1914)
5. Brick King, Backstop (1914)
6. The Making of a Big Leaguer (1915)
7. Courtney of the Center Garden (1915)
8. Covering the Look-In Corner (1915)
9. Lefty Locke, Pitcher-Manager (1916)
10. Guarding the Keystone Sack (1917)
11. The Man on First (1920)
12. Lego Lamb, Southpaw (1923)
13. The Grip of the Game (1924)
14. Lefty Locke, Owner (1925)
15. Lefty Locke Wins Out (1926)
16. Crossed Signals (1928)

124. BIG PICTURE
author: [unknown]
publisher: McLoughlin Bros.
1. Cock Robin (1839)

125. BIG WAR
author: Ross Kay
publisher: Barse & Hopkins
1. The Search for the Spy; the Adventures of an American Boy at the Outbreak of the War (1914)
2. The Air Scout; an American Boy's Adventures When the Big War Began (1914)
3. Dodging the North Sea Mines; the Adventures of an American Boy (1915)
4. With Joffre on the Battle Line; the Adventures of an American Boy in the Trenches (1915)
5. Fighting in France (1916)
6. Battling on the Somme (1917)
7. With Pershing at the Front
8. Smashing the Hindenburg Line; the Adventures of Two American Boys in the Last Drive (1919)
9. The Underground Spy (1920)

126. BILL BOLTON, NAVY AVIATOR
author: Noel Sainsbury, Jr.
publisher: Gold
1. Bill Bolton, Flying Midshipman (1933)
2. Bill Bolton and the Flying Fish (1933)
3. Bill Bolton and the Hidden Danger (1933)

4. Bill Bolton and the Winged Cartwheels (1933)

127. BILL BROWN
author: Wayne Whipple
publisher: Hurst
1. Bill Brown's Radio (1922)
2. Bill Brown Listens In (1922)

128. BILL BRUCE AIR PILOT
author: Henry Arnold
publisher: A. L. Burt
1. Bill Bruce and the Pioneer Aviators (1929)
2. Bill Bruce, the Flying Cadet (1929)
3. Bill Bruce Becomes an Ace (1929)
4. Bill Bruce on the Border Patrol (1929)
5. Bill Bruce and the Trans-Continental Race (1929)
6. Bill Bruce on Far East Patrol (1929)

129. BILLABONG
author: Mary Grant Bruce
publisher: Ward Lock
1. A Little Bush Maid (1910)
2. Mates at Billabong (1911)
3. Norah of Billabong (1913)
4. From Billabong to London (1915)
5. Back to Billabong (1921)
6. Billabong's Daughter (1924)
7. Billabong Adventurers (1927)
8. Bill of Billabong (1931)
9. Billabong's Luck (1933)
10. Wings Above Billabong (1935)
11. Billabong Gold (1937)
12. Son of Billabong (1939)
13. Billabong Riders (1942)

130. BILLIE BRADLEY
author: Janet D. Wheeler [pseudonym of the Stratemeyer Syndicate]
illustrators: Howard L. Hastings and Walter S. Rogers
publishers: Sully [1–5]; Cupples & Leon [6–9]
1. Billie Bradley and Her Inheritance; or, The Queer Homestead at Cherry Corners (1920)
2. Billie Bradley at Three-Towers Hall; or, Leading a Needed Rebellion (1920)
3. Billie Bradley on Lighthouse Island; or, The Mystery of the Wreck (1920)

4. Billie Bradley and Her Classmates; or,
   The Secret of the Locked Tower (1921)
5. Billie Bradley at Twin Lakes; or, Jolly
   Schoolgirls Afloat and Ashore (1922)
6. Billie Bradley at Treasure Cove; or, The
   Old Sailor's Secret (1928)
7. Billie Bradley at Sun Dial Lodge; or,
   School Chums Solving a Mystery
   (1929)
8. Billie Bradley and the School Mystery;
   or, The Girl from Oklahoma (1930)
9. Billie Bradley Winning the Trophy; or,
   Scoring Against Big Odds (1932)

131. BILLY BUNNY BOOKS
author: David Magie Cory
publishers: Cupples & Leon; George H.
Doran
1. Billy Bunny and His Friends (1917)
2. Billy Bunny and the Friendly Elephant
   (1920)
3. Billy Bunny and Daddy Fox (1920)
4. Billy Bunny and Uncle Bull Frog
   (1920)
5. Billy Bunny and Uncle Lucky Left-
   hindfoot (1920)
6. Billy Bunny and Robbie Redbreast
   (1921)

132. BILLY TO-MORROW
author: Sarah Pratt Carr
publisher: A.C. McClurg
1. [title unknown]
2. Billy To-Morrow in Camp (1910)

133. BILLY TOPSAIL
author: Norman Duncan
publisher: Fleming H. Revell
1. The Adventures of Billy Topsail (1906)
2. Billy Topsail & Company; a Story for
   Boys (1910)

134. BILLY WHISKERS
author: Frances Trego Montgomery
publisher: Saalfield
1. Billy Whiskers; the Autobiography of a
   Goat (1902)
2. Billy Whiskers' Kids; or, Day and
   Night; A Sequel to Billy Whiskers
   (1903)
3. Billy Whiskers, Jr. (1904)
4. Billy Whiskers' Friends (1906)

5. Billy Whiskers' Travels (1907)
6. Billy Whiskers, Jr. and His Chums
   (1907)
7. Billy Whiskers at the Circus (1908)
8. Billy Whiskers' Vacation (1908)
9. Billy Whiskers at the Fair (1909)
10. Billy Whiskers' Grandchildren (1909)
11. Billy Whiskers Kidnaped (1910)
12. Billy Whiskers' Twins (1911)
13. Billy Whiskers in an Aeroplane (1912)
14. Billy Whiskers in Town (1913)
15. Billy Whiskers in Panama (1914)
16. Billy Whiskers on the Mississippi
    (1915)
17. Billy Whiskers at the Exposition
    (1915)
18. Billy Whiskers Out West (1916)
19. Billy Whiskers in the South (1917)
20. Billy Whiskers in Camp (1918)
21. Billy Whiskers' Adventures (1920)
22. Billy Whiskers in the Movies (1921)
23. Billy Whiskers Out for Fun (1922)
24. Billy Whiskers' Frolics (1923)
25. Billy Whiskers at Home (1924)
26. Billy Whiskers' Pranks (1925)
27. Billy Whiskers in Mischief; Continu-
    ing the Famous Billy Whiskers Series
    (1926)
28. Billy Whiskers and the Radio; Con-
    tinuing the Famous Billy Whiskers
    Series (1927)
29. Billy Whiskers' Treasure Hunt; Con-
    tinuing the Famous Billy Whiskers
    Series (1928)
30. Billy Whiskers Tourist; Continuing
    the Famous Billy Whiskers Series
    (1929)
31. Billy Whiskers Stowaway; Continuing
    the Famous Billy Whiskers Series
    (1930)

135. BIRD BOYS [also called AERO-
PLANE BOYS] [see also AIR-
PLANE BOYS]
author: John Luther Langworthy
publisher: M. A. Donohue
1. The Bird Boys; or, The Young Pilot's
   First Air Voyage (1912)
2. The Bird Boys on the Wing; or, Aeroplane Chums in the Tropics (1912)
3. The Bird Boys Among the Clouds; or,
   Young Aviators in a Wreck (1912)

4. The Bird Boys' Flight; or, A Hydro-plane Round-up (1914)
5. The Bird Boys' Aeroplane Wonder; or, Young Aviators on a Cattle Ranch (1914)

136. BIRTHDAY
author: Harriet Burn McKeever
publisher: Porter and Coates
3. Lucy Forrester's Triumph (1867)

137. BLACK EAGLE PATROL
author: Leslie W. Quirk
publisher: Little, Brown
1. The Boy Scouts of the Black Eagle Patrol (1915)
2. The Boy Scouts on Crusade
3. The Boy Scouts of Lakeville High (1920)

138. BLACK HERITAGE LIBRARY COLLECTION
author: Oliver Optic [pseudonym of William Taylor Adams]
publisher: Books for Libraries Press
1. Hatchie, the Guardian Slave

139. BLACK RIDER [see also ADVENTURE AND MYSTERY]
authors: Capwell Wyckoff (1–2); Milton Richards [pseudonym of Milo Milton Dolinger] (3)
publisher: Saalfield
1. The Mystery at Lake Retreat (1931)
2. In the Camp of the Black Rider (1937)
3. Tom Blake's Mysterious Adventure (1937)

140. BLACK SHADOW
author: Ernest L. Thurston
publisher: Saalfield
1. The Black Shadow (1934)

BLACKIE'S EASY TO READ BOOKS
see EASY TO READ

141. BLACKIE'S STORY BOOK READERS
author: [unknown]
publisher: Blackie & Son
1. Cornet Walter, from Orange and Green (1899)
2. Cast Ashore, from Under Drake's Flag (1899)

142. BLONDIE AND DAGWOOD
author: Chic Young
publisher: Whitman
1. Blondie and Dagwood's Secret Service (1945)
2. Blondie and Dagwood's Snapshot Clue
3. Blondie and Dagwood's Adventure in Magic
4. Blondie and Dagwood's Footlight Folly (1951)

143. BLOSSOM SHOP BOOKS
author: Isla May Mullins
publisher: L. C. Page
1. The Blossom Shop: A Story of the South (1913)
2. Anne of the Blossom Shop: or, The Growing Up of Anne Carter (1914)
3. Anne's Wedding: a Blossom Shop Romance (1916)
4. The Mt. Blossom Girls: or, New Paths from the Blossom Shop (1918)
5. Tweedie (1919)
6. Uncle Mary (1922)

144. BLUE AND BUFF
author: Everett Titsworth Tomlinson
publisher: A. L. Burt
1. A Prisoner in Buff; A Boy's Story of Old New York in 1776 (1900)
2. In Days of Peril; A Boy's Story of the Massacre in the Wyoming Valley in 1778 (1901)

145. BLUE AND GRAY [see also BLUE AND GRAY AFLOAT; BLUE AND GRAY ARMY; BLUE AND GRAY ON LAND]
author: Oliver Optic [pseudonym of William Taylor Adams]
publisher: Lee & Shepard
1. Taken by the Enemy (1888)
2. Fighting for the Right (1892)
3. On the Staff (1896)
4. Stand By the Union (1891)
5. A Victorious Union (1894)

146. BLUE AND GRAY AFLOAT [see also BLUE AND GRAY; BLUE AND GRAY ARMY; BLUE AND GRAY ON LAND]

author: Oliver Optic [pseudonym of William Taylor Adams]
publisher: Lee & Shepard
1. [title unknown]
2. Within the Enemy's Lines (1889)
3. On the Blockade (1890)
4. Stand By the Union (1891)
5. Fighting for the Right (1892)
6. A Victorious Union (1893)

147. BLUE AND GRAY ARMY [see also BLUE AND GRAY; BLUE AND GRAY AFLOAT; BLUE AND GRAY ON LAND]

author: Oliver Optic [pseudonym of William Taylor Adams]
publisher: Lee & Shepard
1. In the Saddle (1895)
2. Brother Against Brother; or, The War on the Border (1894)

148. BLUE AND GRAY ON LAND [see also BLUE AND GRAY; BLUE AND GRAY ARMY]

author: Oliver Optic [pseudonym of William Taylor Adams]
publisher: Lee & Shepard
1. Brother Against Brother; or, The War on the Border (1894)
2. In the Saddle (1897)
3. At the Front (1897)
4. On the Staff (1896)

149. BLUE-BELL

author: Eleanor Catherine Price
publisher: Marcus Ward
1. The Story of a Demoiselle (1880)

150. BLUE BIRD

author: Lilian Elizabeth (Becker) Roy
publisher: Platt & Peck; Platt & Nourse
1. The Blue Birds of Happy Times Nest (1914)
2. The Blue Birds' Winter Nest (1916)
3. The Blue Birds' Uncle Ben (1917)
4. The Blue Birds at Happy Hills (1919)

151. BLUE BONNET

authors: Caroline Elliott Jacobs [1–4]; Edyth Ellerbeck Read [2]; Lela Horn Richards [3–7]
publisher: L. C. Page

1. A Texas Blue Bonnet (1910)
2. Blue Bonnet's Ranch Party (1912)
3. Blue Bonnet in Boston (1914)
4. Blue Bonnet Keeps House (1916)
5. Blue Bonnet: Debutante (1917)
6. Blue Bonnet of the Seven Stars (1919)
7. Blue Bonnet's Family (1929)

152. BLUE DOMER SERIES

author: Jean Finley
publisher: A. L. Burt
1. The Blue Domers (1928)
2. The Blue Domers' Alphabet Zoo (1928)
3. The Blue Domers and the Wishing Tree (1928)
4. The Blue Domers and the Magic Flute (1928)
5. The Blue Domers in the Deep Woods (1928)
6. The Blue Domers Under Winter Skies (1928)
7. The Blue Domers and the Hidden Shanty (1930)
8. The Blue Domers' Nest (1930)

153. BLUE GRASS SEMINARY GIRLS

author: Carolyn Judson Burnett
publisher: A. L. Burt
1. The Blue Grass Seminary Girls' Vacation Adventures; or, Shirley Willing to the Rescue (1916)
2. The Blue Grass Seminary Girls' Christmas Holidays; or, A Four Weeks' Tour with the Glee Club (1916)
3. The Blue Grass Seminary Girls in the Mountains; or, Shirley Willing on a Mission of Peace (1916)
4. The Blue Grass Seminary Girls on the Water; or, Exciting Adventures on a Summer's Cruise Through the Panama Canal (1916)

154. BLUE WATER

author: Charles Pendexter Durell
publisher: Milton Bradley
1. The Skipper of the Cynthia B (1921)
2. Heave Short! (1926)

155. BLYTHE GIRLS BOOKS

author: Laura Lee Hope [pseudonym of the Stratemeyer Syndicate]

illustrator: Thelma Gooch
publisher: Grosset & Dunlap
1. The Blythe Girls: Helen, Margy and Rose; or, Facing the Great World (1925)
2. The Blythe Girls: Margy's Queer Inheritance; or, The Worth of a Name (1925)
3. The Blythe Girls: Rose's Great Problem; or, Face to Face with a Crisis (1925)
4. The Blythe Girls: Helen's Strange Boarder; or, The Girl from Bronx Park (1925)
5. The Blythe Girls: Three on a Vacation; or, The Mystery at Peach Farm (1925)
6. The Blythe Girls: Margy's Secret Mission; or, Exciting Days at Shadymere (1926)
7. The Blythe Girls: Rose's Odd Discovery; or, The Search for Irene Conroy (1927)
8. The Blythe Girls: The Disappearance of Helen; or, The Art Shop Mystery (1928)
9. The Blythe Girls: Snowbound in Camp; or, The Mystery at Elk Lodge (1929)
10. The Blythe Girls: Margy's Mysterious Visitor; or, Guarding the Pepper Fortune (1930)
11. The Blythe Girls: Rose's Hidden Talent (1931)
12. The Blythe Girls: Helen's Wonderful Mistake; or, The Mysterious Necklace (1932)

156. BOAT-BUILDER

author: Oliver Optic [pseudonym of William Taylor Adams]
publishers: Lee & Shepard; Charles T. Dillingham
1. All Adrift; or, The Goldwing Club (1882)
2. Snug Harbor; or, The Champlain Mechanics (1883)
3. Square and Compasses; or, Building the House (1884)
4. Stem to Stern; or, Building the Boat (1886)
5. All Taut; or, Rigging the Boat (1886)
6. Ready About; or, Sailing the Boat (1887)

157. BOAT CLUB

author: Oliver Optic [pseudonym of William Taylor Adams]

publishers: Caldwell; Henneberry; Mershon; M. A. Donohue
1. The Boat Club; or, The Bunkers of Rippleton: A Tale for Boys (1884)
2. All Aboard; or, Life on the Lake: A Sequel to "The Boat Club" (1855)
3. Now or Never; or, The Adventures of Bobby Bright: A Story for Young Folks (1858)
4. Try Again; or, The Trials and Triumphs of Harry West: A Story for Young Folks (1850)
5. Poor and Proud; or, The Fortunes of Katy Redburn: A Story for Little Folks (1858)
6. Little by Little; or, The Cruise of the Flyaway: A Story for Young Folks (1866)

158. BOB CHASE BIG GAME

author: Frank A. Warner [pseudonym of the Stratemeyer Syndicate]
illustrator: David Randolph
publisher: Barse & Company
1. Bob Chase with the Big Moose Hunters (1929)
2. Bob Chase after Grizzly Bears (1929)
3. Bob Chase in the Tiger's Lair (1929)
4. Bob Chase with the Lion Hunters (1930)

159. BOB COOK

author: Paul G. Tomlinson
publisher: Barse & Hopkins
1. Bob Cook and the German Spy (1917)
2. Bob Cook and the German Air Fleet
3. Bob Cook's Brother in the Trenches (1918)
4. Bob Cook and the Winged Messengers (1919)

160. BOB DEXTER MYSTERY

author: Willard F. Baker
publisher: Cupples & Leon
1. Bob Dexter and the Club-House Mystery; or, The Missing Golden Eagle (1925)
2. Bob Dexter and the Beacon Beach Mystery; or, The Wreck of the Sea Hawk
3. Bob Dexter and the Storm Mountain Mystery; or, The Secret of the Log Cabin

4. Bob Dexter and the Aeroplane Mystery; or, The Secret of the Jint San (1930)
5. Bob Dexter and the Seaplane Mystery; or, The Secret of the White Stones
6. Bob Dexter and the Red Auto Mystery; or, The Secret of the Flying Car
7. Bob Dexter and the Radio Mystery; or, The Secret of the Counterfeiters (1932)

BOB HAMILTON *see* **UNCLE SAM'S ARMY BOYS**

161. BOB HANSON
author: Russell Gordon Carter
publisher: Penn
1. Bob Hanson, Tenderfoot (1921)
2. Bob Hanson, Scout (1921)
3. Bob Hanson, First Class Scout (1922)
4. Bob Hanson, Eagle Scout (1923)

162. BOB HUNT
author: George W. Orton
publishers: Jacobs; Whitman
1. Bob Hunt at Camp Pontiac (1914)
2. Bob Hunt, Senior Camper
3. Bob Hunt in Canada (1916)

163. BOB KNIGHT'S DIARY
author: Charlotte Curtis Smith
publisher: E. P. Dutton
1. Bob Knight's Diary at Poplar Hill School (1900)
2. Bob Knight's Diary, Camping Out (1902)
3. Bob Knight's Diary with the Circus (1908)
4. Bob Knight's Diary on a Farm (1911)

BOB STEELE *see* **MOTOR POWER**

164. BOB THORPE
author: Austin Bishop
publisher: Harcourt, Brace and Howe
1. Bob Thorpe, Sky Fighter in the Lafayette Flying Corps (1919)
2. Bob Thorpe, Sky Fighter in Italy (1920)

165. BOB WAKEFIELD
author: Harold Blaine Miller
publisher: Dodd, Mead

1. Bob Wakefield, Naval Aviator (1936)
2. Bob Wakefield, Naval Inspector (1937)

166. BOBBSEY TWINS
author: Laura Lee Hope [pseudonym of the Stratemeyer Syndicate]
illustrators: Walter S. Rogers [1, 8–15, 17, 22–24]; Charles Nuttall [2–3]; Marie Schubert [1–2, 4, 25, 27–30, 32–37]; Margaret Temple Braley [26]; Gloria Singer [73x]; Ruth Sanderson [74x–76x]; Martha E. Miller [1–3]; Henry E. Vallely [1]; Janet Laura Scott [1–3]; Corinne Dillon [1]
publishers: Grosset & Dunlap; Simon & Schuster
1. The Bobbsey Twins; or, Merry Days Indoors and Out (1904)
2. The Bobbsey Twins in the Country (1904)
3. The Bobbsey Twins at the Seashore (1907)
4. The Bobbsey Twins at School (1913)
5. The Bobbsey Twins at Snow Lodge (1913)
6. The Bobbsey Twins on a Houseboat (1915)
7. The Bobbsey Twins at Meadowbrook (1915)
8. The Bobbsey Twins' Big Adventure at Home (1916)
9. The Bobbsey Twins in a Great City (1917)
10. The Bobbsey Twins on Blueberry Island (1917)
11. The Bobbsey Twins on the Deep Blue Sea (1918)
12. The Bobbsey Twins in Washington (1919)
13. The Bobbsey Twins in the Great West (1920)
14. The Bobbsey Twins at Cedar Camp (1921)
15. The Bobbsey Twins at the County Fair (1922)
16. The Bobbsey Twins Camping Out (1923)
17. The Bobbsey Twins and Baby May (1924)
18. The Bobbsey Twins Keeping House (1925)

19. The Bobbsey Twins at Cloverbank (1926)
20. The Bobbsey Twins at Cherry Corner (1927)
21. The Bobbsey Twins and Their Schoolmates (1928)
22. The Bobbsey Twins Treasure Hunting (1929)
23. The Bobbsey Twins at Spruce lake (1930)
24. The Bobbsey Twins' Wonderful Secret (1931)
25. The Bobbsey Twins at the Circus (1932)
26. The Bobbsey Twins on an Airplane Trip (1933)
27. The Bobbsey Twins Solve a Mystery (1934)
28. The Bobbsey Twins on a Ranch (1935)
29. The Bobbsey Twins in Eskimo Land (1936)
30. The Bobbsey Twins in a Radio Play (1937)
31. The Bobbsey Twins at Windmill Cottage (1938)
32. The Bobbsey Twins at Lighthouse Point (1939)
33. The Bobbsey Twins at Indian Hollow (1940)
34. The Bobbsey Twins at the Ice Carnival (1941)
35. The Bobbsey Twins in the Land of Cotton (1942)
36. The Bobbsey Twins in Echo Valley (1943)
37. The Bobbsey Twins on the Pony Trail (1944)
38. The Bobbsey Twins at Mystery Mansion (1945)
39. The Bobbsey Twins at Sugar Maple Hill (1946)
40. The Bobbsey Twins in Mexico (1947)
41. The Bobbsey Twins' Toy Shop (1948)
42. The Bobbsey Twins in Tulip Land (1949)
43. The Bobbsey Twins' Own Little Railroad (1951)
44. The Bobbsey Twins in Rainbow Valley (1950)
45. The Bobbsey Twins at Whitesail Harbor (1952)
46. The Bobbsey Twins and the Horseshoe Riddle (1953)
47. The Bobbsey Twins at Big Bear Pond (1953)
48. Meet the Bobbsey Twins (1954)
49. The Bobbsey Twins on a Bicycle Trip (1954)
50. The Bobbsey Twins' Own Little Ferryboat (1956)
51. The Bobbsey Twins at Pilgrim Rock (1956)
52. The Bobbsey Twins' Forest Adventure (1957)
53. The Bobbsey Twins at London Tower (1959)
54. The Bobbsey Twins in the Mystery Cave (1960)
55. The Bobbsey Twins of Lakeport (1961)
56. The Bobbsey Twins in Volcano Land (1961)
57. The Bobbsey Twins and the Goldfish Mystery (1962)
58. The Bobbsey Twins and the Big River Mystery (1963)
59. The Bobbsey Twins and the Greek Hat Mystery (1964)
60. The Bobbsey Twins' Search for the Green Rooster (1965)
61. The Bobbsey Twins and Their Camel Adventure (1966)
62. The Bobbsey Twins' Mystery of the King's Puppet (1967)
63. The Bobbsey Twins and the Secret of Candy Castle (1968)
64. The Bobbsey Twins' Adventures with Baby May (1968)
65. The Bobbsey Twins and the Doodlebug Mystery (1969)
66. The Bobbsey Twins and the Talking Fox Mystery (1970)
67. The Bobbsey Twins: The Red, White and Blue Mystery (1971)
68. The Bobbsey Twins and Dr. Funnybone's Secret (1972)
69. The Bobbsey Twins and the Tagalong Giraffe (1973)
70. The Bobbsey Twins and the Flying Clown (1974)
71. The Bobbsey Twins on the Sun-Moon Cruise (1975)
72. The Bobbsey Twins and the Freedom Bell (1977)

73. The Bobbsey Twins and the Smoky Mountain Mystery (1977)
74. The Bobbsey Twins in the T.V. Mystery Show (1978)
75. The Bobbsey Twins and the Coral Turtle Mystery (1979)
76. The Bobbsey Twins and the Blue Poodle Mystery (1980)
77. The Bobbsey Twins and the Secret of the Pirate's Cave (1980)
78. The Bobbsey Twins and the Dune Buggy Mystery (1981)
79. The Bobbsey Twins and the Missing Pony Mystery (1981)
80. The Bobbsey Twins and the Rose Parade Mystery (1981)
81. The Bobbsey Twins and the Camp Fire Mystery (1982)
82. The Bobbsey Twins and Double Trouble (1982)
83. The Bobbsey Twins and the Mystery of the Laughing Dinosaur (1983)
84. The Bobbsey Twins and the Missing Box Mystery (1983)
85. The Bobbsey Twins and the Ghost in the Computer (1984)
86. The Bobbsey Twins and the Haunted House Mystery (1985)
87. The Bobbsey Twins and the Mystery of the Hindu Temple (1985)
[Note: This series is followed by a series called The New Bobbsey Twins]

167. BOBBY BLAKE

author: Frank A. Warner [pseudonym of the Statemeyer Syndicate]
illustrators: R. Emmett Owen [1–7]; Charles L. Wrenn [8]; E. J. Dinsmore [9]; Walter S. Rogers [10–11]; Oriet Williams [12]
publishers: Barse & Hopkins; Grosset & Dunlap
1. Bobby Blake at Rockledge School; or, Winning the Medal of Honor (1915)
2. Bobby Blake at Bass Cove; or, The Hunt for the Motor Boat "Gem" (1915)
3. Bobby Blake on a Cruise; or, The Castaways of Volcano Island (1915)
4. Bobby Blake and His School Chums; or, The Rivals of Rockledge (1916)
5. Bobby Blake at Snowtop Camp; or, Winter Holidays in the Big Woods (1916)

6. Bobby Blake on the School Nine; or, The Champions of Monotook Lake League (1917)
7. Bobby Blake on a Ranch; or, The Secret of the Mountain Cave (1918)
8. Bobby Blake on an Auto Tour; or, The Mystery of the Deserted House (1920)
9. Bobby Blake on the School Eleven; or, Winning the Banner of Blue and Gold (1921) [alternate subtitle: The Winning Touchdown]
10. Bobby Blake on a Plantation; or, Lost in the Great Swamp (1922) [alternate subtitle: The Secret of the Old Cabin]
11. Bobby Blake in the Frozen North; or, The Old Eskimo's Last Message (1923) [alternate subtitle: Lost in the Land of Ice]
12. Bobby Blake on Mystery Mountain; or, The Ghost of the Crags (1926)

168. BOB'S HILL

author: Charles Pierce Burton
publishers: H. Holt; Grosset & Dunlap
1. The Boys of Bob's Hill; Adventures of Tom Chapin and the "Band," as Told by the "Secretary" (1915)
2. The Bob's Hill Cave Boys; A Sequel to "The Boys of Bob's Hill" (1909)
3. The Bob's Hill Braves (1910)
4. The Boy Scouts of Bob's Hill (1912)
5. The Camp on Bob's Hill (1915) [alternate title: Camp Bob's Hill]
6. The Raven Patrol of Bob's Hill
7. The Trail Makers
8. Treasure Hunters of Bob's Hill (1926)
9. Bob's Hill Meets the Andes; Doings of the "Band" in South America as Told in the "Minutes of the Meeting" (1928)
10. Bob's Hill Trails
11. Bob's Hill Boys on the Air; Some Adventures that the Secretary Failed to Record in the "Minutes of the Meeting" (1934)
12. Bob's Hill Boys in Virginia (1939)
13. Bob's Hill Boys in the Everglades

169. BOMBA THE JUNGLE BOY

author: Roy Rockwood [pseudonym of the Statemeyer Syndicate]

illustrators: Walter S. Rogers [1–6];
Howard L. Hastings [7–11; 13–14]; A.
Suk [12]

publishers: Cupples & Leon; Clover
Books

1. Bomba the Jungle Boy; or, The Old Naturalist's Secret (1926)
2. Bomba the Jungle Boy at the Moving Mountain; or, The Mystery of the Caverns of Fire (1926)
3. Bomba the Jungle Boy at the Giant Cataract; or, Chief Nascanora and His Captives (1926)
4. Bomba the Jungle Boy on Jaguar Island; or, Adrift on the River of Mystery (1927)
5. Bomba the Jungle Boy in the Abandoned City; or, A Treasure Ten Thousand Years Old (1927)
6. Bomba the Jungle Boy on Terror Trail; or, The Mysterious Men from the Sky (1928)
7. Bomba the Jungle Boy in the Swamp of Death; or, The Sacred Alligators of Abarago (1929)
8. Bomba the Jungle Boy Among the Slaves; or, Daring Adventures in the Valley of Skulls (1929)
9. Bomba the Jungle Boy on the Underground River; or, The Cave of Bottomless Pits (1930)
10. Bomba the Jungle Boy and the Lost Explorers; or, A Wonderful Revelation (1930)
11. Bomba the Jungle Boy in a Strange Land; or, Facing the Unknown (1931)
12. Bomba the Jungle Boy Among the Pygmies; or, Battling with Stealthy Foes (1931)
13. Bomba the Jungle Boy and the Cannibals; or, Winning Against Native Dangers (1932)
14. Bomba the Jungle Boy and the Painted Hunters; or, A Long Search Rewarded (1932)
15. Bomba the Jungle Boy and the River Demons; or, Outwitting the Savage Medicine Man (1933)
16. Bomba the Jungle Boy and the Hostile Chieftain; or, A Hazardous Trek to the Sea (1934)
17. Bomba the Jungle Boy Trapped by the Cyclone; or, Shipwrecked on the Swirling Seas (1935)
18. Bomba the Jungle Boy in the Land of Burning Lava; or, Outwitting Superstitious Natives (1936)
19. Bomba the Jungle Boy in the Perilous Kingdom; or, Braving Strange Hazards (1937)
20. Bomba the Jungle Boy in the Steaming Grotto; or, Victorious Through Flame and Fury (1938)

170. BONNIE

author: Rebecca Caudill
publisher: Winston

1. Happy Little Family (1947)
2. The Schoolhouse in the Woods (1949)
3. Up and Down the River (1951)
4. Schoolroom in the Parlor (1959)

171. BORDER BOYS

author: Fremont B. Deering [pseudonym of John Henry Goldfrap]
illustrator: Charles L. Wrenn
publishers: A. L. Burt; Hurst

1. The Border Boys on the Trail (1911)
2. The Border Boys Across the Frontier (1911)
3. The Border Boys with the Mexican Rangers (1911)
4. The Border Boys with the Texas Rangers (1912)
5. The Border Boys in the Canadian Rockies (1913)
6. The Border Boys Along the St. Lawrence (1914)

172. BOUND TO SUCCEED

author: Edward Stratemeyer
publisher: Lee & Shepard

1. Richard Dare's Venture; or, Striking Out for Himself (1899)
2. Oliver Bright's Search; or, The Mystery of a Mine (1899)
3. To Alaska for Gold; or, The Fortune Hunters of the Yukon (1899)

173. BOUND TO WIN I

author: Edwin Alger
publisher: Grosset & Dunlap

1. Phil Hardy's Struggle (1930)

2. Phil Hardy's Triumph (1930)
3. Phil Hardy's Greatest Test (1930)

174. BOUND TO WIN II
author: Arthur M. Winfield [pseudonym
of Edward Stratemeyer]
publisher: M. A. Donohue
[1 to 10 titles unknown]
11. By Pluck, Not Luck; or, Dan
Granbury's Struggle to Rise (1905)

175. BOUND TO WIN III
author: Ralph Bonehill
publisher: W. L. Allison
1. Leo the Circus Boy; or, Life Under the
Great White Canvas (1897)

176. BOXCAR CHILDREN
author: Gertrude Chandler Warner
publishers: Rand McNally [1]; Scott [2];
Albert Whitman [3–19]
1. The Boxcar Children (1924)
2. Surprise Island (1949)
3. The Yellow House Mystery (1953)
4. Mystery Ranch (1958)
5. Mike's Mystery (1960)
6. Blue Bay Mystery (1961)
7. The Woodshed Mystery (1962)
8. The Lighthouse Mystery (1963)
9. The Mountain Top Mystery (1964)
10. Schoolhouse Mystery (1965)
11. Caboose Mystery (1966)
12. Houseboat Mystery (1967)
13. Snowbound Mystery (1968)
14. Treehouse Mystery (1969)
15. Bicycle Mystery (1970)
16. Mystery in the Sand (1971)
17. Mystery Behind the Wall (1973)
18. Bus Station Mystery (1974)
19. Benny Uncovers a Mystery (1976)

177. BOY ADVENTURERS
author: Alpheus Hyatt Verrill
publisher: Putnam
1. The Boy Adventurers in the Forbidden
land (1922)
2. The Boy Adventurers in the land of El
Dorado (1923)
3. The Boy Adventurers in the Land of
the Monkey Men (1923)
4. The Boy Adventurers in the Unknown
Land (1924)

178. BOY ALLIES WITH THE ARMY [see also BOY ALLIES WITH THE NAVY]
author: Robert L. Drake [pseudonym of
Clair Wallace Hayes]
publisher: A. L. Burt
1. The Boy Allies at Liege; or, Through
Lines of Steel (1915)
2. The Boy Allies on the Firing Line; or,
Twelve Days' Battle Along the Marne
(1915)
3. The Boy Allies with the Cossacks; or,
A Wild Dash over the Carpathian
Mountains (1915) [alternate subtitle:
A Wild Dash over the Carpathians]
4. The Boy Allies in the Trenches; or,
Midst Shot and Shell Along the Aisne
(1915)
5. The Boy Allies in Great Peril; or, With
the Italian Army in the Alps (1916)
6. The Boy Allies in the Balkan Campaign; or, The Struggle to Save a
Nation (1916)
7. The Boy Allies on the Somme; or,
Courage and Bravery Rewarded (1917)
8. The Boy Allies at Verdun; or, Saving
France from the Enemy (1917)
9. The Boy Allies Under the Stars and
Stripes; or, Leading the American
Troops to the Firing Line (1918)
10. The Boy Allies with Haig in Flanders;
or, The Fighting Canadians of Vimy
Ridge (1918)
11. The Boy Allies with Pershing in
France; or, Over the Top at Chateau
Thierry (1919)
12. The Boy Allies with the Great
Advance; or, Driving the Enemy
Through France and Belgium (1919)
13. The Boy Allies with Marshal Foch; or,
The Closing Days of the Great World
War (1919)

179. BOY ALLIES WITH THE NAVY [see also BOY ALLIES WITH THE ARMY]
author: Robert L. Drake [pseudonym of
Clair Wallace Hayes]
publisher: A. L. Burt
1. The Boy Allies on the North Sea
Patrol; or, Striking the First Blow at
the German Fleet (1915)

2. The Boy Allies Under Two Flags; or, Sweeping the Enemy from the Seas (1915)
3. The Boy Allies with the Flying Squadron; or, The Naval Raiders of the Great War (1915)
4. The Boy Allies with the Terror of the Sea; or, The Last Shot of Submarine D-16 (1915)
5. The Boy allies Under the Sea; or, The Vanishing Submarine (1916)
6. The Boy Allies in the Baltic; or, Through Fields of Ice to Aid the Czar (1916)
7. The Boy Allies at Jutland; or, The Greatest Naval Battle of History (1917)
8. The Boy Allies with Uncle Sam's Cruisers; or, Convoying the American Army Across the Atlantic (1918)
9. The Boy Allies with the Submarine D-32; or, The Fall of the Russian Empire (1918)
10. The Boy Allies with the Victorious Fleets; or, The Fall of the German Navy (1919)

180. BOY AVIATORS

author: Captain Wilbur Lawton [pseudonym of John Henry Goldfrap]
illustrator: Charles L. Wrenn
publisher: Hurst

1. The Boy Aviators in Nicaragua; or, In League with the Insurgents (1910)
2. The Boy Aviators on Secret Service; or, Working with Wireless (1910)
3. The Boy Aviators in Africa; or, An Aerial Ivory Trail (1910)
4. The Boy Aviators' Treasure Quest; or, The Golden Galleon (1910)
5. The Boy Aviators in Record Flight; or, The Rival Aeroplane (1910)
6. The Boy Aviators' Polar Dash; or, Facing Death in the Antarctic (1910)
7. The Boy Aviators' Flight for a Fortune (1912)
8. The Boy Aviators with the Air Raiders; A Story of the Great World War (1915)

181. BOY CHUMS

author: Wilmer Mateo Ely
publisher: A. L. Burt

1. The Boy Chums on Indian River; or, The Boy Partners of the Schooner "Orphan" (1905)
2. The Boy Chums on Haunted Island; or, Hunting for Pearls in the Bahama Islands (1909)
3. The Boy Chums in the Forest; or, Hunting for Plume Birds in the Florida Everglades (1910) [alternate title: The Young Plume Hunters; The Adventures of Charley West and Walter Hazard Hunting the Treasure of the Everglades]
4. The Boy Chums' Perilous Cruise; or, Searching for Wreckage on the Florida Coast (1911)
5. The Boy Chums in the Gulf of Mexico; or, On a Dangerous Cruise Among the Greek Spongers (1913)
6. The Boy Chums Cruising in Florida Waters; or, The Perils and Dangers of the Fishing Fleet (1914)
7. The Boy Chums in the Florida Jungle; or, Charlie West and Walter Hazard with the Seminole Indians (1915)
8. The Boy Chums in Mystery Land; or, Charlie West and Walter Hazard Among the Mexicans (1916)

182. BOY EXPLORERS [*see also* DICK]

author: Warren Hastings Miller
publisher: Harper

1. The Boy Explorers in Darkest New Guinea (1921)
2. The Boy Explorers in Borneo (1922)
3. The Boy Explorers and the Ape-Man of Sumatra
4. The Boy Explorers on Tiger Trails in Burma (1925)
5. The Boy Explorers in the Pirate Archipelago (1926)

183. BOY FORTUNE HUNTERS

author: Floyd Akers [pseudonym of Lyman Frank Baum]
publisher: Reilly & Britton

1. The Boy Fortune Hunters in Alaska (1908)
2. The Boy Fortune Hunters in Panama (1908)

3. The Boy Fortune Hunters in Egypt (1908)
4. The Boy Fortune Hunters in China (1909)
5. The Boy Fortune Hunters in Yucatan
6. The Boy Fortune Hunters in the South Seas (1911)

184. BOY GLOBE TROTTERS
author: Elbert Curtiss Fisher
publishers: New York Book; M. A. Donohue
1. The Boy Globe Trotters — From New York to the Golden Gate (1915)
2. The Boy Globe Trotters — From San Francisco to Japan (1915)
3. The Boy Globe Trotters — From Tokyo to Bombay (1915)
4. The Boy Globe Trotters — From India to the War Zone

185. BOY HIKERS
author: Chelsea Curtis Fraser
publishers: World; Thomas Y. Crowell
1. The Boy Hikers; or, Doing Their Bit for Uncle Sam (1918)

186. BOY HUNTERS
author: Ralph Bonehill [pseudonym of the Stratemeyer Syndicate]
publisher: Cupples & Leon
1. Four Boy Hunters; or, The Outing of the Gun Club (1906)
2. Guns and Snowshoes; or, The Winter Outing of the Young Hunters (1907)
3. Young Hunters of the Lake; or, Out with Rod and Gun (1908)
4. Out with Gun and Camera; or, The Boy Hunters in the Mountains (1910)

187. BOY INVENTORS
author: Richard Bonner
publishers: Hurst; M. A. Donohue
1. The Boy Inventors' Wireless Telegraph (1912)
2. The Boy Inventors' Vanishing Gun (1912)
3. The Boy Inventors' Diving Torpedo Boat (1912)
4. The Boy Inventors' Flying Ship
5. The Boy Inventors' Electric Hydroaeroplane (1914)

6. The Boy Inventors' Radio-Telephone (1915)

188. BOY RANCHERS
author: Willard F. Baker
publisher: Cupples & Leon
1. The Boy Ranchers; or, Solving the Mystery at Diamond X (1921)
2. The Boy Ranchers in Camp; or, The Water Fight at Diamond X (1921)
3. The Boy Ranchers on the Trail; or, The Diamond X After Cattle Rustlers (1921)
4. The Boy Ranchers Among the Indians; or, The Diamond X Trailing the Yaquis (1922)
5. The Boy Ranchers at Spur Creek; or, The Diamond X Fighting the Sheep Herders (1923)
6. The Boy Ranchers in the Desert; The Diamond X and the Lost Mine (1924)
7. The Boy Ranchers on Roaring River; or, The Diamond X and the Chinese Smugglers (1926)
8. The Boy Ranchers in Death Valley; or, The Diamond X and the Poison Mystery (1928)
9. The Boy Ranchers in Terror Canyon; or, The Diamond X Winning Out (1930)

BOY SCOUT AND NATURE ADVENTURE see BOY SCOUTS XIX

BOY SCOUT LIFE see BOY SCOUTS XIII

189. BOY SCOUTS I
author: John Blaine
illustrators: E. A. Furman [1–7]; F. Schwankovsky, Jr. [8]; Clare Angell [9]
publisher: Saalfield
1. The Boy Scouts in Germany; On Board the Mine-Laying Cruiser (1916)
2. The Boy Scouts in England; Facing the German Foe (1916)
3. The Boy Scouts in France (1916)
4. The Boy Scouts in Italy; Fighting in the Alps (1916)
5. The Boy Scouts in Russia (1916)
6. The Boys Scouts in Servia (1916)

7. The Boys Scouts in the Netherlands; The Belgians to the Front (1916)
8. The Boy Scouts in Turkey; Shelled by an Unseen Foe (1916)
9. The Boy Scouts on a Submarine (1918)

190. BOY SCOUTS II
author: Thornton Waldo Burgess
illustrators: Charles S. Corson [1–3]; F. A. Anderson [4]
publisher: Penn
1. The Boy Scouts of Woodcraft Camp (1912)
2. The Boy Scouts on Swift River (1913)
3. The Boy Scouts on Lost Trail (1914)
4. The Boy Scouts in a Trapper's Camp (1915)

191. BOY SCOUTS III
author: Herbert Carter
publisher: A. L. Burt
1. The Boy Scouts' First Camp Fire; or, Scouting with the Silver Fox Patrol (1913)
2. The Boy Scouts in the Blue Ridge; or, Marooned Among the Moonshiners (1913)
3. The Boy Scouts on the Trail; or, Scouting Through the Big Game Country (1913)
4. The Boy Scouts in the Maine Woods; or, The New Test for the Silver Fox Patrol (1913)
5. The Boy Scouts Through the Big Timber; or, The Search for the Lost Tenderfoot (1913)
6. The Boy Scouts in the Rockies; or, The Secret of the Hidden Silver Mine (1913)
7. The Boy Scouts on Sturgeon Island; or, Marooned Among the Game Fish Poachers (1914)
8. The Boy Scouts Down in Dixie; or, The Strange Secret of Alligator Swamp (1914)
9. The Boy Scouts at the Battle of Saratoga; or, The Story of General Burgoyne's Defeat in 1777 (1909)
10. Boy Scouts Along the Susquehanna; or, The Silver Fox Patrol Caught in a Flood (1915)

11. The Boy Scouts on War Trails in Belgium; or, Caught Between the Hostile Armies (1916)
12. The Boy Scouts Afoot in France; or, With the Red Cross Corps at the Marne (1917)

192. BOY SCOUTS IV
author: Brewer Corcoran
illustrator: John Goss
publisher: L. C. Page
1. The Boy Scouts of Kendallville (1918)
2. The Boy Scouts of the Wolf Patrol (1920)
3. The Boy Scouts at Camp Lowell (1922)

193. BOY SCOUTS V
authors: Irving Crump [1]; F. Moulton McLane [2]; Frank Hobart Cheley [3]; Charles Henry Lerrigo [4, 7, 11–12]; Walter Walden [5]; Franklin K. Matthews [6]; John Garth [8]; Corcoran [9]
illustrator: Charles L. Wrenn
publishers: Barse & Hopkins [1–9]; Little, Brown [10]
1. The Boy Scout Fire Fighters (1917)
2. The Boy Scouts of the Lighthouse Troop; or, The Surprising Adventures of a New York Schoolboy (1917)
3. The Boy Scout Trail Blazers; or, Scouting for Uncle Sam on the Pike National Forest (1917)
4. The Boy Scout Treasure Hunters; or, The Lost Treasure of Buffalo Hollow (1917)
5. The Boy Scouts Afloat; or, Scouting on the Mississippi in a Houseboat (1918)
6. Boy Scouts Courageous; Stories of Scout Valor and Daring (1918)
7. The Boy Scouts to the Rescue (1920)
8. The Boy Scouts on the Trail (1920)
9. The Boy Scouts in Africa (1923)
10. The Boy Scouts of Round Table Patrol (1924)
11. The Boy Scouts on Special Service (1922)
12. The Merry Men of Robin Hood Patrol (1927)

194. BOY SCOUTS VI

author: George Durston [pseudonym of Georgia Roberts] [1–3; 5; 8–12; 15; 19–26]; Robert Maitland [4; 6–7, 13–14; 16–18]

publisher: Saalfield

1. The Boy Scouts in Camp; or, Jack Danby's Courage (1912)
2. The Boy Scouts to the Rescue; or Jack Danby's Fighting Chance (1912)
3. The Boy Scouts on the Trail; or, Jack Danby's Strange Hunt (1912)
4. The Boy Scout Firefighters; or, Jack Danby's Bravest Deed (1912)
5. The Boy Scouts Afloat (1921)
6. The Boy Scouts Pathfinders; or, Jack Danby's Best Adventure
7. The Boy Scouts Automobilists
8. The Boy Scouts Aviators; or, Jack Danby's Fine Skill (1912)
9. The Boy Scouts' Champion Recruit; or, Tom Peck's Courage (1912)
10. The Boy Scouts' Defiance; or, Will Ransier's Heroic Act (1912)
11. The Boy Scouts' Challenge; or, Will Ransier's Great Problem (1912)
12. The Boy Scouts' Victory; or, Bob Morrison's Lone Struggle (1912)
13. The Boy Scouts with King George; or, Harry Fleming's Ordeal (1915)
14. The Boy Scouts with the Allies; or, Frank Barnes' Exploit (1915)
15. The Boy Scouts Under the Star and Stripes; or, Serving on Land and Sea (1918)
16. The Boy Scouts at Liege; or, Paul Latour's Patriotism (1915)
17. The Boy Scouts with the Cossacks; or, Fred Waring's Service (1915)
18. The Boy Scouts Before Belgrade; or, Dick Warner's Mission (1915)
19. The Boy Scouts' Test; or, A Son of Italy (1916)
20. A Boy Scout's Campaign (1927)
21. A Boy Scout's Secret (1927)
22. The Boy Scouts Under the Red Cross; or, Back of the Fighting Line (1916)
23. The Boy Scouts in the War Zone
24. The Boy Scouts in Front of Warsaw; or, In the Wake of War (1916)
25. The Boy Scouts with Joffre (1919)
26. The Boy Scouts Under Fire in France; or, Abroad for Uncle Sam (1919)
27. The Boy Scouts' Discovery (1927)
28. The Boy Scouts' Mission (1927)
29. The Boy Scouts Under the Kaiser; or, Karl Adler's Devotion (1915)

195. BOY SCOUTS VII

author: Walter Prichard Eaton
illustrators: Charles Copeland; Frank T. Merrill
publisher: W. A. Wilde

1. The Boy Scouts of the Berkshires (1912)
2. The Boy Scouts in the Dismal Swamp (1913)
3. The Boy Scouts in the White Mountains; The Story of a Long Hike (1914)
4. The Boy Scouts of the Wildcat Patrol; The Adventures of Peanut as a Young Scout Master (1915)
5. The Boy Scouts in Glacier Park; The Adventures of Two Young Easterners in the Heart of the High Rockies (1918)
6. The Boy Scouts at Crater Lake; A Story of Crater Lake National Park and High Cascades (1922)
7. The Boy Scouts on Katahdin; A Story of the Maine Woods (1924)
8. The Boy Scouts on the Green Mountain Trail; A Story of the Long Trail (1929)
9. The Boy Scouts at the Grand Canyon; A Story of the Rainbow Country (1932)
10. The Boy Scouts in Death Valley (1939)

196. BOY SCOUTS VIII

author: Archibald Lee Fletcher
publisher: M. A. Donohue

1. Boy Scout Rivals; or, A Leader of the Tenderfoot Patrol (1913)
2. Boy Scouts' Test of Courage; or, Winning the Merit Badge (1913)
3. Boy Scouts' Signal Sender; or, When Wigwag Knowledge Paid (1913)
4. Boy Scouts on a Long Hike; or, To the Rescue in the Black Water Swamp (1913)
5. Boy Scouts' Woodcraft Lesson; or,

Proving their Mettle in the Field (1913)
6. Boy Scout Pathfinders; or, The Strange Hunt for the Beaver Patrol (1913)
7. Boy Scouts on Old Superior; or, The Tale of the Pictured Rocks (1913)
8. Boy Scouts in the Everglades; or, The Island in Lost Channel (1913)
9. Boy Scouts in Northern Wilds; or, The Signal from the Hills (1913)
10. Boy Scouts on the Great Divide; or, The Ending of the Trail (1913)
11. Boy Scouts in the Coal Caverns; or, The Light in Tunnel Six (1913)
12. Boy Scouts in Alaska; or, The Camp on the Glacier (1913)

197. BOY SCOUTS IX
author: Edward Griggs
publisher: Saalfield
1. The Boy Scout's Destiny (1921)
2. The Boy Scout's Holiday (1921)
3. The Boy Scout's Courage (1921)
4. The Boy Scout's Daring (1921)
5. The Boy Scout's Patriot (1921)
6. The Boy Scout's Adventure (1921)
7. The Boy Scout's Struggle (1921)
8. The Boy Scout's Success (1921)

198. BOY SCOUTS X
author: William Heyliger
publisher: David Appleton
1. Don Strong of the Wolf Patrol (1916)
2. Don Strong, Patrol Leader
3. Don Strong, American (1920)

199. BOY SCOUTS XI
author: Rupert Sargent Holland
illustrators: Herbert Pullinger [1]; Will Thomson [2]
publisher: J. B. Lippincott
1. The Boy Scouts of Birch-Bark Island (1911)
2. The Boy Scouts of Snow-Shoe Lodge (1915)

200. BOY SCOUTS XII
authors: James Otis [pseudonym of James Otis Kaler] [1–2]; P. K. Fitzhugh [3–5]; Edwin Legrand Sabin [6]

illustrator: Clarence H. Rowe
publisher: Thomas W. Crowell
1. Boy Scouts in the Maine Woods (1911)
2. Boy Scouts in a Lumber Camp (1913)
3. Along the Mohawk Trail; or, Boy Scouts on Lake Champlain (1912)
4. For Uncle Sam, Boss; or, Boy Scouts at Panama (1913)
5. In the Path of LaSalle; or, Boy Scouts on the Mississippi (1914)
6. Pluck on the Long Trail; or, Boy Scouts in the Rockies (1912)

201. BOY SCOUTS XIII
author: Howard Payson [pseudonym of John Henry Goldfrap]
illustrators: Charles L. Wrenn; Arthur O. Scott; R.M. Brinkerhoff
publishers: Hurst; A. L. Burt
1. The Boy Scouts of the Eagle Patrol (1911)
2. The Boy Scouts on the Range (1911)
3. The Boy Scouts and the Army Air-Ship (1911)
4. The Boy Scouts' Mountain Camp (1912)
5. The Boy Scouts for Uncle Sam (1912)
6. The Boy Scouts at the Panama Canal (1913)
7. The Boy Scouts Under Fire in Mexico (1914)
8. The Boy Scouts on Belgian Battle-fields (1915)
9. The Boy Scouts with the Allies in France (1915)
10. The Boy Scouts at the Panama-Pacific Exposition (1915)
11. The Boy Scouts Under Sealed Orders (1916)
12. The Boy Scouts' Campaign for Preparedness (1916)
13. The Boy Scouts' Badge of Courage (1917)
14. The Boy Scouts at the Canadian Border (1918)

202. BOY SCOUTS XIV
author: Leslie W. Quirk
illustrator: William Kirkpatrick
publishers: Little,Brown; Grosset & Dunlap

1. The Boy Scouts of Black Eagle Patrol (1915)
2. The Boy Scouts on Crusade (1917)
3. The Boy Scouts of Lakeville High (1920)

203. BOY SCOUTS XV
author George Harvey Ralphson
publisher: M. A. Donahue

1. Boy Scouts in Mexico; or, On Guard with Uncle Sam (1911)
2. Boy Scouts in the Canal Zone; or, The Plot Against Uncle Sam (1911)
3. Boy Scouts in the Philippines; or, The Key to the Treaty Box (1911)
4. Boy Scouts in the Northwest; or, Fighting Forest Fires (1911)
5. Boy Scouts in a Motor Boat; or, Adventures on the Columbia River (1912)
6. Boy Scouts in an Airship; or, The Warning from the Sky (1912)
7. Boy Scouts in a Submarine; or, Searching an Ocean Floor (1912)
8. Boy Scouts on Motorcycles; or, With the Flying Squadron (1912)
9. Boy Scouts Beyond the Arctic Circle; or, The Lost Expedition (1913)
10. Boy Scout Camera Club; or, The Confession of a Photograph (1913)
11. Boy Scout Electricians; or, The Hidden Dynamo (1913)
12. Boy Scouts in California; or, The Flag on the Cliff (1913)
13. Boy Scouts on Hudson Bay; or, The Disappearing Fleet (1914)
14. Boy Scouts in Death Valley; or, The City in the Sky (1914)
15. Boy Scouts on Open Plains; or, The Roundup Not Ordered (1914)
16. Boy Scouts in Southern Waters; or, The Spanish Treasure Chest (1915)
17. Boy Scouts in Belgium; or, Under Fire in Flanders (1914) [alternate subtitle: Imperiled in a Trap]
18. Boy Scouts in the North Sea; or, The Mystery of U-13 (1915) [alternate subtitle: The Mystery of a Sub]
19. Boy Scouts Under the Kaiser; or, The Uhlan's Escape (1916) [alternate subtitle: The Uhlans in Peril]
20. Boy Scouts with the Cossacks; or,

Poland Recaptured (1916) [alternate subtitle: A Guilty Secret]
21. Boy Scouts' Mysterious Signal; or Perils of the Black Bear Patrol (1916) [alternate title: Boy Scouts In the Verdun Attack]
22. Boy Scouts in Belgium; or, Imperiled in a Trap (1912)
23. Boy Scouts Afloat; or, Adventures on Watery Trails (1917)
24. Boy Scouts on the Open Plains; or, The Round-Up Not Ordered
25. Boy Scouts on Old Superior; or, The Tale of the Pictured Rocks (1913)

204. BOY SCOUTS XVI
author: Robert Shaler
publisher: Hurst

1. The Boy Scouts of the Life Saving Crew (1914)
2. The Boy Scouts as Forest Fire Fighters (1915)
3. The Boy Scouts at Mobilization Camp (1914)
4. The Boy Scouts of the Signal Corps (1912)
5. The Boy Scouts of Pioneer Camp (1914)
6. The Boy Scouts of the Geological Survey (1914)
7. [title unknown]
8. The Boy Scouts on Picket Duty (1914)
9. The Boy Scouts of the Flying Squadron (1914)
10. The Boy Scouts and the Prize Pennant (1914)
11. The Boy Scouts of the Naval Reserve (1914)
12. The Boy Scouts in the Saddle (1914)
13. The Boy Scouts for City Improvement (1914)
14. The Boy Scouts in the Great Flood (1915)
15. The Boy Scouts of the Field Hospital (1915)
16. The Boy Scouts with the Red Cross (1915)
17. The Boy Scouts as County Fair Guides (1915)
18. The Boy Scouts on the Roll of Honor (1916)

19. The Scouts with the Motion Picture
    Players (1916)

205. BOY SCOUTS XVII
author: V. T. Sherman
publisher: M. A. Donahue
  1. The Boy Scouts with Joffre; or, In the
     Trenches in Belgium (1912)
  2. The Boy Scouts' Signal; or, The
     Camp on the Cliff (1913)
  3. Scouting the Balkans in a Motor
     Boat; or, An Escape from the Dard-
     anelles (1913)
  4. Capturing a Spy; or, A New Peril
     (1913)
  5. The Boy Scouts in the War Zone;
     or, Boy Scouts of the North Sea
     (1915)
  6. Lost Patrol; or, Scout Tactics to the
     Front (1913)
  7. The War Zone of the Kaiser; or, Boy
     Scouts in the North Sea
  8. An Interrupted Wig Wag; or, A Boy
     Scout Trick (1913)
  9. The Call of the Beaver Patrol; or, A
     Break in the Glacier (1913)
 10. The Perils of An Air-Ship; or, Boy
     Scouts in the Sky (1912)
 11. The Runaway Balloon; or, The
     Besieged Scouts (1913)

206. BOY SCOUTS XVIII
author: Ralph Victor
illustrator: Ralph Mencl
publishers: A. L. Chatterton; Platt &
  Peck; Hurst
  1. The Boy Scouts' Patrol (1910)
  2. The Boy Scouts' Motor Cycles (1911)
  3. The Boy Scouts' Canoe Trip (1911)
  4. The Boy Scouts in the Canadian Rock-
     ies (1911)
  5. The Boy Scouts' Air Craft (1912)
  6. The Boy Scouts on the Yukon (1912)
  7. The Boy Scouts in the North Woods
     (1913)
  8. The Boy Scouts in the Black Hills
     (1913)

207. BOY SCOUTS OF THE AIR
author: Gordon Stuart [pseudonym of
  Harry Lincoln Sayler, G.N. Madison,
  and H. Bedford]

illustrators: Norman P. Hall [1–9]; Harry
  W. Armstrong [14]; Charles E. Meister
  [10]; Joseph W. Wyckoff [11] Kirke
  Bride [12]
publishers: Reilly & Britton; Reilly &
  Lee
  1. The Boy Scouts of the Air at Eagle
     Camp (1912)
  2. The Boy Scouts of the Air at Green-
     wood School (1912)
  3. The Boy Scouts of the Air in Indian
     Land (1912)
  4. The Boy Scouts of the Air in North-
     ern Wilds (1912)
  5. The Boy Scouts of the Air on Flathead
     Mountain (1913)
  6. The Boy Scouts of the Air on the
     Great Lakes (1914)
  7. The Boy Scouts of the Air in Belgium
     (1915)
  8. The Boy Scouts of the Air in the Lone
     Star Patrol (1916)
  9. The Boy Scouts of the Air on Lost
     Island (1917)
 10. The Boy Scouts of the Air on The
     French Front (1918)
 11. The Boy Scouts of the Air with Persh-
     ing (1919)
 12. The Boy Scouts of the Air in the Dis-
     mal Swamp (1920)
 13. The Boy Scouts of the Air at Cape
     Peril (1921)
 14. The Boy Scouts of the Air on Bald-
     crest (1922)

208. BOY SPIES
authors: James Otis [pseudonym of James
  Otis Kaler] [1, 3–11] and William
  Pendleton Chipman [2, 12]
publisher: A. L. Burt
  1. The Boy Spies at the Battle of New
     Orleans; A Boy's Story of the Greatest
     Battle of the War of 1812 (1896)
  2. The Boy Spies at the Defense of Fort
     Henry; A Story of Wheeling Creek in
     1777 (1900)
  3. The Boy Spies at the Battle of Bunker
     Hill; A Story of the Siege of Boston
     (1898)
  4. The Boy Spies at the Siege of Detroit;
     A Story of the Ohio Boys in the War of
     1812 (1904)

5. The Boy Spies with Lafayette at York-town; The Story of How Two Boys Joined the Continental Army (1895) [alternate Title: The Boy Spies at Yorktown; The Story of How the Young Spies Helped General Lafayette in the Siege of Yorktown (1899)]
6. The Boy Spies on Chesapeake Bay; The Story of Two Young Spies Under Commodore Barney (1907)
7. The Boy Spies with the Regulators; The Story of How the Boys Assisted the Carolina Patriots to Drive the British from the State (1901)
8. The Boy Spies with the Swamp Fox; The Story of General Marion and His Young Spies (1899)
9. [title unknown]
10. The Boy Spies of Philadelphia; The Story of How The Young Spies Helped the Continental Army at Valley Forge (1897)
11. The Boy Spies at Fort Griswald; The Story of the Part the Young Spies Took in its Brave Defense (1900)
12. The Boy Spies of Old New York; The Story of How the Young Spies Prevented the Capture of General Washington (1899)

209. BOY TRAPPER
author: Harry Castlemon [pseudonym of Charles Austin Fosdick]
publishers: Porter and Coates; J. C. Winston
1. The Buried Treasure; or, Old Jordan's "Haunt" (1877)
2. The Boy Trapper (1878)
3. The Mail Carrier (1879)

210. BOY TROOPERS
author: Clair Wallace Hayes
publisher: A. L. Burt
1. The Boy Troopers on the Trail (1922)
2. The Boy Troopers in the Northwest (1922)
3. The Boy Troopers on Strike Duty (1922)
4. The Boy Troopers Among the Wild Mountaineers (1922)

211. BOY VOLUNTEERS
author: Kenneth Ward
publisher: New York Book Co.
1. The Boy Volunteers on the Belgian Front (1917)
2. The Boy Volunteers With the French Airmen (1917)
3. The Boy Volunteers With the British Artillery (1917)
4. The Boy Volunteers With the Submarine Fleet
5. The Boy Volunteers With the American Infantry (1918)

BOY WITH THE U.S. SERVICE see
U.S. SERVICE

212. BOYS' ADVENTURE I [see also ADVENTURE AND MYSTERY]
authors: DeWitt Hanes [1]; G. Hunting [2]; Van Powell [3]
publisher: Saalfield
1. The Big Opportunity (1929)
2. Barry Dare and the Mysterious Box
3. The Ghost of Mystery Airport

213. BOYS' ADVENTURE II [see also BUFFALO BILL]
authors: Elmer Sherwood [pseudonym of Samuel Leuwenkrohn]
publisher: Whitman
1. Buffalo Bill's Boyhood
2. Buffalo Bill and the Pony Express
3. Ted Marsh, the Boy Scout
4. Ted Marsh on an Important Mission
5. Ted Marsh, the Young Volunteer
6. Ted Marsh and the Enemy

214. BOYS' ADVENTURE III
authors: Robert Leighton [1]; Oswald Dallas [3]; Edith Janice Craine [5–7]
publisher: World Syndicate
1. Sergeant Silk, the Prairie Scout (1929)
2. [title unknown]
3. The Treasures of Asshur (1929)
4. [title unknown]
5. The Grist Mill Ghost (1931)
6. David, the Incorrigible (1928)
7. Canny the Courageous (1931)

215. BOYS' ADVENTURE IV
author: Percy Francis Westerman

publisher: S. W. Partridge
1. The Mystery of Stockmere School (1924)

216. BOYS AND GIRLS OF COLONIAL DAYS
author: Carolyn Sherwin Bailey
[titles unknown]

217. BOYS AND GIRLS OF DIS-COVERY DAYS
author: Carolyn Sherwin Bailey
[titles unknown]

218. BOYS AND GIRLS OF PIO-NEER DAYS
author: Carolyn Sherwin Bailey
[titles unknown]

219. BOYS AND GIRLS OF TODAY
author: Carolyn Sherwin Bailey
[titles unknown]

220. BOYS AT THE FRONT IN THE GREAT WAR
author: Allan Grant
publisher: George H. Doran
1. In Defense of Paris; An American Boy in the Trenches: A Story of Infantry and the Big Guns (1915)

221. BOYS' BANNER
author: Oliver Optic [pseudonym of William Taylor Adams]
publisher: M. A. Donohue
1–3. [titles unknown]
  4. In School and Out
5–8. [titles unknown]
  9. Little by Little
 10. [title unknown]
 11. Now or Never

222. BOYS' BIG GAME
author: Elliott Whitney [pseudonym]
publisher: Reilly & Britton; Reilly & Lee
1. The Giant Moose (1912)
2. The King Bear of Kodiak Island (1912)
3. The White Tiger of Nepal (1912)
4. The Blind Lion of the Congo (1912)
5. The Rogue Elephant (1913)
6. The Pirate Shark (1914)
7. The King Condor of the Andes (1915)

8. The Black Fox of Yukon (1917)
9. The Bobcat of Jump Mountain (1920)
10. The Crazy Elk of Terrapin Swamp (1921)

BOYS' EXPLORERS *see* DICK

223. BOYS' GOLDEN WEST
author: William S. Hart
publishers: Houghton Mifflin; Grosset & Dunlap
1. Injun and Whitey (1920)
2. Injun and Whitey Strike Out for Themselves
3. Injun and Whitey to the Rescue (1922)

BOYS' INDIAN *see* BRADEN

224. BOY'S LIBERTY
author: Oliver Optic [pseudonym of William Taylor Adams]
publisher: M. A. Donohue
 8. Little by Little
12. Poor and Proud
18. Try Again

225. BOYS' MYSTERY [*see also* ADVENTURE AND MYSTERY]
author: Capwell Wycoff
publisher: Saalfield
1. The Mystery of Gaither Cove
2. The North Point Cabin Mystery
3. The Secret of the Armor Room

226. BOYS OF BUSINESS [*see also* ALLEN CHAPMAN]
author: Allen Chapman [pseudonym of Edward Stratemeyer]
illustrators: Charles Nuttall [1–3]; Alex Levy [4]
publishers: Cupples & Leon
1. The Young Express Agent; or, Bart Stirling's Road to Success (1906)
2. Two Boy Publishers; or, From Typecase to Editor's Chair (1906)
3. Mail Order Frank; or, A Smart Boy and His Chances (1907)
4. A Business Boy; or, Winning Success (1907)
5. The Young Land Agent; or, The Secret of the Borden Estate (1907)

227. BOYS OF COLUMBIA HIGH
[*see also* FRANK ALLEN]
authors: Graham B. Forbes [pseudonym of the Stratemeyer Syndicate]; St. George Rathborn
publisher: Grosset & Dunlap
1. The Boys of Columbia High: or, The All Around Rivals of the School (1911)
2. The Boys of Columbia High on the Diamond; or, Winning Out by Pluck (1911)
3. The Boys of Columbia High on the River; or, The Boat Race Plot that Failed (1911)
4. The Boys of Columbia High on the Gridiron; or, The Struggle for the Silver Cup (1911)
5. The Boys of Columbia High on the Ice; or, Out for the Hockey Championship (1911)
6. The Boys of Columbia High in Track Athletics; or, A Long Run that Won (1913)
7. The Boys of Columbia High in Winter Sports; or, Stirring Doings on Skates and Iceboats (1915)
8. Boys of Columbia High in Camp; or, The Rivalry of the Old School League (1920)

BOYS OF PLUCK *see* BOYS OF BUSINESS

BOYS OF STEEL *see* IRON BOYS

BOYS OF THE ARMY *see* UNCLE SAM'S BOYS

BOYS OF THE ROYAL MOUNTED POLICE *see* DICK KENT

228. BOYS' OWN AUTHOR
author: Paschal Grouset
publisher: Dana Estes
1. Schoolboy Days in France (1896)

229. BOYS' OWN LIBRARY
author: Oliver Optic [pseudonym of William Taylor Adams]
publishers: Federal Book Co.; McKay; Street & Smith
1. Giant Islanders

2. How He Won
3. Nature's Young Noblemen
4. The Rival Battalions
5. All Aboard
6. The Boat Club
7. Little by Little
8. Now or Never
9. Poor and Proud
10. Try Again
11. The Young Actor

230. BOYS' PIONEER [*see also* BRADEN]
author: James Andrew Braden
publisher: Saalfield
1–2. [titles unknown]
   3. Connecticut Boys in the Western Reserve; A Tale of the Moravian Massacre (1927)
   4. [title unknown]
   5. Captives Three (1927)

231. BOYS' POPULAR LIBRARY
author: Oliver Optic [pseudonym of William Taylor Adams]
publishers: Street & Smith; McKay; Federal Book Co.
1. All Aboard
3. The Boat Club
24. Little by Little
31. Now or Never
45. Try Again

232. BOYS' PRIZE LIBRARY
author: R. Banner [1]; Rathborne [2, 3, 10]; H. Castlemon [pseudonym of Charles Austin Fosdick] [4]; Foster [5]; Mark Overton [6, 7]; Whipple [8, 9]; Philips [11]
publisher: M. A. Donohue
1. The Boy Inventors' Flying Ship
2. Camp Mates in Michigan
3. Chums in Dixie
4. Frank in the Woods
5. Frozen Ship Among the Sealers
6. Jack Winter's Campmates
7. Jack Winter's Gridiron Chums
8. Radio Boys' Cronies
9. Radio Boys' Loyalty
10. Rocky Mountain Boys
11. Two Young Crusoes
12. Young Hunters in Puerto Rico

233. BOYS' STORY OF THE ARMY
author: Florence Kimball Russel
publisher: L. C. Page
1. Born to the Blue; A Story of the Army (1906)
2. In West Point Grays as Plebe and Yearling (1908)

234. BOYS' STORY OF THE RAILROAD
author: Burton Egbert Stevenson
publisher: L. C. Page
1. [title unknown]
2. The Young Train Dispatcher (1907)
3. The Young Train Master (1909)

235. BRADEN [alternate title: BOYS INDIAN] [see also INDIAN and BOYS' PIONEER]
author: James Andrew Braden
publisher: Saalfield
1. Far Past the Frontier (1902)
2. Two Boy Pioneers (1902)
3. Captives Three
4. The Lone Indian (1907)
5. Connecticut Boys in the Western Reserve; A Tale of the Moravian Massacre
6. The Cabin in the Clearing (1904)
7. The Trail of the Seneca (1907)

236. BRAIN AND BRAWN
author: William Drysdale
publisher: W. A. Wilde
1. The Young Reporter — A Story of Printing House Square
2. The Fast Mail — The Story of a Train Boy
3. The Beach Patrol — A Story of the Life Saving Service
4. The Young Supercargo — A Story of the Merchant Marine

237. BRENDA
author: Helen Leah Reed
publisher: Little, Brown
1. Miss Theodora: West End Story (1898)
2. Brenda, Her School and Her Club (1900)
3. Brenda's Summer at Rockley (1901)
4. Brenda's Cousin at Radcliffe (1902)
5. Brenda's Bargain (1903)
6. Amy in Acadia (1905)
7. Brenda's Ward (1906)

238. BRIGHT AND BOLD
author: Arthur M. Winfield (pseudonym of Edward Stratemeyer)
publisher: M. A. Donohue
1. Poor but Plucky; or, The Mystery of a Flood (1905)
2. School Days of Fred Harley; or, Rivals for all Honors (1905)
3. By Pluck, Not Luck; or, Dan Granbury's Struggle to Rise (1905)
4. The Missing Tin Box; or, The Stolen Railroad Bonds (1905)

239. BRIGHT EYE
author: [unknown]
publisher: M. A. Donohue
1. The Angels (1869)
2. The Children's Hour (1900)

240. BRIGHTON BOYS
author: James R. Driscoll
publisher: Winston
1. The Brighton Boys with the Flying Corps (1918)
2. The Brighton Boys in the Trenches (1918)
3. The Brighton Boys with the Battle Fleet (1918)
4. The Brighton Boys in the Radio Service (1918)
5. The Brighton Boys in the Submarine Fleet (1918)
6. The Brighton Boys with the Engineers at Cantigny (1919)
7. The Brighton Boys at Chateau-Thierry (1919)
8. The Brighton Boys at St. Mihiel (1919)
9. The Brighton Boys in the Argonne Forest (1920)
10. The Brighton Boys in Transatlantic Flight (1920)
11. The Brighton Boys in the Submarine Treasure Ship (1920)

241. BRONCHO RIDER BOYS
author: Frank Fowler
publisher: A. L. Burt
1. The Broncho Rider Boys at Keystone Ranch; or, Three Chums of the Saddle and Lariat (1914)
2. The Broncho Rider Boys Down in

Arizona; or, A Struggle for the Great Copper Load (1914)
3. The Broncho Rider Boys Along the Border; or, The Hidden Treasure of the Zuni Medicine Man (1914)
4. The Broncho Rider Boys on the Wyoming Trail; or, The Mystery of the Prairie Stampede (1914)
5. The Broncho Rider Boys with the Texas Rangers; or, The Capture of the Smugglers on the Rio Grande (1915)
6. The Broncho Rider Boys with Funston at Vera Cruz; or, Upholding the Honor of the Stars and Stripes (1916)

242. BROOKSIDE
author: Madeline Leslie
publishers: Henry A. Young; Henry A. Sumner
1. Stopping the Leak (1865)
2. Lost But Found; or, The Jewish Home (1867)
3. The Hole in the Pocket (1865)
4. Fashion and Folly (1867)

243. BROTHER AND SISTER
author: Josephine Lawrence
publisher: Cupples & Leon
1. Brother and Sister (1921)
2. Brother and Sister's Holidays (1921)
3. Brother and Sister's Schooldays (1921)
4. Brother and Sister's Vacation (1922)
5. Brother and Sister at Bayport (1922)
6. Brother and Sister Keep House (1927)

244. BROTHER SUNSHINE'S SERIES
author: [unknown]
publisher: Dean & Son
1. The Affecting Story of the Children in the Wood (1850)
2. Nursery Ditties (1855)
3. The Death and Burial of Poor Cock Robin (1858)

245. BROWNIE
author: [unknown]
publisher: Hubbard
1. [title unknown]
2. Cock Robin and Other Stories
3–5. [titles unknown]
6. Merry Mice (1896)

246. BROWNIE SCOUTS
author: Mildred Augustine Wirt
publisher: Cupples & Leon
1. The Brownie Scouts at Snow Valley (1949)
2. The Brownie Scouts in the Circus (1949)
3. The Brownie Scouts in the Cherry Festival (1950)
4. The Brownie Scouts and Their Tree House (1951)
5. The Brownie Scouts at Silver Beach (1952)
6. The Brownie Scouts at Windmill Farm (1953)

247. BUCK AND LARRY BASEBALL STORIES
author: Elmer A. Dawson [pseudonym of the Stratemeyer Syndicate]
illustrators: Walter S. Rogers [1–4]; W. B. Grubb [5]
publisher: Grosset & Dunlap
1. The Pick-up Nine; or, The Chester Boys on the Diamond (1930)
2. Buck's Winning Hit; or, The Chester Boys Making a Record (1930)
3. Larry's Fadeaway; or, The Chester Boys Saving the Nine (1930)
4. Buck's Home Run Drive; or, The Chester Boys Winning Against Odds (1931)
5. Larry's Speedball; or, The Chester Boys and the Diamond Secret (1932)

248. BUCK JONES
author: Richmond Pearson Hobson
publisher: David Appleton
1. Buck Jones at Annapolis (1907)
2. In Line of Duty (1910)

249. BUD BRIGHT
author: A. Van Buren Powell
publisher: Penn
1. Bud Bright, Boy Detective (1929)
2. Bud Bright and the Bank Robbers (1929)
3. Bud Bright and the Kidnappers (1930)
4. Bud Bright and the Drug Ring (1931)
5. Bud Bright and the Counterfeiters (1931)

250. BUDDY BOOKS
author: Howard Roger Garis
publisher: Cupples & Leon
  1. Buddy on the Farm; or, A Boy and His Prize Pumpkin (1929)
  2. Buddy in School; or, A Boy and His Dog (1929)
  3. Buddy and His Winter Fun; or, A Boy in a Snow Camp (1929)
  4. Buddy at Rainbow Lake; or, A Boy and His Boat (1930)
  5. Buddy and His Chum; or, A Boy's Queer Search (1930)
  6. Buddy at Pine Beach; or, A Boy on the Ocean (1931)
  7. Buddy and His Flying Balloon; or, A Boy's Mysterious Airship (1931)
  8. Buddy on Mystery Mountain; or, A Boy's Strange Discovery (1932)
  9. Buddy on Floating Island; or, A Boy's Wonderful Secret (1933)
  10. Buddy and the Secret Cave; or, A Boy and the Crystal Hermit (1934)
  11. Buddy and His Cowboy Pal; or, A Boy on a Ranch (1935)
  12. Buddy and the Indian Chief; or, A Boy Among the Navajos (1936)
  13. Buddy and the Arrow Club; or, A Boy and the Long Bow (1937)
  14. Buddy at Lost River; or, A Boy and a Gold Mine (1938)
  15. Buddy on the Trail; or, A Boy Among the Gypsies (1939)
  16. Buddy in Deep Valley; or, A Boy on a Bee Farm (1940)
  17. Buddy at Red Gate; or, A Boy on a Chicken Farm (1941)
  18. Buddy in Dragon Swamp; or, A Boy on a Strange Hunt (1942)
  19. Buddy's Victory Club; or, A Boy and a Salvage Campaign (1943)
  20. Buddy and the G-Man Mystery; or, A Boy and a Strange Cipher (1944)
  21. Buddy and His Fresh-Air Camp; or, A Boy and the Unlucky Ones (1947)

251. BUDDY BOOKS FOR BOYS
authors: Percy Kees Fitzhugh [1–8]; Harold M. Sherman [9–13]; J. Allen Dunn [14–15]; Edward Bacon [16]; William Heyliger [19–20]
publisher: Grosset & Dunlap

  1. Lefty Lieghton
  2. Spiffy Henshaw
  3. Wigwag Wiegand
  4. Hervey Willets
  5. Skinny McCord
  6. Mark Gilmore, Scout of the Air
  7. The Story of Terrible Terry
  8. Cameron McBain, Backwoodsman
  9. Number 44
  10. Don Rader, Trailblazer
  11. Ding Palmer, Air Detective
  12. Beyond the Dog's Nose
  13. The Land of Monsters
  14. Buffalo Boy
  15. The Young Eagle of the Trail
  16. Tuck Simms, Fortyniner
  17. Quarterback Hothead
  18. Hot Dog Partners
  19. Bean Ball Bill
  20. Bill Darrow's Victory

252. BUFFALO BILL [see also BOYS ADVENTURE II]
author: Elmer Sherwood (pseudonym of Samuel Lewenkrohn)
publisher: Whitman
  1. Buffalo Bill's Boyhood
  2. Buffalo Bill and the Pony Express

253. BUNCHY
author: Joyce Lankaster Brisley
publisher Harrap
  1. Bunchy (1937)
  2. Another Bunchy Book (1951)

254. BUNGALOW BOYS
author: Dexter J. Forrester [pseudonym of John Henry Goldfrap]
illustrators: J. Paul Burnham; Charles L. Wrenn
publishers: Hurst
  1. The Bungalow Boys (1911)
  2. The Bungalow Boys Marooned in the Tropics (1911)
  3. The Bungalow Boys in the Great North West (1911)
  4. The Bungalow Boys on the Great Lakes (1912)
  5. The Bungalow Boys Along the Yukon (1913)
  6. The Bungalow Boys North of Fifty-Three (1914)

255. BUNNY BROWN AND HIS SISTER SUE
author: Laura Lee Hope [pseudonym of the Stratemeyer Syndicate]
illustrators: Florence England Nosworthy [1–7] Thelma Gooch [8]; Walter S. Rogers [9–20]
publisher: Grosset & Dunlap
1. Bunny Brown and His Sister Sue (1916)
2. Bunny Brown and His Sister Sue on Grandpa's Farm (1916)
3. Bunny Brown and His Sister Sue Playing Circus (1916)
4. Bunny Brown and His Sister Sue at Camp Rest-a-While (1916)
5. Bunny Brown and His Sister Sue at Aunt Lu's City Home (1916)
6. Bunny Brown and His Sister Sue in the Big Woods (1917)
7. Bunny Brown and His Sister Sue on an Auto Tour (1917)
8. Bunny Brown and His Sister Sue and Their Shetland Pony (1918)
9. Bunny Brown and His Sister Sue Giving A Show (1919)
10. Bunny Brown and His Sister Sue at Christmas Tree Cove (1920)
11. Bunny Brown and His Sister Sue in the Sunny South (1921)
12. Bunny Brown and His Sister Sue Keeping Store (1922)
13. Bunny Brown and His Sister Sue and their Trick Dog (1923)
14. Bunny Brown and His Sister Sue at a Sugar Camp (1924)
15. Bunny Brown and His Sister Sue on the Rolling Ocean (1925)
16. Bunny Brown and His Sister Sue on Jack Frost Island (1927)
17. Bunny Brown and His Sister Sue at Shore Acres (1928)
18. Bunny Brown and His Sister Sue at Berry Hill (1929)
19. Bunny Brown and His Sister Sue at Sky Top (1930)
20. Bunny Brown and His Sister Sue at the Summer Carnival (1931)

256. BUSINESS
author: Harry S. Morrison
publisher: L. C. Page
1. The Adventures of a Boy Reporter (1898)
2. A Yankee Boy's Success (1900)

257. BUSINESS VENTURE
author: James Otis [pseudonym of James Otis Kaler]
illustrator: J. W. Ferguson Kennedy
publisher: D. Estes
1. The Cruise of the Phoebe; or, A Story of Lobster Buying on the Eastern Coast (1908)
2. Sarah Hane, Dicky Dalton; A Story of Tugboating in Portland Harbor (1909)
3. Captain Dicky Dalton

258. BUTT CHANDLER
author: James Shelley Hamilton
publisher: David Appleton
1. Butt Chandler, Freshman (1908)
2. The New Sophomore (1909)
3. Junior Days
4. Senior Sports

259. BY AND BY
author: Mrs. Frederick Field
publisher: Ward & Drummond
1. I Forgot; or, Will Leonard (1879)

260. BY SEA AND SHORE
author: Wilhelm Herchenbach
publisher: D. & J. Sadlier
1. The Voyage of the Veronica (1886)
2. Angel Hilda (1886

261. CAMBRIDGE CLASSICS
author: Oliver Optic [pseudonym of William Taylor Adams]
publisher: Hurst
1. In School and Out
2. Little by Little
3. Rich and Humble

CAMERA BOYS *see* **MOTION PICTURE COMRADS**

262. CAMP AND CANOE
author: George Rathborne
publisher: David McKay
1. [title unknown]
2. Paddling Under Palmettos (1901)
3. Rival Canoe Boys; or, With Pack and Paddle on the Nipigon (1902)

263. CAMP AND TRAIL
author: Hugh Pendexter
publisher: Small, Maynard
1. The Young Timber-Cruisers; or, Fighting the Spruce Pirates (1911)
2. The Young Gem-Hunters; or, The Mystery of the Haunted Camp (1911)
3. [title unknown]
4. The Young Trappers; or, The Quest of the Giant Moose (1913)

264. CAMP BRADY
author: Lewis Edwin Theiss
publisher: W.A. Wilde
1. In Camp at Fort Brady (1914)
2. [title unknown]
3. The Wireless Patrol at Camp Brady (1917)

265. CAMP FIRE
author: Edward Sylvester Ellis
publisher: Thompson & Thomas
1. Red Plume; or, A Friendly Redskin (1902)

266. CAMP LENAPE
author: Carl Saxon
publisher: Books
1. Blackie Thorne at Camp Lenape (1931)
2. The Mystery at Camp Lenape (1940)
3. Camp Lenape on the Long Trail (1940)

267. CAMP LIFE
author: Raymond Smiley Spears
publisher: Harper & Brothers
1. Camping on the Great River; the Adventures of a Boy Afloat on the Mississippi (1912)

268. CAMPAIGN
author: Horatio Alger
publisher: H.T. Coates
1. Paul Prescott's Charge; A Story for Boys (1893)

269. CAMPBELLS
author: Janet Lambert
publisher: Dutton
1. The Precious Days (1957)
2. For Each Other (1959)
3. Forever and Ever (1961)
4. Five's a Crowd (1963)
5. First of All (1966)

270. CAMPFIRE AND TRAIL
author: Lawrence Leslie
publishers: New York Books; M. A. Donohue
1. In Camp on the Big Sunflower (1913)
2. Rivals of the Trail
3. The Strange Cabin on Catamount Island
4. Lost in the Great Dismal Swamp
5. With Trapper Jim in the North Woods
6. Caught in a Forest Fire
7. Chums of the Campfire
8. Afloat on the Flood
9. The Cruise of the Houseboat
10. At Whispering Pine Lodge (1918)

271. CAMPFIRE BOYS I
author: Oliver Lee Clifton [pseudonym of George Rathborne]
publisher: Barse & Hopkins
1. The Campfire Boys at Log Cabin Bend; or, Four Chums Afloat in the Tall Timber (1923)
2. The Campfire Boys in Muskrat Swamp; or, a Hunt for the Missing Plane Pilot
3. The Campfire Boys at Silver Fox Farm; or, A Lively Week in the Wilderness
4. The Campfire Boys' Canoe Cruise; or, Stormbound on the Upper Rockaway
5. The Campfire Boys' Tracking Squad; or, Where Woodcraft Paid Big Dividends (1926)

272. CAMPFIRE BOYS II
author: Latharo Hoover
publisher: A. L. Burt
1. The Campfire Boys' Treasure Quest (1929)
2. The Campfire Boys in the Brazilian Wilderness
3. The Campfire Boys in the South Seas
4. The Campfire Boys in the African Jungles
5. The Campfire Boys in Borneo
6. The Campfire Boys in the Philippines
7. The Campfire Boys in the Australian Gold Fields (1932)

273. CAMPFIRE GIRLS I
author: Marion Davidson [pseudonym of Howard Roger Garis]

publishers: R. F. Fenno and M. A. Donahue

1. The Campfire Girls on the Ice; or, The Mystery of a Winter Cabin (1913)
2. The Campfire Girls; or, The Secret of an Old Mill (1913)

274. CAMPFIRE GIRLS II

author: Julianne DeVries [pseudonym of Julian DeVries]
publisher: World Syndicate

1. The Campfire Girls on Caliban Island (1933)
2. The Campfire Girls Flying Around the Globe (1933)
3. The Campfire Girls at Holly House (1933)
4. The Campfire Girls as Detectives (1933)
5. The Camp Fire Girls at the White House (1935)
6. The Camp Fire Girls as Federal Investigators (1935)

275. CAMPFIRE GIRLS III

authors: Stella M. Francis [1-6]; Irene Elliott Benson [7-10]
publisher: M. A. Donohue

1. The Campfire Girls at Twin Lakes; or, The Quest of a Summer Vacation (1918)
2. The Campfire Girls in the Allegheny Mountains; or, A Christmas Success Against Odds (1918)
3. The Campfire Girls in the Country; or, The Secret Aunt Hannah Forgot (1918)
4. The Campfire Girls on a Hike; or, Lost in the Great North Woods (1918)
5. The Campfire Girls' Outing; or, Ethel Hollister's Second Summer in Camp (1918)
6. The Campfire Girls' Trip Up the River; or, Ethel Hollister's First Lesson (1918)
7. The Campfire Girls' Rural Retreat; or, The Quest of a Secret (1918)
8. The Campfire Girls in the Forest; or, The Lost Trail Found (1918)
9. The Campfire Girls Mountaineering; or, Overcoming all Obstacles (1918)
10. The Campfire Girls' Lake Camp; or, Searching for New Adventures (1918)

276. CAMPFIRE GIRLS IV

author: Hildegard Gertrude Frey
publisher: A. L. Burt

1. The Camp Fire Girls at Onoway House; or, The Magic Garden (1916)
2. The Camp Fire Girls at School; or, The Wokelo Weavers (1916)
3. The Camp Fire Girls Go Motoring; or, Along the Road that Leads the Way (1916)
4. The Camp Fire Girls in the Maine Woods; or, The Winnebagos Go Camping (1916)
5. The Camp Fire Girls' Larks and Pranks; or, the House of the Open Door (1917)
6. The Camp Fire Girls on Ellen's Isle; or, The Trail of the Seven Cedars (1917)
7. The Camp Fire Girls on the Open Road; or, Glorify Work (1918)
8. The Camp Fire Girls Solve a Mystery; or, The Christmas Adventure at Carver House (1919)
9. The Camp Fire Girls do Their Bit; or, Over the Top with the Winnebagos (1919)
10. The Camp Fire Girls at Camp Keewaydin; or, Down Paddles (1920)

277. CAMPFIRE GIRLS V

author: Harriet Pyne Grove
publisher: A. L. Burt

1. The Campfire Girls of Wyandotte Camp (1931)
2. The Campfire Girls on the Trail (1931)

278. CAMPFIRE GIRLS VI

author: Helen Hart [pseudonym of Samuel E. Lowe]
illustrators: Violet Moore Higgins [1-2]; Alice Carsey (3-4)
publisher: Whitman

1. The Camp Fire Girls' Duty Call (1920)
2. The Campfire Girls at Work (1920)
3. The Campfire Girls in High School
4. The Campfire Girls' Success

279. CAMPFIRE GIRLS VII

author: Isabel Katherine Hornibrook
illustrator: John Goss
publisher: Lothrop, Lee & Shepard

1. The Girls of the Morning-Glory Camp Fire (1916)
2. The Camp Fire Girls and Mount Greylock (1917)
3. The Campfire Girls in War and Peace (1919)

280. CAMPFIRE GIRLS VIII

author: Margaret Penrose [pseudonym of the Stratemeyer Syndicate]
publisher: Goldsmith
1. The Campfire Girls of Roselawn; or, A Strange Message from the Air (1930)
2. The Campfire Girls on the Program; or, Singing and Reciting at the Sending Station (1930)
3. The Campfire Girls on Station Island; or, The Wireless from the Steam Yacht (1930)
4. The Campfire Girls at Forest Lodge; or, The Strange Hut in the Swamp (1930)

281. CAMPFIRE GIRLS IX

author: Harriet Rietz
illustrator: Alice Carsey
publisher: Whitman
1. The Campfire Girls and Aunt Madge
2. The Campfire Girls' Week-End Party

282. CAMPFIRE GIRLS X

author: Margaret Love Sanderson [pseudonym ?]
illustrators: Mildred Webster [5]; Alice Carsey [4]; Bernice C. Tapp [3]; Maude Martin Evers [7]; Harry W. Armstrong [8]
publishers: Reilly & Britton [1-4]; Reilly & Lee [6-7]
1. The Camp Fire Girls at Hillside (1913)
2. The Camp Fire Girls at Pine-Tree Camp (1914)
3. The Camp Fire Girls at Top o' the World (1916)
4. The Camp Fire Girls at Lookout Pass (1917)
5. The Camp Fire Girls at Driftwood Heights (1918)
6. The Camp Fire Girls in Old Kentucky (1919)
7. The Camp Fire Girls on a Yacht (1920)
8. The Camp Fire Girls on Hurricane Island (1921)

283. CAMPFIRE GIRLS XI

author: Jane L. Stewart
publisher: Saalfield
1. The Camp Fire Girls' First Council Fire (1914) [alternate title: The Camp Fire Girls in the Woods; or, Bessie King's First Council Fire]
2. The Campfire Girls' Chum (1914) [alternate title: The Camp Fire Girls on the Farm; or, Bessie King's New Chum]
3. The Campfire Girl in summer Camp (1914) [alternate title: The Camp Fire Girls at Long Lake; or, Bessie King in Summer Camp]
4. The Campfire Girls in the Mountains (1914) [alternate title: A Campfire Girl's Adventure; or, Bessie King's Happiness]
5. The Campfire Girl's Test of Friendship (1914) [alternate title: Camp Fire Girls on the March; or, Bessie King's Test of Friendship]
6. The Campfire Girl's Happiness (1914) [alternate title: The Camp Fire Girls at the Seashore; or, Bessie King's Happiness]

284. CAMPFIRE GIRLS XII

author: Margaret O'Bannon Womack Vandercook
publisher: John C. Winston
1. The Camp Fire Girls Amid the Snows (1913)
2. The Camp Fire Girls at Sunrise Hill (1913)
3. The Camp Fire Girls Across the Seas (1914)
4. The Camp Fire Girls in the Outside World (1914)
5. The Camp Fire Girls on the Edge of the Desert (1914)
6. The Camp Fire Girls' Careers (1915)
7. The Camp Fire Girls in After Years (1915)
8. The Camp Fire Girls at the End of the Trail (1917)
9. The Camp Fire Girls Behind the Lines (1918)
10. The Camp Fire Girls in Glorious France (1919)
11. The Camp Fire Girls in Merrie England (1920)

12. The Camp Fire Girls at Half Moon Lake (1921)

285. CAN AND CAN'T
author: Catherine Lydia Burnham
publisher: Ward & Drummond
1. I'll Try; or, Sensible Daisy (1879)
2. I Can; or, Charlie's Motto (1879)
3. I Can't; or, Nelly and Lucy (1870)

286. CANDY KANE
author: Janet Lambert
publisher: Dutton
1. Candy Kane (1943)
2. Whoa, Matilda! (1944)
3. One for the Money (1946)

287. CANOE AND CAMPFIRE
author: George Henry Rathborne
publisher: M. A. Donohue
1. Canoe Mates in Canada; or, Three Boys Afloat on the Saskatchewan (1912)
2. The Young Fur-Takers; or, Traps and Trails in the Wilderness (1912)
3. The House-Boat Boys; or, Drifting Down to the Sunny South (1912)
4. Chums in Dixie; or, The Strange Cruise of a Motorboat
5. Camp Mates in Michigan; or, With Pack and Paddle in the Pine Woods (1913)
6. Rocky Mountain Boys; or, Camping in the Big Game Country (1913)

288. CAPTAIN JANUARY
author: Laura Elizabeth Howe Richards
publisher: L.C. Page
1. Narcissa (1894)
2. Captain January (1891)
3. Star Bright: A Sequel to Captain January (1927)

CAROL PAGE *see* CAROL STAGE

289. CAROL STAGE
author: Helen Dore Boylston
publisher: Little, Brown; Lane
1. Carol Goes Backstage (1941) [alternate title: Carol Goes on the Stage]
2. Carol Plays Summer Stock (1942) [alternate title: Carol in Repertory]

3. Carol on Broadway (1945) [alternate title: Carol Comes to Broadway]
4. Carol on Tour (1946)

290. CAROLINE
author: Lela Horn Richards
publisher: Little, Brown
1. Then Came Caroline (1921)
2. Caroline at College (1922)
3. Caroline's Career (1923)

291. CAROLYN
author: Ruth Belmore Endicott [pseudonym of the Stratemeyer Syndicate]
illustrator: Edward C. Caswell
publisher: Dodd, Mead & Company
1. Carolyn of the Corners (1918)
2. Carolyn of the Sunny Heart (1919)

292. CARTER GIRLS
author: Nell Speed
publisher: Hurst
1. The Carter Girls (1917)
2. The Carter Girls' Week-End Camp (1919)
3. The Carter Girls' Mysterious Neighbors (1921)
4. The Carter Girls of Carter House (1921)

CASTLEMON'S WAR *see* WAR

293. CATAMOUNT CAMP
author: Edward Sylvester Ellis
publisher: J.C. Winston
1. Catamount Camp (1910)

294. CATHY LEONARD
author: Catherine Woolley
publisher: Morrow
1. A Room for Cathy (1956)
2. Miss Cathy Leonard (1958)
3. Cathy Leonard Calling (1960)
4. Cathy's Little Sister (1964)
5. Chris in Trouble (1968)
6. Cathy and the Beautiful People (1971)
7. Cathy Uncovers a Secret (1972)

295. CATTY ATKINS
author: Charles Buddington Kelland
publisher: Harper
1. Catty Atkins (1920)

2. Catty Atkins, Riverman
3. Catty Atkins, Sailorman
4. Catty Atkins, Financier
5. Catty Atkins, Bandmaster (1924)

CENTRAL HIGH GIRLS *see* **GIRLS OF CENTRAL HIGH**

296. CHALET SCHOOL GIRLS
author: Elinor M. Brent-Dyer
publisher: Chambers
  1. The School at the Chalet (1925)
  2. Jo of the Chalet School (1926)
  3. The Princess of the Chalet School (1927)
  4. The Head Girl of the Chalet School (1928)
  5. The Rivals of the Chalet School (1929)
  6. Eustacia Goes to the Chalet School (1930)
  7. The Chalet School and Jo (1931)
  8. The Chalet Girls in Camp (1932)
  9. The Exploits of the Chalet Girls (1933)
  10. A Rebel at the Chalet School (1934)
  11. The Chalet School and the Lintons (1934)
  12. The New House at the Chalet School (1935)
  13. Jo Returns to the Chalet School (1936)
  14. The New Chalet School (1938)
  15. The Chalet School in Exile (1940)
  16. The Chalet School Goes to It (1941)
  17. The Highland Twins at the Chalet School (1942)
  18. Lavender Laugh in the Chalet School (1943)
  19. Gay from China at the Chalet School (1944)
  20. Jo to the Rescue (1945)
  21. Three Go to the Chalet School (1949)
  22. Peggy of the Chalet School (1950)
  23. The Chalet School and the Island (1950)
  24. The Chalet School and Rosalie (1951)
  25. Carola Storms the Chalet School (1951)
  26. The Chalet School in the Oberland (1952)
  27. The Wrong Chalet School (1952)
  28. Shocks for the Chalet School (1952)
  29. Bride Leads the Chalet School (1953)
  30. Changes for the Chalet School (1953)
  31. The Chalet School Fete
  32. The Chalet School and Barbara (1954)
  33. A Chalet Girl from Kenya (1955)
  34. The Chalet School Does It Again (1955)
  35. Tom Tackles the Chalet School (1955)
  36. A Problem for the Chalet School (1956)
  37. Mary-Lou of the Chalet School (1956)
  38. A Genius at the Chalet School (1956)
  39. Excitements at the Chalet School (1957)
  40. The New Mistress at the Chalet School (1957)
  41. The Chalet School and Richenda (1958)
  42. The Coming-of-Age of the Chalet School (1958)
  43. Theodora and the Chalet School (1959)
  44. Trials for the Chalet School (1959)
  45. A Leader in the Chalet School (1961)
  46. The Chalet School Wins the Trick (1961)
  47. The Feud in the Chalet School (1962)
  48. The Chalet School Reunion (1963)
  49. The Chalet School Triplets (1963)
  50. Jane at the Chalet School (1964)
  51. Redheads at the Chalet School (1964)
  52. Summer Term at the Chalet School (1964)
  53. Adrienne and the Chalet School (1967)
  54. Two Sams at the Chalet School (1967)
  55. Althea Joins the Chalet School (1969)
  56. Prefects of the Chalet School (1970)

297 CHAMPION SPORTS
authors: Noel Everingham Sainsbury, Jr. [1-3]; Charles Lawton [pseudonym of Sainsbury] [4-8]
publisher: Cupples & Leon
  1. Cracker Stanton; or, The Making of a Batsman (1934)
  2. Gridiron Grit; or, The Making of a Fullback (1934)
  3. The Fighting Five; or, The Kidnaping of the Clarksville Basketball Team (1934)

4. Clarkville's Battery; or, Baseball Versus Gangsters (1937)
5. Ros Hackney, Halfback; or, How Clarkville's Captain Made Good (1937)
6. The Winning Forward Pass; or, Onward to the Orange Bowl Game (1940)
7. Home Run Hennessey; or, Winning the All-Star Game (1941)
8. Touchdown to Victory; or, The Touchdown Express Makes Good (1942)

298. CHANNERY
author: Ralph Henry Barbour
publisher: David Appleton
1. The Last Play (1926)
2. The Long Pass (1927)
3. The Relief Pitcher (1927)

299. CHELTHAM
author: Ralph Henry Barbour
publishers: Farrar-Rinehart; David Appleton
1. Candidate for the Line (1930)
2. Flashing Oars (1930)
3. Squeeze Play (1931)

300. CHENANGO TOYS
author: [unknown]
publisher: Williams & Hunt
1. The Little Convert (1833)

CHERRY see TWO WILD CHERRIES

301. CHERRY AMES, NURSE
authors: Helen Wells [1-10, 18-24]; Julia Campbell Tatham [10-17]
publisher: Grosset & Dunlap
1. Cherry Ames, Student Nurse (1943)
2. Cherry Ames, Senior Nurse (1944)
3. Cherry Ames, Army Nurse (1944)
4. Cherry Ames, Chief Nurse (1944)
5. Cherry Ames, Flight Nurse (1945)
6. Cherry Ames, Veteran's Nurse (1946)
7. Cherry Ames, Private Duty Nurse (1946)
8. Cherry Ames, Visiting Nurse (1947)
9. Cherry Ames, Cruise Nurse (1948)
10. Cherry Ames at Spencer (1949)
11. Cherry Ames, Night Supervisor (1950)
12. Cherry Ames, Moutaineer Nurse (1951)
13. Cherry Ames, Clinic Nurse (1952)
14. Cherry Ames, Dude Ranch Nurse (1953)
15. Cherry Ames, Rest Home Nurse (1954)
16. Cherry Ames, Country Doctor's Nurse (1955)
17. Cherry Ames, Boarding School Nurse (1956)
18. Cherry Ames, Department Store Nurse (1957)
19. Cherry Ames, Camp Nurse (1958)
20. Cherry Ames at Hilton Hospital (1959)
21. Cherry Ames, Island Nurse (1960)
22. Cherry Ames, Rural Nurse (1961)
23. Cherry Ames, Staff Nurse (1962)
24. Cherry Ames, Companion Nurse (1964)
25. Cherry Ames, Jungle Nurse (1965)

CHESTER BOYS see BUCK AND LARRY BASEBALL STORIES

302. CHICKEN LITTLE JANE
author: Lily Munsel Ritchie
publishers: Britton [1-3]; Barse & Hopkins [4-5]
1. Chicken Little Jane (1918)
2. Chicken Little Jane on the "Big John" (1919)
3. Adventures of Chicken Little Jane (1920)
4. Chicken Little Jane Comes to Town (1921)
5. Chicken Little Jane in the Rockies (1926)

303. CHILDHOOD OF FAMOUS AMERICANS
authors: Marguerite Henry [58]; Helen Boyd Higgins [1]; Jean Brown Wagoner [2]; Mabel Cleland Widdemer [4, 6]; Dorothea J. Snow [34]; Miriam Evangeline Mason [8]; Augusta Stevenson [12, 40]; Olive Woolley Burt [45]
publisher: Spencer Books
[series numbers for the first batch following are uncertain]
1. Stephen Foster, Boy Minstrel (1944)
2. Jane Addams, Little Lame Girl (1944)
3. David Farregut, Boy Midshipman (1950)

4. [see below]
5. Julia Ward Howe, Girl of Old New York (1945)
6. Peter Stuyvesant, Boy with Wooden Shoes (1950)
7. Oliver Hazard Perry, Boy of the Sea (1949)
8. Mary Mapes Dodge, Jolly Girl 1949)
[series numbers below are correct; missing numbers are unknown titles]
4. Aleck Bell, Ingenious Boy (1947)
12. Booker T. Washington, Ambitious Boy (1950)
34. John Paul Jones, Salt-Water Boy (1950)
40. Kit Carson, Boy Trapper (1945)
45. Luther Burbank, Boy Wizard (1948)

304. CHILDREN OF ALL LANDS STORIES

authors: Madeline Brandeis [1-14]; Bernadine Bailey [15-16] Gladys Shaw Erskine [17]; Margaret Sutton [18]
publisher: Grosset & Dunlap
1. The Little Dutch Tulip Girl (1929)
2. Little Jeanne of France (1930)
3. Shaun o'Day of Ireland (1930)
4. Little Anne of Canada (1931)
5. The Little Mexican Donkey Boy (1931)
6. Little Philippe of Belgium (1931)
7. Mitz and Fritz of Germany (1933)
8. Little Tony of Italy (1934)
9. Little Tom of England (1935)
10. The Little Spanish Dancer (1936)
11. The Little Indian Weaver (1937)
12. The Little Swiss Wood-Carver (1937)
13. The Wee Scotch Piper (1937)
14. Little Erik of Sweden (1938)
15. Little Greta of Denmark (1939)
16. Little Lauri of Finland (1940)
17. Little Pepito of Central America (1941)
18. A Shepherd Boy of Australia (1941)

305. CHILDREN OF AMERICA STORIES

authors: Madeline Brandeis [1-4]; Bernadine Bailey [5]; Margaret Sutton [6]
publisher: Grosset & Dunlap
1. Little Carmen of the Golden Coast (1935)

2. Little Rose of the Mesa (1935)
3. Little John of New England (1936)
4. Little Farmer of the Middle West (1937)
5. Little Woodsman of the North (1940)
6. Two Boys of the Ohio Valley (1943)

306. CHILDREN OF STANTOUN-CORBET

author: Lucy Ellen Guernsey
publisher: American Sunday School Union
1. Lady Lucy's Secret; or, The Gold Thimble (1869)

307. CHILDREN'S FAVORITE

author: Raymond H. Garman
publisher: Ideal Book Builders
1-2. [titles unknown]
3. Moving-Picture Circus; Greatest Show on Earth (1909)
4. [title unknown]
5. Moving-Picture Fair (1912)

308. CHILDREN'S FRIEND

author: Louise Chandler Moulton [1]; Catharine Maria Trowbridge [2]
publisher: Little, Brown
1. Her Baby Brother (1901)
2. Mistakes (1880)

309. CHILDREN'S HOUR

authors: Ouida [1]; Carolyn Sherwin Bailey [2]
publishers: H.M Caldwell; Milton Bradley; Maria Edgeworth
1. The Child of Urbino; and, Moufflou (1913)
2. Everyday Stories (1920)
3. Holiday Time (1891)
4. Forgive and Forget (1908)
5. Hero Stories (1917)
6. Folk Stories and Fables (1916)
7. Broad Stripes and Bright Stars (1919)

310. CHILHOWEE

author: Sarah E. Morrison
publisher: Thomas Y. Crowell
1. Chilhowee Boys (1895)
2. Chilhowee Boys at College
3. Chilhowee Boys in Harness
4. Chilhowee Boys in War Time (1898)

311. CHIMNEY CORNER
author: [unknown]
publisher: McLoughlin
1. Old Mother Hubbard and Other Stories (1880)
2. Three Little Kittens and Three Blind Mice (1889)
3. Abner Holden's Bound Boy (1890)

312. CHRISTMAS STOCKING
author: John Howard Jewett
publisher: Frederick A. Stokes
1. Con, the Wizard (1905)
2. Little Christmas (1906)
3. Cinderella and Sleeping Beauty (1905)
4. Fairy Tales from Andersen (1905)
5. Fairy Tales from Grimm (1905)
6. The Night Before Christmas (1905)
7. Snuggy Bedtime Stories (1906)
8. Animal ABC: A Child's Visit to the Zoo (1907)

313. CINDA HOLLISTER
author: Janet Lambert
publisher: Dutton
1. Cinda (1954)
2. Fly Away (1956)
3. Big Deal (1958)
4. Triple Trouble (1965)
5. Love to Spare (1967)

314. CINDERELLA
author: [unknown]
publisher: McLoughlin Brothers
1. Some Adventures in the Life of a Cockatoo (1872)
2. Puss in Boots (1897)

315. CIRCUS
authors: Stanley Norris [1-4]; Victor St. Clair [6]; George Waldo Browne [5]
publishers: Street & Smith; David McKay
1. Phil the Showman; or, Life in the Sawdust Ring (1902)
2. The Young Showman's Rivals; or, Ups and Downs of the Road (1903)
3. The Young Showman's Pluck; or, An Unknown Rider in the Ring (1903)
4. The Young Showman's Triumph; or, A Grand Tour on the Road (1903)
5. Zig-Zag, The Boy Conjurer; or, Life On and Off the Stage (1903)

6. Zip, the Acrobat; or, The Old Showman's Secret

316. CIRCUS ANIMAL STORIES
author: Howard Roger Garis
publisher: R. F. Fenno
1. Snarlie the Tiger (1916)
2. Woo-Uff, the Lion (1917)

317. CIRCUS BOYS
author: Edgar B. P. Darlington
publisher: Henry Altemus
1. The Circus Boys on the Flying Rings; or, Making a Start in the Saw Dust Life (1910)
2. The Circus Boys Across the Continent; or, Winning New Laurels on the Tanbark (1911)
3. The Circus Boys in Dixie Land; or, Winning the Plaudits of the Sunny South (1911)
4. The Circus Boys on the Mississippi; or, Afloat with the Big Show on the Big River (1912)
5. The Circus Boys on the Plains; or, Young Advance Agents Ahead of the Show (1920)

318. CIVIL WAR
author: Joseph Alexander Altsheler
publisher: David Appleton-Century
1. The Guns of Bull Run; A Story of the Civil War's Eve (1914)
2. The Guns of Shiloh; A Story of the Great Western Campaign (1914)
3. The Scouts of Stonewall; A Story of the Great Valley Campaign (1914)
4. The Sword of Antietam; A Story of the Nation's Crisis (1914)
5. The Star of Gettysburg; A Story of Southern High Tide (1915)
6. The Rock of Chickamauga; A Story of the Western Crisis (1915)
7. The Shades of the Wilderness; A Story of Lee's Great Stand (1916)
8. The Tree of Appomattox; A Story of the Civil War's Close (1916)

319. CLARA
authors: Caroline Lewis [pseudonym of Harold Begbie; J. Stafford Ransome; M. H. Temple]

publisher: Heinemann
1. Clara in Blunderland (1902)
2. Lost in Blunderland; the Further Adventures of Clara (1903)

320. CLASSMATES
author: Paul G. Tomlinson
publisher: Charles Scribner's
1. To the Land of the Caribou; The Adventures of Four Classmates on a Cruise to Labrador (1914)
2. In Camp on Bass Island; What Happened to Four Classmates on the St. Lawrence (1915)
3. Strange Gray Canoe (1916)

321. CLEO [see also LILIAN GARIS BOOKS]
author: Lilian C. McNamara Garis
publisher: Grosset & Dunlap
1. Cleo's Misty Rainbow (1927)
2. Cleo's Conquest (1927)

322. CLEVER POLLY
author: Catherine Storr
publisher: Faber
1. Clever Polly and Other Stories (1952)
2. Clever Polly and the Stupid Wolf (1955)
3. Polly, the Giant's Bride (1956)
4. The Adventures of Polly and the Wolf (1957)

CLIF FARADAY see TRUE BLUE; STIRRING STORIES OF NAVAL ACADEMY LIFE

323. CLIF STIRLING
author: Burt L. Standish [pseudonym of Gilbert Patten]
publisher: David McKay
1. Clif Stirling, Captain of the Nine (1910)
2. Clif Stirling Behind the Line (1911)
3. Clif Stirling, Stroke of the Crew (1912)
4. Clif Stirling, Freshman at Stormbridge (1913)
5. Clif Stirling, Sophomore at Stormbridge (1916)

324. CLINT WEBB
author: Walter Bertram Foster

publisher: M. A. Donohue
1. Swept Out to Sea; or, Clint Webb Among the Whalers (1913)
2. The Frozen Ship; or, Clint Webb Among the Sealers (1913)
3. From Sea to Sea; or, Clint Webb on a Windjammer [alternate Subtitle: Clint Webb's Cruise on the Windjammer] (1914)
4. The Ocean Express; or, Clint Webb Aboard the Sea Tramp (1914)

325. CLOUD PATROL
author: Irving Crump
publisher: Grosset & Dunlap
1. The Cloud Patrol (1929)
2. Pilot of the Cloud Patrol (1930)
3. Craig of the Cloud Patrol (1931)

326. CLOVERFIELD FARM
author: Helen Fuller Orton
publisher: Stokes
1. Bobby of Cloverfield Farm (1922)
2. Prince and Rover of Cloverfield Farm (1922)
3. Summer at Cloverfield Farm (1924)
4. Winter at Cloverfield Farm (1926)

327. CO-ED
author: Alice Louise Lee
publisher: Penn
1. A Freshman Co-Ed (1910)
2. A Sophomore Co-Ed (1911)
3. A Junior Co-Ed (1912)
4. A Senior Co-Ed (1913)

328. COCK ROBIN [NOTE: there may be two series conflated in the following list; see dates]
author: [unknown]
publishers: McLoughlin; Blackie
1. Careless Content (1814)
2. Tom Thumb (1888)
3. Goody Two-Shoes (1888)
4. An Elegy on the Death and Burial of Cock Robin (1932)
5. Tally Goes Joy-Riding (1955)
6. Three by Tey (1954)

329. COLLEGE ATHLETIC
author: Thomas Truxton Hare
publisher: Penn

1. Making the Freshman Team (1907)
2. A Sophomore Half-back (1910)
3. A Junior in the Line (1909)
4. A Senior Quarter-back (1910)
5. A Graduate Coach (1911)

COLLEGE GIRLS *see* **GRACE HAR-LOWE AT COLLEGE**

330. COLLEGE LIFE
author: Burt L. Standish [pseudonym of Gilbert Patten]
publisher: Barse & Hopkins
1. Boltwood of Yale (1914)
2. The College Rebel (1914)
3. On College Battlefields (1917)
4. The Call of the Varsity (1920)
5. Sons of Old Eli (1923)
6. Ben Oakman, Stroke (1925)

331. COLLEGE SPORTS I
author: Lester Chadwick [pseudonym of the Stratemeyer Syndicate]
publisher: Cupples & Leon
1. The Rival Pitchers; A Story of College Baseball (1910)
2. A Quarter-back's Pluck; A Story of College Football (1910)
3. Batting to Win; A Story of College Baseball (1911)
4. The Winning Touch Down; A Story of College Football (1911)
5. For the Honor of Randall; A Story of College Athletic (1912)
6. The Eight-Oared Victors; A Story of College Water Sports (1913)

COLLEGE SPORTS II *see* **ALL-AMERICAN SPORTS**

332. COLONIAL I
author: Everett Titsworth Tomlinson
publisher: W. A. Wilde
1. With Flintlock and Fife; A Tale of the French and Indian Wars (1903)
2. The Fort in the Forest; A Story of the Fall of Fort William Henry in 1757 (1904)
3. A Soldier of the Wilderness; A Story of Abercrombie's Defeat and the Fall of Fort Frontenac in 1758 (1905)

4. The Young Rangers; A Story of the Conquest of Canada (1906)

333. COLONIAL II
author: Edward Stratemeyer
publishers: Lee & Shepard; Lothrop, Lee & Shepard
1. With Washington in the West; Or, A Soldier Boy's Battles in the Wilderness (1901)
2. Marching on Niagara; or, The Soldier Boys of the Old Frontier (1902)
3. At the Fall of Montreal; or, A Soldier Boy's Final Victory (1903)
4. On the Trail of Pontiac; or, The Pioneer Boys of the Ohio (1904)
5. The Fort in the Wilderness; or, The Soldier Boys of the Indian Trails (1905)
6. Trail and Trading Post; or, The Young Hunters of the Ohio (1906)

334. COLONIAL III
author: Edward Sylvester Ellis
publisher: H. T. Coates
1-2. [titles unknown]
3. The Last Emperor of the Old Dominion (1904)

335. COLUMBUS [*see also* GOLDEN TREASURY *and* OXFORD series]
author: Thomas Hughes
publisher: International Book
1. Tom Brown's School Days at Rugby (1890)

336. COMIC ANIMAL
author: [unknown]
publisher: McLoughlin Brothers
1. Fun and Fancy; Wonder Tales for Children from Seven to Seventy (1885)
2. The Funny Household (1898)
3. Early Cares (1898)

337. COMRADES
author: Ralph Victor
illustrators: S. Schneider and Rudolf Mencl
publishers: Chatterton-Peck; Platt & Peck; Hurst
1. Comrades in Camp; or, On Lake and River (1908)
2. Comrades in New York,; or, Snaring the Smugglers (1908)

3. Comrades on the Ranch; or, Secret the of Lost River (1908)
4. Comrades in New Mexico; or, The Round-Up (1908)
5. Comrades on the Farm; or, The Deep Gulch Mystery (1908)
6. Comrades on the Great Divide; or, The Aztec Search (1909)
7. Comrades at School (1909)
8. Comrades at Winton Hall; or, Cadet Pranks and Winter Sports (1909)
9. Comrades on Winton Oval; or, The Fight for the Silver Pennant (1909)
10. Comrades on River and Lake (1910)
11. Comrades with the Winton Cadets; or, Leading the Yearlings Against the Plebes (1911)

338. CONNIE LORING [see also LILIAN GARIS BOOKS]
author: Lilian C. McNamara Garis
publisher: Grosset & Dunlap
1. Connie Loring; or, Connie Loring's Ambition (1925)
2. Gypsy Friend; or Connie Loring's Dilemma (1925)

339. CONNIE MORGAN
author: James Beardsley Hendryx
publishers: Putnam [1-6,9-10]; Jarrclos [7]; Doudleday, Doran [8]
1. Connie Morgan in Alaska (1916)
2. Connie Morgan with the Mounties (1918)
3. Connie Morgan in the Lumber Camps (1919)
4. Connie Morgan in the Fur Country (1921)
5. Connie Morgan in the Cattle Country (1923)
6. Connie Morgan with the Forest Rangers (1925)
7. Connie Morgan, Prospector
8. Connie Morgan Hits the Trail (1929)
9. Connie Morgan in the Arctic (1936)
10. Connie Morgan in the Barren Lands (1937)

340. CONQUEST OF THE UNITED STATES
author: Harrie Irving Hancock
publisher: Henry Altemus

1. The Invasion of the United States; or, Uncle Sam's Boys at the Capture of Boston (1916)
2. In the Battle for New York; or, Uncle Sam's Boys in the Desperate Struggle for the Metropolis (1916)
3. At the Defense of Pittsburgh; or, The Struggle to Save America's "Fighting Steel" Supply (1916)
4. Making the Last Stand for Old Glory; or, Uncle Sam's Boys in the Last Frantic Drive (1916)

341. COOPER LAKE
author: Ralph Henry Barbour
publisher: David Appleton-Century
1. Rivals on the Mound (1938)
2. Fighting Guard (1938)
3. Ninth Inning Rally (1940)

CORNER see FOUR CORNER HOUSE GIRLS

342. CORNER HOUSE GIRLS
author: Grace Brooks Hill [pseudonym of the Stratemeyer Syndicate]
illustrators: Thelma Gooch [10-12]; R. Emmett Owen [1-9]; Howard L. Hastings [13]
publisher: Barse & Hopkins
1. The Corner House Girls; How They Moved to Milton, What They Found, and What They Did (1915)
2. The Corner House Girls at School; How They Entered, How They Met, and What They Did (1915)
3. The Corner House Girls Under Canvas; How They Reached Pleasant Cove and What Happened Afterwards (1915)
4. The Corner House Girls in a Play; How They Rehearsed, How They Acted, and What The Play Brought In (1916)
5. The Corner House Girls' Odd Find; Where They Made It, and What the Strange Discovery Led To (1916)
6. The Corner House Girls on a Tour; Where They Went, What They Saw, and What They Found (1917)
7. The Corner House Girls Growing Up; What Happened First, What Came Next, and How It Ended (1918)

8. The Corner House Girls Snowbound; How They Went Away, What They Discovered, and How It Ended (1919)
9. The Corner House Girls on a House-boat; How They Sailed Away, What Happened on the Voyage, and What Was Discovered (1920)
10. The Corner House Girls Among the Gypsies; How They Met, What Happened, and How It Ended (1921)
11. The Corner House Girls on Palm Island; Looking for Adventure, How They Found It, and What Happened (1922)
12. The Corner House Girls Solve a Mystery; What It Was, Where It Was, and Who Found It (1923)
13. The Corner House Girls Facing the World; Why They Had To, How They Did It, and What Came of It (1926)

343. CORWIN'S NEST
author: Madeline Leslie
publisher: A.F. Graves
1. Little Tot's Lessons (1869)

344. COSMO
author: Palmer Cox
publisher: Century
1. Palmer Cox's Brownie Book (1900)

345. COSY CORNER [see also LIT-TLE COLONEL]
authors: Annie Fellows Johnston [1-13]; Sir Charles George Douglas Roberts [14]; Dinah Maria Mulock Craik 15, 18]; Edna S. Brainerd [16]; Ouida [17]
illustrators: W. L. Taylor [9]; Sears Gallagher [8]; E. F. Bonsall [10]; Diantha W. Horne [12]; Emily B. Waite [13]; Frank T. Merrill [5]; Mary G. Johnston [2]; Amy M. Sacker [2]; Etheldred B. Barry [1, 3-7, 11];
publisher: L. C. Page
1. Big Brother (1893)
2. Ole Mammy's Torment (1897)
3. The Giant Scissors (1898)
4. Gate of the Giant Scissors (1898)
5. Two Little Knights of Kentucky Who Were the "Little Colonel's" Neighbors (1899)
6. Story of Dago (1900)
7. Little Colonel (1901)
8. Cicely and Other Stories (1903)
9. Aunt 'Liza's Hero and Other Stories (1903)
10. Flip's "Islands of Providence" (1903)
11. The Quilt That Jack Built; How He Won the Bicycle (1904)
12. Mildred's Inheritance; Just Her Way; Ann's Own Way (1906)
13. Little Man in Motley (1918)
14. The Young Acadian; or, The Raid from Beausejour (1894)
15. The Little Lame Prince (1898)
16. Millicent in Dreamland (1903)
17. A Dog of Flanders; A Christmas Story (1897)
18. The Adventures of a Brownie as Told to my Child (1897)

346. COUSIN ROSEBUD
author: [unknown]
publisher: S. Marks & Sons
1. The Adventures of Dame Crump and Her Little White Pig (1880)

347. CROWN LIBRARY
author: George Ernest Rochester
publisher: Warne
1. White Wings and Blue Water; a Story of Adventure in the South Seas (1952)
2. The "Black Octopus" (1954)

348. CUFFY BEAR
author: Arthur Scott Bailey
illustrators: Ernest Vetsch, Harry L. Smith
publisher: Grosset & Dunlap
1. Tale of Cuffy Bear (1915)
2. Tale of Cuffy Bear and the Circus (1929)
3. Tale of Cuffy Bear and the Scarecrow (1929)
4. Tale of Cuffy Bear and the Snow Man (1929)
5. Tale of Cuffy Bear's Holidays (1929)

349. CURLYTOPS
author: Howard Roger Garis
illustrator: Julia Greene
publisher: Cupples & Leon
1. The Curlytops Snowed in; or, Grand Fun with Skates and Sleds (1918)

2. The Curlytops at Cherry Farm; or, Vacation Days in the Country (1918)
3. The Curlytops on Star Island; or, Camping Out with Grandpa (1918)
4. The Curlytops at Uncle Frank's Ranch; or, Little Folks on Ponyback (1918)
5. The Curlytops at Silver Lake; or, On the Water with Uncle Ben (1920)
6. The Curlytops and Their Pets; or, Uncle Toby's Strange Collection (1921)
7. The Curlytops and Their Playmates; or, Jolly Times Through the Holidays (1922)
8. The Curlytops in the Woods; or, Fun at the Lumber Camp (1923)
9. The Curlytops at Sunset Beach; or, What Was Found in the Sand (1924)
10. The Curlytops Touring Around; or, The Missing Photograph Albums (1925)
11. The Curlytops in a Summer Camp; or, Animal Joe's Menagerie (1927)
12. The Curlytops Growing Up; or, Winter Sports and Summer Pleasures (1928)
13. The Curlytops at Happy House; or, The Mystery of the Chinese Vase (1931)
14. The Curlytops at the Circus; or, The Runaway Elephant (1932)

350. DADDY SERIES FOR LITTLE FOLKS

author: Howard Roger Garis
illustrators: Eva Dean, Edyth Garside Powers
publishers: R. F. Fenno; M.A. Donahue; A.L. Burt
1. Daddy Takes Us Camping (1914)
2. Daddy Takes Us Fishing (1914)
3. Daddy Takes Us Skating (1914)
4. Daddy Takes Us to the Circus (1914)
5. Daddy Takes Us Coasting (1914)
6. Daddy Takes Us to the Woods (1914)
7. Daddy Takes Us to the Farm (1914)
8. Daddy Takes Us Hunting Birds (1914)
9. Daddy Takes Us Hunting Flowers (1914)
10. Daddy Takes Us to the Garden (1914)

351. DAISY

author: George Alfred Henty
publisher: F.M. Lupton
1. Among Malay Pirates (1909)

352. DAISY DELL

author: Phillip Findlay
publishers: Henry A. Young; C.E. Brown
1. Sadie's Dream; or, The Would-Be Runaway (1869)
2. Going into the Country (1869)
3. Playing Soldier (1869)
4. Little Alice and the Ox-Goad (1869)
5. The Shepherdess of Daisy Dell (1869)

353. DANA GIRL MYSTERY STORIES

author: Lilian C. McNamara Garis
publisher: Grosset & Dunlap
1. The Mystery of Stingyman's Alley (1938)

354. DANA GIRLS

author: Carolyn Keene [pseudonym of the Stratemeyer Syndicate]
publisher: Grosset & Dunlap
1. By the Light of the Study Lamp (1934)
2. The Secret at Lone Tree Cottage (1934)
3. In the Shadow of the Tower (1934)
4. A Three-Cornered Mystery (1935)
5. The Secret at the Hermitage (1936)
6. The Circle of Footprints (1937)
7. The Mystery of the Locked Room (1938)
8. The Clue in the Cobweb (1939)
9. The Secret at the Gatehouse (1940)
10. The Mysterious Fireplace (1941)
11. The Clue of the Rusty Key (1942)
12. The Portrait in the Sand (1943)
13. The Secret in the Old Well (1944)
14. The Clue in the Ivy (1952)
15. The Secret of the Jade Ring (1953)
16. The Mystery at the Crossroads (1954)
17. The Ghost in the Gallery (1955)
18. The Clue of the Black Flower (1956)
19. The Winking Ruby Mystery (1957)
20. The Secret of the Swiss Chalet (1958)
21. The Haunted Lagoon (1959)
22. The Mystery of the Bamboo Bird (1960)

23. The Sierra Gold Mystery (1961)
24. The Secret of Lost Lake (1963)
25. The Mystery of the Stone Tiger (1963)
26. The Riddle of the Frozen Fountain (1964)
27. The Secret of the Silver Dolphin (1965)
28. The Mystery of the Wax Queen (1966)
29. The Secret of the Minstrel's Guitar (1967)
30. The Phantom Surfer (1968)
31. The Curious Coronation (1976)
32. The Hundred-Year Mystery (1977)
33. The Mountain Peak Mystery (1978)
34. The Witch's Omen (1979)

355. DANDELION COTTAGE

author: C. W. Rankin
publisher: Holt
1. Dandelion Cottage (1904)
2. The Girls of Gardenville (1906)
3. The Adopting of Rosa Marie (1908)
4. The Castaways of Pete's Patch (1911)
5. The Girls of Highland Hall (1921)

356. DARE BOYS

author: Stephen Angus Cox
illustrator: Rudolf Mencl
publishers: A. L. Chatterton; Platt & Peck; Hurst
1. The Dare Boys of 1776 (1910)
2. The Dare Boys on the Hudson (1910)
3. The Dare Boys in Trenton (1910)
4. The Dare Boys on the Brandywine (1910)
5. The Dare Boys in the Red City (1910)
6. The Dare Boys After Benedict Arnold (1910)
7. The Dare Boys in Virginia (1910)
8. The Dare Boys with General Greene (1910)
9. The Dare Boys with Lafayette (1910)
10. The Dare Boys and the "Swamp Fox" (1910)
11. The Dare Boys in Vincennes (1912)
12. The Dare Boys in the Northwest (1913)

357. DAREWELL CHUMS

author: Allen Chapman [pseudonym of Edward Stratemeyer]
illustrators: Clare Angell [1]; Charles Nuthall [2–4]; H. Richard Boehm [5]

publishers: Cupples & Leon; M. A. Donohue
1. The Darewell Chums; or, The Heroes of the School (1908) [alternate title: The Heroes of the School; or, The Darewell Chums Through Thick and Thin]
2. The Darewell Chums in the City; or, The Disappearance of Ned Wilding (1908) [alternate title: Ned Wilding's Disappearance; or, The Darewell Chums in the City]
3. The Darewell Chums in the Woods,; or, Frank Roscoe's Secret (1908) [alternate title: Frank Roscoe's Secret; or, The Darewell Chums in the Woods]
4. The Darewell Chums on a Cruise; or, Fenn Masterson's Odd Discovery (1909) [alternate title: Fenn Masterson's Discovery; or, The Darewell Chums on a Cruise]
5. The Darewell Chums in a Winter Camp; or, Bart Keene's Best Shot (1911) [alternate title: Bart Keen's Hunting Days; or, The Darewell Chums in a Winter Camp]

358. DARING TWINS

author: Lyman Frank Baum
publisher: Reilly & Britton
1. The Daring Twins
2. Phoebe Daring; A Story for Young Folk (1912)

359. DAVE DARRIN [see also ALTEMUS' ANNAPOLIS SERIES]

author: Harrie Irving Hancock
publishers: Henry Altemus; Saalfield
1. Dave Darrin at Vera Cruz; or, Fighting with the United States Navy in Mexico (1914)
2. Dave Darrin on Mediterranean Service; or, With Dan Dalzell on European Duty (1919)
3. Dave Darrin's South American Cruise; or, Two Innocent Young Naval Tools of an Infamous Conspiracy (1919)
4. Dave Darrin after the Mine Layers; or, Hitting the Enemy a Hard Naval Blow (1919)
5. Dave Darrin on the Asiatic Station; or, Winning Lieutenant's Commissions on the Admiral's Flagship (1919)

6. Dave Darrin and the German Submarines; or, Making a Clean-up of the Hun Sea Monsters (1919)

360. DAVE DASHAWAY

author: Roy Rockwood [pseudonym of the Stratemeyer Syndicate]
illustrator: R. Blass
publisher: Cupples & Leon

1. Dave Dashaway the Young Aviator; or, In the Clouds for Fame and Fortune (1913)
2. Dave Dashaway and His Hydroplane; or, Daring Adventures Over the Great Lakes (1913)
3. Dave Dashaway and His Giant Airship; or, A Marvelous Trip Across the Atlantic (1913)
4. Dave Dashaway Around the World; or, A Young Yankee Aviator Among Many Nations (1913)
5. Dave Dashaway, Air Champion; or, Wizard Work in the Clouds (1915)

361. DAVE DAWSON [alternate title: WAR ADVENTURE]

author: Robert Sidney Bowen
publishers: Saalfield; Crown

1. Dave Dawson at Dunkirk (1941)
2. Dave Dawson with the R.A.F. (1941)
3. Dave Dawson in Libya (1941)
4. Dave Dawson on Convoy Patrol (1941)
5. Dave Dawson, Flight Lieutenant (1941)
6. Dave Dawson at Singapore (1942)
7. Dave Dawson with the Pacific Fleet (1942)
8. Dave Dawson with the Air Corps (1942)
9. Dave Dawson on the Russian Front (1943)
10. Dave Dawson with the Commandos (1942)
11. Dave Dawson with the Flying Tigers (1943)
12. Dave Dawson on Guadalcanal (1943)
13. Dave Dawson at Casablanca (1944)
14. Dave Dawson with the Eighth Air Force (1944)
15. Dave Dawson over Japan
16. Dave Dawson at Truk (1946)

362. DAVE FEARLESS

author: Roy Rockwood [pseudonym of the Stratemeyer Syndicate]
illustrators: A. B. Shute, Clare Angell, Charles Nuttall
publishers: George Sully [1–3]; Garden City Publishing [4–17]

1. Dave Fearless After a Sunken Treasure; or, The Rival Ocean Divers (1918)
2. Dave Fearless on a Floating Island; or, The Cruise of the Treasure Ship (1918)
3. Dave Fearless and the Cave of Mystery; or, Adrift on the Pacific (1926)
4. Dave Fearless Among the Icebergs; or, The Secret of the Eskimo Igloo (1926)
5. Dave Fearless Wrecked Among Savages; or, The Captives of the Head Hunters (1926)
6. Dave Fearless and His Big Raft; or, Alone on the Broad Pacific (1926)
7. Dave Fearless on Volcano Island; or, The Magic Cave of Blue Fire (1926)
8. Dave Fearless Captured by Apes; or, Lost in Gorilla Land (1926)
9. Dave Fearless and the Mutineers; or, Prisoners on the Ship of Death (1926)
10. Dave Fearless Under the Ocean; or, The Treasure of the Lost Submarine (1926)
11. Dave Fearless in the Black Jungle; or, Lost Among the Cannibals (1926)
12. Dave Fearless Near the South Pole; or, The Giant Whales of Snow Island (1926)
13. Dave Fearless Caught by Malay Pirates; or, The Secret of Bamboo Island (1926)
14. Dave Fearless on the Ship of Mystery; or, The Strange Hermit of Shark Cove (1927)
15. Dave Fearless on the Lost Brig; or, Abandoned in the Big Hurricane (1927)
16. Dave Fearless at Whirlpool Point; or, The Mystery of the Water Cave (1927)
17. Dave Fearless Among the Cannibals; or The Defense of the Hut in the Swamp (1927)

363. DAVE PERRY ADVENTURE STORIES

author: Kent Sagendorph

publisher: Cupples & Leon
1. Radium Island (1938)
2. Beyond the Amazon (1938)
3. Sin-Kiang Castle (1938)

364. DAVE PORTER
author: Edward Stratemeyer
publisher: Lothrop, Lee & Shepard
1. Dave Porter at Oak Hall; or, The Schooldays of an American Boy (1905)
2. Dave Porter in the South Seas; or, The Strange Cruise of the Stormy Petrel (1906)
3. Dave Porter's Return to school; or, Winning the Medal of Honor (1907)
4. Dave Porter in the Far North; or, The Pluck of an American School Boy (1908)
5. Dave Porter and His Classmates; or, For the Honor of Oak Hall (1909)
6. Dave Porter at Star Ranch; or, The Cowboy's Secret (1910)
7. Dave Porter and His Rivals; or, The Chums and Foes of Oak Hall (1911)
8. Dave Porter on Cave Island; or, A Schoolboy's Mysterious Mission (1912)
9. Dave Porter and the Runaways; or, Last Days at Oak Hall (1913)
10. Dave Porter in the Gold Fields; or, The Search for the Landslide Mine (1914)
11. Dave Porter at Bear Camp; or, The Wild Man of Mirror Lake (1915)
12. Dave Porter and His Double; or, The Disappearance of the Basswood Fortune (1916)
13. Dave Porter's Great Search; or, The Perils of a Young Civil Engineer (1917)
14. Dave Porter Under Fire; or, A Young Army Engineer in France (1918)
15. Dave Porter's War Honors; or, At the Front with the Flying Engineers (1919)

365. DAVID
author: David Binney Putman
publisher: Brewer, Warren & Putnam
1. David Goes Voyaging (1925)
2. David Goes to Greenland (1926)
3. David Goes to Baffin Island (1927)
4. David Sails the Viking Trail (1931)

366. DEAR LITTLE GIRL
author: Amy E. Blanchard
publisher: Jacobs
1. A Dear Little Girl (1897)
2. A Dear Little Girl at School (1910)
3. A Dear Little Girl's Summer Holidays (1911)
4. A Dear Little Girl's Thanksgiving Holidays (1912)

367. DEEP SEA
author: Roy Rockwood [pseudonym of the Stratemeyer Syndicate]
illustrators: A. B. Shute [1]; Clare Angell [2]; Charles Nuttall [3–4];
publishers: Stitt [1–2]; Grosset & Dunlap [3–4]
1. The Rival Ocean Divers; or, The Search for a Sunken Treasure (1905) [alternate subtitle: After a Sunken Treasure]
2. The Cruise of the Treasure Ship; or, The Castaways of Floating Island (1907)
3. Adrift on the Pacific; or, The Secret of the Island Cave (1908)
4. Jack North's Treasure Hunt; or, Daring Adventures in South America (1908)

368. DEEP SEA HUNTERS
author: Alpheus Hyatt Verrill
publisher: David Appleton
1. Deep Sea Hunters; Adventures on a Whaler (1922)
2. Deep Sea Hunters in the Frozen Seas (1923)
3. Deep Sea Hunters in the South Seas (1924)

369. DEER LODGE
author: William Gordon Parker
publisher: Lee & Shepard
1–2. [titles unknown]
3. Rival Boy Sportsmen; or, The Mink Lake Regatta (1900)

370. DENEWOOD
authors: E. B. and A. A. Knipe
publisher: Century
1. The Lucky Sixpence (1912)
2. Beatrice of Denewood (1913)

3. Peg o' the Ring, a Maid of Denewood (1915)
4. The Luck of Denewood (1921)

371. DERIC
author: Deric Nusbaum
publisher: G. P. Putnam's Sons
1. Deric in Mesa Verde (1926)
2. Deric with the Indians (1927)

372. DIANE
author: Betty Cavanna
publisher: Macrae
1. A Date for Diane (1946)
2. Diane's New Love (1955)
3. Toujours Diane (1957)

373. DICK
author: Anthone Weston Dimock
publisher: F.A. Stokes
1. Dick in the Everglades (1909)
2. Dick Among the Lumber-Jacks (1910)
3. Dick Among the Seminoles (1911)
4. Dick Among the Miners (1913)

374. DICK AND DOLLY
author: Carolyn Wells
illustrators: Ada Budell [1]; Mayo Bunker [2]
publisher: Grosset & Dunlap
1. Dick and Dolly (1909)
2. Dick and Dolly's Adventures (1910)

375. DICK AND JANET CHERRY
author: Howard Roger Garis
publisher: McLaughlin Bros.
1. The Bear Hunt (1930)
2. The Gypsy Camp (1930)
3. Saving the Old Mill (1930)
4. Shipwrecked on Christmas Island (1930)

376. DICK ARNOLD
author: Earl Reed Silvers
publisher: David Appleton
1. Dick Arnold of Raritan College (1920)
2. Dick Arnold of the Varsity (1921)

377. DICK HAMILTON
author: Howard Roger Garis
publishers: Grosset & Dunlap; Gold; Saalfield

1. Dick Hamilton's Fortune; or, The Stirring Doings of a Millionaire's Son (1909)
2. Dick Hamilton's Cadet Days; or, The Handicap of a Millionaire's Son (1910)
3. Dick Hamilton's Steam Yacht; or, A Young Millionaire and the Kidnappers (1911)
4. Dick Hamilton's Football Team; or, A Young Millionaire on the Gridiron (1912)
5. Dick Hamilton's Touring Car; or, A Young Millionaire's Race for a Fortune (1913)
6. Dick Hamilton's Airship; or, A Young Millionaire in the Clouds (1914)

378. DICK KENT [alternate title: BOYS OF THE ROYAL MOUNTED POLICE]
author: Milton Richards [pseudonym of Milo Milton Oblinger]
publisher: A. L. Burt
1. Dick Kent with the Mounted Police (1927)
2. Dick Kent in the Far North (1927)
3. Dick Kent with the Eskimos (1927)
4. Dick Kent, Fur Trader (1927)
5. Dick Kent and the Malemute Mail (1927)
6. Dick Kent on Special Duty (1928)
7. Dick Kent at Half Way House (1929)
8. Dick Kent, Mounted Police Deputy (1933)
9. Dick Kent's Mysterious Mission (1933)
10. Dick Kent and the Mine Mystery (1934)

DICK PRESCOTT see UNCLE SAM'S BOYS; WEST POINT II

379. DIMSIE
author: Dorita Fairlie Bruce
publisher: Oxford University Press
1. The Senior Prefect (1921) [alternate title: Dimsie Goes to School]
2. Dimsie Moves Up (1921)
3. Dimsie Moves Up Again (1922)
4. Dimsie Among the Prefects (1923)
5. Dimsie Grows Up (1924)
6. Dimsie, Head-Girl (1925)

7. Dimsie Goes Back (1927)
8. Dimsie Intervenes (1937)
9. Dimsie Carries On (1942)

380. DINNY GORDON
author: Anne Emery
publisher: Macrae
1. Dinny Gordon, Freshman (1959)
2. Dinny Gordon, Sophomore (1961)
3. Dinny Gordon, Junior (1964)
4. Dinny Gordon, Senior (1965)

"DO SOMETHING" BOOKS see JAN-
ICE DAY

381. DOCTOR DOOLITTLE
author: Hugh John Lofting
publisher: J. B. Lippincott
1. The Story of Doctor Doolittle, Being
the History of His Peculiar Life at
Home and Astonishing Adventures in
Foreign Parts (1920)
2. The Voyages of Doctor Doolittle (1922)
3. Doctor Doolittle's Post Office (1923)
4. The Story of Mrs. Tubbs (1923)
5. Doctor Doolittle and the Green
Canary (1924)
6. Doctor Doolittle's Circus (1924)
7. Porridge Poetry (1924)
8. Doctor Doolittle's Zoo (1925)
9. Doctor Doolittle's Caravan (1926)
10. Doctor Doolittle's Garden (1927)
11. Doctor Doolittle in the Moon (1928)
12. Noisy Nora (1929)
13. Gub Gub's Book, or, An Encyclope-
dia of Food (1932)
14. Doctor Doolittle's Return (1933)
15. Doctor Doolittle's Birthday Book
(1935)
16. Tommy, Tilly and Mrs. Tubbs (1936)
17. Doctor Doolittle and the Secret Lake
(1948)

382. DOCTOR'S LITTLE GIRL
author: Marion Ames
publisher: L. C. Page
1. The Doctor's Little Girl (1907)
2. Sweet Nancy (1909)
3. Nancy, the Doctor's Little Partner
(1911)
4. Nancy Porter's Opportunity (1912)
5. Nancy and the Coggs Twins (1914)

383. DODD'S YOUNG PEOPLE'S LIBRARY
authors: Cyrus Townsend Brady [1];
Alpheus Hyatt Verrill [2]; Charles
James Louis Gilson [3]
publisher: Dodd, Mead
1. Bob Dashaway, Privateersman; An Old
Time Sea Tale of Good Fun and Good
Fighting (1911)
2. The Boy's Book of Whalers (1927)
3. The Scarlet Hand (1927)

384. DOLLY AND MOLLY
author: Elizabeth Gordon
publisher: Rand McNally
1. Dolly and Molly at the Circus (1914)
2. Dolly and Molly and the Farmer Man
(1914)
3. Dolly and Molly at the Sea Shore
(1914)
4. Dolly and Molly on Christmas Day
(1914)

385. DON HALE
author: William Henry Crispin Sheppard
publisher: Penn
1. Don Hale in the War Zone (1917)
2. Don Hale Over There (1918)
3. Don Hale with the Flying Squadron
(1919)
4. Don Hale with the Yanks (1919)

386. DON KIRK
author: Gilbert Patten
publisher: David McKay
1. The Boy Cattle King; or, Don Kirk
2. The Boy from the West
3. Don Kirk's Mine; or, The Flight for a
Lost Treasure

387. DON STURDY
author: Victor Appleton [pseudonym of
the Stratemeyer Syndicate]
illustrators: Walter S. Rogers [1–11]; Nat
Falk [12–15]
publisher: Grosset & Dunlap
1. Don Sturdy on the Desert of Mystery;
or, Autoing in the Land of Caravans
(1925)
2. Don Sturdy with the Big Snake
Hunters; or, Lost in the Jungles of the
Amazon (1925)

3. Don Sturdy in the Tombs of Gold; or, The Old Eygptian's Great Secret (1925)
4. Don Sturdy Across the North Pole; or, Castaway in the Land of Ice (1925)
5. Don Sturdy in the Land of Volcanoes; or, The Trail of the Ten Thousand Smokes (1925)
6. Don Sturdy in the Port of Lost Ships; or, Adrift in the Sargasso Sea (1926)
7. Don Sturdy Among the Gorillas; or, Adrift in the Great Jungle (1927)
8. Don Sturdy Captured by Head Hunters; or, Adrift in the Wilds of Borneo (1928)
9. Don Sturdy in Lion Land; or, The Strange Clearing in the Jungle (1929)
10. Don Sturdy in the Land of Giants; or, Captives of the Savage Patagonians (1930)
11. Don Sturdy on the Ocean Bottom; or, The Strange Cruise of the Phantom (1931)
12. Don Sturdy in the Temples of Fear; or, Destined for a Strange Sacrifice (1932)
13. Don Sturdy Lost in Glacier Bay; or, The Mystery of the Moving Totem Poles (1933)
14. Don Sturdy Trapped in the Flaming Wilderness; or, Unearthing Secrets in Central Asia (1934)
15. Don Sturdy with the Harpoon Hunters; or, The Strange Cruise of the Whaling Ship (1935)

388. DON WINSLOW

author: Frank Victor Martinek
publishers: Grosset & Dunlap [1–4]; Rosenow [5]
1. Don Winslow of the Navy (1940)
2. Don Winslow Face to Face with the Scorpion (1940)
3. Don Winslow Breaks the Spy Net (1941)
4. Dow Winslow Saves the Secret Formula (1941)
5. Don Winslow, USN in Ceylon

389. DONALD KIRK

author: Edward Mott Woolley
publisher: Little, Brown
1. Donald Kirk, the Morning Record Copy-Boy (1912)

390. DONCHESTER

author: Arthur Duffey
publisher: Lothrop, Lee & Shepard
1. On the Cinder Path; or, Archie Hartley's First Year at Donchester (1911)
2. For Old Donchester; or, Archie Hartley and His Schoolmates (1912)

391. DORIS FORCE

author: Julia K. Duncan [pseudonym of the Stratemeyer Syndicate]
illustrator: Thelma Gooch
publisher: Henry Altemus
1. Doris Force at Cloudy Cove; or, The Old Miser's Signature (1931)
2. Doris Force at Locked Gates; or, Saving a Mysterious Fortune (1931)
3. Doris Force at Barry Manor; or, Mysterious Adventures Between Classes (1932)
4. Doris Force at Raven Rock; or Uncovering the Secret Oil Well (1932)

392. DOROTHY

author: Evelyn Raymond
publishers: Grosset & Dunlap [1]; Chatterton [2–11]
1. Dorothy Chester at Skyrie (1907)
2. Dorothy's House Party (1908)
3. Dorothy's Schooling (1908)
4. Dorothy's Travels (1908)
5. Dorothy (1909)
6. Dorothy in California (1909)
7. Dorothy on a House Boat (1909)
8. Dorothy on a Ranch (1909)
9. Dorothy at Oak Knowe (1910)
10. Dorothy's Tour (1912)
11. Dorothy's Triumph (1913)

393. DOROTHY BROOKE

author: Frances Campbell Sparhawk
publisher: Thomas Y. Crowell
1. Dorothy Brooke's School Days (1909)
2. Dorothy Brooke's Vacation (1910)
3. Dorothy Brooke's Experiments (1911)
4. Dorothy Brooke at Ridgemore (1912)
5. Dorothy Brooke Across the Sea (1913)

394. DOROTHY DAINTY

author: Amy Brooks
illustrator: Amy Brooks
publishers: Lothrop, Lee & Shepard

1. Dorothy Dainty (1902)
2. Dorothy's Playmates (1903)
3. Dorothy Dainty at School (1904)
4. Dorothy Dainty at the Shore (1905)
5. Dorothy Dainty in the City (1906)
6. Dorothy Dainty at Home (1907)
7. Dorothy Dainty's Gay Times (1908)
8. Dorothy Dainty in the Country (1909)
9. Dorothy Dainty's Winter (1910)
10. Dorothy Dainty at the Mountains (1911)
11. Dorothy Dainty's Holidays (1912)
12. Dorothy Dainty's Vacation (1913)
13. Dorothy Dainty's Visit (1914)
14. Dorothy Dainty at Crestville (1915)
15. Dorothy Dainty's New Friends (1916)
16. Dorothy Dainty at Glenmore (1917)
17. Dorothy Dainty at Foam Ridge (1918)
18. Dorothy Dainty at Gem Island (1920)
19. Dorothy Dainty's Red Letter Days (1921)
20. Dorothy Dainty's Castle (1923)

395. DOROTHY DALE

author: Margaret Penrose [pseudonym of the Stratemeyer Syndicate]
illustrators: Charles Nuttall [1–5]; H. Richard Boehm [6]; Walter S. Rogers [9–10]; R. Emmett Owen [11–12]
publisher: Cupples & Leon
1. Dorothy Dale: A Girl of Today (1908)
2. Dorothy Dale at Glenwood School (1908)
3. Dorothy Dale's Great Secret (1909)
4. Dorothy Dale and Her Chums (1909)
5. Dorothy Dale's Queer Holidays (1910)
6. Dorothy Dale's Camping Days (1911)
7. Dorothy Dale's School Rivals (1912)
8. Dorothy Dale in the City (1913)
9. Dorothy Dale's Promise (1914)
10. Dorothy Dale in the West (1915)
11. Dorothy Dale's Strange Discovery (1916)
12. Dorothy Dale's Engagement (1917)
13. Dorothy Dale to the Rescue (1924)

396. DOROTHY DIXON

author: Dorothy Wayne
publisher: Goldsmith Publishing
1. Dorothy Dixon Solves the Conway Case (1933)
2. Dorothy Dixon and the Double Cousin (1933)
3. Dorothy Dixon and the Mystery Plane (1933)
4. Dorothy Dixon Wins Her Wings (1933)

397. DOT AND DASH

author: Dorothy West
publisher: Cupples & Leon
1. Dot and Dash at the Maple Sugar Camp
2. Dot and Dash at Happy Hollow
3. Dot and Dash in the North Woods (1938)
4. Dot and Dash in the Pumpkin Patch

398. DOTTY DIMPLE STORIES
[alternative title: EDITHA II] [see also LITTLE PRUDY]

author: Sophie May [pseudonym of Rebecca Sophia Clarke]
illustrators: Amy Brooks; Bertha G. Davidson
publishers: Lee & Shepard; H. M. Caldwell; M.A. Donohue; Charles T. Dillingham
1. Little Prudy's Dotty Dimple (1865)
2. Dotty Dimple at Her Grandmother's (1867)
3. Dotty Dimple Out West (1864)
4. Dotty Dimple at Play (1868)
5. Dotty Dimple at School (1869)
6. Dotty Dimple's Flyaway (1870)
7. Dotty Dimple at Home (1868)

399. DREADNOUGHT BOYS

author: Wilbur Lawton [pseudonym of John Henry Goldfrap]
illustrator: Charles L. Wrenn
publisher: Hurst
1. The Dreadnought Boys on Battle Practice (1911)
2. The Dreadnought Boys Aboard a Destroyer (1911)
3. The Dreadnought Boys on a Submarine (1911)
4. The Dreadnought Boys on Aero Service (1912)
5. The Dreadnought Boys' World Cruise (1913)

6. The Dreadnought Boys in Home Waters (1914)

400. DRIA MEREDITH
author: Janet Lambert
publisher: Dutton
1. Star Dream (1951)
2. Summer for Seven (1952)
3. High Hurdles (1955)

401. EAGLE LAKE
authors: Levi Parker Wyman [1, 2]; Philip Hart [3]
publisher: Saalfield
1. Blind Man's Inlet (1932)
2. The Mystery of Eagle Lake (1931)
3. The Strange Teepee (1931)

402. EAGLE SCOUT
author: Norton Hughes Jonathan
publisher: M. A. Donohue
1. The Movie Scout; or, The Thrill Hunters (1934)
2. The Speedway Cyclone; or, Driving to Win (1933)
3. The Lost Empire; or, Larry Hannon Carries On (1934)

403. EASTERN INDIAN
author: Elmer Russell Gregor
publisher: David Appleton
1. Running Fox (1818)
2. Spotted Deer (1922)
3. The War Eagle (1826)
4. The Mystery Trail (1927)

404. EASY TO READ
authors: Edith Ellen Ellsworth [1, 2, 6]; Margaret L. Mitchell [3]; Josephine Pollard [4]; Lewis Carroll [5]
publishers: Blackie; McLoughlin Brothers; Saalfield
1. The Adventures of Gulliver (1950)
2. Children of the Old Testament and Children of the New Testament (1954)
3. Tippy's Story (1950)
4. Easy Word Stories (1900)
5. Through the Looking-Glass (1920)

EDDIE *see* **BETSY**

405. EDITHA I
authors: Margaret Penrose and Frances Hodgson Burnett
illustrator: Frank T. Merrill
publisher: H. M. Caldwell
1. Editha's Burglar (1888)
2. Editha's Burglar and Sara Crewe (1890)
3. The Burglar's Daughter; or, A True Heart Wins Friends (1899)

EDITHA II *see* **DOTTY DIMPLE STORIES**

406. EDITHA III
author: Dinah Maria Mulock
publisher: Caldwell
1. The Adventures of a Brownie (1907)

407. EIGHTEENPENCE JUVENILE SERIES
author: Cycla
publisher: James Nisbet
1. Daybreak; or, Right, Struggling and Triumphant (1879)

408. ELIZABETH ANN
author: Josephine Lawrence
publishers: Barse & Hopkins [1–6]; Grosset & Dunlap [7–8]
1. The Adventures of Elizabeth Ann (1923)
2. Elizabeth Ann at Maple Spring (1923)
3. Elizabeth Ann's Six Cousins (1924)
4. Elizabeth Ann and Doris (1925)
5. Elizabeth Ann's Borrowed Grandma (1926)
6. Elizabeth Ann's Spring Vacation (1927)
7. Elizabeth Ann and Uncle Doctor (1928)
8. Elizabeth Ann's Houseboat (1929)

409. ELSIE
author: Martha Finley [pseudonym of Martha Farquharson]
publisher: Dodd, Mead
1. Elsie Dinsmore (1867)
2. Elsie's Girlhood (1872)
3. Elsie's Womanhood (1875)
4. Elsie's Motherhood (1876)
5. Elsie's Children (1877)
6. Elsie's Widowhood (1880)
7. Grandmother Elsie (1882)

8. Elsie's New Relations (1883)
9. Elsie at Nantucket (1884)
10. The Two Elsies (1885)
11. Elsie's Kith and Kin (1886)
12. Elsie's Friends at Woodburn (1887)
13. Christmas with Grandma Elsie (1888)
14. Elsie and the Raymonds (1889)
15. Elsie Yachting with the Raymonds (1890)
16. Elsie's Vacation and After Events (1891)
17. Elsie at Viamede (1892)
18. Elsie at Ion (1893)
19. Elsie at the World's Fair (1894)
20. Elsie's Journey on Inland Waters (1895)
21. Elsie at Home (1897)
22. Elsie on the Hudson and Elsewhere (1898)
23. Elsie in the South (1899)
24. Elsie's Young Folks in Peace and War (1900)
25. Elsie's WinterTrip (1902)
26. Elsie and Her Loved Ones (1903)
27. Elsie and Her Namesakes (1905)
28. Elsie's Holidays at Roseland (1906)

410. EMILY
author: L. M. Montgomery
publisher: Hodder & Stoughton
1. Emily's Quest (1922)
2. Emily of New Moon (1923)
3. Emily Climbs (1925)

411. EMPIRE EDITION
author: Oliver Optic [pseudonym of William Taylor Adams]
publisher: American News
1. Now or Never
2. Try Again
3. All Aboard
4. The Boat Club

412. ERSKINE
author: Ralph Henry Barbour
publisher: David Appleton
1. Behind the Line; A Story of College Life and Football (1902)
2. Weatherby's Inning; A Story of College Life and Baseball (1903)
3. On Your Mark! A Story of College Life and Athletics (1904)

413. ETHEL MORTON
author: Mabell S. C. Smith
publisher: New York Books
1. Ethel Morton and the Christmas Ship (1915)
2. Ethel Morton at Chautauqua (1915)
3. Ethel Morton at Rose House (1915)
4. Ethel Morton at Sweetbriar Lodge (1915)
5. Ethel Morton's Enterprise (1915)
6. Ethel Morton's Holidays (1915)

414. EUROPEAN WAR
author: Franklin T. Ames
publisher: Grosset & Dunlap
1. Between the Lines in Belgium; a Boy's Story of the Great European War (1915)
2. Between the Lines in France; a Boy's Story of the Great European War (1915)

415. EVERY BOY'S ADVENTURE
authors: William Heyliger [1]; Walter E. Butts, Jr. [2]; Graham M. Dean [3]
publisher: Gold; Goldsmith
1. Detectives Incorporated
2. Brothers of the Senecas (1925)
3. The Racer Boys

416. EVERY BOY'S MYSTERY
authors: Edwin Green [1–2]; George Morse [3–5]
publisher: Goldsmith
1. Air Monster (1932)
2. Secret Flight (1933)
3. Extra! (1932)
4. Circus Dan (1933)
5. Vanishing Liner (1934)

417. EVERYDAY SUSAN
author: Mary F. Leonard
publisher: Thomas Y. Crowell
1. Everyday Susan (1912)
2. Christmas Tree House (1913)
3. Susan Grows Up (1914)

418. EVERYHOME [see also FRONTIER I]
authors: Charles H. Pearson [1]; Cousin Mary [2]
publisher: Lothrop, Lee & Shepard
1. The Young Pioneers of the North-West (1870)

2. Country Life, and Other Stories (1910)

419. EXPLORATION
author: James H.Foster
publishers: A. L. Burt; Saalfield
1. Lost in the Wilds of Brazil (1933)
2. Captured by the Arabs (1933)
3. Secrets of the Andes (1933)
4. The Forest of Mystery (1935)

420. FAIRMOUNT GIRLS
author: Etta Anthony Baker
publisher: Little, Brown
1. The Girls of Fairmount (1909)
2. Frolics at Fairmount (1910)
3. The Fairmount Girls in School and Camp (1911)
4. Fairmount's Quartette (1914)

421. FAIRVIEW BOYS [see also UP AND DOING]
author: Frederick Gordon [pseudonym of the Stratemeyer Syndicate]
illustrators: R. Mencl [4–5]; R. Emmett Owen [6]
publishers: Graham & Matlack; C. E. Graham
1. Fairview Boys Afloat and Ashore; or, The Young Crusoes of Pine Island (1912)
2. Fairview Boys on Eagle Mountain; or, Sammy Brown's Treasure Hunt (1912)
3. Fairview Boys and Their Rivals; or, Bob Bouncer's Schooldays (1912)
4. Fairview Boys at Camp Mystery; or, The Old Hermit and His Secret (1914)
5. Fairview Boys at Lighthouse Cove; or, Carried Out to Sea (1914)
6. Fairview Boys on a Ranch; or, Riding with the Cowboys (1917)

422. FAIRVIEW HIGH
author: William Heyliger
publisher: David Appleton
1. Captain Fair and Square (1916)
2. County Pennant
3. Fighting for Fairview (1918)

423. FAIRY MOONBEAMS
author: [unknown]
publisher: McLoughlin Brothers

1. The Frog Who Would a Wooing Go (1861)
2. Cinderella and the Little Glass Slipper (1879)
3. Hop o' My Thumb (1890)
4. The Three Bears (1899)
5. Sleeping Beauty in the Woods (1900)

424. FAITH PALMER
author: Lazelle Thayer Woolley
publisher: Penn
1. Faith Palmer at the Oaks (1912)
2. Faith Palmer at Fordyce Hall (1913)
3. Faith Palmer in New York (1914)
4. Faith Palmer in Washington (1915)

425. FAMILIAR
author: [unknown]
publisher: McLoughlin Brothers
1. The Story of Cock Robin (1890)

426. FAMILY FROM ONE END STREET
author: Eve C. R. Garnett
publisher: Vanguard
1. One End Street (1937)
2. The Family from One End Street; and Some of Their Adventures (1938)
3. Further Adventures of the Family from One End Street (1956)

427. FAMOUS ADVENTURE
author: Oliver Optic [pseudonym of William Taylor Adams]
publisher: David McKay
5. How He Won

428. FAMOUS BOOKS FOR BOYS
author: Oliver Optic [pseudonym of William Taylor Adams]
publisher: Caldwell
1. All Aboard
2. The Boat Club

429. FATHER TAKES
author: Grace Humphrey
publisher: Penn
1. Father Takes Us to New York (1927)
2. Father Takes Us to Boston (1928)
3. Father Takes Us to Philadelphia (1929)
4. Father Takes Us to Washington (1931)

**430. FATHER TUCK'S "CHIL-
DREN'S HOUR"**
author: [unknown]
publisher: Raphael Tuck & Sons
1. Meadowsweet Farm (1910)

**431. FATHER TUCK'S LITTLE
DARLING**
author: Helen Marion Burnside
publisher: Raphael Tuck & Sons
1. Robinson Crusoe (1890)

**432. FATHER TUCK'S LITTLE
PETS**
author: [unknown]
publisher: Raphael Tuck & Sons
1. Three Little Kittens (1880)
2. The Three Little Pigs (1890)
3. More About the Three Little Kittens
(1900)
4. Puss in Boots (1900)

**433. FATHER TUCK'S "LITTLE
TREASURES"**
author: [unknown]
publisher: Raphael Tuck & Sons
1. Doggy's Doings (1898)

**434. FATHER TUCK'S "PLAY
AND PLEASURE"**
author: [unknown]
publisher: Raphael Tuck & Sons
1. Robinson Crusoe (1900)
2. Three Little Kittens (1900)
3. The Three Bears (1900)
4. Daisy Dell Farm ABC (1900)

**435. FATHER TUCK'S TINY
TOTS**
author: [unknown]
publisher: Raphael Tuck & Sons
1. Robinson Crusoe (1897)
2. Who Killed Cock Robin (1902)

**436. FATHER TUCK'S USEFUL
KNOWLEDGE**
author: [unknown]
publisher: Raphael Tuck & Sons
1. Red Riding Hood (1900)

437. FAVORITE
author: George Alfred Henty

publishers: Griffith, Farran, Browne;
McLoughlin Brothers
1. In Times of Peril: A Tale of India
(1881)
2. Favorite Animals and Birds (1866)
3. Who Killed Cock Robin and Other
Rhymes (1900)

438. FELICIA
author: Elizabeth Lincoln Gould
publisher: Penn
1. Felicia (1908)
2. Felicia's Friends (1909)
3. Felicia's Visits (1910)
4. Felicia's Folks (1911)

439. FERRY HILL
author: Ralph Henry Barbour
publisher: Century
1–2. [titles unknown]
    3. Harry's Island (1908)
    4. Captain Chub (1909)

440. FIGHTERS FOR FREEDOM
authors: Gaylord Dubois [2]; Marshall
McClintock [5,7]; Roy Judson Snell
[1,6]; Ruby Lorrain Radford [3,4]
illustrator: J. R. White
publisher: Whitman
1. Sally Scott of the WAVES (1943)
2. Barry Blake of the Flying Fortress
(1943)
3. Nancy Dale, Army Nurse (1944)
4. Kitty Carter, Canteen Girl (1944)
5. Dick Donnelly of the Paratroops
(1944)
6. Norma Kent of the WACS (1943)
7. March Anson and Scoot Bailey of the
U.S. Navy (1944)

441. FIRESIDE I
author: Benjamin Broadaxe
publisher: International Book
[only one title known in this series]
34. The Bad Boy and His Sister (1887)

442. FIRESIDE II
author: Louis Rousselet
publisher: Donohue Brothers
1. The Ocean Rovers; or, Two Cabin
Boys (1892)

443. FIRESIDE III
author: Oliver Optic [pseudonym of
William Taylor Adams]
publisher: Hurst
1. Oliver Optic's New Story Book

444. FIRESIDE HENTY I
authors: Oliver Optic [pseudonym of
William Taylor Adams][1]; Thomas
McLean Newson [2]; Friedrich Ger-
stacker [3]; George Alfred Henty
[4–6,9]; William Francis Butler [7];
Mayne Reid [8]
publisher: M. A. Donohue
1. The Boat Club
2. Forest and Frontiers; or, Adventures
Among the Indians (1884)
3. Adventures in the Tropics (1900)
4. Thrilling Adventures at Sea; or, Noted
Shipwrecks and Famous Sailors
(1890)
5. Captain Bayley's Heir; A Tale of the
Gold Fields of California (1900)
6. With Wolfe in Canada; or, The Winning of a Continent (1890)
7. The Hero of Pine Ridge; A Story of the
Great Prairie (1904)
8. The Boy Hunters; Adventures in Search
of a White Buffalo (1900)
9. Col. Thorndyke's Secret (1911)

445. FIRESIDE HENTY II [see also
HENTY]
author: George Alfred Henty
publisher: M.A. Donohue
1. Thrilling Adventures at Sea; or, Noted
Shipwrecks and Famous Sailors (1890)
2. Captain Bayley's Heir; A Tale of the
Gold Fields of California (1890)
3. The Young Franc-Tireurs and Their
Adventures in the Franco-Prussian War
(1890)
4. Bonnie Prince Charlie; A Tale of
Fontenoy and Culloden (1891)
5. For Name and Fame; or, Through
Afghan Passes (1890)
6. In Freedom's Cause; A Story of Wallace
and Bruce (1900)
7. In the Reign of Terror; The Adventures
of a Westminister Boy (1890)
8. With Clive in India; or, The Beginnings of an Empire (1900)

9. With Wolfe in Canada; or, The Winning of a Continent (1890)
10. Facing Death; or, The Hero of the
Vaughan Pit: A Tale of the Coal
Mines (1901)
11. Col. Thorndyke's Secret (1910)
12. Maori and Settler; A Story of the New
Zealand War (1900)
13. Jack Archer; A Tale of the Crimea
(1900)

446. FIRESIDE SERIES FOR
BOYS [see also FIRESIDE HENTY
II; HENTY]
author: George Alfred Henty
publisher: William L. Allison
1. Under Drake's Flag; a Tale of the Spanish Main (1900)
2. The Young Franc-Tireurs and Their
Adventures in the Franco-Prussian War
(1890)
3. On the Pampas; or, The Young Settlers
(1900)
4. The Boy Knight; A Tale of the Crusade
(1900)
5. In Times of Peril; A Tale of India
(1900)
6. Orange and Green; A Tale of the
Boyne and Limerick (1890)
7. Through the Fray; A Tale of the Luddite Riots (1897)

447. FIVE CHUMS
author: Norman Brainerd
publisher: Lothrop, Lee & Shepard
1. Winning His Shoulder Straps; or, Bob
Anderson at Chatham Military School
(1909)
2. Winning the Eagle Prize; or, The Pluck
of Billy Hazen (1910)
3. Winning the Junior Cup; or, The
Honor of Stub Barrows
4. Winning His Army Blue; or, The
Honor Graduate (1917)

448. FIVE LITTLE PEPPERS
author: Margaret Sidney [pseudonym of
Harriet Mulford (Stone) Lothrop]
illustrators: Sears Gallagher [6]; Arthur
Becker; Eugenie M. Wireman [9];
Fanny Y. Cory [7]; Hermann Heyer [8,
11]; George Giguere, Fred D. Lohman,

William Sharp, Roberta Paflin, Mente, W.L. Taylor, Alice Barber Stephens [12]; Jessie McDermott [3–5]; Etheldred B. Barry [5]
publisher: Lothrop
1. The Five Little Peppers and How They Grew (1880)
2. The Five Little Peppers Midway; A Sequel to Five Little Peppers and How They Grew (1890)
3. The Five Little Peppers Grown Up; A Sequel to The Five Little Peppers Midway (1892)
4. Phronsie Pepper; The Youngest of the "Five Little Peppers (1897) [alternate title: The Last of the "Five Little Peppers"]
5. Stories Polly Pepper Told To the Five Little Peppers in the Little Brown House (1899)
6. The Adventures of Joel Pepper (1900)
7. The Five Little Peppers Abroad (1902)
8. The Five Little Peppers at School (1903)
9. The Five Little Peppers and Their Friends (1904)
10. Ben Pepper (1905)
11. The Five Little Peppers in the Little Brown House (1907)
12. Our Davie Pepper (1916)
13. The Stories of Joel Pepper

449. FIVE LITTLE STARRS
author: Lilian Elizabeth (Becker) Roy
publishers: Nourse; Platt & Nourse; A. L. Burt; Platt & Peck
1. The Five Little Starrs (1913)
2. The Five Little Starrs on a Canal Boat (1913)
3. The Five Little Starrs on a Ranch (1913)
4. The Five Little Starrs in an Island Cabin (1914)
5. The Five Little Starrs in the Canadian Forest (1915)
6. The Five Little Starrs in Alaska (1915)
7. The Five Little Starrs on a Motor Tour (1916)
8. The Five Little Starrs in Hawaii (1919)

450. FLAG AND COUNTRY
author: Paul G. Tomlinson
publisher: Barse & Hopkins

1. Bob Cook and the German Spy (1917)
2. Bob Cook and the German Air Fleet (1918)
3. Bob Cook's Brother in the Trenches (1918)
4. Bob Cook and the Winged Messenger (1919)
5. Bob Cook and the Bomb Plot (1920)

451. FLAG OF FREEDOM
author: Ralph Bonehill [pseudonym of Edward Stratemeyer]
publishers: Mershon; Grosset & Dunlap
1. When Santiago Fell; or, The War Adventures of Two Chums (1899)
2. A Sailor Boy with Dewey; or, Afloat in the Philippines (1899)
3. Off for Hawaii; or, The Mystery of a Great Volcano (1899)
4. The Young Bandmaster; or, Concert, Stage and Battlefield (1900)
5. Boys of the Fort; or, A Young Captain's Pluck (1901)
6. With Custer in the Black Hills; or, A Young Scout Among the Indians (1902)

452. FLASHLIGHT DETECTIVE
authors: [as noted below]
publisher: M. A. Donohue
34. The Red Revenger; or, The Pirate King of the Floridas (1900) [au: Ned Buntline]
38. The Royal Yacht; or, Logan the Warlock (1893) [au: Sylvanus Cobb]
41. The Secrets of the Coast; or, A Life for a Life (1899) [au: Sylvanus Cobb]
54. A Case of Identity (1905) [au: Arthur Conan Doyle]
61. Escaped from Sing Sing (1892) [au: John Arthur Fraser]
67. A Freak of Fate; or, Lawyer Manton of Chicago (1899) [au: J. M. Jelly]
70. Jack the Ripper; or, London's Greatest Mystery (1890) [au: N. T. Oliver]
73. Jim Cummings; or, The Crime of the 'Frisco Express (1899) [au: Francis Farrars]
87. A Singular Escape; or, Kit Carson Among the Indians (1899) [au: Edward Sylvester Ellis]
[unknown #]: The Sorceress of the Cannibal Islands (1912) [au: Colonel Brenet]

453. FLEMING STONE
author: Carolyn Wells
publishers: J. B. Lippincott
1. Omnibus Fleming Stone (1923)
2. Spooky Hollow; A Fleming Stone Story (1923)
3. Prilligirl; A Fleming Stone Story (1924)
4. Furthest Fury; A Fleming Stone Story (1924)
5. Anything But the Truth; A Fleming Stone Story (1925)
6. The Daughter of the House; A Fleming Stone Story (1925)
7. The Bronze Hand; A Fleming Stone Story (1926)
8. The Red-haired Girl; A Fleming Stone Story (1926)
9. All at Sea; A Fleming Stone Story (1927)
10. Where's Emily; A Fleming Stone Story (1927)
11. The Crime in the Crypt; A Fleming Stone Story (1928)
12. The Tannahill Tangle; A Fleming Stone Story (1928)
13. The Tapestry Room Murder; A Fleming Stone Story (1929)
14. The Triple Murder; A Fleming Stone Story (1929)
15. The Doomed Fire; A Fleming Stone Story (1930)
16. The Ghosts' High Noon; A Fleming Stone Story (1930)
17. The Umbrella Murder; A Fleming Stone Story (1931)
18. The Horror House; A Fleming Stone Story (1931)
19. Fuller's Earth; A Fleming Stone Detective Story (1932)
20. The Roll-top Desk Mystery; A Fleming Stone Story (1932)
21. The Broken O; A Fleming Stone Detective Novel (1933)
22. The Clue of the Eyelash; A Fleming Stone Detective Story (1933)
23. The Master Murderer: A Fleming Stone Detective Novel (1933)
24. The Visiting Villain; A Fleming Stone Detective Novel (1934)
25. The Eyes in the Wall; A Fleming Stone Detective Novel (1934)
26. The Wooden Indian; A Fleming Stone Detective Novel (1935)
27. For Goodness' Sake; A Fleming Stone Detective Novel (1935)
28. The Money Musk; A Fleming Stone Detective Novel (1936)
29. Murder in the Bookshop; A Fleming Stone Detective Novel (1936)
30. The Huddle; A Fleming Stone Detective Novel (1936)
31. The Mystery of the Tarn; A Fleming Stone Detective Novel (1937)
32. The Radio Studio Murder; A Fleming Stone Detective Novel (1937)
33. The Gilt Edged Guilt; A Fleming Stone Detective Novel (1938)
34. The Missing Link; A Fleming Stone Detective Novel (1938)
35. The Killer; A Fleming Stone Detective Novel (1938)
36. The Importance of Being Murdered; A Fleming Stone Detective Novel (1939)
37. Calling All Suspects; A Fleming Stone Detective Novel (1939)
38. Crime Tears On; A Fleming Stone Detective Novel (1939)
39. The Crime Incarnate; A Fleming Stone Detective Novel (1940)
40. Murder on Parade; A Fleming Stone Detective Novel (1940)
41. Murder Plus; A Fleming Stone Detective Novel (1940)
42. The Devil's Work; A Fleming Stone Detective Novel (1940)
43. The Black Night Murders; A Fleming Stone Story (1941)
44. Murder at the Casino; A Fleming Stone Mystery Novel (1941)
45. Murder Will In; A Fleming Stone Detective Novel (1942)
46. Who Killed Caldwell?; A Fleming Stone Detective Novel (1942)

454. FLICKA, RICKA, DICKA
author: Lindman
publisher: A. Whitman
1. Flicka, Ricka, Dicka and the New Dotted Dresses (1939)
2. Flicka, Ricka, Dicka and the Girl Next Door (1940)
3. Flicka, Ricka, Dicka and the Three Kittens (1941)

4. Flicka, Ricka, Dicka and Their New Friend (1942)
5. Flicka, Ricka, Dicka and the Strawberries (1943)
6. Flicka, Ricka, Dicka and a Little Dog (1946)
7. Flicka, Ricka, Dicka and Their New Skates (1939)
8. Flicka, Ricka, Dicka Bake a Cake (1955)
9. Flicka, Ricka, Dicka Go to Market (1958)
10. Flicka, Ricka, Dicka and the Big Red Hen (1960)

455. FLOWERETS; A SERIES OF STORIES ON THE COMMANDMENTS
author: Joanna Hooe Mathews
publisher: Robert Carter & Brothers
1–2. [titles unknown]
3. Daisy's Work: The Third Commandment (1870)
4. Rose's Temptation: The Fourth Commandment (1870)
5. Hyacynthe and Her Brothers (1870)
[other titles unknown]

456. FLYAWAY STORIES
author: Alice Dale Hardy [pseudonym of the Stratemeyer Syndicate]
illustrator: Walter S. Rogers
publisher: Grosset & Dunlap
1. The Flyaways and Cinderella (1925)
2. The Flyaways and Goldilocks (1925)
3. The Flyaways and Little Red Riding Hood (1925)

457. FLYING BUDDIES [*see also* **AIRPLANE BOYS**]
author: Edith Janice Craine
publisher: World Syndicate
1. Flying to Amy-Ran Fastness (1930)

458. FLYING GIRL
author: Edith Van Dyne [pseudonym of Lyman Frank Baum]
publisher: Reilly & Britton
1. The Flying Girl
2. The Flying Girl and Her Chum

459. FLYING MACHINE BOYS
author: Frank Walton
publisher: A. L. Burt
1. The Flying Machine Boys in Mexico; or, The Secret of the Crater (1913)
2. The Flying Machine Boys on Duty; or, The Clue Above the Clouds (1913)
3. The Flying Machine Boys in the Wilds; or, The Mystery of the Andes (1913)
4. The Flying Machine Boys on Secret Service; or, The Capture in the Air (1913)
5. The Flying Machine Boys in Deadly Peril; or, Lost in the Clouds (1914)
6. The Flying Machine Boys in the Frozen North; or, The Trail in the Snow (1915)

460. FLYING STORIES
authors: Irving Crump [1–3]; Harold Sherman [4]; P. K. Fitzhugh [5–7]
publisher: Grosset & Dunlap
1. The Cloud Patrol (1929)
2. Pilot of the Cloud Patrol
3. Craig of the Cloud Patrol
4. Ding Palmer, Air Detective
5. Mark Gilmore, Scout of the Air
6. Mark Gilmore: Speed Flyer
7. Mark Gilmore's Lucky Landing (1931)

461. FOOTBALL ELEVEN
author: Ralph Henry Barbour
publishers: Dodd, Mead; Grosset & Dunlap
1. Left End Edwards (1914)
2. Left Tackle Thayer (1915)
3. Left Guard Gilbert (1916)
4. Center Rush Roland (1917)
5. Full-back Foster (1919)
6. Quarter-back Bates (1920)
7. Left Half Hamon (1921)
8. Right End Emerson (1922)
9. Right Guard Grant (1923)
10. Right Tackle Todd (1924)
11. Right Half Hollins (1925)
12. Coach Carson (1927)

462. FOR THE CHILDREN'S HOUR
author: Carolyn Sherwin Bailey
publisher: Milton Bradley
1. Folk Stories and Fables (1916)
2. Hero Stories (1917)

3. Broad Stripes and Bright Stars: Stories of American History (1919)

463. FOREIGN ADVENTURE
author: Edward Sylvester Ellis
publisher: J. C. Winston
1. [title unknown]
2. River and Jungle (1906)
3. The Hunt of the White Elephant (1906)

464. FOREST AND STREAM
author: Harry Castlemon [pseudonym of Charles Austin Fosdick]
publisher: Porter & Coates
1. Snagged and Sunk; or, The Adventures of a Canvas Canoe (1888)
2. The Steel Horse; or, The Rambles of a Bicycle (1888)
3. Joe Wayring at Home (1895)

465. FOREST CITY
author: Mary S. Deering
publisher: Dresser, McLellan
1. [title unknown]
2. Phil, Rob, and Louis; or Haps and Mishaps of Three Average Boys (1878)

466. FOREST, FIELD AND STREAM STORIES
author: Carolyn Sherwin Bailey

467. FOREST GLEN
author: Elijah Kellogg
publisher: Lee & Shepard
1. Sowed by the Wind; or, The Poor Boy's Fortune (1874)
2. Burying the Hatchet; or, The Young Brave of the Delawares (1878)
3. Brought to the Front; or, The Young Defenders (1875)
4. Wolf Run; or, Boys of the Wilderness (1875)
5. Forest Glen; or, The Mohawk's Friendship (1877)

FORTUNE HUNTERS *see* TED JONES

468. FOULSHAM HENTY LIBRARY [*see also* HENTY]
author: George Alfred Henty
publisher: Foulsham

1. In the Reign of Terror; The Adventures of a Westminister Boy (1953)
2. In the Heart of the Rockies; A Story of Adventure in Colorado (1953)
3. Bonnie Prince Charlie; A Tale of Fontenoy and Culloden (1954)
4. When London Burned; A Story of Restoration Times and the Great Fire (1954)
5. Through Russian Snows; A Story of Napoleon's Retreat from Moscow (1954)

469. FOUR BOYS
author: Everett Titsworth Tomlinson
publishers: Lothrop, Lee & Shepard; Grosset & Dunlap
1. Four Boys in the Yellowstone; How They Went and What They Did (1906)
2. Four Boys in the Land of Cotton; Where They Went, What They Saw, and What They Did (1907)
3. Four Boys on the Mississippi; Where They Went, What They Did and What They Saw (1908)
4. Four Boys and a Fortune; Why They Went to England, and What They Found (1910)
5. Four Boys in the Yosemite (1911)
6. Four Boys on Pike's Peak; Where They Went, What They Did, and What They Saw (1911)

470. FOUR CORNER HOUSE GIRLS
author: Amy Ella Blanchard
publisher: G. W. Jacobs
1. The Four Corners (1906)
2. The Four Corners in California (1907)
3. The Four Corners at School (1908)
4. The Four Corners Abroad (1909)
5. The Four Corners in Camp (1910)
6. The Four Corners at College (1911)
7. The Four Corners in Japan (1912)
8. The Four Corners in Egypt (1913)

471. FOUR LITTLE BLOSSOMS
author: Mabel C. Hawley [pseudonym of the Stratemeyer Syndicate]
illustrators: Robert Gaston Herbert [1–3]; Walter S. Rodgers [4]

publishers: Sully [1–5]; Cupples & Leon [6–7]

1. Four Little Blossoms at Brookside Farm (1920)
2. Four Little Blossoms at Oak Hill School (1920)
3. Four Little Blossoms and Their Winter Fun (1920)
4. Four Little Blossoms on Apple Tree Island (1921)
5. Four Little Blossoms Through the Holidays (1922)
6. Four Little Blossoms at Sunrise Beach (1929)
7. Four Little Blossoms Indoors and Out (1930)

472. FRANCIE
author: Emily Hahn
publisher: Watts
1. Francie (1951)
2. Francie Again (1953)
3. Francie Comes Home (1956)

473. FRANK ALLEN [see also BOYS OF COLUMBIA HIGH]
author: Graham B. Forbes [pseudonym of the Stratemeyer Syndicate]
publisher: Garden City Publishing Company
1. Frank Allen's Schooldays; or, The All-Around Rivals of Columbia High (1926)
2. Frank Allen Playing to Win; or, The Boys of Columbia High on the Ice (1926)
3. Frank Allen in Winter Sports; or, Columbia High on Skates and Iceboats (1926)
4. Frank Allen and His Rivals; or, The Boys of Columbia High in Track Athletics (1926)
5. Frank Allen — Pitcher; or, The Boys of Columbia High on the Diamond (1926)
6. Frank Allen — Head of the Crew; or, The Boys of Columbia High on the River (1926)
7. Frank Allen in Camp; or, Columbia High and the School League Rivals (1926)
8. Frank Allen at Rockspur Ranch; or, The Old Cowboy's Secret (1926)
9. Frank Allen at Gold Fork; or, Locating the Lost Claim (1926)
10. Frank Allen and His Motor Boat; or, Racing to Save a Life (1926)
11. Frank Allen — Captain of the Team; or, The Boys of Columbia High on the Gridiron (1926)
12. Frank Allen at Old Moose Lake; or, The Trail in the Snow (1926)
13. Frank Allen at Zero Camp; or, The Queer Old Man of the Hills (1926)
14. Frank Allen Snowbound; or, Fighting for Life in the Big Blizzard (1927)
15. Frank Allen After Big Game; or, With Guns and Snowshoes in the Rockies (1927)
16. Frank Allen with the Circus; or, The Old Ringmaster's Secret (1927)
17. Frank Allen Pitching His Best; or, The Baseball Rivals of Columbia High (1927)

474. FRANK AND ANDY [see also RACER BOYS]
author: Vance Barnum [pseudonym of the Stratemeyer Syndicate]
publishers: George Sully; Whitman
1. Frank and Andy Afloat; or, The Cave on the Island (1921)
2. Frank and Andy at Boarding School; or, Rivals for Many Honors (1921)
3. Frank and Andy in a Winter Camp; or, The Young Hunters' Strange Discovery (1921)

FRANK AND ARCHIE see GUNBOAT

475. FRANK ARMSTRONG
author: Matthew M. Colton [pseudonym of Walter Chauncey Camp]
illustrators: Martin Lewis [1–3]; Arthur O. Scott [4–6]
publishers: Hurst; A. L. Burt
1. Frank Armstrong's Vacation (1911)
2. Frank Armstrong at Queen's (1911)
3. Frank Armstrong's Second Term (1911)
4. Frank Armstrong, Drop Kicker (1912)
5. Frank Armstrong, Captain of the Nine (1913)
6. Frank Armstrong at College (1914)

476. FRANK MERRIWELL
author: Burt L. Standish [pseudonym of
Gilbert Patten]
publisher: David McKay
1. Frank Merriwell's School Days (1901)
2. Frank Merriwell's Chums
3. Frank Merriwell's Foes (1902)
4. Frank Merriwell's Trip West (1902)
5. Frank Merriwell Down South (1903)
6. Frank Merriwell's Bravery (1903)
7. Frank Merriwell's Races (1903)
8. Frank Merriwell's Hunting Tour
   (1903)
9. Frank Merriwell at Yale (1903)
10. Frank Merriwell's Sports Afield (1903)
11. Frank Merriwell's Courage (1903)
12. Frank Merriwell's Daring (1903)
13. Frank Merriwell's Skill (1903)
14. Frank Merriwell's Champions
15. Frank Merriwell's Return to Yale
    (1904)
16. Frank Merriwell's Secret (1897)
17. Frank Merriwell's Loyalty (1898)
18. Frank Merriwell's Reward (1900)
19. Frank Merriwell's Faith (1900)
20. Frank Merriwell's Victories (1900)
21. Frank Merriwell's Power (1900)
22. Frank Merriwell's Set-Back; A Story
    for Boys (1900)
23. Frank Merriwell's False Friend; A
    Story for Boys (1901)
24. Frank Merriwell's Brother; or, The
    Greatest Triumph of All (1901)
25. Frank Merriwell in Camp (1898)
26. Frank Merriwell's Vacation; or, A
    Visit to Fardale (1898)
27. Frank Merriwell's Cruise (1898)
28. Frank Merriwell's Lads; or, The Boys
    Who Got Another Chance (1911)

477. FRANK NELSON
author: Harry Castlemon [pseudonym of
Charles Austin Fosdick]
publisher: Porter & Coates
1. The Sportsman's Club in the Saddle
   (1873)
2. The Sportsman's Club Afloat
3. Snowed Up; or, The Sportsman's Club
   in the Mountains (1876)
4. Frank Nelson in the Forecastle; or, The
   Sportsman's Club Among the Whalers
   (1876)

5. Boy Traders; or, The Sportsman's Club
   Among the Boers (1877)

478. FRANKLIN HIGH
author: Ralph Henry Barbour
publisher: David Appleton
1. Merritt Leads the Nine (1935)
2. Watch That Pass (1936)
3. The Score Is Tied (1937)

479. FRED FENTON
author: Allen Chapman [pseudonym of
Edward Stratemeyer]
illustrator: Walter S. Rogers
publisher: Cupples & Leon
1. Fred Fenton, the Pitcher; or The Rivals
   of Riverport School (1913)
2. Fred Fenton in the Line; or, The Football Boys of Riverport School (1913)
3. Fred Fenton on the Crew; or, The
   Young Oarsmen of Riverport School
   (1913)
4. Fred Fenton on the Track; or, The
   Athletes of Riverport School (1913)
5. Fred Fenton Marathon Runner; or,
   The Great Race at Riverport School
   (1915)

480. FREDDY CARR
author: Richard Philip Garrold
publisher: Benziger Brothers
1. [title unknown]
2. Freddy Carr and His Friends; A Day-
   School Story (1910)
3. Freddy Carr's Adventures; A Sequel to
   Freddy Carr and His Friends (1911)

481. FRENCH AND INDIAN WAR
author: Joseph Alexander Altsheler
publisher: David Appleton
1. The Hunters of the Hills; A Story of
   the Great French and Indian War
   (1916)
2. The Shadow of the North; A Story of
   Old New York and a Last Campaign
   (1917)
3. The Rulers of the Lakes; A Story of
   George and Champlain (1917)
4. The Masters of the Peaks; A Story of
   the Great North Woods (1918)
5. The Lords of the Wild; A Story of the
   Old New York Border (1919)

6. The Sun of Quebec; A Story of a Great Crisis (1919)

482. FRIENDLY ANIMAL
author: Warner Carr
publisher: McLoughlin Brothers; Whitman
1. Lammie on a Frolic (1900)
2. Lammie Wants to Learn (1900)
3. Outdoor Friends (1904)

483. FRIENDLY TERRACE
author: Harriet Lummis Smith
publisher: L. C. Page
1. The Girls of Friendly Terrace; or, Peggy Raymond's Success (1912)
2. Peggy Raymond's Vacation; or, Friendly Terrace Transplanted (1913)
3. Peggy Raymond's School Days; or, Old Girls and New (1916)
4. The Friendly Terrace Quartette; How Peggy and Priscilla and Amy and Ruth Did Their Share on the Farm and in the Shop (1920)
5. Peggy Raymond's Way; or, Blossom Time at Friendly Terrace (1922)

484. FRIPSEY
author: Madge Lee Chastain
publisher: Harcourt
1. Bright Days (1952)
2. Fripsey Summer (1953)
3. Fripsey Fun (1955)
4. Leave It to the Fripseys (1957)

485. FROLIC
author: Sarah Catherine Martin
publisher: McLoughlin
1. Mother Hubbard and Her Dog (1880)

486. FRONTIER I
author: Charles H. Pearson
publisher: Lee & Shepard
1. The Cabin on the Prairie (1869)
2. The Young Pioneers of the North-West (1870)

487. FRONTIER II
author: Ralph Bonehill [pseudonym of the Stratemeyer Syndicate]
publishers: Mershon; Grosset & Dunlap

1. With Boone on the Frontier; or, The Pioneer Boys of Old Kentucky (1903)
2. Pioneer Boys of the Great Northwest; or, With Lewis and Clark Across the Rockies
3. Pioneer Boys of the Gold Fields; or, The Nugget Hunters of '49 (1906)

488. FRONTIER BOYS
author: Captain Wyn Roosevelt
publishers: Platt & Peck; Hurst; A. L. Chatterton
1. Frontier Boys on Overland Trail; or, Across the Plains of Kansas (1908)
2. Frontier Boys in Colorado; or, Captured by Indians (1911)
3. Frontier Boys in the Rockies; or, Lost in the Mountains [alternate subtitle: A Winter in the Big Canyon] (1909)
4. Frontier Boys in the Grand Canyon; or, A Search for Treasure
5. Frontier Boys In Mexico; or, Mystery Mountain (1908)
6. Frontier Boys on the Coast; or, In the Pirate's Power (1909)
7. Frontier Boys in Hawaii; or, The Mystery of the Hollow Mountain (1909)
8. Frontier Boys in the Sierras; or, The Lost Mine (1909)
9. Frontier Boys in the Saddle (1910)
10. Frontier Boys in Frisco (1911)
11. Frontier Boys in the South Seas (1912)

489. FRONTIER GIRL
author: Alice Turner Curtis
publisher: Penn
1. A Frontier Girl of Virginia (1929)
2. A Frontier Girl of Massachusetts (1930)
3. A Frontier Girl of New York (1931)
4. A Frontier Girl of Chesapeake Bay (1934)
5. A Frontier Girl of Pennsylvania (1937)

490. FROST'S JUVENILE SERIES
author: [unknown]
publisher: Lippincott, Grambo & Co.
1. Herman and Other Stories for the Entertainment and Instruction of the Young (1852)

491. FUN LOVING GANG
author: Harold M. Sherman

publisher: Gold
1. In Wrong Right (1934)
2. Always Up to Something (1934)

492. FUNNY ANIMAL
author: [unknown]
publisher: J.E. Potter; T. Nelson & Sons
1. The Robber Kitten (1800)
2. Chit Chat by a Motherly Cat (1855)

493. G-MAN'S SON
authors: Edward O'Connor [1]; Warren F.
    Robinson [2–3]
publisher: Goldsmith
1. The G-Man's Son (1936)
2. The G-Man's Son at Porpoise Island
    (1937)
3. The Phantom Whale (1937)

494. G-MEN
authors: William Engle [1]; Laurence
    Dwight Smith [2–3]
publisher: Grosset and Dunlap
1. The G-Men Smash the "Professor's
    Gang" (1936)
2. The G-Men in Jeopardy (1938)
3. The G-Men Trap the Spy Ring (1939)

495. GARRY GRAYSON FOOT-
BALL STORIES
author: Elmer A. Dawson [pseudonym of
    the Stratemeyer Syndicate]
illustrators: Walter S. Rogers [1–9]; G.
    Condon [10]
publisher: Grosset & Dunlap
1. Garry Grayson's Hill Street Eleven; or,
    The Football Boys of Lenox (1926)
2. Garry Grayson at Lenox High; or, The
    Champions of the Football League
    (1926)
3. Garry Grayson's Football Rivals; or,
    The Secret of the Stolen Signals (1926)
4. Garry Grayson Showing His Speed; or,
    A Daring Run on the Gridiron (1927)
5. Garry Grayson at Stanley Prep; or, The
    Football Rivals of Riverview (1927)
6. Garry Grayson's Winning Kick; or,
    Battling for Honor (1928)
7. Garry Grayson Hitting the Line; or,
    Stanley Prep on a New Gridiron
    (1929)
8. Garry Grayson's Winning Touchdown;

or, Putting Passmore Tech on the Map
    (1930)
9. Garry Grayson's Double Signals; or,
    Vanquishing the Football Plotters
    (1931)
10. Garry Grayson's Forward Pass; or,
    Winning in the Final Quarter (1932)

496. GENEVA BOOK
author: Oliver Optic [pseudonym of
    William Taylor Adams]
publisher: Carlton Press
1. The Boat Club

497. GILT TOP
author: Oliver Optic [pseudonym of
    William Taylor Adams]
publisher: Hurst
1. Little by Little

498. GINNIE
author: Catherine Woolley
publisher: Morrow
1. Ginnie and Geneva (1948)
2. Ginnie Joins In (1951)
3. Ginnie and the New Girl (1954)
4. Ginnie and the Mystery House (1957)
5. Ginnie and the Mystery Doll (1960)
6. Ginnie and Her Juniors (1963)
7. Ginnie and the Cooking Contest (1966)
8. Ginnie and the Wedding Bells (1967)
9. Ginnie and the Mystery Cat (1969)

499. GINNY GORDON
author: Julie Campbell [pseudonym of
    Julie Tatham]
publisher: Whitman
1. Ginny Gordon and the Mystery of the
    Disappearing Candlesticks (1948)
2. Ginny Gordon and the Missing Heir-
    loom (1950)
3. Ginny Gordon and the Mystery of the
    Old Barn (1951)
4. Ginny Gordon and the Lending
    Library (1954)
5. Ginny Gordon and the Broadcast Mys-
    tery (1956)

500. GIRL AVIATORS
author: Margaret Burnham
illustrator: Charles L. Wrenn
publishers: Hurst; M. A. Donohue

1. The Girl Aviators and the Phantom Airship (1911)
2. The Girl Aviators on Golden Wings (1911)
3. The Girl Aviators' Sky Cruise (1911)
4. The Girl Aviators' Motor Butterfly (1912)

501. GIRL FLYER

author: Bess Moyer
publisher: Goldsmith
1. Gypsies of the Air (1932)
2. On Adventure Island (1932)

502. GIRL SCOUTS I

author: Virginia Fairfax
publisher: A. L. Burt
1. The Mysterious Camper (1933)
2. The Secret of Camp Pioneer (1933)
3. The Secret of Halliday House (1933)
4. The Trail of the Gypsy Eight (1933)
5. The Curious Quest (1934)
6. The Camp's Strange Visitors (1936)

503. GIRL SCOUTS II

author: Katherine Keene Galt
publisher: Saalfield
1. The Girl Scouts at Home; or, Rosanna's Beautiful Day (1921)
2. The Girl Scouts Rally; or, Rosanna Wins (1921)
3. The Girl Scouts' Triumph; or, Rosanna's Sacrifice (1921)

504. GIRL SCOUTS III

author: Lilian C. McNamara Garis
publisher: Cupples & Leon
1. The Girl Scouts at Bellaire; or, Maid Mary's Awakening (1920)
2. The Girl Scout Pioneers; or, Winning the First B.C. (1920)
3. The Girl Scouts at Sea Crest; or, The Wig Wag Rescue (1920)
4. The Girl Scouts at Camp Comealong; or, Peg of Tamarack Hills (1921)
5. The Girl Scouts at Rocky Ledge; or, Nora's Real Vacation (1922)

505. GIRL SCOUTS IV

authors: Edith Lavell [1–10]; Harriet Pyne Grove [11]
publisher: A. L. Burt

1. The Girl Scouts at Camp (1922)
2. The Girl Scouts at Miss Allen's School (1922)
3. The Girl Scouts' Canoe Trip (1922)
4. The Girl Scouts' Good Turn (1922)
5. The Girl Scouts' Rivals (1922)
6. The Girl Scouts on the Ranch (1923)
7. The Girl Scouts' Motor Trip (1924)
8. The Girl Scouts' Vacation Adventures (1924)
9. The Girl Scouts' Captain (1925)
10. The Girl Scouts' Director (1925)
11. The Girl Scouts' Problem Solved (1931)

506. GIRL SCOUTS V [probably subsuming GIRL SCOUTS MOUNTAIN and GIRL SCOUTS COUNTRY LIFE]

author: Lilian Elizabeth (Becker) Roy
illustrator: H.S. Barbour
publishers: George Scully; Grosset & Dunlap; A. L. Burt
1. The Girl Scouts in the Rockies (1921)
2. Natalie: a Garden Scout (1921)
3. The Girl Scouts at Dandelion Camp (1921)
4. The Girl Scouts in the Adirondacks (1921)
5. Janet: a Stock-Farm Scout (1925)
6. Norma: a Flower Scout (1925)
7. The Girl Scouts in the Redwoods (1926)
8. The Girl Scouts in the Magic City (1927)
9. The Girl Scouts in Glacier Park (1928)

507. GIRL SCOUTS VI

author: Margaret O'Bannon Womack Vandercook
publisher: John C. Winston
1. The Girl Scouts in Beechwood Forest (1921)
2. The Girl Scouts of the Eagle's Wing (1921)
3. The Girl Scouts of the Round Table (1921)
4. The Girl Scouts and the Open Road (1923)
5. The Girl Scouts in Mystery Valley (1923)

508. GIRL SCOUTS VII
author: Mildred Augustine Wirt
illustrator: Marguerite Gayer
publisher: Cupples & Leon
1. The Girl Scouts at Penguin Pass; or,
   Trail of the Snowman (1953)
2. The Girl Scouts at Singing Sands (1955)
3. The Girl Scouts at Mystery Mansion
   (1957)

GIRL SCOUTS COUNTRY LIFE *see*
GIRL SCOUTS IV

GIRL SCOUTS MOUNTAIN *see* **GIRL SCOUTS IV**

GIRL SCOUTS MYSTERY *see* **GIRL SCOUTS VII**

509. GIRLS' ADVENTURE
authors: Grace May North [pseudonym of
   Carol Norton] [1]; Mary Dickerson
   Donahey
publisher: Saalfield
1. Meg of Mystery Mountain (1926)
2. Mystery in the Pines (1950)

**510. GIRLS' HOME AND
   SCHOOL**
author: [unknown]
publisher: [unknown]
1. The Girls of St. Bede's
2. Angela Goes to School
3. The Doings of Denys
4. The Responsibility of Ruffles

511. GIRLS OF CENTRAL HIGH
author: Gertrude W. Morrison [pseudo-
   nym of the Stratemeyer Syndicate]
illustrators: Dick Richards [1,4]; Jim
   Richards [2]; Walter S. Rogers [6]; R.
   Emmett Owen [7]
publisher: Grosset & Dunlap
1. The Girls of Central High; or, Rivals
   for All Honors (1914)
2. The Girls of Central High on Lake
   Luna; or, The Crew That Won (1914)
3. The Girls of Central High at Basketball; or, The Great Gymnasium Mystery (1914)
4. The Girls of Central High on the Stage;
   or, The Play That Took the Prize (1914)

5. The Girls of Central High on Track
   and Field; or, The Champions of the
   School League (1914)
6. The Girls of Central High in Camp;
   or, The Old Professor's Secret (1915)
7. The Girls of Central High Aiding the
   Red Cross; or, Amateur Theatricals for
   a Worthy Cause (1919)

**512. GIRLS OF FRIENDLY TER-
   RACE**
author: Harriet Lummis Smith
publisher: L. C. Page
1. The Girls of Friendly Terrace; or,
   Peggy Raymond's Success (1912)
2. Peggy Raymond's Vacation; or, Friendly
   Terrace Transplanted (1913)
3. Peggy Raymond's School Days; or, Old
   Girls and New (1916)
4. The Friendly Terrace Quartette; or,
   How Peggy and Priscilla and Amy and
   Ruth Did Their Share on the Farm and
   in the Shop (1920)
5. Peggy Raymond's Way; or, Blossom
   Time at Friendly Terrace (1922)

GLAD BOOKS *see* **POLLYANNA**

513. GLENDALE
author: Ralph Henry Barbour
publisher: Farrar and Rinehart
1. Skate, Glendale! The Story of Hockey,
   Battles and Victory (1932)

514. GLENLOCK GIRLS
author: Grace M. Remich
publisher: Penn
1. Glenloch Girls (1909)
2. Glenloch Girls Abroad (1910)
3. Glenloch Girls' Club (1911)
4. Glenloch Girls at Camp West (1912)

**515. GLOBE TROTTER ADVEN-
   TURE**
authors: Edith Janice Craine and Lotta
   Bacskai
illustrator: Charlotte Lederer
publisher: World Syndicate
1. Out of the Jungle (1932)
2. Head of the House of Chang (1932)
3. The Call of the Veldt (1932)
4. The Lost Prince (1932)

516. GLORIA

author: Lilian C. McNamara Garis
publisher: Grosset & Dunlap
1. Gloria: A Girl and Her Dad
2. Gloria at Boarding School
3. Joan: Just Girl (1924)
4. Joan's Garden of Adventure (1925)

517. GO-AHEAD

author: Harry Castlemon [pseudonym of
   Charles Austin Fosdick]
publisher: Porter & Coates
1. No Moss; or, The Career of a Rolling
   Stone (1864)
2. Tom Newcombe; or, The Boy of Bad
   Habits (1867)
3. Go-Ahead; or, The Fisher-Boy's Motto
   (1867)

518. GO AHEAD BOYS

author: Ross Kay
publishers: Goldsmith; Barse & Hopkins
1. The Go Ahead Boys on Smuggler's
   Island (1916)
2. The Go Ahead Boys and the Treasure
   Cave (1916)
3. The Go Ahead Boys and the Mysterious Old House (1916)
4. The Go Ahead Boys in the Island
   Camp (1916)
5. The Go Ahead Boys and the Racing
   Motor Boat (1916)
6. The Go Ahead Boys and Simon's Mine
   (1916)

519. GOLD

author: Oliver Optic [pseudonym of
   William Taylor Adams]
publisher: F. M. Lupton
1. All Aboard
2. The Boat Club

520. GOLDEN ACORN

author: Mrs. J.H. Riddell [1]; Ethel Coxon
   [2]
publishers: Office of London Society; J.B.
   Lippincott
1. The Curate of Lowood; or, Every Man
   Has His Golden Chance (1882)
2. A Brave Boy's Trial; or, Say Well Is a
   Good Word, but Do Well Is a Better
   (1881)

521. GOLDEN BOYS

author: Levi Parker Wyman
publisher: A. L. Burt
1. The Golden Boys and Their New
   Electric Cell (1922)
2. The Golden Boys at the Fortress (1922)
3. The Golden Boys in the Maine
   Woods (1922)
4. The Golden Boys with the Lumber
   Jacks (1923)
5. The Golden Boys on the River Drive
   (1923)
6. The Golden Boys Rescued by Radio
   (1923)
7. The Golden Boys Along the River
   Allagash (1923)
8. The Golden Boys at the Haunted
   Camp (1924)
9. The Golden Boys Save the Chamber-
   lain Dam (1927)
10. The Golden Boys on the Trail (1927)

522. GOLDEN CROWN SERIES OF BOOKS FOR THE YOUNG

author: Louisa M. Gray
publisher: Thomas Nelson & Sons
1. Nelly's Teachers and What They
   Learned (1880)
2. Ada and Gerty; or, Hand in Hand
   Heavenward (1885)

523. GOLDEN DAYS

author: [unknown]
publisher: M.A. Donohue
1. The Adventures of Robin Crusoe
   (1930)

524. GOLDEN HOUR

author: James Otis [pseudonym of James
   Otis Kaler]
publisher: Thomas Y. Crowell
1. How the Twins Captured a Hessian: A
   Story of Long Island in 1776 (1902)
2. The I Can School (1902)
3. Molly (1902)

525. GOLDEN LADDER I

author: [unknown]
publisher: Robert Carter & Brothers
1. Nettie's Mission
2. Little Margery

3. Margery's City Home
4. The Crossing-Sweeper
5. Rosy Conroy's Lessons (1871)
6. Ned Dolan's Garret

526. GOLDEN LADDER II
author: Anna Bartlett Warner
publisher: James Nisbet
1. The Three Little Spades (1873)

527. GOLDEN MOTTO
author: Phebe Ann Hanaford [1–2]; Mary Atkins [3]
publisher: Henry A. Sumner; H.A. Young; Young & Bartlett
1. The Golden Motto; or, He Can Conquer Who Thinks He Can (1881)
2. Frank Nelson; or, The Runaway Boy (1865)
3. Earl Whiting; or, The Career of a Nameless Boy (1881)

528. GOLDEN SPRING
author: Madeline Leslie
publisher: Andrew F. Graves
1. Behind the Curtain; or, Leelinau (1869)
2. The Breach of Trust; or, The Professor and Possessor of Piety (1869)

529. GOLDEN TREASURY [NOTE: These may represent different series: see dates]
1. Days of Old; Three Stories from Old English History, for the Young (1865)
2. Rose in Bloom (1933)
3. Tom Brown's School Days (1868)

530. GOOD COMPANY
author: Oliver Optic [pseudonym of William Taylor Adams]
publishers: Lee & Shepard; C. T. Dillingham
1–2. [titles unknown]
3. Three Millions! or, The Way of the World (1866)

531. GRACE HARLOWE AT COLLEGE
author: Jessie Graham Flower [pseudonym of Josephine Chase]
publisher: Henry Altemus

1. Grace Harlowe's First Year at Overton College (1914)
2. Grace Harlowe's Second Year at Overton College (1914)
3. Grace Harlowe's Third Year at Overton College (1914)
4. Grace Harlowe's Fourth Year at Overton College (1914)
5. Grace Harlowe's Return to Overton Campus (1915)
6. Grace Harlowe's Problem (1916)
7. Grace Harlowe's Golden Summer (1917)

532. GRACE HARLOWE AT HIGH SCHOOL
author: Jessie Graham Flower [pseudonym of Josephine Chase]
publisher: Henry Altemus
1. Grace Harlowe's Plebe Year at High School; or, The Merry Doings of the Oakdale Freshman Girls (1910)
2. Grace Harlowe's Sophomore Year at High School; or, The Record of the Girl Chums in Work and Athletics (1911)
3. Grace Harlowe's Junior Year at High School; or, Fast Friends in the Sororities (1911)
4. Grace Harlowe's Senior Year at High School; or, The Parting of the Ways (1911)

533. GRACE HARLOWE OVERSEAS
author: Jessie Graham Flower [pseudonym of Josephine Chase]
publisher: Henry Altemus
1. Grace Harlowe with the U. S. Troops in the Argonne (1920)
2. Grace Harlowe Overseas (1920)
3. Grace Harlowe with the Red Cross in France (1920)
4. Grace Harlowe with the American Army on the Rhine (1920)
5. Grace Harlowe with the Marines at Chateau Thierry (1920)
6. Grace Harlowe with the Yankee Shock Boys at St. Quentin (1920)

534. GRACE HARLOWE'S OVERLAND RIDERS
author: Jessie Graham Flower [pseudonym of Josephine Chase]

publishers: Henry Altemus
1. Grace Harlowe's Overland Riders Among the Kentucky Mountaineers (1921)
2. Grace Harlowe's Overland Riders in the Great North Woods (1921)
3. Grace Harlowe's Overland Riders on the Great American Desert (1921)
4. Grace Harlowe's Overland Riders on the Old Apache Trail (1921)
5. Grace Harlowe's Overland Riders at Circle O Ranch (1923)
6. Grace Harlowe's Overland Riders in the Black Hills (1923)
7. Grace Harlowe's Overland Riders in the High Sierras (1923)
8. Grace Harlowe's Overland Riders in the Yellowstone National Park (1923)
9. Grace Harlowe's Overland Riders on the Lost River Trail (1924)
10. Grace Harlowe's Overland Riders Among the Border Guerrillas (1924)
11. Grace Harlowe Stories

535. GRAFTON
author: Ralph Henry Barbour
publisher: David Appleton
1. Rivals for the Team; A Story of School Life and Football (1916)
2. Winning His Game (1917)
3. Hitting the Line (1917)

536. GRAMMAR SCHOOL BOYS
[see also HIGH SCHOOL BOYS]
author: Harrie Irving Hancock
publisher: Henry Altemus
1. The Grammar School Boys of Gridley; or, Dick & Co. Start Things Moving (1911)
2. The Grammar School Boys Snowbound; or, Dick & Co. at Winter Sports (1911)
3. The Grammar School Boys in the Woods; or, Dick & Co. Trail Fun and Knowledge (1911)
4. The Grammar School Boys in Summer Athletics; or, Dick & Co. Make Their Fame Secure (1911)

537. GRANDPA'S LITTLE GIRLS
author: Alice Turner Curtis
publisher: Penn

1. Grandpa's Little Girls (1907)
2. Grandpa's Little Girls at School (1908)
3. Grandpa's Little Girls and Their Friends (1909)
4. Grandpa's Little Girls' House-boat Party (1910)
5. Grandpa's Little Girls and Miss Abitha (1911)
6. Grandpa's Little Girls Grown Up (1912)

538. GRAPER GIRLS
author: Elizabeth Corbet
publisher: Century [1–2]; Appleton-Century [3–4]
1. The Graper Girls (1931)
2. The Graper Girls Go to College (1932)
3. Growing Up with the Grapers (1934)
4. Beth and Ernestine Graper (1936)

539. GREAT ACE
author: Noel Everingham Sainsbury, Jr.
publisher: Cupples & Leon
1. Billy Smith — Exploring Ace; or, By Airplane to New Guinea [alternate subtitle: or, Into the Heart of Savage New Guinea by Airplane] (1928)
2. Billy Smith — Secret Service Ace; or, Airplane Adventures in Arabia (1932)
3. Billy Smith — Mystery Ace; or, Airplane Discoveries in South America (1932)
4. Billy Smith — Trail Eater Ace; or, Into the Wilds of Northern Alaska by Airplane (1933)
5. Billy Smith — Shanghaied Ace; or, Malay Pirates and Solomon Islands Cannibals (1934)

540. GREAT ADMIRAL
author: James Otis [pseudonym of James Otis Kaler]
illustrators: William F. Stecher [1–2]; E. Tallok [3]
publisher: W. A. Wilde
1. With Preble at Tripoli; A Story of "Old Ironsides" and the Tripolitan War (1900)
2. With Porter in the Essex; A Story of His Famous Cruise in Southern Waters During the War of 1812 (1901)
3. With Rodgers on the President; The Story of the Cruise Wherein the Flag-

ship Fired the First Hostile Shot in the War with Great Britain for the Rights of American Seamen (1903)

541. GREAT AMERICAN INDUSTRIES
author: Hugh Cosgro Weir
publisher: W. A. Wilde
1. With the Flag in Panama (1913)
2. The Young Shipper of the Great Lakes; A Story of the Commerce of the Great Lakes (1912)
3. "Cinders" — The Young Apprentice of the Steel Mills (1914)
4. The Young Wheat Scout; Being the Story of the Growth, Harvesting, and Distribution of the Great Wheat Crop of the United States (1915)

542 GREAT INDIAN CHIEFS
author: Paul Greene Tomlinson
publisher: David Appleton
1. Trail of the Mohawk Chief; A Story of Brant (Thayendanegea) (1916)
2. The Trail of Tecumseh (1917)

543. GREAT INDIAN SCOUTS
author: Paul G. Tomlinson
publisher: David Appleton
1. The Trail of Black Hawk (1915)
2. The Trail of Tecumseh (1917)

544. GREAT MARVEL
author: Roy Rockwood [pseudonym of the Stratemeyer Syndicate]
illustrators: Charles Nuttall [1–3]; G.M. Kizer [4]; Ernest Townsend [7]; Ed Whittemore [8]; C.R. Shaare [9]
publisher: Cupples & Leon
1. Through the Air to the North Pole; or, The Wonderful Cruise of the Electric Monarch (1906)
2. Under the Ocean to the South Pole; or, The Strange Cruise of the Submarine Wonder (1907)
3. Five Thousand Miles Underground; or, The Mystery of the Center of the Earth (1908)
4. Through Space to Mars; or, The Most Wonderful Trip on Record [alternate subtitle: The Longest Journey on Record (1910)

5. Lost on the Moon; or, In Quest of the Field of Diamonds (1911)
6. On a Torn-Away World; or, Captives of the Great Earthquake (1913)
7. The City Beyond the Clouds; or, Captured by the Red Dwarfs (1925)
8. By Air Express to Venus; or, Captives of a Strange People (1929)
9. By Space Ship to Saturn; or, Exploring the Ringed Planet (1935)

545. GREAT NEWSPAPER [see also LARRY DEXTER and YOUNG REPORTER]
author: Howard Roger Garis
publishers: Chatterton-Peck; Grosset & Dunlap
1. From Office Boy to Reporter; or, The First Step in Journalism (1907)
2. Larry Dexter, Reporter; or, Strange Adventures in a Great City (1907)
3. Larry Dexter's Great Search; or, The Hunt for the Missing Millionaire (1909)

546. GREAT RIVER
author: Edward Sylvester Ellis
publishers: Cassell; Mershon
1. Down the Mississippi (1886)
2. Up the Tapajos; or, Adventures in Brazil (1881)

GREAT WAR see TWO AMERICAN BOYS

547. GREAT WEST I
author: Joseph Alexander Altsheler
publisher: David Appleton
1. The Great Sioux Trail; A Story of Mountain and Plain (1918)
2. The Lost Hunters; A Story of Wild Man and Great Beasts (1918)

548. GREAT WEST II
author: Edward Legrand Sabin
publisher: Thomas Y. Crowell
1. The Boy Settler; or, Terry in the New West
2. The Great Pike's Peak Rush; or, Terry in the Gold Fields
3. On the Overland Stage; or, Terry as a King Whip Cub

4. Opening the Iron Trail; or, Terry in the Great Railroad Race [alternate subtitle: Terry as a "U.Pay." Man (A Semicentennial Story)] (1919)

549. GREAT WESTERN

author: Oliver Optic [pseudonym of William Taylor Adams]
publisher: Lee & Shepard
1. Lake Breezes; or, The Cruise of the Sylvania (1878)
2. Up the River; or, Yachting on the Mississippi (1881)
3. Going West; or, The Perils of a Poor Boy (1875)
4. Going South; or, Yachting on the Atlantic Coast (1879)
5. Down South; or, Yacht Adventures in Florida (1880)
6. Out West; or, Roughing It on the Great Lakes (1877)

550. GREEN MEADOW

author: Thornton W. Burgess
publisher: Little, Brown
1. Happy Jack
2. Mrs. Peter Rabbit
3. Bowser the Hound
4. Old Granny Fox

551. GREENACRES

author: Izola L. Forrester
publisher: Jacobs
1. Greenacre Girls (1915)
2. Jean of Greenacres (1917)
3. Kit of Greenacre Farm (1919)

552. GREYCLIFF GIRLS

author: Harriet Pyne Grove
publisher: A. L. Burt
1. Cathaline at Greycliff (1923)
2. The Girls of Greycliff (1923)
3. Greycliff Wings (1923)
4. The Greycliff Girls in Camp (1923)
5. Greycliff Heroines (1923)
6. The Greycliff Girls Ranching (1925)
7. The Greycliff Girls' Great Adventure (1925)
8. The Greycliff Girls in Georgia (1925)

553. GREYFRIARS

author: Frank Richards
publisher: Charles Skilton
1. Billy Bunter Among the Cannibals (1950)

554. GRIDIRON STORIES

authors: Eddie Dooley [1]; Harold M. Sherman [2–9]
publisher: Grosset & Dunlap
1. Under the Goal Posts
2. One Minute to Play
3. Touchdown
4. Block That Kick
5. Crashing Through
6. Fight 'em, Big Three
7. Goal to Go
8. Hold That Line
9. Number 44

555. GUNBOAT

author: Harry Castlemon [pseudonym of Charles Austin Fosdick]
publisher: Porter & Coates
1. Frank Before Vicksburg (1864)
2. Frank on a Gun-Boat (1864)
3. Frank the Young Naturalist (1864)
4. Frank on the Prairie (1865)
5. Frank in the Woods (1865)
6. Frank on the Lower Mississippi (1867)
7. Frank in the Mountains (1868)

556. GYPSY [see also LILY]

author: Elizabeth Stuart Phelps
publishers: Graves & Young; Dodd, Meade; A.D. Porter; Dutton; Henry A. Young
1. Gypsy Breynton (1865)
2. Gypsy's Sowing and Reaping (1866)
3. Gypsy's Cousin Joy (1866)
4. Gypsy's Year at the Golden Crescent (1867)

557. HAL KEEN MYSTERY

author: Hugh Lloyd [pseudonym of Percy Kees Fitzhugh]
publisher: Grosset & Dunlap
1. The Hermit of Gordon's Creek (1931)
2. Kidnapped in the Jungle
3. The Copperhead Trail Mystery
4. The Smuggler's Secret
5. The Mysterious Arab

6. The Lonesome Swamp Mystery
7. The Clue at Skeleton Rocks
8. The Doom of Stark House
9. The Lost Mine of the Amazon
10. The Mystery of Dark Star Ranch

HAMLET CLUB *see* **ABBEY GIRLS**

558. HAPPY DAY
author: [unknown]
publisher: McLoughlin
1. Golden Days Story Book (1905)

559. HAPPY HEART
author: Elizabeth M. Bruce
publisher: Charles Caverly, Jr.
1. Borrowing (1874)
2. The May Party (1874)
3. Merry Madge (1874)

560. HAPPY HOLLISTERS
author: Jerry West [pseudonym of the
     Stratemeyer Syndicate]
illustrator: Helen S. Hamilton
publisher: Doubleday
1. The Happy Hollisters (1953)
2. The Happy Hollisters on a River Trip (1953)
3. The Happy Hollisters at Sea Gull Beach (1953)
4. The Happy Hollisters and the Indian Treasure (1953)
5. The Happy Hollisters at Mystery Mountain (1954)
6. The Happy Hollisters at Snowflake Camp (1954)
7. The Happy Hollisters and the Trading Post Mystery (1954)
8. The Happy Hollisters at Circus Island (1955)
9. The Happy Hollisters and the Secret Fort (1955)
10. The Happy Hollisters and the Merry-Go-Round Mystery (1955)
11. The Happy Hollisters at Pony Hill Farm (1956)
12. The Happy Hollisters and the Old Clipper Ship (1956)
13. The Happy Hollisters at Lizard Cove (1957)
14. The Happy Hollisters and the Scarecrow Mystery (1957)
15. The Happy Hollisters and the Mystery of the Totem Faces (1958)
16. The Happy Hollisters and the Ice Carnival Mystery (1958)
17. The Happy Hollisters and the Mystery in Skyscraper City (1959)
18. The Happy Hollisters and the Mystery of the Little Mermaid (1960)
19. The Happy Hollisters and the Mystery at Missile Town (1961)
20. The Happy Hollisters and the Cowboy Mystery (1961)
21. The Happy Hollisters and the Haunted House Mystery (1962)
22. The Happy Hollisters and the Secret of the Lucky Coins (1962)
23. The Happy Hollisters and the Castle Rock Mystery (1963)
24. The Happy Hollisters and the Cuckoo Clock Mystery (1963)
25. The Happy Hollisters and the Swiss Echo Mystery (1963)
26. The Happy Hollisters and the Sea Turtle Mystery (1964)
27. The Happy Hollisters and the Punch and Judy Mystery (1964)
28. The Happy Hollisters and the Whistle-Pig Mystery (1964)
29. The Happy Hollisters and the Ghost Horse Mystery (1965)
30. The Happy Hollisters and the Mystery of the Golden Witch (1966)
31. The Happy Hollisters and the Mystery of the Mexican Idol (1967)
32. The Happy Hollisters and the Monster Mystery (1969)
33. The Happy Hollisters and the Mystery of the Midnight Trolls (1970)

561. HAPPY HOME
author: Howard R. Garis
publisher: Grosset & Dunlap
1. Adventures of the Galloping Gas Stove (1926)
2. Adventures of the Runaway Rocking Chair (1926)
3. Adventures of the Sailing Sofa (1926)
4. Adventures of the Sliding Foot Stool (1926)
5. Adventures of the Traveling Table (1926)
6. Adventures of the Prancing Piano (1926)

562. HAPPY HOUR
author: Elizabeth Hoyt
publishers: W.A. Wilde; Lothrop
1. Santa Claus' Dolls (1911)
2. Little Friends: for Sweet Childhood
    Days (1897)
3. Picture Joys for Girls and Boys: to
    Laugh at, to Color, and to Draw
    (1887)
4. The Little Chum Club (1910)
5. Play Days (1909)
6. The Dolls' Story-Book (1908)

563. HAPPY THOUGHT
author: Oliver Optic [pseudonym of
    William Taylor Adams]
publisher: Street & Smith
1–4. [titles unknown]
5. The Young Pilot; or, Steady Hand and
    True Eye (1887)

564. HARDY BOYS
author: Franklin W. Dixon [pseudonym of
    the Stratemeyer Syndicate]
illustrators: Walter S. Rogers [1–10];
    Clemens Gretter [11–15]; Paul Laune
    [16–23]; Russell H. Tandy [24–30];
    Roy Pell [31–32]; Leslie Morrill
    [59–66]
publishers: Grosset & Dunlap [1–58, 67,
    68–69]; Simon & Schuster [59–66,
    70–71]
1. The Tower Treasure (1927)
2. The House on the Cliff (1927)
3. The Secret of the Old Mill (1927)
4. The Missing Chums (1928)
5. Hunting for Hidden Gold (1928)
6. The Shore Road Mystery (1928)
7. The Secret of the Caves (1929)
8. The Mystery of Cabin Island (1929)
9. The Great Airport Mystery (1930)
10. What Happened at Midnight (1931)
11. While the Clock Ticked (1932)
12. The Footprints Under the Window
    (1933)
13. The Mark on the Door (1934)
14. The Hidden Harbor Mystery (1935)
15. The Sinister Signpost (1936)
16. The Figure in Hiding (1937)
17. The Secret Warning (1938)
18. The Twisted Claw (1939)
19. The Disappearing Floor (1940)

20. The Mystery of the Flying Express
    (1941)
21. The Clue of the Broken Blade (1942)
22. The Flickering Torch Mystery (1943)
23. The Melted Coins (1944)
24. The Short-Wave Mystery (1945)
25. The Secret Panel (1946)
26. The Phantom Freighter (1947)
27. The Secret of Skull Mountain (1948)
28. The Sign of the Crooked Arrow
    (1949)
29. The Secret of the Lost Tunnel (1950)
30. The Wailing Siren Mystery (1951)
31. The Secret of Wildcat Swamp (1952)
32. The Criss-Cross Shadow (1953)
33. The Yellow Feather Mystery (1953)
34. The Hooded Hawk Mystery (1954)
35. The Clue in the Embers (1955)
36. The Secret of Pirates' Hill (1956)
37. The Ghost at Skeleton Rock (1958)
38. The Mystery at Devil's Paw (1959)
39. The Mystery of the Chinese Junk
    (1960)
40. The Mystery of the Desert Giant
    (1961)
41. The Clue of the Screeching Owl
    (1962)
42. The Viking Symbol Mystery (1963)
43. The Mystery of the Aztec Warrior
    (1964)
44. The Haunted Fort (1965)
45. The Mystery of the Spiral Bridge
    (1966)
46. The Secret Agent on Flight 101 (1967)
47. The Mystery of the Whale Tattoo
    (1968)
48. The Arctic Patrol Mystery (1969)
49. The Bombay Boomerang (1970)
50. The Danger on Vampire Trail (1971)
51. The Masked Monkey (1972)
52. The Shattered Helmet (1973)
53. The Clue of the Hissing Serpent
    (1974)
54. The Mysterious Caravan (1975)
55. The Witch-Master's Key (1976)
56. The Jungle Pyramid (1977)
57. The Firebird Rocket (1978)
58. The Sting of the Scorpion (1979)
59. The Night of the Werewolf (1979)
60. The Mystery of the Samurai Sword
    (1979)
61. The Pentagon Spy (1979)

62. The Apeman's Secret (1980)
63. The Mummy Case (1980)
64. The Mystery of Smuggler's Cove (1980)
65. The Mystery of the Stone Idol (1981)
66. The Vanishing Thieves (1981)
related titles:
67. The Hardy Boys' Detective Handbook (1959)
68. The Hardy Boys and Nancy Drew Meet Dracula (1978)
69. The Haunted House and Flight to Nowhere (1978)
70. The Hardy Boys' Handbook: Seven Stories of Survival (1980)
71. The Hardy Boys' Who-Dunnit Mystery Book (1980)

HARKAWAY SERIES FOR BOYS *see* **JACK HARKAWAY SERIES FOR BOYS**

565. HARPER'S YOUNG PEOPLE SERIES
author: William Livingston Alden
publisher: Harper & Brothers
1. A New Robinson Crusoe (1899)
2. The Adventures of a Brownie; As Told to My Child (1900)

566. HARRY HARDING
author: Alfred Raymond
publisher: Cupples & Leon
1. Harry Harding — Messenger "45" (1917)
2. Harry Harding's Year of Promise (1917)

567. HEARTHSTONE
author: Oliver Optic [pseudonym of William Taylor Adams]
publisher: Lee & Shepard
4. Getting an Indorser and Other Stories

568. HELEN
author: Beth Bradford Gilchrist
publisher: Penn
1. Helen Over-the-Wall; The Adventure with the Fairy Godmother (1912)
2. Helen and the Uninvited Guests; The Adventure with the Yellow-Goggles Lady (1913)
3. Helen and the Find-Out-Club; The

Adventure with the Girl Across the Street (1914)
4. Helen and the Fifth Cousins; The Adventure with Judith, the Hermit and Some Other People (1915)

569. HELEN GRANT
author: Amanda M. Douglas
publishers: Lee & Shepard [1–2]; Lothrop, Lee & Shepard [3–9]
1. Helen Grant's Schooldays (1903)
2. Helen Grant's Friends (1904)
3. Helen Grant at Aldred House (1905)
4. Helen Grant in College (1906)
5. Helen Grant, Senior (1907)
6. Helen Grant, Graduate (1908)
7. Helen Grant, Teacher (1909)
8. Helen Grant's Decision (1910)
9. Helen Grant's Harvest Year (1911)

570. HELPFUL HAND
author: Elizabeth M. Bruce
publisher: Charles Caverly
1. Robby and Nellie and Susie (1880)

571. HENLEY SCHOOLBOYS
author: Frank Ernest Channon
publishers: Lee & Shepard; Little, Brown
1. An American Boy at Henley (1910)
2. Jackson and His Henley Friends (1911)
3. Henley's American Captain (1911)
4. Henley on the Battle Line (1911)

572. HENTY [*see also* **FIRESIDE HENTY II, FOULSHAM HENTY LIBRARY, SCRIBNER SERIES FOR YOUNG PEOPLE**]
author: George Alfred Henty
publishers: Donohue Brothers; William Allison
[the first group of series numbers are correct]
3. Bonnie Prince Charlie; A Tale of Fontenoy and Culloden (1890)
4. The Bravest of the Brave; or, With Peterborough in Spain (1900)
8. By Sheer Pluck; A Tale of the Ashanti War (1900)
18. In Times of Peril; A Tale of India (1900)
35. The Young Buglers (1897)
47. Orange and Green; A Tale of Waterloo (1900)

[the true series numbers of the following are unknown]

1. Under Drake's Flag; A Tale of the Spanish Main (1900)
2. St. George for England; A Tale of Cressy and Poitiers (1889)
3. By England's Aid; or, The Freeing of the Netherlands (1899)
4. Through the Fray; A Tale of the Luddite Riots (1890)
5. By Pike and Dyke; A Tale of the Rise of the Dutch Republic (1890)
6. With Wolfe in Canada; or, The Winning of a Continent (1900)
7. With Lee in Virginia; A Story of the American Civil War (1890)
8. Maori and Settler; A Story of the New Zealand War (1900)
9. Among Malay Pirates; A Tale of Adventure and Peril (1900)
10. True to the Old Flag; A Tale of the American War of Independence (1890)
11. The Young Carthaginian; A Story of the Times of Hannibal (1900)
12. Out on the Pampas; or, The Young Settlers (1900)
13. One of the 28th; A Tale of Waterloo (1900)
14. Facing Death; or, The Hero of the Vaughan Pit: A Tale of the Coal Mines (1890)
15. The Lion of St. Mark; A Story of Venice in the Fourteenth Century (1912)
16. The Young Franc-Tireurs and Their Adventures in the Franco-Prussian War (1900)

573. HENTY SERIES FOR BOYS
[see also HENTY, FIRESIDE HENTY, FOULSHAM HENTY]
author: George Alfred Henty
publisher: Hurst
1. The Boy Knight; A Tale of the Crusade (1890)
2. Among Malay Pirates; A Tale of Adventure and Peril (1900)
3. Out on the Pampas; or, The Young Settlers (1900)
4. By Pike and Dyke; A Tale of the Rise of the Dutch Republic (1890)

5. A Final Reckoning; A Tale of Bush Life in Australia (1890)
6. The Lost Heir (1904)
7. The Young Carthaginian; A Story of the Times of Hannibal (1900)
8. The Young Midshipman; A Story of the Bombardment of Alexandria (1900)
9. By England's Aid; or, The Freeing of the Netherlands (1899)
10. Through the Fray; A Tale of the Luddite Riots (1890)
11. For Name and Fame; or, Through Afghan Passes (1900)
12. True to the Old Flag; A Tale of the American War of Independence (1890)
13. With Clive in India; or, The Beginnings of an Empire (1890)
14. In the Reign of Terror; The Adventures of a Westminister Boy (1890)
15. In Times of Peril; A Tale of India (1900)
16. Captain Bayley's Heir; A Tale of the Gold Fields of California (1900)
17. By Right of Conquest; or, With Cortez in Mexico (1989)
18. The Young Franc-Tireurs and Their Adventures in the Franco-Prussian War (1900)
19. Under Drake's Flag; A Tale of the Spanish Main (1900)
20. The Young Colonists (1890)
21. Jack Archer; A Tale of the Crimea (1900)
22. The Lion of the North; A Tale of the Times of Gustavus Adolphus and the Wars of Religion (1900)
23. For the Temple; A Tale of the Fall of Jerusalem (1900)
24. In Freedom's Cause; A Story of Wallace and Bruce (1902)
25. The Dragon and the Raven; or, The Days of King Alfred (1890)

574. HERB KENT WEST POINT
author: Graham M. Dean
publisher: Goldsmith
1. Herb Kent, West Point Cadet (1936)
2. Herb Kent, West Point Fullback (1936)

575. HESTER
author: Jean K. Baird
publisher: Lothrop, Lee & Shepard

1. The Coming of Hester (1909)
2. Hester's Counterpart; a Story of Boarding School Life (1910)
3. Hester's Wage-Earning (1912)

576. HICKORY RIDGE BOY SCOUTS [alternate title: VICTORY BOY SCOUTS]
author: Alan Douglas
publishers: New York Book Company; M. A. Donohue
[titles also published omitting the initial words "The Hickory Ridge Boy Scouts"]
1. Campfires of the Wolf Patrol (1912)
2. The Hickory Ridge Boy Scouts' Woodcraft; or, How a Patrol Leader Made Good
3. The Hickory Ridge Boy Scouts' Pathfinder; or, The Missing Tenderfoot
4. The Hickory Ridge Boy Scouts' Fast Nine; or, A Challenge from Fairfield
5. The Hickory Ridge Boy Scouts' Great Hike; or, The Pride of the Khaki Troop
6. The Hickory Ridge Boy Scouts' Endurance Test; or, How Clear Grit Won the Day
7. The Hickory Ridge Boy Scouts Under Canvas; or, The Search for the Carteret Ghost
8. The Hickory Ridge Boy Scouts Snowbound; or, A Vacation Among the Snow Drifts
9. The Hickory Ridge Boy Scouts Afloat; or, Adventures on Watery Trails (1917)
10. The Hickory Ridge Boy Scouts' Tenderfoot Squad; or, Camping at Raccoon Bluff (1918)

577. HIGH BENTON
author: William Heyliger
publisher: David Appleton
1. High Benton (1919)
2. High Benton: Worker (1921)

578. HIGH SCHOOL BOYS [see also GRAMMAR SCHOOL BOYS; HIGH SCHOOL BOYS VACATION SERIES]
author: Harrie Irving Hancock
publisher: Henry Altemus

1. The High School Freshmen; or, Dick & Co.'s First Year Pranks and Sports (1910)
2. The High School Pitcher; or, Dick & Co. on the Gridley Diamond (1910)
3. The High School Left End; or, Dick & Co. Grilling on the Football Gridiron (1910) [alternate subtitle: Dick & Co. on the Football Field]
4. The High School Captain of the Team; or, Dick & Co. Leading the Athletic Vanguard (1910)

579. HIGH SCHOOL BOYS VACATION SERIES
author: Harrie Irving Hancock
publisher: Henry Altemus
1. The High School Boys' Canoe Club; or, Dick & Co.'s Rivals on Lake Pleasant (1912)
2. The High School Boys in Summer Camp; or, The Dick Prescott Six Training for the Gridley Eleven (1912)
3. The High School Boys' Fishing Trip; or, Dick & Co. in the Wilderness (1913)
4. The High School Boys' Training Hike; or, Making Themselves "Hard as Nails" (1913)

HIGH SCHOOL GIRLS see GRACE HARLOWE AT HIGH SCHOOL

580. HIGHWOOD
author: Ralph Henry Barbour
publisher: David Appleton
1. Hunt Holds the Center (1928)
2. Lovell Leads Off (1928)
3. Grantham Gets On (1929)

581. HILDA
author: Mary Pemberton Ginther
publisher: Penn
1. Hilda of Grey Cottage (1922)
2. Hilda of Landis and Co. (1924)
3. Hilda of the Green Smock (1925)
4. Hilda of the Three Star Ranch (1926)

582. HILLSFIELD
author: Ralph Henry Barbour
publisher: David Appleton
1. The Fumbled Pass (1935)

2. Hero of the Camp (1932)
3. The Cub Battery (1934)
4. Goal to Go (1935)
5. Beaton Runs the Mile (1933)
6. Southworth Scores (1934)

583. HILLTOP BOYS
author: Cyril Burleigh
publishers: New York Book Company;
World Syndicate
1. The Hilltop Boys; or, A Story of
School Life (1917)
2. The Hilltop Boys in Camp; or, The
Rebellion at the Academy (1917)
3. The Hilltop Boys on Lost Island; or,
An Unusual Adventure (1917)
4. The Hilltop Boys on the River; or, A
Cruise Up the Hudson (1917)
5. The Hilltop Boys Doing Their Bit; or,
The Young Farmers of the Highlands
(1918)

584. HILTON
author: Ralph Henry Barbour
publisher: David Appleton
1. The Halfback; A Story of School,
Football and Golf (1899)
2. For the Honor of the School (1900)
3. Captain of the Crew (1901)

HIRAM *see* **BACK TO THE SOIL**

585. HOCKEY [*see also* SPORTS STORIES]
author: Harold Morrow Sherman
publisher: Grosset & Dunlap
1. Flashing Steel (1929)
2. Flying Heels
3. Slashing Sticks and Other Hockey Stories (1931)

586. HOLIDAY
author: Evelyn Lance
publishers: The Holiday Publishing Company; Shug
1. A Letter to Santa Claus and Other Stories (1906)
2. School Days; or, Bad Boy Bob (1872)

587. HOLLYTREE
author: Harrie Irving Hancock
illustrator: J.C. Claghorn

publisher: Henry Altemus
1. Chuggins, the Youngest Hero with the
Army; A Tale of the Capture of Santiago (1904)

588. HOME
author: [unknown]
publisher: McLoughlin Brothers
1. Puss in Boots (1880)

589. HOME LIFE
author: Madeline Leslie
publisher: Lee & Shepard
1. Cora and the Doctor; or, Revelations
of a Physician's Wife (1874)
2–3. [titles unknown]
4. Juliette; or, Now and Forever (1869)

590. HOME SERIES FOR GIRLS
author: Oliver Optic [pseudonym of
William Taylor Adams]
publisher: Hurst
1. The Do-somethings (1905)
2. Proud and Lazy (1905)

591. HOMERUN [*see also* SPORT STORIES]
author: Harold Morrow Sherman
publisher: Grosset & Dunlap
1. Bases Full! "Ernie Challenges the
World" (1928)
2. Hit By Pitcher (1928)
3. Safe! (1928)
4. Hit and Run! (1929)
5. Batter Up! A Story of American Legion
Junior Baseball (1930)
6. Double Play! And Other Baseball Stories (1932)

592. HONEY BUNCH [*see also* HONEY BUNCH AND NORMAN in which several of these books were republished with slightly variant titles]
author: Helen Louise Thorndyke [pseudo-
nym of the Stratemeyer Syndicate]
illustrators: Walter S. Rogers [1–12]; Marie
Schubert [13–23, 28]
publisher: Grosset & Dunlap
1. Honey Bunch: Just a Little Girl (1923)
2. Honey Bunch: Her First Visit to the
City (1923)

3. Honey Bunch: Her First Days on the Farm (1923)
4. Honey Bunch: Her First Visit to the Seashore (1924)
5. Honey Bunch: Her First Little Garden (1924)
6. Honey Bunch: Her First Days in Camp (1925)
7. Honey Bunch: Her First Auto Tour (1926)
8. Honey Bunch: Her First Trip on the Ocean (1927)
9. Honey Bunch: Her First Trip West (1928)
10. Honey Bunch: Her First Summer on an Island (1929)
11. Honey Bunch: Her First Trip on the Great Lakes (1930)
12. Honey Bunch: Her First Trip in an Airplane (1931)
13. Honey Bunch: Her First Visit to the Zoo (1932)
14. Honey Bunch: Her First Big Adventure (1933)
15. Honey Bunch: Her First Big Parade (1934)
16. Honey Bunch: Her First Little Mystery (1935)
17. Honey Bunch: Her First Little Circus (1936)
18. Honey Bunch: Her First Little Treasure Hunt (1937)
19. Honey Bunch: Her First Little Club (1938)
20. Honey Bunch: Her First Trip in a Trailer (1939)
21. Honey Bunch: Her First Trip to a Big Fair (1940)
22. Honey Bunch: Her First Twin Playmates (1941)
23. Honey Bunch: Her First Costume Party (1943)
24. Honey Bunch: Her First Trip in a Houseboat (1945)
25. Honey Bunch: Her First Winter at Snowtop (1946)
26. Honey Bunch: Her First Trip to the Big Woods (1947)
27. Honey Bunch: Her First Little Pet Show (1948)
28. Honey Bunch: Her First Trip to a Lighthouse (1949)
29. Honey Bunch: Her First Visit to a Pony Ranch (1950)
30. Honey Bunch: Her First Tour of Toy Town (1951)
31. Honey Bunch: Her First Visit to Puppyland (1952)
32. Honey Bunch: Her First Trip to Reindeer Farm (1953)

593. HONEY BUNCH AND NORMAN [see also HONEY BUNCH]
author: Helen Louise Thorndyke [pseudonym of the Stratemeyer Syndicate]
publisher: Grosset & Dunlap
1. Honey Bunch and Norman Ride with the Sky Mailman (1954)
2. Honey Bunch and Norman Visit Beaver Lodge (1955)
3. Honey Bunch and Norman (1957)
4. Honey Bunch and Norman Tour Toy Town (1957)
5. Honey Bunch and Norman on Lighthouse Island (1957)
6. Honey Bunch and Norman Play Detective at Niagara Falls (1957)
7. Honey Bunch and Norman in the Castle of Magic (1958)
8. Honey Bunch and Norman Visit Reindeer Farm (1958)
9. Honey Bunch and Norman Solve the Pine Cone Mystery (1960)
10. Honey Bunch and Norman and the Paper Lantern Mystery (1961)
11. Honey Bunch and Norman and the Painted Pony (1962)
12. Honey Bunch and Norman and the Walnut Tree Mystery (1963)

594. HOUSEHOLD LIBRARY
author: Oliver Optic [pseudonym of William Taylor Adams]
publisher: Lee & Shepard
1. In Doors and Out; or, Views from the Chimney Corner
2. Living Too Fast
3. The Way of the World

595. HUNNIWELL BOYS
author: Levi Parker Wyman
publisher: A. L. Burt
1. The Hunniwell Boys in the Air (1928)
2. The Hunniwell Boys' Victory (1928)

3. The Hunniwell Boys in the Secret Service (1928)
4. The Hunniwell Boys and the Platinum Mystery (1928)
5. The Hunniwell Boys' Longest Flight (1928)
6. The Hunniwell Boys in the Gobi Desert (1930)
7. The Hunniwell Boys in the Caribbean (1930)
8. The Hunniwell Boys' Non-Stop Flight Around the World (1931)

596. HUNTING
author: Harry Castlemon [pseudonym of Charles Austin Fosdick]
publisher: Porter and Coates
1. Camp in the Foot-Hills; or, Oscar on Horseback (1893)
2. Oscar in Africa (1894)

597. HURRICANE KIDS
author: Oskar Lebeck
publisher: Grosset & Dunlap
1. The Hurricane Kids on the Lost Islands (1944)

598. IKE PARTINGTON
author: Benjamin Penhallow Shillaber
publishers: Lee & Shepard; Charles T. Dillingham
1. Ike Partington; or, The Adventures of a Human Boy and His Friends (1878) [alternate title: "Lively Boys! Lively Boys!" Ike Partington...]
2. Cruises with Captain Bob on Sea and Land (1879)
3. The Double-Runner Club; or, The Lively Boys of Rivertown (1881)

599. IN DAYS OF OLD
author: Henry Gilbert
publisher: T. Nelson & Sons
1. Robin Hood and His Merry Men (1914)

600. INDIAN
author: James Braden
publisher: Saalfield
1. Far Past the Frontier
2. The Lone Indian
3. The Trail of the Seneca

INJUN AND WHITEY *see* BOYS' GOLDEN WEST

601. IRON BOYS
author: James R. Mears
publisher: Henry Altemus
1. The Iron Boys in the Mines; or, Starting at the Bottom of the Shaft (1912)
2. The Iron Boys as Foremen; or, Heading the Diamond Drill Shaft (1912)
3. The Iron Boys on the Ore Boats; or, Roughing it on the Great Lakes (1913)
4. The Iron Boys in the Steel Mills; or, Beginning Anew in the Cinder Pits (1913)

602. ISABEL CARLETON
author: Margaret Ashmun
publisher: Macmillan
1. Isabel Carleton's Year (1916)
2. The Heart of Isabel Carleton (1917)
3. Isabel Carleton's Friends (1918)
4. Isabel Carleton in the West (1919)
5. Isabel Carleton at Home (1920)

603. ISLAND
author: Earl C. McAllister
publisher: Dana Estes
1. On Tower Island (1907)

604. ISLAND BOYS
author: Howard Roger Garis
publisher: R. F. Fenno
1. The Island Boys; or, Fun and Adventures on Lake Modok (1912)

605. JACK
author: George Bird Grinnell
publisher: Stokes
1. Jack, The Young Ranchman; or, A Boy's Adventures in the Rockies (1899)
2. Jack Among the Indians; or, A Boy's Summer on the Buffalo Plains
3. Jack in the Rockies; or, A Boy's Adventures with a Pack Train
4. Jack, The Young Canoeman; or, An Eastern Boy's Voyage in a Chinook Canoe
5. Jack, The Young Trapper; or, An Eastern Boy's Fur Hunting in the Rocky Mountains

6. Jack, the Young Explorer; or, A Boy's Experiences in the Unknown Northwest
7. Jack, The Young Cowboy; or, An Eastern Boy's Experience on a Western Round-up (1913)

606. JACK ARMSTRONG
author: Stanley J. Wallace
publisher: Cupples & Leon
1. Jack Armstrong's Mystery Eye (1936)
2. Jack Armstrong's Mystery Crystal (1936)

607. JACK HALL
author: Robert Grant
publisher: Charles Scribner's Sons
1. Jack in the Bush; or, A Summer on a Salmon River (1906)

608. JACK HARKAWAY SERIES FOR BOYS
author: Bracebridge Hemyng
publisher: Federal Book Company
 1. Jack Harkaway's Duel (1911)
 2. Jack Harkaway After Schooldays (1870)
 3. Jack Harkaway's Adventures Afloat and Ashore; A Sequel to Jack Harkaway After Schooldays (1900)
 4. [title unknown]
 5. Jack Harkaway at Oxford (1900)
 6. Jack Harkaway Among the Brigands of Italy (1900)
 7. Jack Harkaway Among Brigands (1900)
 8. Jack Harkaway and His Son's Adventures Round the World (1900)
 9. Jack Harkaway's Adventures in America and Cuba (1870)
10. Jack Harkaway's Capture (1900)
11. Jack Harkaway and His Son's Adventures in Greece (1896)
12. [title unknown — possibly part 2 of number 11]
13. Jack Harkaway and His Son's Adventures in Australia (1912)
14. Adventures of Young Jack Harkaway and His Boy Tinker (1896)
15. Jack Harkaway's Boy Tinker Among the Turks; Being the Conclusion of the Adventures of Young Jack Harkaway and His Boy Tinker (1900)
16–21. [titles unknown]

22. Jack Harkaway's Confidence (1904)
23. Jack Harkaway's Duel (1904)
unknown series numbers:
 1. Jack Harkaway's Schooldays (1989)
 2. Jack Harkaway and His Son's Adventures in China (1870)

609. JACK HEATON
author: Archie Frederick Collins
publisher: Frederick A. Stokes
1. Jack Heaton, Wireless Operator (1919)
2. Jack Heaton, Oil Prospector (1920)

610. JACK LORIMER
author: Wynn Standish [pseudonym of Walter Leon Sawyer]
illustrators: Arthur William Brown [1]; Louis D. Gowing [1]; Harold J. Cue [5]; James K. Bonnar [2]; Frank P. Fairbanks [3]; John Goss [4]
publishers: A. L. Burt; L. C. Page
1. Captain Jack Lorimer; or, The Young Athletes of Millvale High (1906)
2. Jack Lorimer's Champions; or, Sports on Land and Lake (1907)
3. Jack Lorimer's Holidays; or, Millvale High in Camp (1908)
4. Jack Lorimer's Substitute; or, The Acting Captain of the Team (1909)
5. Jack Lorimer, Freshman; or, From Millvale High to Exmouth (1912)

611. JACK RACE
author: Harry Hale
publisher: Heart's International Library Co.
1. Jack Race at Boarding School; or, The Leader of Merrivale Academy (1915)
2. Jack Race's Baseball Nine; or, Winning the Junior League Pennant
3. Jack Race, Speed King; or, A Trip Across the Continent [alternate subtitle: Racing Across the Continent] (1915)
4. Jack Race, Air Scout; or, Adventures in a War Aeroplane
5. Jack Race on the Ranch; or, The Triumphs of a Tenderfoot

612. JACK RANGER
author: Clarence Young [pseudonym of the Stratemeyer Syndicate]

illustrator: Charles Nuttall
publisher: Cupples & Leon
1. Jack Ranger's Schooldays; or, The Rivals of Washington Hall (1907)
2. Jack Ranger's Western Trip; or, From Boarding School to Ranch and Range (1908)
3. Jack Ranger's School Victories; or, Track, Gridiron and Diamond (1908)
4. Jack Ranger's Ocean Cruise; or, The Wreck of the Polly Ann (1909)
5. Jack Ranger's Gun Club; or, From Schoolroom to Camp and Trail (1910)
6. Jack Ranger's Treasure Box; or, The Outing of the Schoolboy Yachtsmen (1911)

613. JACK STRAW

author: Irving Crump
publisher: McBride
1. Jack Straw in Mexico; or, How the Engineer Defined the Great Hydroelectric Plant (1914)
2. Jack Straw, Lighthouse Builder (1915)

614. JACK WINTER [alternate title: AMERICAN BOYS' SPORTS]

author: Mark Overton
publisher: M. A. Donohue
1. Jack Winter's Baseball Team; or, Rivals of the Diamond (1919)
2. Jack Winter's Campmates; or, Vacation Days in the Woods (1919)
3. Jack Winter's Gridiron Chums; or, When the Halfback Saved the Day (1919)
4. Jack Winter's Iceboat Wonder; or, Leading the Hockey Team to Victory (1919)

615. JAMES OTIS' COLONY SERIES [see also JAMES OTIS' PIONEER SERIES]

author: James Otis [pseudonym of James Otis Kaler]
publisher: American Book
1. Richard of Jamestown; A Story of the Virginia Colony (1910)
2. Stephen of Philadelphia; A Story of Penn's Colony (1910)
3. Ruth of Boston; A Story of the Massachusetts Bay Colony (1910)

616. JAMES OTIS' PIONEER SERIES [see also JAMES OTIS' COLONY SERIES]

author: James Otis [pseudonym of James Otis Kaler]
publisher: American Book
1. Hannah of Kentucky; A Story of the Wilderness Road (1912)
2. Mary of Plymouth; A Story of the Pilgrim Settlement (1910)
3. Seth of Colorado; A Story of the Settlement of Denver (1912)
4. Antoine of Oregon; A Story of the Oregon Trail (1912)
5. Martha of California; A Story of the California Trail (1913)
6. Philip of Texas; A Story of Sheep Raising in Texas (1913)

617. JANE ALLEN COLLEGE SERIES [see also MYSTERY AND ADVENTURE SERIES FOR GIRLS]

author: Edith Bancroft
publisher: Cupples & Leon
1. Jane Allen of the Sub-Team (1917)
2. Jane Allen: Right Guard (1918)
3. Jane Allen: Center (1920)
4. Jane Allen: Junior (1921)
5. Jane Allen: Senior (1922)

618. JANE STUART

author: Grace M. Remick
publisher: [unknown]
1. Jane Stuart, Twin (1913)
2. Jane Stuart's Chum (1914)
3. Jane Stuart at Rivercroft (1915)
4. Jane Stuart, Comrade (1916)

619. JANICE DAY

author: Helen Beecher Long [pseudonym of the Stratemeyer Syndicate]
illustrators: Walter S. Rogers [1]; Corinne Turner [2–5]
publisher: Sully and Kleinteich
1. Janice Day (1914) [alternate title: Janice Day at Poketown]
2. The Testing of Janice Day (1915)
3. How Janice Day Won (1916)
4. The Mission of Janice Day (1917)
5. Janice Day, the Young Homemaker (1919)

620. JANIE MARSHAL
author: Dorothy Simpson
publisher: J. B. Lippincott
1. Island in the Bay (1956)
2. The Honest Dollar (1957)
3. A Lesson for Janie (1958)
4. A Matter of Pride (1959)
5. New Horizons (1961)
6. Visitor from the Sea (1965)

621. JAPANESE FAIRY TALE
author: [unknown]
publisher: Griffith, Farran & Co.
1. Momotaro; or, Little Peachling (1892)
2–9. [titles unknown]
10. The Matsuyama Mirror (1892)
11. The Hare of Inaba (1892)

622. JEAN CABOT
author: Gertrude Fisher Scott
publisher: Lothrop, Lee & Shepard
1. Jean Cabot at Ashton (1912)
2. Jean Cabot in the British Isles   (1913)
3. Jean Cabot in Cap and Gown (1914)
4. Jean Cabot at the House with the Blue Shutters (1915)

623. JEAN CRAIG
author: Kay Littleton [pseudonym of Mary Anne Amsbary]
publisher: World Syndicate
1. Jean Craig Grows Up (1948)
2. Jean Craig in New York (1948)
3. Jean Craig Finds Romance (1948)
4. Jean Craig, Nurse (1949)
5. Jean Craig, Graduate Nurse (1950)

624. JEAN MARY
author: Ella Lee
publisher: A. L. Burt
1. Jean Mary's Adventures (1931)
2. Jean Mary in Virginia (1931)
3. Jean Mary's Romance (1931)
4. Jean Mary's Summer Mystery (1931)
5. Jean Mary Solves the Mystery (1933)

625. JEANNE
author: Alice Ross Colver
publisher: Penn
1. Jeanne (1922)
2. Jeanne's House Party (1923)

3. Jeanne's Happy Year (1925)
4. Jeanne at Rainbow Lodge (1926)

626. JENNIFER
author: Eunice Young Smith
publisher: Bobbs-Merrill
1. The Jennifer Wish (1949)
2. The Jennifer Gift (1950)
3. The Jennifer Prize (1951)
4. Jennifer Is Eleven (1952)
5. Jennifer Dances (1954)
6. High Heels for Jennifer (1964)

627. JERRY FORD WONDER STORIES
author: Fenworth Moore [pseudonym of the Stratemeyer Syndicate]
illustrator: Russell H. Tandy [1–4]
publisher: Cupples & Leon
1. Wrecked on Cannibal Island; or, Jerry Ford's Adventure Among Savages (1931)
2. Lost in the Caves of Gold; or, Jerry Ford Among the Mountains of Mystery (1931)
3. Castaway in the Land of Snow; or, Jerry Ford Among the Polar Bears (1931)
4. Prisoners on the Pirate Ship; or, Jerry Ford and the Yellow Men (1932)
5. Thrilling Stories for Boys (1937) [contains titles 1–3]

628. JERRY FOSTER
author: Elmer Ellsworth Ferris
publisher: Doubleday
1. Jerry of Seven Mile Creek (1938)
2. Jerry at the Academy (1940)
3. Jerry Foster, Salesman (1942)

629. JERRY HICKS
author: William Heyliger
publisher: Grosset & Dunlap
1. Yours Truly, Jerry Hicks (1929)
2. Jerry Hicks: Ghost Hunter (1927)
3. Jerry Hicks and His Gang (1929)
4. Jerry Hicks: Explorer (1930)
5. Jerry Hicks and the Lucky Rabbit's Foot (1931)

630. JERRY TODD
author: Leo Edwards [pseudonym of Edward Edson Lee]

illustrators: Bert N. Salg [1–13]; Herman Bacharach [16]; Myrtle Sheldon [14–15]
publisher: Grosset & Dunlap
1. Jerry Todd and the Whispering Mummy (1924)
2. Jerry Todd and the Rose-Colored Cat (1924)
3. Jerry Todd and the Oak Island Treasure (1925)
4. Jerry Todd and the Waltzing Hen (1924)
5. Jerry Todd and the Talking Frog (1925)
6. Jerry Todd and the Purring Egg (1926)
7. Jerry Todd in the Whispering Cave (1927)
8. Jerry Todd, Pirate (1928)
9. Jerry Todd and the Bob-tailed Elephant (1929)
10. Jerry Todd, Editor-in-Grief (1930)
11. Jerry Todd, Caveman (1932)
12. Jerry Todd and the Flying Flapdoodle (1934)
13. Jerry Todd and the Buffalo Bill Bathtub (1936)
14. Jerry Todd's Up-the-Ladder Club (1937)
15. Jerry Todd's Poodle Parlor (1938)
16. Jerry Todd's Cuckoo Camp (1940)

631. JESSICA TRENT
author: Evelyn Hunt Raymond
publishers: Street & Smith [1]; David McKay [2–3]
1. Jessica Trent, Her Life on a Ranch (1902)
2. Jessica, the Heiress (1904)
3. Jessica Trent's Inheritance (1907)

JEWEL see ADVENTURE BOYS

632. JIM MASON
author: Elmer Russell Gregor
publisher: David Appleton
1. [title unknown]
2. Jim Mason, Scout (1923)
3. Captain Jim Mason (1924)
4. Mason and His Rangers (1926)

633. JIM SPURLING
author: Albert Walter Tolman

publisher: Harper & Brothers
1. Jim Spurling, Fisherman; or, Making Good (1918)
2. Jim Spurling, Millman (1921)
3. Jim Spurling, Leader; or, Ocean Camp (1926)
4. Jim Spurling, Trawler; or, Fishing with Cap'n John (1927)

634. JIMMY DRURY
author: David O'Hara [pseudonym of A. Van Buren Powell]
publisher: Grosset & Dunlap
1. Candid Camera Detective (1938)
2. What the Dark Room Revealed
3. Caught by the Camera
4. By Bursting Flash Bulbs (1941)

635. JIMMY KIRKLAND
author: Hugh S. Fullerton
publisher: Winston
1. Jimmy Kirkland of the Shasta Boys' Team (1915)
2. Jimmy Kirkland of the Cascade College Team (1915)
3. Jimmy Kirkland and the Plot for a Pennant (1915)

636. JOAN I
author: Lilian C. McNamara Garis
publisher: Grosset & Dunlap
1. Joan, Just a Girl
2. Joan's Garden of Adventure

637. JOAN II
authors: Emilia Elliot [pseudonym of Caroline E. Jacobs] [1–5]; Lucy Mansfield Mason [5]
publisher: Jacobs
1. Joan of Juniper Inn (1907)
2. Joan's Jolly Vacation (1909)
3. Patricia (1910)
4. S. W. F. Club (1912)
5. Joan's California Summer (1917)

638. JOAN AND BILL
author: Ellsworth Newcomb
publisher: Dutton
1. Anchor for Her Heart (1947)
2. Window on the Sea (1948)
3. Stars Above (1949)
4. With This Ring (1951)

639. JOAN FOSTER
author: Alice Ross Colver
publisher: Dodd, Mead
1. Joan Foster, Freshman, the Story of a Girl of Today (1942)
2. Joan Foster, Sophomore (1948)
3. Joan Foster, Junior (1949)
4. Joan Foster, Senior (1950)
5. Joan Foster in Europe (1951)
6. Joan Foster, Bride (1952)

640. JOE STRONG
author: Vance Barnum [pseudonym of the Stratemeyer Syndicate]
illustrators: Walter S. Rogers; Jerome L. Kroeger; Erwin L. Hess
publishers: George Sully; Whitman; Hearst's International Library
1. Joe Strong, the Boy Wizard; or, The Mysteries of Magic Exposed. (1916)
2. Joe Strong on the Trapeze; or, The Daring Feats of a Young Circus Performer (1916)
3. Joe Strong, the Boy Fish; or, Marvelous Doings in a Big Tank (1916)
4. Joe Strong on the High Wire; or, Motorcycle Perils of the Air (1916)
5. Joe Strong and His Wings of Steel; or, A Young Acrobat in the Clouds (1916)
6. Joe Strong and His Box of Mystery; or, The Ten Thousand Dollar Prize Trick (1916)
7. Joe Strong, the Boy Fire-Eater; or, The Most Dangerous Performance on Record (1916)

641. JOHN AND BETTY
author: Margaret Williamson
publisher: Lothrop, Lee & Shepard
1. John and Betty's English History Visit (1910)
2. John and Betty's Scotch History Visit (1912)
3. John and Betty's Irish History Visit (1914)

642. JOHN NEWBERRY
author: Dinah Maria Mulock Craik
publisher: Saalfield
1.The Adventures of a Brownie (1927)

643. JOLLY SANTA CLAUS
author: [unknown]
publisher: McLoughlin
1. Fun for Christmas Time (1899)

644. JONAS'S STORIES [see also ROLLO I and LUCY]
author: Jacob Abbott
publishers: Clark & Maynard; Clark, Austin & Smith
1. Jonas's Stories: Related to Rollo and Lucy (1839)
2. Jonas on a Farm in Winter (1841)
3. Jonas on a Farm in Summer (1841)
4. Jonas as Judge; or, Law Among the Boys (1944)
5. Caleb in the Country: A Story for Children (1854)
6. Caleb in Town: A Story for Children (1856)

645. JORDONS
author: Janet Lambert
publisher: Dutton
1. Just Jennifer (1945)
2. Friday's Child (1947)
3. Confusion By Cupid (1950)
4. A Dream for Susan (1954)
5. Love Taps Gently (1955)
6. A Song in Their Hearts (1956)
7. Myself and I (1957)
8. The Stars Hang High (1960)
9. Wedding Bells (1961)
10. A Bright Tomorrow (1965)
11. Here's Marny (1969)

646. JOSIE O'GORMAN
author: Emma Speed Sampson [pseudonym of Lyman Frank Baum]
publisher: Reilly & Lee
1. Mary Louise and Josie O'Gorman (1922)
2. Josie O'Gorman (1923)
3. Josie O'Gorman and the Meddlesome Major (1924)

647. JOYCE PAYTON
author: Dorothy Whitehill
publishers: Barse & Hopkins [1–5]; Grosset & Dunlap [6]
1. Joy and Gypsy Joe (1927)
2. Joy and Pam (1927)

3. Joy and Her Chums (1928)
4. Joy and Pam at Brookside (1929)
5. Joy and Pam A-Sailing (1930)
6. Joy and Pam as Seniors (1932)

648. JUDY BOLTON
author: Margaret Sutton
publisher: Grosset & Dunlap
1. The Haunted Attic (1932)
2. The Invisible Chimes (1932)
3. The Seven Strange Clues (1932)
4. The Vanishing Shadow (1932)
5. The Ghost Parade (1933)
6. The Yellow Phantom (1934)
7. The Mystic Ball (1934)
8. The Voice in the Suitcase (1935)
9. The Mysterious Half Cat (1936)
10. The Riddle of the Double Ring (1937)
11. The Unfinished House (1938)
12. The Midnight Visitor (1939)
13. The Name on the Bracelet (1940)
14. The Clue in the Patchwork Quilt (1941)
15. The Mark on the Mirror (1942)
16. The Secret of the Barred Window (1943)
17. The Rainbow Riddle (1946)
18. The Living Portrait (1947)
19. The Secret of the Musical Tree (1948)
20. The Warning on the Window (1949)
21. The Clue of the Stone Lantern (1950)
22. The Spirit of Fog Island (1951)
23. The Black Cat's Clue (1952)
24. The Forbidden Chest (1953)
25. The Haunted Road (1954)
26. The Clue in the Ruined Castle (1955)
27. The Trail of the Green Doll (1956)
28. The Haunted Fountain (1957)
29. The Clue of the Broken Wing (1958)
30. The Phantom Friend (1959)
31. The Discovery at the Dragon's Mouth (1960)
32. The Whispered Watchword (1961)
33. The Secret Quest (1962)
34. The Puzzle in the Pond (1963)
35. The Hidden Clue (1964)
36. The Pledge of the Twin Knights (1965)
37. The Search for the Glowing Hat (1966)
38. The Secret of the Sand Castle (1967)

649. JUDY JORDAN
author: Lilian C. Gariis
publisher: Grosset & Dunlap
1. Judy Jordan (1931)
2. Judy Jordan's Discovery (1931)
3. Judy Jordan's Mystery

650. KATHIE ALSTON
author: Amanda M. Douglas
publisher: Lothrop, Lee & Shepard
1. Kathie's Summer at Cedarwood (1898)
2. Kathie's Three Wishes (1898)
3. Kathie's Soldiers
4. In the Ranks

651. KATRINKA
author: Helen Eggleston Haskell
publisher: Dutton
1. Katrinka, the Story of a Russian Child (1915)
2. Katrinka Grows Up (1932)
3. Peter, Katrinka's Brother (1933)
4. Peggy Keeps House (1935)
5. Nadya Makes Her Bow (1939)

652. KAY TRACEY
author: Frances K. Judd
publisher: Cupples & Leon
1. The Secret of the Red Scarf (1934)
2. The Strange Echo (1934)
3. The Shadow on the Door (1935)
4. The Mystery of the Swaying Curtains (1935)
5. The Green Cameo Mystery (1936)
6. The Six Fingered Glove Mystery (1936)
7. The Secret at the Windmill (1937)
8. Beneath the Crimson Briar Bush (1937)
9. The Message in the Sand Dunes (1938)
10. The Murmuring Portrait (1938)
11. In the Sunken Garden (1939)
12. When the Key Turned (1939)
13. The Forbidden Tower (1940)
14. The Sacred Feather (1940)
15. The Double Disguise (1941)
16. The Lone Footprint (1941)
17. The Mansion of Secrets (1942)
18. The Mysterious Neighbors (1942)

653. KEN
author: Basil Miller
publisher: Zondervan

1. Ken Rides the Range; A Boy's Story of the Painted Desert (1941)
2. Ken Bails Out; A High Sierra Adventure for Boys (1942)
3. Ken Follows the Chuck Wagon
4. Ken's Mercy Flight to Australia (1944)
5. Ken in Alaska (1944)
6. Ken Saddles Up (1945)
7. Ken South of the Border (1947)
8. Ken on the Argentine Pampas (1947)
9. Ken on the Navajo Trail (1948)

654. KENNETH CARLISLE DETECTIVE STORIES
author: Carolyn Wells
publisher: Doubleday, Doran
1. The Doorstep Murders, a Kenneth Carlisle Detective Story (1930)
2. The Skeleton at the Feast, a Kenneth Carlisle Detective Story (1931)

655. KHAKI BOYS
author: Gordon Bates [pseudonym of Josephine Chase]
publisher: Cupples & Leon
1. The Khaki Boys at Camp Sterling; or, Training for the Big Fight in France (1918)
2. The Khaki Boys on the Way; or, Doing Their Bit on Sea and Land (1918)
3. The Khaki Boys at the Front; or, Shoulder to Shoulder in the Trenches (1918)
4. The Khaki Boys Over the Top; or, Doing and Daring for Uncle Sam (1919)
5. The Khaki Boys Fighting to Win; or, Smashing the German Lines (1919)
6. The Khaki Boys Along the Rhine; or, Winning the Honors of War (1919)

656. KHAKI GIRLS
author: Edna Brooks
publisher: Cupples & Leon
1. The Khaki Girls of the Motor Corps; or, Finding Their Places in the Big War (1918)
2. The Khaki Girls Behind the Lines; or, Driving with the Ambulance Corps (1918)
3. The Khaki Girls at Windsor Barracks; or, "Standing To" with the "Trusty Twenty" (1919)

4. The Khaki Girls in Victory; or, Home with the Heroes (1920)

657. KIDNAPPED CAMPERS
author: Flavia Camp Canfield
publisher: Harper & Brothers
1. The Kidnapped Campers; A Story of Out-of-Doors (1908)

658. KING'S HIGHWAY
author: Carolyn Sherwin Bailey
publisher: Macmillan
1. The Way of the Gate (1917)
2. The Way of the Green Pastures (1917)
3. The Way of the Rivers (1916)
4. The Way of the Hills (1916)
5. The Way of the Mountains
6. The Way of the Stars (1916)
7. The Way of the King's Gardens
8. The Way of the King's Palace (1916)

659. KITUK
author: Roy Judson Snell
publisher: Little, Brown
1. [title unknown]
2. Captain Kituk (1918)

660. KOKO
author: Basil Miller
publisher: Zondervan
1. Koko — King of the Arctic Trail (1947)
2. Koko of the Airways
3. Koko and the Eskimo Doctor

661. KRISS KRINGLE
author: [unknown]
publisher: McLoughlin Brothers
1. Robinson Crusoe (1897)
2. Tom Thumb (1897)
3. Doings of Kriss Kringle (1897)
4. Apple-Pie ABC (1897)

662. KRISTY
author: Olive Thorne Miller
publisher: Houghton-Mifflin
1. Kristy's Queer Christmas (1904)
2. Kristy's Surprise Party (1905)
3. Kristy's Rainy Day Picnic (1906)

663. LAKE SHORE
author: Oliver Optic [pseudonym of William Taylor Adams]

publisher: Lee & Shepard; Dillingham
1. Through by Daylight; or, The Young Engineer of the Lake Shore Railroad (1869)
2. Lightning Express; or, The Rival Academies (1870)
3. On Time; or, The Young Captain of the Ucayga Steamer (1869)
4. Switch Off; or, The War of the Students (1869)
5. Brake Up; or, The Young Peacemakers (1870)
6. Bear and Forbear; or, The Young Skipper of Lake Ucayga (1869)

664. LAKEPORT

author: Ralph Bonehill [pseudonym of Edward Stratemeyer?]
illustrators: Charles Nuttall [1–3]; Max Klepper [4]; John Goss [5]; H. Richard Boehm [6]
publisher: Lothrop, Lee & Shepard
1. The Gun Club Boys of Lakeport; or, The Island Camp (1908)
2. The Baseball Boys of Lakeport; or, The Winning Run (1908)
3. The Boat Club Boys of Lakeport; or, The Water Champions (1908)
4. The Football Boys of Lakeport; or, More Goals Than One (1909)
5. The Automobile Boys of Lakeport; or, A Run for Fun and Fame (1910)
6. The Air Craft Boys of Lakeport; or, Rivals of the Clouds (1912)

665. LAKERIM

author: Robert Hughes
publisher: Century
1. The Lakerim Cruise (1910)
2. The Lakerim Athletic Club (1910)
3. The Dozen from Lakerim (1910)

666. LAKEWOOD BOYS

author: Levi Parker Wyman
publisher: A. L. Burt
1. The Lakewood Boys on the Lazy S (1925)
2. The Lakewood Boys and the Lost Mine (1925)
3. The Lakewood Boys in the Frozen North (1925)

4. The Lakewood Boys and the Polo Ponies (1925)
5. The Lakewood Boys in the South Sea Islands (1925)
6. The Lakewood Boys in Montana (1927)
7. The Lakewood Boys in the African Jungle (1927)

667. LAND OF THE FREE

authors: Elsie Singmaster [1]; Erick Berry [2]; Jo Evalin Lundy [3, 10]; Walter Havighurst [4, 15]; Gertrude Robinson [5]; Virginia Armstrong Oakes [6]; Elizabeth Jane Coatsworth [7]; Florence Crannell Means [8]; Alida Maldus [9]; Joseph H. Gage [11]; Herbert Best [12]; Arna Wendell Bontemps [13]; Olive Woolley Burt [14]; Charles Minor Blackford [16]; Maude Morgan Thomas [17]; Elsie Reif Ziegler [18]
publishers: Holt, Rinehart & Winston; J.C. Winston
1. I Heard of a River; The Story of the Germans in Pennsylvania (1948)
2. Seven Beaver Skins; A Story of the Dutch in New Amsterdam (1948)
3. Tidewater Valley; A Story of the Swiss in Oregon (1949)
4. Song of the Pines; A Story of Norwegian Lumbering in Wisconsin (1949)
5. The Sign of the Golden Fish; A Story of the Cornish Fishermen in Maine (1949)
6. Footprints of the Dragon; A Story of the Chinese and the Pacific Railways (1949)
7. Door to the North; A Saga of Fourteenth Century America (1950)
8. The Silver Fleece; A Story of the Spanish in New Mexico (1950)
9. Colt of Destiny; A Story of the California Missions (1950)
10. Seek the Dark Gold; A Story of the Scots Fur Traders (1951)
11. The Beckoning Hills (1951)
12. Watergate; A Story of the Irish on the Erie Canal (1951)
13. Chariot in the Sky; A Story of the Jubilee Singers (1951)
14. The Oak's Long Shadow; A Story of the Basque Shepherders in Idaho (1952)

15. Climb a Lofty Ladder; A Story of Swedish Settlement in Minnesota (1952)
16. Deep Treasure; A Story of the Greek Sponge Fishers of Florida (1954)
17. Sing in the Dark; A Story of the Welsh in Pennsylvania (1954)
18. The Blowing Wand; A Story of Bohemian Glassmaking in Ohio (1955)

668. LANKY LAWSON
author: Harry Mason Roe [pseudonym of the Stratemeyer Syndicate]
illustrator: David Randolph
publisher: Barse & Company
1. Lanky Lawson, the Boy from Nowhere: How He Arrived at Beanville, What Beanville Did to Him, and What He Did to Beanville (1929)
2. Lanky Lawson with the One-Ring Circus: How He Joined the Show, What He Did to the Wild Animals, What Happened When the Circus Collapsed (1929)
3. Lanky Lawson and His Trained Zebra: How He Happened to Get the Beast, How the Cantankerous Animal Performed, and What Happened at the County Fair (1930)
4. Lanky Lawson Somewhere on the Ocean (1930)

669. LANSING
authors: William Heyliger [1–3]; Hawley Williams [4]
publisher: David Appleton
1. Batter Up (1912)
2. The Winning Hit
3. Fair Play (1915)
4. Quarterback Reckless (1912)

670. LARRY BURKE
author: Frank I. Odell
publisher: Lothrop, Lee & Shepard
1. Larry Burke, Freshman
2. Larry Burke, Sophomore (1911)

671. LARRY DEXTER [*see also* **GREAT NEWSPAPER** *and* **YOUNG REPORTER**]
authors: Howard Roger Garis and Raymond Sperry [pseudonym of Howard Roger Garis]

publishers: Grosset & Dunlap; Garden Publishing Co.
1. Larry Dexter and the Missing Millionaire; or, The Great Search (1900) [alternate titles: Larry Dexter's Great Search; or, The Hunt for a Missing Millionaire. The Young Reporter and the Missing Millionaire; or, A Strange Disappearance]
2. Larry Dexter at the Big Flood; or, The Perils of a Reporter (1907) [alternate titles: From Office Boy to Reporter; or, The First Step in Journalism. The Young Reporter at the Big Flood; or, The Perils of News Gathering]
3. Larry Dexter and the Land Swindlers; or, Queer Adventures in a Great City (1907) [alternate titles: Larry Dexter, The Young Reporter; or, Strange Adventures in a Great City. The Young Report and the Land Swindlers; or, Queer Adventures in a Great City]
4. Larry Dexter and the Bank Mystery; or, Exciting Days in Wall Street [alternate titles: Larry Dexter and the Bank Mystery; or A Young Reporter in Wall Street. The Young Reporter and The Bank Mystery; or, Stirring Doings in Wall Street]
5. The Young Reporter and the Stolen Boy; or, A Chase on the Great Lakes (1912) [alternate titles: Larry Dexter and the Stolen Boy; or, A Young Reporter on the Lakes. The Young Reporter and the Stolen Boy; or, A Chase on the Great Lakes]
6. Larry Dexter at the Battle Front; or, A War Correspondent's Double Mission [alternate titles: Larry Dexter in Belgium; or, A Young War Correspondent's Double Mission. The Young Reporter at the Battle Front; or, A War Correspondent's Double Mission]
7. Larry Dexter and the Ward Diamonds; or, The Young Reporter at Sea Cliff
8. Larry Dexter's Great Chase; or, The Young Reporter Across the Continent

672. LAURELHURST
author: Oliver Optic [pseudonym of William Taylor Adams]
publisher: Hurst

1. In School and Out
2. Little by Little
3. Rich and Humble

673. LEATHERCLAD TALES
author: Oliver Optic [pseudonym of William Taylor Adams]
publishers: Lovell; United States Book Co.
6. Nature's Young Noblemen
27. The Young Actor
29. The Rival Battalions

674. LEND-A-HAND BOYS
author: George Rathborne
publisher: Goldsmith
1. Lend-A-Hand Boys of Carthage; or, Waking up the Home Town (1931)
2. Lend-A-Hand Boys' Sanitary Squad; or, When the Fever Came to Blairstown (1931)
3. Lend-A-Hand Boys' Teamwork; or, Putting Their Shoulders to the Wheel (1931)
4. Lend-A-Hand Boys as Wild Game Protectors; or, The Little Four-Footed Brother in the Fur Coat (1931)

675. LET'S MAKE BELIEVE AND PLAY
author: Lilian C. McNamara Garis
publisher: R.F. Fenno
1. Let's Make Believe We're Soldiers (1918)

676. LETTY
author: Helen Sherman Griffith
publisher: Penn
1. Letty and the Twins (1910)
2. Letty of the Circus (1910)
3. Letty's New Home (1911)
4. Letty's Sister (1912)
5. Letty's Treasure (1913)
6. Letty's Good Luck (1914)
7. Letty at the Conservatory (1915)
8. Letty's Springtime (1916)
9. Letty and Miss Grey (1917)
10. Letty Grey, Heiress (1918)

677. LIBRARY FOR YOUNG PEOPLE
author: Oliver Optic [pseudonym of William Taylor Adams]

publishers: Hurst; Rickey, Mallory
1. All Aboard
2. The Boat Club
3. Little by Little; or, The Cruise of the Flyaway: A Story for Young Folks (1861)
4. Now or Never
5. Poor and Proud
6. Try Again

678. LIFE AND ADVENTURE
author: C. Bernard Rutley
publisher: Blackie & Son
1. Island of Secrets (1948)

679. LILIAN GARIS BOOKS [see also CLEO, CONNIE LORING, BARBARA HALE, GLORIA]
author: Lilian C. McNamara Garis
publisher: Grosset & Dunlap
[titles are simply the sum of the 4 series listed above]

680. LILY [see also GYPSY]
author: Elizabeth Stuart Phelps
publisher: Ward, Lock, Bowden
1. Gypsy Breynton (1892)

681. LINDA CARLTON
author: Edith Lavell
publisher: A. L. Burt
1. Linda Carlton, Air Pilot (1931)
2. Linda Carlton, Island Adventure (1931)
3. Linda Carlton's Ocean Flight (1931)
4. Linda Carlton's Perilous Summer (1932)
5. Linda Carlton's Hollywood Flight (1933)

682. LINDA LANE
author: Josephine Lawrence
publisher: Barse & Hopkins
1. Linda Lane (1925)
2. Linda Lane Helps Out (1925)
3. Linda Lane's Plan (1926)
4. Linda Lane's Experiments (1927)
5. Linda Lane's Problem (1928)
6. Linda Lane's Big Sister (1929)

683. LINGER-NOTS
author: Agnes Miller
publisher: Cupples & Leon

1. The Linger-Nots and the Mystery House; or, The Story of Nine Adventurous Girls (1923)
2. The Linger-Nots and the Valley Feud; or, The Great West Point Chain (1923)
3. The Linger-Nots and Their Golden Quest; or, The Log of the Ocean Monarch (1923)
4. The Linger-Nots and the Whispering Charm; or, The Secret from Old Alaska (9125)
5. The Linger-Nots and the Secret Maze; or, Treasure-Trove on Battlefield Hill (1931)

684. LISA, EMMY AND DODIE
author: Madge Lee Chastain
publisher: Harcourt
1. Dark Treasure (1954)
2. Emmy Keeps a Promise (1956)
3. Magic Island (1964)

685. LITTLE AGNES [*see also* MRS. LESLIE'S JUVENILE SERIES]
author: Madeline Leslie
publisher: Ward
1. Trying to be Useful (1858)
2. Art and Art Lessness (1864)

686. LITTLE BOY BLUE
authors: Amanda Minnie Douglas [1]; Ella Farman [2]
publisher: David Lothrop
1. Tim's Partner, and Other Stories (1877)
2. Strangers from the South, and Other Stories (1877)

687. LITTLE CHARLEY'S LIBRARY
author: [unknown]
publisher: C. G. Henderson
1. Little Charley's Country Walk (1852)

688. LITTLE COCKALORUM
author: Wallis Simkins
publisher: Penn
1. The Little Cockalorum (1922)
2. The Little Cockalorum Crows Again (1923)
3. The Little Cockalorum on Her Own (1924)

4. The Little Cockalorum Finds Romance (1925)

689. LITTLE COLONEL [*see also* COSY CORNER]
author: Annie Fellows Johnston
illustrators: Etheldred B. Barry, Mary G. Johnston, Harold Cue, P. Verburg, John Goss, Louis Meynall, L.J. Bridgman
publishers: L. C. Page; J. Knight
1. The Little Colonel (1895)
2. The Giant Scissors (1898)
3. Two Little Knights of Kentucky
4. The Little Colonel Stories [contains 1–3]
5. The Little Colonel's House Party (1900)
6. The Little Colonel's Holidays (1901)
7. The Little Colonel's Hero (1902)
8. The Little Colonel's Good Times Book (1902)
9. The Little Colonel at Boarding School (1903)
10. The Little Colonel in Arizona (1904)
11. The Little Colonel's Christmas Vacation (1906)
12. The Little Colonel: Maid of Honor (1906)
13. The Little Colonel's Knight Comes Riding (1907)
14. The Little Colonel's Chum: Mary Ware (1908) [alternate title: Mary Ware: The Little Colonel's Chum]
15. The Rescue of the Princess Winsome; A Fairy Play for Old and Young (1908)
16. Mary Ware in Texas (1910)
17. The Little Colonel Doll Book Representing Characters and Costumes from the Books of the Little Colonel Series (1910)
18. Mary Ware in Texas (1910)
19. Story of the Red Cross as Told to the Little Colonel (1918)

690. LITTLE COLONEL STORIES
author: Annie Fellows Johnston
publisher: [unknown]
1. Ole Mammy's Torment
2. The Three Tremonts
3. The Little Colonel in Switzerland

691. LITTLE COUSIN

authors: Elizabeth Borton [78,80]; Eva Cannon Brooks [40]; E. C. Butler [25]; Claire Martha Coburn [30]; Julia Darrow Cowles [46, 51, 54]; Mabel Farnum [79]; Isaac Taylor Headland [11]; Tehyi Hsieh [77]; Luna May Innes [44]; Charles H. L. Johnston [58]; Mellicent Humason Lee [24, 83]; Elizabeth Roberts Macdonald [16]; Blanch McManus Mansfield [22–23, 26, 28, 32, 34, 36, 41]; Florence Mendel [45, 47]; Gladys M. Morgan [70]; Emily F. Murphy [68]; Mary F. Nixon-Roulet [29, 31, 33, 35, 37–38]; H. Pike [24, 27]; Feodor A. Postnikov [56]; Laura E. Richards [66]; E. A. Sawyer [43]; Mary S. Saxe [63]; E. Shedd [39; Anna B. Sloane [73]; Phyllis Ayer Sowers [81–82]; Evaleen Stein [55, 59, 61, 65]; Emily Goddard Taylor [67]; Mary Hazelton Blanchard Wade [1–10, 12–15, 17–21]; Anna C. Winlow [71–72, 74–76]; Clara V. Winlow[48, 50, 53, 60, 62, 64, 69, 71

illustrators: L. J. Bridgman; John Goss; Diantha Horne Marlowe; Harold Cue; Louis de Meserac; Ivan Doseff; Thelma Gooch; Walter S. Rogers; Charles E. Meister; Elizabeth Otis; Josephine Bruce; Harriet O'Brian; Leslie W. Lee; Gertrude Herrick; John M. Foster; H. W. Packard; R. C. Woodberry; Elizabeth R. Withington; Monica Beaton

publisher: L. C. Page

1. Our Little Indian Cousin (1901)
2. Our Little Japanese Cousin (1901)
3. Our Little Malayan Cousin (1901)
4. Petrovna, Our Little Russian Cousin (1901)
5. Our Little African Cousin (1902)
6. Our Little Cuban Cousin (1902)
7. Our Little Eskimo Cousin (1902)
8. Our Little Hawaiian Cousin (1902)
9. Our Little Philippine Cousin (1902)
10. Our Little Porto Rican Cousin (1902)
11. Our Little Chinese Cousin (1903)
12. Our Little Italian Cousin (1903)
13. Our Little Norwegian Cousin (1903)
14. Our Little Siamese Cousin (1903)
15. Our Little Swiss Cousin (1903)
16. Our Little Canadian Cousin (1904)
17. Our Little German Cousin (1904)
18. Our Little Irish Cousin (1904)
19. Our Little Jewish Cousin (1904)
20. Our Little Turkish Cousin (1904)
21. Our Little Armenian Cousin (1905)
22. Our Little English Cousin (1905)
23. Our Little French Cousin (1905)
24. Our Little Korean Cousin (1905)
25. Our Little Mexican Cousin (1905)
26. Our Little Dutch Cousin (1906)
27. Our Little Panama Cousin (1906)
28. Our Little Scotch Cousin (1906)
29. Our Little Spanish Cousin (1906)
30. Our Little Swedish Cousin (1906)
31. Our Little Alaskan Cousin (1907)
32. Our Little Arabian Cousin (1907)
33. Our Little Brazilian Cousin (1907)
34. Our Little Hindu Cousin (1907)
35. Our Little Australian Cousin (1908)
36. Our Little Egyptian Cousin (1908)
37. Our Little Grecian Cousin (1908)
38. Our Little Hungarian Cousin (1909)
39. Our Little Persian Cousin (1909)
40. Our Little Argentine Cousin (1910)
41. Our Little Belgian Cousin (1911)
42. Our Little Bohemian Cousin (1911)
43. Our Little Portuguese Cousin (1911)
44. Our Little Danish Cousin (1912)
45. Our Little Polish Cousin (1912)
46. Our Little Athenian Cousin of Long Ago (1913)
47. Our Little Austrian Cousin (1913)
48. Our Little Bulgarian Cousin (1913)
49. Our Little Roman Cousin of Long Ago (1913)
50. Our Little Servian Cousin (1913)
51. Our Little Spartan Cousin of Long Ago (1914)
52. Our Little Boer Cousin (1915)
53. Our Little Carthaginian Cousin of Long Ago (1915)
54. Our Little Macedonian Cousin of Long Ago (1915)
55. Our Little Norman Cousin of Long Ago (1915)
56. Our Little Cossack Cousin (1916)
57. Our Little Saxon Cousin of Long Ago (1916)
58. Our Little Viking Cousin of Long Ago (1916)
59. Our Little Frankish Cousin of Long Ago (1917)

60. Our Little Roumanian Cousin (1917)
61. Our Little Celtic Cousin of Long Ago (1918)
62. Our Little Finnish Cousin (1918)
63. Our Little Quebec Cousin (1919)
64. Our Little Czecho-Slovak Cousin (1920)
65. Our Little Crusader Cousin of Long Ago (1921)
66. Our Little Feudal Cousin of Long Ago (1922)
67. Our Little West Indian Cousin (1922)
68. Our Little Canadian Cousin of the Great Northwest (1923)
69. Our Little Jugoslav Cousin (1923)
70. Our Little Welsh Cousin (1924)
71. Our Little Ukranian Cousin (1925)
72. Our Little Lithuanian Cousin (1926)
73. Our Little Lapp Cousin (1927)
74. Our Little Chilean Cousin (1928)
75. Our Little Florentine Cousin of Long Ago (1929)
76. Our Little Burmese Cousin (1931)
77. Our Little Manchurian Cousin (1933)
78. Our Little Aztec Cousin of Long Ago (1934)
79. Our Little Vatican City Cousin (1934)
80. Our Little Ethiopian Cousin (1935)
81. Our Little Mongolian Cousin (1936)
82. Our Little Corinthian Cousin of Long Ago (1937)
83. Our Little Guatamalan Cousin (1937)

692. LITTLE DOT
author: [unknown]
publisher: McLoughlin Brothers
1. Three Little Kittens (1899)
2. The Frog Who Would A Wooing Go (1900)
3. Three Bears (1880)
4. Cinderella; or, The Little Glass Slipper (1879)
5. Sad Fate of Poor Robin (1879)
6. Sleeping Beauty (1899)

693. LITTLE FOLK'S SERIES
author: [unknown]
publisher: McLoughlin Brothers
1. The Five Little Pigs
2. Old Mother Goose
3. Old Woman Who Lived in a Shoe
4. The Three Bears

5. Dame Trot and Her Cat
6. Jack and the Bean-Stalk
7. Sing a Song of Sixpence
8. Story of Three Little Pigs
9. Babes in the Woods
10. Diamonds and Toads
11. My First Alphabet
12. Little Bo-Peep

LITTLE FRANKIE see MRS. LESLIE'S BOOKS FOR LITTLE CHILDREN

694. LITTLE GIRL
author: Amanda Minnie Douglas
publisher: Dodd, Mead
1. A Little Girl in Old New York (1896)
2. Hannah Ann; a Sequel to A Little Girl in Old New York (1896)
3. A Little Girl of Long Ago (1897)
4. A Little Girl in Old Boston (1898)
5. A Little Girl in Old Philadelphia (1899)
6. A Little Girl in Old Washington (1900)
7. A Little Girl in Old New Orleans (1901)
8. A Little Girl in Old Detroit (1902)
9. A Little Girl in Old St. Louis (1903)
10. A Little Girl in Old Chicago (1904)
11. A Little Girl in Old San Francisco (1905)
12. A Little Girl in Old Quebec (1906)
13. A Little Girl in Old Baltimore (1907)
14. A Little Girl in Old Salem (1908)
15. A Little Girl in Old Pittsburgh (1909)

695. LITTLE HAZEL
author: Matilda Horsburgh
publisher: T. Nelson & Sons
1. The Guiding Pillar; or, Pansy's Perfect Trust (1889)

696. LITTLE HOUSE ON THE PRAIRIE
author: Laura Ingalls Wilder
publisher: Harper
1. Little House on the Prairie (1935)
2. Little House in the Big Woods (1932)
3. Farmer Boy (1933)
4. On the Banks of Plum Creek (1937)
5. By the Shores of Silver Lake (1939)
6. The Long Winter (1940)

7. Little Town on the Prairie (1941)
8. These Happy Golden Years (1943)
9. The First Four Years (1971)

697. LITTLE KITTENS
author: Sarah Catherine Martin
publisher: Charles E. Graham
1. Three Little Kittens (1895)
2–7. [titles unknown]
   8. Old Mother Hubbard and Her Dog
      (1899)

698. LITTLE LUCIA
author: Mabel L. Robinson
publisher: Dutton
1. Dr. Tam O'Shanter (1921)
2. Little Lucia (1922)
3. Little Lucia and Her Puppy (1923)
4. All By Ourselves (1924)
5. Little Lucia's Island Camp (1924)
6. Little Lucia's School (1926)
7. Sarah's Dakin (1927)

699. LITTLE MAID
author: Alice Turner Curtis
publisher: Penn
1. A Little Maid of Province Town
   (1913)
2. A Little Maid of Massachusetts
   Colony (1914)
3. A Little Maid of Narragansett Bay
   (1915)
4. A Little Maid of Bunker Hill (1916)
5. A Little Maid of Ticonderoga (1917)
6. A Little Maid of Old Connecticut
   (1918)
7. A Little Maid of Old Philadelphia
   (1919)
8. A Little Maid of Old Maine (1920)
9. A Little Maid of Old New York (1921)
10. A Little Maid of Virginia (1922)

700. LITTLE MISS CRICKET
author: Gabrielle E. Jackson
publisher: David Appleton
1. Little Miss Cricket (1905)
2. Little Miss Cricket's New Home (1907)
3. Little Miss Cricket at School (1908)

701. LITTLE MOTHER
author: John Howard Jewett
publisher: Nister

1. The Toy Bearkins Christmas Tree (1905)
2. The Three Baby Bears (1865)

702. LITTLE ORPHAN ANNIE
author: [unknown]
publisher: Cupples & Leon
1. Little Orphan Annie
2. Little Orphan Annie in Cosmic City
3. Little Orphan Annie in the Great
   Depression
4. Little Orphan Annie 1
5. Little Orphan Annie 2
6. Annie

703. LITTLE PEOPLE'S LIBRARY
author: [unknown]
publishers: Aldine; Juvenile Productions;
   D & J Saddler
   1. The Children of the New Forest
      (1899)
   2. Three Little Kittens: Nursery Rhymes
      (1952)
   3. The Children's Treasury (1952)
   4. The Children's Picture ABC (1952)
   5. The Children's Fun Fair (1952)
   6. The Pleasure Book for Boys and Girls
      (1953)
   7. The Novelty Box for Boys and Girls
      (1953)
   8. My Toyland A.B.C. (1953)
   9. Mother Goose Nursery Rhymes
      (1953)
10. Charlie and Beatrice; and Other Sto-
    ries (1899)
11. Little James; or, Busy as Bees: and
    Other Stories (1899)
12. Short Tales and Parables for Little
    Children (1857)

704. LITTLE PIG
author: [unknown]
publisher: McLoughlin Brothers
1. 3 Little Pigs (1904)

705. LITTLE PILGRIM
author: Ella Rodman Church
publisher: American Sunday-School Union
1. Little Pilgrim at Aunt Lori's (1879)

706. LITTLE PRINCESS
author: Aileen Cleveland Higgins
publisher: Penn

1. A Little Princess of Tenopah (1909)
2. A Little Princess of the Pines (1910)
3. A Little Princess of the Patio (1911)
4. A Little Princess of the Ranch (1914)
5. A Little Princess of the Stars and Stripes (1915)

707. LITTLE PRUDY [*see also* **DOTTY DIMPLE STORIES; EDITHA II**]
author: Sophie May [pseudonym of Rebecca Sophia Clarke]
publishers: Saalfield; Lee & Shepard; Hurst
1. Little Prudy (1800)
2. Little Prudy's Cousin Grace (1800)
3. Little Prudy's Fairy Book (1865)
4. Little Prudy's Captain Horace (1892)
5. Little Prudy's Sister Susy (1890)
6. Little Prudy's Dotty Dimple (1865)
7. Little Prudy's Story Book

708. LITTLE PRUDY'S FLYAWAY
author: Sophie May [pseudonym of Rebecca Sophia Clarke]
publishers: Lee & Shepard; Lothrop, Lee & Shepard; Lee, Shepard & Dillingham
1. Little Folks Astray (1870)
2. Prudy Keeping House (1870)
3. Aunt Madge's Story (1871)
4. Little Grandmother (1870)
5. Little Grandfather (1875)
6. Miss Thistledown (1901)

709. LITTLE PURITAN
author: Edith Robinson
publishers: Knight (1); L. C. Page (2–8)
1. A Loyal Little Maid (1897)
2. A Little Puritan Rebel (1898)
3. A Little Daughter of Liberty (1899)
4. A Little Puritan's First Christmas (1900)
5. A Little Puritan Pioneer (1901)
6. A Puritan Knight Errant (1903)
7. A Little Puritan Bound Girl (1904)
8. A Little Puritan Cavalier (1905)

710. LITTLE READERS
author: Carolyn Sherwin Bailey
publisher: McLoughlin Brothers
1. Adventure Stories (1934)

711. LITTLE RED HOUSE CHILDREN
author: Amanda M. Douglas
publisher: Lothrop, Lee & Shepard
1. The Children in the Little Old Red House (1912)
2. The Red House Children at Grafton (1913)
3. The Red House Children's Vacation (1914)
4. The Red House Children's Year (1915)
5. The Red House Children Growing Up (1916)

712. LITTLE RUNAWAYS
author: Alice Turner Curtis
publisher: Penn
1. The Little Runaways (1906)
2. The Little Runaways at Home (1912)
3. The Little Runaways and Mother (1913)
4. The Little Runaways at Orchard House (1914)

713. LITTLE SALLY SMITH
author: Elizabeth Coatsworth
publisher: Macmillan
1. Away Goes Sally (1934)
2. Five Bushel Farm (1939)
3. The "Fair America" (1940)

714. LITTLE SANTA CLAUS
author: [unknown]
publisher: McLoughlin Brothers
1. Santa Claus and His Doings (1906)

715. LITTLE SUNBEAM
author: [unknown]
publisher: De Wolfe, Fiske
1. Merry Chimes for Happy Times (1890)
2. Animal Stories and Pictures: Amusing and Instructive Stories about Beasts, Birds, Reptiles and Fishes (1899)

716. LITTLE WASHINGTONS
authors: Lilian Elizabeth Becker Roy [2, 3, 5, 6]; S. Waukley Roy Nourse [1, 4]
publisher: Grosset & Dunlap
1. The Little Washingtons (1918)
2. The Little Washingtons' Travels (1918)
3. The Little Washingtons' Relatives (1918)

4. The Little Washingtons at School (1920)
5. The Little Washingtons' Holidays (1925)
6. The Little Washingtons: Farmers (1926)

717. LITTLE WIZARD
author: Lyman Frank Baum
publisher: Reilly & Britton
1. [title unknown]
2. Little Dorothy and Toto (1913)
3. Tiktok and the Nome King (1913)

718. LITTLE WOMEN
author: Louisa May Alcott
publisher: Little
1. Little Women; or, Meg, Jo, Beth and Amy (1868)
2. Little Women Married (1869)
3. Little Men: Life at Plumfield with Jo's Boys (1871)
4. Jo's Boys, and How They Turned Out (1886)

719. LITTLE WORKERS
author: [unknown]
publisher: McLoughlin Brothers
1. The Little Farmer Girl; and Other Stories (1899)
2. The Little Housemaid; and Other Stories (1901)
3. The Little Joiner; and Other Stories (1904)

720. LIVE DOLLS
author: Josephine Scribner Gates
publishers: Bowen-Merrill (1); Franklin (2, 3); Bobbs (4–11)
1. The Story of the Live Dolls (1901)
2. The Doll That Was Lost and Found (1903)
3. More About Live Dolls (1903)
4. The Story of the Three Dolls (1905)
5. The Live Dolls' House Party (1906)
6. The Live Dolls' Busy Days (1907)
7. The Live Dolls' Play Days (1908)
8. The April Fool Doll (1909)
9. The Live Dolls' Party Days (1910)
10. The Live Dolls in Fairyland (1912)
11. The Live Dolls in Wonderland (1912)

721. LOG CABIN
author: Edward Sylvester Ellis
publisher: Cassell
1. The Lost Trail (1891)
2. Footprints in the Forest (1897)

722. LOG CABIN LIBRARY [alternate title: YOUNG AMERICA AFLOAT]
author: Oliver Optic [pseudonym of William Taylor Adams]
publisher: Log Cabin Press
1–15. [titles unknown]
16. Outward Bound (1867)

723. LONE RANGER
author: Fran Striker
publisher: Grosset & Dunlap
1. The Lone Ranger (1936)
2. The Lone Ranger and the Mystery Ranch
3. The Lone Ranger and the Gold Robbery
4. The Lone Ranger and the Outlaw Stronghold
5. The Lone Ranger and Tonto
6. The Lone Ranger at the Hunted Gulch
7. The Lone Ranger Traps the Smugglers
8. The Lone Ranger Rides Again
9. The Lone Ranger Rides North
10. The Lone Ranger and the Silver Bullet
11. The Lone Ranger on Powderhorn Trail
12. The Lone Ranger in Wild Horse Canyon
13. The Lone Ranger West of Maverick Pass
14. The Lone Ranger on Gunsight Mesa
15. The Lone Ranger and the Bitter Spring Feud
16. The Lone Ranger and the Code of the West
17. The Lone Ranger: Trouble on the Santa Fe
18. The Lone Ranger on Red Butte Trail (1956)

724. LONG AGO
author: Ellis Gray
publisher: Lockwood, Brooks
1. The Cedars; More of Child Life (1878)

725. LONG TRAIL BOYS

author: Dale Wilkins [pseudonym of Josephine Chase]
publisher: Winston
1. The Long Trail Boys at Sweet Water Ranch; or, The Mystery of the White Shadow (1923)
2. The Long Trail Boys and the Gray Cloaks; or, A Mystery of the Oregon Forests
3. The Long Trail Boys and the Scarlet Sign
4. The Long Trail Boys and the Vanishing Rider
5. The Long Trail Boys and the Mystery of the Fingerprints
6. The Long Trail Boys and the Mystery of the Unknown Messenger (1928)

726. LORAINE AND THE LITTLE PEOPLE

author: Elizabeth Gordon
publisher: Rand
1. Loraine and the Little People (1915)
2. Loraine and the Little People of Spring (1918)
3. Loraine and the Little People of Summer (920)
4. Loraine and the Little People of the Ocean (1922)

727. LORNE

author: Daniel Defoe [1]
publisher: Gall and Inglis
1. The Life and Adventures of Robinson Crusoe of York, Mariner (1890)

728. LOUIE MAUDE

author: Helen Sherman
publisher: Penn
1. Louie Maude (1924)
2. The Roly Poly Family (1924)
3. Louie Maude and the Caravan (1925)
4. Louie Maude and the Mary Ann (1927)

729. LUCILE

author: Elizabeth M. Duffield
publisher: Sully
1. Lucile, the Torch Bearer (1915)
2. Lucile, Triumphant (1916)
3. Lucile, Bringer of Joy (1917)
4. Lucile on the Heights (1918)

730. LUCK AND PLUCK [see also ALGER; ALGER SERIES FOR BOYS]

author: Horatio Alger
publishers: Porter & Coates; John C. Winston; Henry T. Coates; M.A. Donohue; A.L. Burt
first series:
1. Luck and Pluck; or, John Oakley's Inheritance (1869)
2. Sink or Swim; or Harry Raymond's Resolve (1870)
3. [title unknown]
4. Strive and Succeed; or, The Progress of Walter Conrad (1872)
second series:
1. [title unknown]
2. Bound to Rise; or, Harry Walton's Motto (1873)
3. Risen from the Ranks; or, Harry Walton's Success (1874)
[# unknown]: Herbert Carter's Legacy; or, The Inventor's Son (1875)
series unknown:
[1] Try and Trust; or, The Story of a Bound Boy (1873)
[2] Strong and Steady; or, Paddle Your Own Canoe (1871)

731. LUCKY I

author: Oliver Optic [pseudonym of William Taylor Adams]
publisher: George Munro's Sons
1. The Boat Club

732. LUCKY II

author: Elmer Sherwood [pseudonym of Samuel Leuwenkrohn]
publisher: Whitman
1. Lucky, the Boy Scout (1916)
2. Lucky and His Friend Steve (1922)
3. [title unknown]
4. Lucky, the Young Volunteer (1917)
5. Lucky Finds a Friend
6. [title unknown]
7. Lucky, the Young Soldier (1917)
8. Lucky, the Young Navyman (1917)

733. LUCKY TERRELL FLYING STORIES

author: Canfield Cook
publisher: Grosset & Dunlap

1. Spitfire Pilot (1942)
2. Sky Attack
3. Secret Mission
4. Lost Squadron
5. Springboard to Tokyo
6. Wings Over Japan
7. The Flying Jet
8. The Flying Wing (946)

734. LUCKY TOM

author: Harry Castlemon [pseudonym of
Charles Austin Fosdick]
publisher: Porter & Coates
1. Our Fellows (1895)
2. Elam Storm, the Wolfer; or, The Lost
Nugget (1895)
3. Missing Pocket-Book; or, Tom Mason's
Luck (1895)

735. LUCY

author: Jacob Abbott
publisher: Thomas Y. Crowell
1. Stories Told to Rollo's Cousin Lucy
When She Was a Little Girl (1909)
2. Cousin Lucy at Play (1909)
3. Cousin Lucy at Study (1909)
4. Cousin Lucy on the Sea-Shore (1909)
5. Cousin Lucy Among the Mountains;
and Cousin Lucy on the Seashore
6. Cousin Lucy's Conversations

736. LUCY GORDON

author: Aline Howard
publisher: Penn
1. Captain Lucy and Lieutenant Bob
(1918)
2. Captain Lucy in France (1919)
3. Captain Lucy's Flying Ace (1920)
4. Captain Lucy in the Home Sector (1921)

737. LUPTON GILT TOP

author: Oliver Optic [pseudonym of
William Taylor Adams]
publisher: Federal
1. All Aboard
2. The Boat Club
3. Now or Never
4. Poor and Proud
5. Try Again

738. MACLELLAN BOOKS

author: Oliver Optic [pseudonym of
William Taylor Adams]

publisher: MacLellan
1. Outward Bound

739. MADGE MORTON

author: Amy D. V. Chalmers
publisher: Henry Altemus
1. Madge Morton — Captain of the Merry
Maid
2. Madge Morton's Secret
3. Madge Morton's Trust (1914)
4. Madge Morton's Victory (1914)

740. MAGIC MAKERS

author: Margaret Sutton
publisher: Grosset & Dunlap
1. The Magic Makers and the Bramble
Bush Man (1936)
2. The Magic Makers and the Golden
Charm (1936)
3. The Magic Makers in Backwards Land
(1936)

741. MAIDA

author: Inez Haynes Irwin
publishers: Huebsch [1,2]; Viking [3];
Grosset & Dunlap [4–15]
1. Maida's Little Shop (1909)
2. Maida's Little House (1921)
3. Maida's Little School (1926)
4. Maida's Little Island (1939)
5. Maida's Little Camp (1940)
6. Maida's Little Village (1942)
7. Maida's Little Houseboat (1943)
8. Maida's Little Theater (1946)
9. Maida's Little Cabins (1947)
10. Maida's Little Zoo (1949)
11. Maida's Little Lighthouse (1951)
12. Maida's Little Hospital (1952)
13. Maida's Little Farm (1953)
14. Maida's Little House Party (1954)
15. Maida's Little Treasure Hunt (1955)

742. MAIL PILOT

author: Lewis Edwin Theiss
publisher: W.A. Wilde
1. Flying the U.S. Mail to South America;
How Pan American Airships Carry on
in Sun and Storm above the Rolling
Caribbean (1933)
2. The Mail Pilot of the Caribbean; The
Adventures of Ginger Hale above the
Southern Seas (1934)

3. [title unknown]
4. From Coast to Coast with the U.S. Air Mail (1936)
5. Flood Mappers Aloft; How Ginger Hale and the Scouts of the Bald Eagle Patrol Surveyed the Watershed of the Susquehanna (1937)
6. Wings over the Andes (1939)

743. MAKE BELIEVE STORIES
author: Laura Lee Hope [pseudonym of Stratemeyer Syndicate]
illustrator: Harry L. Smith
publisher: Grosset & Dunlap
1. The Story of a Sawdust Doll (1920)
2. The Story of a White Rocking Horse (1920)
3. The Story of a Lamb on Wheels (1920)
4. The Story of a Bold Tin Soldier (1920)
5. The Story of a Candy Rabbit (1920)
6. The Story of a Monkey on a Stick (1920)
7. The Story of a Calico Clown (1920)
8. The Story of a Nodding Donkey (1921)
9. The Story of a China Cat (1921)
10. The Story of a Plush Bear (1921)
11. The Story of a Stuffed Elephant (1922)
12. The Story of a Woolly Dog (1923)

744. MAMMA LOVECHILD'S SERIES
author: [unknown]
publisher: McLoughlin Brothers
1. Cocky Locky and Henny Penny (1850)
2. The Death and Burial of Poor Cock Robin (1850)
3. Three Little Kittens (1850)
4. Prince Arthur's Alphabet; or, A Was an Archer (1859)
5. Old Mother Hubbard (1869)
6. New Nursery Rhymes (1900)
7. Three Tiny Pigs (1859)

745. MARCY
author: Rosamund Du Jardin
publisher: J. B. Lippincott
1. Wait for Marcy (1950)
2. Marcy Catches Up (1952)
3. A Man for Marcy (1954)
4. Senior Prom (1957)

746. MARGARET
author: Laura E. Richards
publishers: Estes & Lauriat (1, 2); Dana Estes (3–5)
1. Three Margarets (1897)
2. Margaret Montfort (1898)
3. Peggy (1899)
4. Rita (1900)
5. Fernley House (1901)

747. MARGERY MORRIS
author: Violet Gordon Gray
publisher: Penn
1. Margery Morris (1917)
2. Margery Morris, Mascot (1919)
3. Margery Morris and Plain Jane (1920)
4. Margery in the Pine Woods (1921)

748. MARILDA
author: Esther Bates
publisher: David McKay
1. Marilda's House (1956)
2. Marilda and the Witness Tree (1957)
3. Marilda and the Bird of Time (1960)

749. MARJORIE I
author: Mrs. George A. Paull
publisher: Jacobs
1. Marjorie's Doings (1900)
2. Marjorie's Play Days (1901)
3. Marjorie Darling (1904)

750. MARJORIE II
author: Alice Turner Curtis
publisher: Penn
1. Marjorie's Way (1905)
2. Marjorie's School Days (1911)
3. Marjorie in the Sunny South (1912)
4. Marjorie on Beacon Hill (1913)

751. MARJORIE III
author: Carolyn Wells
illustrators: Herbert F. Bohnert[(5,6), Julie Carolyn Pratt [4], Mary R. Bassett [3])
publisher: Dodd, Mead
1. Marjorie's Vacation (1907)
2. Marjorie's Busy Days (1908)
3. Marjorie's New Friend (1909)
4. Marjorie in Command (1910)

5. Marjorie's Maytime (1911)
6. Marjorie at Seacote (1912)

752. MARJORIE DEAN COLLEGE SERIES
author: Pauline Lester
publisher: A. L. Burt
1. Marjorie Dean, College Freshman (1922)
2. Marjorie Dean, College Sophomore (1922)
3. Marjorie Dean, College Junior (1922)
4. Marjorie Dean, College Senior (1922)

753. MARJORIE DEAN HIGH SCHOOL SERIES
author: Pauline Lester
publisher: A. L. Burt
1. Marjorie Dean, High School Freshman (1917)
2. Marjorie Dean, High School Sophomore (1917)
3. Marjorie Dean, High School Junior (1917)
4. Marjorie Dean, High School Senior (1917)

754. MARJORIE DEAN POST-GRADUATE SERIES
author: Pauline Lester
publisher: A. L. Burt
1. Marjorie Dean, at Hamilton Arms (1925)
2. Marjorie Dean, Marvelous Manager (1925)
3. Marjorie Dean, Post Graduate (1925)
4. Marjorie Dean' Romance (1925)
5. Marjorie Dean Macy (1926)
6. Marjorie Dean Macy's Hamilton Colony (1930)

755. MARK GILMORE
author: Percy Kees Fitzhugh
illustrator: Howard L. Hastings
publisher: Grosset & Dunlap
1. Mark Gilmore, Scout of the Air (1930)
2. Mark Gilmore, Speed Flyer (1931)
3. Mark Gilmore's Lucky Landing (1931)

756. MARK TIDD
author: Clarence Budington Kelland
publisher: Harpers

1. Mark Tidd (1913)
2. Mark Tidd in the Backwoods (1914)
3. Mark Tidd in Business (1915)
4. Mark Tidd's Citadel (1916)
5. Mark Tidd, Editor (1917)
6. Mark Tidd, Manufacturer (1918)
7. Mark Tidd in Italy (1925)
8. Mark Tidd in Egypt (1926)
9. Mark Tidd in Sicily (1928)

757. MARTHA
author: Julie Lippman
publisher: Holt
1. Martha By-the-Day (1912)
2. Making Over Martha (1913)
3. Martha and Cupid (1914)

758. MARTHA JANE
author: Inez Specking
publishers: Benziger (1,2); Herder (3)
1. Martha Jane: A Western Boarding School (1925)
2. Martha Jane at College (1926)
3. Martha Jane, Sophomore (1929)

759. MARY
author: Emma L. Brock
publisher: Knopf
1. Ballet for Mary (1954)
2. Mary's Secret (1962)
3. Mary's Camera (1963)
4. Mary Makes a Cake (1964)
5. Mary on Roller Skates (1967)

760. MARY AND JERRY MYSTERY STORIES
author: Lew James [pseudonym of Stratemeyer Syndicate]
illustrator: Margaret Ayer (1–5)
publisher: Grosset & Dunlap
1. The Messenger Dog's Secret (1935)
2. The Mystery of the Toy Bank (1935)
3. The Story the Parrot Told (1935)
4. The Secret of the Missing Clown (1936)
5. The Mystery of the Crooked Tree (1937)

761. MARY JANE
author: Clara Ingram Judson
illustrators: Thelma Gooch (5,8); Frances White (1–4, 9, 10, 13–15); Charles L.

Wrenn; Marie Schubert (17–18); Genevieve Foster (19)
publisher: Barse & Hopkins
1. Mary Jane, Her Book (1918)
2. Mary Jane, Her Visit (1918)
3. Mary Jane's Kindergarten (1918)
4. Mary Jane Down South (1919)
5. Mary Jane's City Home (1920)
6. Mary Jane in New England (1921)
7. Mary Jane's Country Home (1922)
8. Mary Jane at School (1923)
9. Mary Jane in Canada (1924)
10. Mary Jane's Summer Fun (1925)
11. Mary Jane's Winter Sports (1926)
12. Mary Jane's Vacation (1927)
13. Mary Jane in England (1928)
14. Mary Jane in Scotland (1929)
15. Mary Jane in France (1930)
16. Mary Jane in Switzerland (1931)
17. Mary Jane in Italy (1933)
18. Mary Jane in Spain (1937)
19. Mary Jane's Friends in Holland (1939)

762. MARY LOU
author: Edith Lavell
publisher: A. L. Burt
1. The Mystery at Dark Cedars (1935)
2. The Mystery of the Fires (1935)
3. The Mystery of the Secret Band (1935)

763. MARY LOUISE
author: Edith Van Dyne and Emma Speed Sampson [pseudonyms of Lyman Frank Baum
publishers: Reilly & Britton (1–3); Reilly & Lee (4–8)
1. Mary Louise (1916)
2. Mary Louise in the Country (1916)
3. Mary Louise Solves a Mystery (1917)
4. Mary Louise and the Liberty Girls (1918)
5. Mary Louise Adopts a Soldier (1919)
6. Mary Louise at Dorfield (1920)
7. Mary Louise Stands the Test (1921)
8. Mary Louise and Josie O'Gorman (1922)

764. MARY-MARY
author: Joan Robinson
publisher: Harrap
1. Mary-Mary (1957)
2. More Mary-Mary (1958)

3. Madam Mary-Mary (1960)
4. Mary-Mary Stories (1965)

765. MARY POPPINS
author: P.L. Travers
publishers: Reynal & Hitchcock [1–3]; Peter Davies [4]; Harcourt [5]; Harcourt Brace [6]; Collins [7]
1. Mary Poppins (1934)
2. Mary Poppins Comes Back (1935)
3. Mary Poppins Opens the Door (1943)
4. Mary Poppins in the Park (1952)
5. Mary Poppins from A to Z (1962)
6. Mary Poppins in the Kitchen: A Cookery Book with a Story by Travers with Maurice Moore-Betty (1975)
7. Mary Poppins in Cherry Tree Lane (1982)

766. MARY ROSE
author: Mary Mabel Wirries
publisher: Benziger
1. Mary Rose at Boarding School (1924)
2. Mary Rose Keeps House (1925)
3. Mary Rose, Sophomore (1925)
4. Mary Rose, Graduate (1926)
5. Mary Rose at Rose Gables (1928)
6. Mary Rose in Friendville (1930)
7. Mary Rose's Sister Bess (1932)

767. MAXIE [*see also* **MYSTERY AND ADVENTURE SERIES FOR GIRLS**]
author: Elsie Bell Gardner
publisher: Cupples & Leon
1. Maxie, an Adorable Girl; or, Her Adventures in the British West Indies (1932)
2. Maxie in Venezuela; or, The Clue to the Diamond Mine (1932)
3. Maxie Searching for Her Parents; or, The Mystery in Australian Waters (1934)
4. Maxie at Brinksome Hall; or, Strange Adventures with Her Chums (1936)
5. Maxie and Her Adventures in Spain; or, The Rescue of a Royalist (1937)
6. Maxie in the Jungle; or, The Temple of the Incas (1937)
7. Maxie and the Golden Bird; or, The Mysterious Council of Seven (1939)

768. MAY BELLS
author: [unknown]
publisher: McLoughlin Brothers
1. The Three Bears (1870)
2. Three Little Pigs (1880)
3. Jack and the Beanstalk (1870)
4. The Babes in the Wood (1870)
5. Diamonds and Toads (1869)

769. MAY IVERSON
author: Elizabeth Jordan
publisher: Harper
1. May Iverson — Her Book (1904)
2. May Iverson Tackles Life (1912)
3. May Iverson's Career (1914)

770. MEADOW-BROOK GIRLS
author: Janet Aldridge
publisher: Henry Altemus
1. The Meadow-Brook Girls Across Country; or, The Young Pathfinders on a Summer Hike (1913)
2. The Meadow-Brook Girls Under Canvas; or, Fun and Frolic in the Summer Camp (1913)
3. The Meadow-Brook Girls Afloat; or, The Stormy Cruise of the Red Rover (1913)
4. The Meadow-Brook Girls in the Hills; or, The Missing Pilot of the White Mountains (1914)
5. The Meadow-Brook Girls by the Sea; or, The Loss of the Lonesome Bar (1914)
6. The Meadow-Brook Girls on the Tennis Courts; or, Winning Out in the Big Tournament (1914)

771. MEDAL LIBRARY
author: Oliver Optic [pseudonym of William Taylor Adams]
publisher: Street & Smith
1. The Boat Club
3. All Aboard
5. Now or Never
9. Try Again
46. Poor and Proud
56. Nature's Young Nobleman
62. How He Won
79. The Rival Battalions
105. The Young Actor
160. Little by Little
174. Haste and Waste
179. Hope and Have
311. Work and Win
315. Watch and Wait
333. Rich and Humble
339. In School and Out
375. The Sailor Boy

772. MELODY LANE MYSTERY STORIES [see also DANA GIRL MYSTERY STORIES]
author: Lilian C. McNamara Garis
publisher: Grosset and Dunlap
1. The Ghost of Melody Lane (1933)
2. The Wild Warning (1934)
3. Terror at Moaning Cliff (1935)
4. Dragon of the Hills (1936)
5. The Mystery of Stingyman's Alley (1938)
6. The Secret of the Kashmir Shawl (1939)
7. The Hermit of Proud Hill (1940)

773. MERCER BOYS
author: Capwell Wyckoff
publishers: A. L. Burt; World Syndicate
1. The Mercer Boys' Cruise in the Lassie (1929)
2. The Mercer Boys at Woodcrest (1929)
3. The Mercer Boys on a Treasure Hunt
4. The Mercer Boys' Mystery Case (1929)
5. The Mercer Boys on the Beach Patrol (1929)
6. The Mercer Boys in Summer Camp (1929)
7. The Mercer Boys as First Classmen (1930)
8. The Mercer Boys and the Indian Gold (1932)
9. The Mercer Boys with the Air Cadets (1932)
10. The Mercer Boys and the Steamboat Riddle (1933)
11. The Mercer Boys with the Coast Guard (1949)

774. MERILYN
author: Harriet Pyne Grove
publisher: A. L. Burt
1. Merilyn at Camp Meenahga (1927)
2. Merilyn Enters Beechwold (1927)

3. Merilyn Forrester, Co-Ed (1927)
4. Merilyn's New Adventure (1927)
5. Merilyn Tests Loyalty (1927)
6. The "Merry Lynn" Mine (1928)
7. Merilyn's Senior Dreams (1929)
8. Merilyn's Rose Garden (1930)

775. MERRIWEATHER GIRLS
author: Lizette Edholm
publisher: Goldsmith
1. The Merriweather Girls and the Mystery of the Queen's Fan (1932)
2. The Merriweather Girls at Good Old Rockhill (1932)
3. The Merriweather Girls in Quest of Treasure (1932)
4. The Merriweather Girls on Campers' Trail (1932)

776. MERRIWELL [see also FRANK MERRIWELL]
author: Burt L. Standish [pseudonym of Gilbert Patten]
publisher: Street & Smith
1. Frank Merriwell's Schooldays; or, A Tale of School Life at Fardale Academy (1901)
2. Frank Merriwell's Chums; or, Tried and True (1902)
3. Frank Merriwell's Foes; or, An Uphill Fight (1902)
4. Frank Merriwell's Trip West; or, Fun and Frolic on the Prairies (1924)
5. Frank Merriwell Down South; or, Amid Perils and Pleasures (1903)
6. Frank Merriwell's Bravery; or, True to His Chums (1903)
7. Frank Merriwell's Hunting Tour; or, Wild Game in Wild Places (1903)
8. Frank Merriwell in Europe; or, Working His Way Upward (1903)
9. Frank Merriwell at Yale; or, Playing a Square Game (1903)
10. Frank Merriwell's Sports Afield; or, The Record Breaker at Work (1903)
11. Frank Merriwell's Races; or, Won by Pluck (1903)
12. Frank Merriwell's Party; or, Fun and Frolic (1903)
13. Frank Merriwell's Bicycle Tour; or, Westward on Wheels (1903)
14. Frank Merriwell's Courage; or, For His Chum's Sake (1903)
15. Frank Merriwell's Daring; or, The Boy Who Was Unafraid (1903)
16. Frank Merriwell's Alarm; or, Doing His Best (1903)
17. Frank Merriwell's Athletes; or, The Boys Who Won (1903)
18. Frank Merriwell's Skill; or, With Might and Main (1903)
19. Frank Merriwell's Champions; or, All in the Game (1904)
20. Frank Merriwell's Return to Yale; or, Welcomed Home (1904)
21. Frank Merriwell's Secret; or, Right vs. Might (1904)
22. Frank Merriwell's Danger; or, Saved by Nerve (1904)
23. Frank Merriwell's Loyalty; or, True to His Friends (1904)
24. Frank Merriwell in Camp; or, Fun in the Open (1904)
25. Frank Merriwell's Vacation; or, Getting Back to Form (1898)
26. Frank Merriwell's Vacation; or, A Visit to Fardale (1898)
27. Frank Merriwell's Chase; or, Excitement for Everybody (1898)
28. Frank Merriwell in Maine; or, The Lure of "Way Down East" (1898)
29. Frank Merriwell's Struggle; or, Fighting Hard for Honor (1898)
30. Frank Merriwell's First Job; or, Bound to Make Good (1898)
31. Frank Merriwell's Opportunity; or, A Question of Honor (1898)
32. Frank Merriwell's Hard Luck; or, The Fight for Right (1898)
33. Frank Merriwell's Protege; or, A Helping Hand (1898)
34. Frank Merriwell on the Road; or, The Show That Broke Records (1898)
35. Frank Merriwell's Own Company; or, Fun Behind the Footlights (1898)
36. Frank Merriwell's Fame; or, A Hard Won Battle (1898)
37. Frank Merriwell's College Chums; or, A Stand for Clean Living (1898)
38. Frank Merriwell's Problem; or, Between Friendship and Honor (1899)
39. Frank Merriwell's Fortune; or, A Streak of Luck (1899)

40. Frank Merriwell's New Comedian; or, The Rise of a Star (1899)
41. Frank Merriwell's Prosperity; or, Honesty Is Best (1899)
42. Frank Merriwell's Stage Hit; or, The Art of "Making Good" (1899)
43. Frank Merriwell's Great Scheme; or, Head and Team Work (1899)
44. Frank Merriwell in England; or, On His Travels (1899)
45. Frank Merriwell on the Boulevards; or, Fun and Excitement in France (1899)
46. Frank Merriwell's Duel; or, Rough Work (1899)
47. Frank Merriwell's Double Shot; or, The Result of Daring (1899)
48. Frank Merriwell's Base Ball Victories; or, The King of the Diamond (1899)
49. Frank Merriwell's Confidence; or, The Boy Who Held On (1899)
50. Frank Merriwell's Auto; or, Fun and Frolic on Wheels (1899)
51. Frank Merriwell's Fun; or, Putting 'Em Over (1899)
52. [title unknown]
53. Frank Merriwell's Tricks; or, Almost a Magician (1900)
54. Frank Merriwell's Temptation; or, Do Right, Fear Nothing (1900)
55. Frank Merriwell on Top; or, Hard to Beat (1900)
56. Frank Merriwell's Luck; or, A Pinch Hit (1900)
57. Frank Merriwell's Mascot; or, A Lucky Find (1900)
58. Frank Merriwell's Reward; or, Work and Win (1900)
59. Frank Merriwell's Phantom; or, The Mystery Finish (1900)
60. Frank Merriwell's Faith; or, True to a Finish (1900)
61. Frank Merriwell's Victories; or, A Well-Placed Hit (1900)
62. Frank Merriwell's Iron Nerve; or, Never Say Die (1900)
63. Frank Merriwell in Kentucky; or, A Blue-Grass Hero (1900)
64. Frank Merriwell's Power; or, Right Makes Might (1900)
65. Frank Merriwell's Shrewdness; or, Brain and Brawn (1900)
66. Frank Merriwell's Setback; or, True Pluck Welcomes Defeat (1901)
67. Frank Merriwell's Search; or, Seek and Find (1900)
68. Frank Merriwell's Club; or, A Warm Reception (1901)
69. Frank Merriwell's Trust; or Never Say Die (1901)
70. Frank Merriwell's False Friend; or, An Investment in Human Nature (1901)
71. Frank Merriwell's Strong Arm; or, Saving an Enemy (1901)
72. Frank Merriwell as Coach; or, The Effort of His Life (1901)
73. Frank Merriwell's Brother; or, The Greatest Triumph of All (1901)
74. Frank Merriwell's Marvel; or, Dick Merriwell's Jump Ball (1901)
75. Frank Merriwell's Support; or, A Triple Play (1901)
76. Dick Merriwell at Fardale; or, The Wonder of the School (1901)
77. Dick Merriwell's Glory; or, Friends and Foes (1901)
78. Dick Merriwell's Promise; or, True to His Word (1901)
79. Dick Merriwell's Rescue; or, Undaunted — Unafraid (1902)
80. Dick Merriwell's Narrow Escape; or, Playing the Game (1902)
81. Dick Merriwell's Racket; or, The Boy Who Would Not Stoop (1902)
82. Dick Merriwell's Revenge; or, Coals of Fire (1902)
83. Dick Merriwell's Ruse; or, A Trap for the Enemy (1902)
84. Dick Merriwell's Delivery; or, Putting It Over (1902)
85. Dick Merriwell's Wonders; or, Good for a Homer (1902)
86. Frank Merriwell's Honor; or, The Fellow Who Cut Corners (1902)
87. Dick Merriwell's Diamond; or, A Game Worth Playing (1902)
88. Frank Merriwell's Winners; or, Out to Clean Up (1902)
89. Dick Merriwell's Dash; or, Fit as a Fiddle (1902)
90. Dick Merriwell's Ability; or, Head-work Wins (1902)
91. Dick Merriwell's Trap; or, The Chap Who Bungled (1902)

144. Dick Merriwell's Joke; or, A Close Shave (1907)
145. Frank Merriwell's Talisman; or, Was It Luck (1907)
146. Frank Merriwell's Horse; or, A Friend in Need (1907)
147. Dick Merriwell's Regret; or, Never Too Late (1907)
148. Dick Merriwell's Magnetism; or, The Boy Who Kept Friends (1907)
149. Dick Merriwell's Backers; or, Well Worth Fighting For (1907)
150. Dick Merriwell's Best Work; or, Clear Head and Stout Heart (1907)
151. Dick Merriwell's Distrust; or, The Boy Who Had to Be Watched (1907)
152. Dick Merriwell's Debt; or, Paid in Like Coin (1907)
153. Dick Merriwell's Mastery; or, The Boy They Could Not Down (1907)
154. Dick Merriwell Adrift; or, A Hard Lesson Well Learned (1907)
155. Frank Merriwell's Worst Boy; or, The Power of a Good Example (1907)
156. Dick Merriwell's Close Call; or, Grit Always Wins (1907)
157. Frank Merriwell's Air Voyage; or, Heroes Undaunted (1907)
158. Dick Merriwell's Black Star; or, The Way to Success (1907)
159. Frank Merriwell in Wall Street; or, Among the Bulls and Bears (1908)
160. Frank Merriwell Facing His Foes; or, Right Makes Might (1908)
161. Dick Merriwell's Stanchness; or, Was It Just Luck? (1908)
162. Frank Merriwell's Hard Case; or, Trying to Be Square (1908)
163. Dick Merriwell's Stand; or, Against Great Temptation (1908)
164. Dick Merriwell Doubted; or, A Fight for Vindication (1908)
165. Frank Merriwell's Steadying Hand; or, The Puzzle of the Weaker Boy (1908)
166. Dick Merriwell's Example; or, Strong and Able (1908)
167. Dick Merriwell in the Wilds; or, Clear Brain and Sharp Eye (1908)
168. Frank Merriwell's Ranch; or, A Struggle Worth While (1908)
169. Dick Merriwell's Way; or, Doing His Best (1908)
170. Frank Merriwell's Lesson; or, The Boy They Could Not Mislead (1908)
171. Dick Merriwell's Reputation; or, Playing to Win (1908)
172. Frank Merriwell's Encouragement; or, The Boy Who Needed Help (1909)
173. Dick Merriwell's Honors; or, Grasping His Opportunities (1909)
174. Frank Merriwell's Wizard; or, Shrewd Brain and Skillful Hand (1909)
175. Dick Merriwell's Race; or, Taking a Slender Chance (1909)
176. Dick Merriwell's Star Play; or, Putting One Over (1909)
177. Frank Merriwell at Phantom Lake; or, At War with the Roughnecks (1909)
178. Dick Merriwell, a Winner; or, The Taming of a "Bad One" (1909)
179. Dick Merriwell at the County Fair; or, Playing the Game (1909)
180. Frank Merriwell's Gift; or, The Power of a Good Example (1910)
181. Dick Merriwell's Power; or, Hold 'Em, Yale! (1909)
182. Frank Merriwell in Peru; or, In the Land of the Incas (1910)
183. Frank Merriwell's Long Chance; or, The Rescue of June Arlington (1910)
184. Frank Merriwell's Old Form; or, On the Slab in the West (1910)
185. Frank Merriwell's Treasure Hunt; or, The Search for Buried Gold (1910)
186. Dick Merriwell Game to the Last; or, Winning from the Bench (1910)
187. Dick Merriwell, Motor King; or, The Wizard of the Road (1910)
188. Dick Merriwell's Tussle; or, The Mystery of Mermaid Island (1910)
189. Dick Merriwell's Aero Dash; or, Winning Above the Clouds (1910)
190. Dick Merriwell's Intuition; or, The Man from Nowhere (1910)
191. Dick Merriwell's Placer Find; or, Game to the Finish (1910)
192. Dick Merriwell's Fighting Chance; or, The Split in the Varsity (1910)
193. Frank Merriwell's Tact; or, The Making of a New Boy (1910)

241. Dick Merriwell's Charm; or, When Disaster Threatened (1914)
242. Frank Merriwell, Jr.'s Fardale Visit; or, Back to Old Friends and Scenes (1914)
243. Frank Merriwell in the Yellowstone; or, Human and Natural Wonders (1915)
244. Frank Merriwell, Jr.'s Yacht Victory; or, Clear Eye and Steady Hand (1915)
245. Frank Merriwell, Jr. and the Talking Head; or, A Mystery Neatly Solved (1915)

777. MERRYVALE BOYS
author: Alice Hale Burnett
publisher: New York Book
1–2. [titles unknown]
3. Picnic Day at Merryvale (1916)
4. Christmas Holidays at Merryvale (1919)

778. MERRYVALE GIRLS
author: Alice Hale Burnett
publisher: New York Book Company
1. Beth's Garden Party (1916)
2. A Day at the County Fair (1916)
3. Geraldine's Birthday Surprise (1916)
4. Mary Entertains the Sewing Club (1916)
5. The Merryvale Girls at the Seaside
6. The Merryvale Girls in the Country

779. MEXICAN WAR
author: Ralph Bonehill [pseudonym of Edward Stratemeyer]
publishers: Dana Estes; Lothrop, Lee & Shepard
1. For the Liberty of Texas (1900)
2. With Taylor on the Rio Grande (1901)
3. Under Scott in Mexico (1902)

780. MIDLAND
author: George Wilbur Peck
publisher: Morrill, Higgins
1. [title unknown]
2. How Private Geo. W. Peck Put Down the Rebellion; or, The Young Experiences of a Raw Recruit (1893)

781. MILDRED
author: Martha Finley [pseudonym of Martha Farquharson]
publisher: A. L. Burt
1. Mildred Keith
2. Mildred at Roselands
3. Mildred and Elsie
4. Mildred's Married Life
5. Mildred at Home

782. MIMI
author: Anne Pence Davis
publisher: Goldsmith
1. Mimi at Camp (1935)
2. Mimi's Houseparty (1936)
3. Mimi at Sheridan School

783. MINUTE BOYS
authors: Edward Stratemeyer [1,2]; James Otis [3–11] [pseudonym of James Otis Kaler]
illustrators: L.J. Bridgman (7,8,10,11); J.W.F. Kennedy (9); A. Burham Shute (3–5)
publishers: Estes & Lauriat; Dana Estes; L. C. Page
1. The Minute Boys of Lexington (1898)
2. The Minute Boys of Bunker Hill (1899)
3. The Minute Boys of the Green Mountains (1904)
4. The Minute Boys of the Mohawk Valley (1905)
5. The Minute Boys of the Wyoming Valley (1906)
6. The Minute Boys of South Carolina; A Story of "How We Boys Aided Marion, the Swamp Fox," as Told by Rufus Randolph (1907)
7. The Minute Boys of Long Island; A Story of New York in 1776 as Told by Ephraim Lyttle (1908)
8. The Minute Boys of New York City, Written by Adam Skidmore (1909)
9. The Minute Boys of Boston (1910)
10. The Minute Boys of Philadelphia (1911)
11. The Minute Boys of Yorktown (1912)

784. MISS BILLY
author: Eleanor Hodgman Porter
publisher: L. C. Page
1. Miss Billy (1911)
2. Miss Billy Married (1911)
3. Miss Billy's Decision (1912)

785. MISS BOO

author: Margaret Lee Rinbeck
publishers: Appleton-Century (1);
    Houghton Mifflin (2)
1. Our Miss Boo (1942)
2. Miss Boo Is Sixteen (1957)

786. MISS MARY MERRY-HEART'S SERIES

author: [unknown]
publishers: McLoughlin Brothers; Dean &
    Son
1. Jack the Giant Killer (1856)
2. History of Austin Brent the Little Midshipman (1856)
3. Robin Hood and Little John (1856)
4. The Story of Little Red Riding Hood (1860)

787. MISS MINERVA

author: Emma Speed Sampson
publisher: Reilly & Lee
1. Billy and the Major (1918)
2. Miss Minerva's Baby (1920)
3. Miss Minerva on the Old Plantation (1923)
4. Miss Minerva Broadcasts Billy (1925)
5. Miss Minerva's Scallywags (1927)
6. Miss Minerva's Neighbors (1929)
7. Miss Minerva Goin' Places (1931)
8. Miss Minerva's Cook Book (1931)
9. Miss Minerva's Mystery (1933)
10. Miss Minerva's Problem (1936)
11. Miss Minerva's Vacation (1939)

788. MISS PAT

author: Mary Pemberton Ginther
publisher: Winston
1. Miss Pat and Her Sisters (1915)
2. Miss Pat at School (1915)
3. Miss Pat in the Old World (1915)
4. Miss Pat and Company, Limited (1916)
5. Miss Pat's Holidays at Greycroft (1916)
6. Miss Pat with the Russian Army (1916)
7. Miss Pat at Artemis Lodge
8. Miss Pat's Problem
9. Miss Pat in Buenos Ayres (1917)
10. Miss Pat's Career (1917)
11. Miss Pat's Great Idea

789. MISS PICKERELL

authors: Ellen MacGregor [1–9]; Dora
    Pantell [5–9]
publisher: Whittlesey
1. Miss Pickerell Goes to Mars (1951)
2. Miss Pickerell and the Geiger Counter (1953)
3. Miss Pickerell Goes Undersea (1953)
4. Miss Pickerell Goes to the Arctic (1954)
5. Miss Pickerell on the Moon (1965)
6. Miss Pickerell Goes on a Dig (1966)
7. Miss Pickerell Harvests the Sea (1968)
8. Miss Pickerell and the Weather Satellite (1971)
9. Miss Pickerell Meets Mr. H.U.M. (1974)
10. Miss Pickerell to the Earthquake Rescue (1977)

790. MODERN BOYS' ADVENTURE

author: George Ernest Rochester
publisher: C.H. Daniels
1. Lair of the Vampire (1949)

791. MOFFATS

author: Eleanor Estes
publisher: Harcourt Brace
1. The Moffats (1941)
2. The Middle Moffat (1942)
3. Rufus Moffat (1943)

792. MOLLY BROWN

author: Nell Speed
publisher: Hurst
1. Molly Brown's Freshman Days (1912)
2. Molly Brown's Sophomore Days (1912)
3. Molly Brown's Junior Days (1912)
4. Molly Brown's Senior Days (1913)
5. Molly Brown's Post-Graduate Days (1914)
6. Molly Brown's Orchard Home (1914)
7. Molly Brown of Kentucky (1917)
8. Molly Brown's College Friends (1921)

793. MOTHER HUBBARD

author: [unknown]
publisher: Donohue Menneneberry
1. Cock Robin and Jenny Wren (1901)

794. MOTHER WEST WIND STORIES

author: Thornton W. Burgess
publisher: Little, Brown
1. Old Mother West Wind
2. Mother West Wind's Children
3. Mother West Wind's Animal Friends
4. Mother West Wind's Neighbors
5. Mother West Wind "Why" Stories
6. Mother West Wind "How" Stories
7. Mother West Wind "When" Stories
8. Mother West Wind "Where" Stories

795. MOTHER'S SERIES

author: [unknown]
publisher: McLaughlin Brothers
1. The Little Sisters (1860)

796. MOTION PICTURE BOYS [see also MOTION PICTURE COMRADES]

author: Elmer Tracey Barnes
publisher: Saalfield
1. The Moving Picture Comrades' Great Venture; or, On the Road with the "Big Round-Top" (1917)
2. The Moving Picture Comrades in African Jungles; or, Camera Boys in Wild Animal Land (1917)
3. The Moving Picture Comrades Producing a Success; or, Featuring a Sensation (1917)

797. MOTION PICTURE CHUMS [see also MOVIE BOYS and MOVING PICTURE BOYS]

author: Victor Appleton [pseudonym of Stratemeyer Syndicate]
publisher: Grosset & Dunlap
1. The Motion Picture Chums' First Venture; or, Opening a Photo Playhouse in Fairlands (1913)
2. The Motion Picture Chums at Seaside Park; or, The Rival Photo Theatres of the Boardwalk (1913)
3. The Motion Picture Chums on Broadway; or, The Mystery of the Missing Cash Box (1914)
4. The Motion Picture Chums' Outdoor Exhibition; or, The Film That Solved a Mystery (1914)
5. The Motion Picture Chums' New Idea; or, The First Educational Photo Playhouse (1914)
6. The Motion Picture Chums at the Fair; or, The Greatest Film Ever Exhibited (1915)
7. The Motion Picture Chums' War Spectacle; or, The Film That Won the Prize (1916)

798. MOTION PICTURE COMRADES [see also MOTION PICTURE BOYS]

author: Elmer Tracey Barnes [pseudonym of Stratemeyer Syndicate]
illustrator: Lester
publishers: New York Book Company; Saalfield
1. The Motion Picture Comrades' Great Venture; or, On the Road with the "Big Round-Top" (1917)
2. The Motion Picture Comrades in African Jungles; or, Camera Boys in Wild Animal Land (1917)
3. The Motion Picture Comrades Along the Orinoco; or, Facing Perils in the Tropics (1917)
4. The Motion Picture Comrades Aboard a Submarine; or, Searching for Treasure Under the Sea (1917)
5. The Motion Picture Comrades Producing a Success; or, Featuring a Sensation (1917)

799. MOTOR BOAT BOYS

author: Louis Arundel
publisher: M. A. Donohue
1. Motor Boat Boys' Cruise Down the Mississippi; or, The Dash for Dixie [alternate title: Motor Boat Boys' Mississippi Cruise] (1910)
2. Motor Boat Boys on the St. Lawrence; or, Solving the Mystery of the Thousand Islands (1912) [also subtitled: Adventures Among the Thousand Islands]
3. Motor Boat Boys on the Great Lakes; or, Exploring the Mystic Isle of Mackinac (1912)
4. Motor Boat Boys Down the Coast; or, Through Storm and Stress to Florida (1913)

5. Motor Boat Boys Among the Florida Keys; or, The Struggle for the leadership (1913)
6. Motor Boat Boys' River Chase; or, Six Chums Afloat and Ashore (1914)
7. Motor Boat Boys Down the Danube; or, Four Chums Abroad (1915)

800. MOTOR BOAT CLUB

author: Harrie Irving Hancock
publisher: Henry Altemus
1. The Motor Boat Club of the Kennebec; or, The Secret of Smugglers' Island (1909)
2. The Motor Boat Club at Nantucket; or, The Mystery of the Dunstan Heir (1909)
3. The Motor Boat Club off Long Island; or, A Daring Marine Game at Racing Speed (1909)
4. The Motor Boat Club and the Wireless; or, The Dot, Dash and Dare Cruise (1909)
5. The Motor Boat Club in Florida; or, Laying the Ghost of Alligator Swamp (1909)
6. The Motor Boat Club at the Golden Gate; or, A Thrilling Capture in the Great Fog (1909)
7. The Motor Boat Club on the Great Lakes; or, The "Flying Dutchman" of the Big Fresh Water (1912)

801. MOTOR BOYS

author: Clarence Young [pseudonym of Stratemeyer Syndicate]
illustrators: Charles Nuttal [1–9]; R. Richards [10–15]; Walter S. Rogers [16–17, 22]; R. Emmett Owen [18–21]
publisher: Cupples & Leon
series 1:
1. The Motor Boys; or, Chums Through Thick and Thin (1906)
2. The Motor Boys Overland; or, A Long Trip for Fun and Fortune (1906)
3. The Motor Boys in Mexico; or, The Secret of the Buried City (1906)
4. The Motor Boys Across the Plains; or, The Hermit of Lost Lake (1907)
5. The Motor Boys Afloat; or, The Stirring Cruise of the Dartaway (1908)
6. The Motor Boys on the Atlantic; or,

The Mystery of the Lighthouse (1908)
7. The Motor Boys in Strange Waters; or, Lost in a Floating Forest (1909)
8. The Motor Boys on the Pacific; or, The Young Derelict Hunters (1909)
9. The Motor Boys in the Clouds; or, A Trip for Fame and Fortune (1910)
10. The Motor Boys Over the Rockies; or, A Mystery of the Air (1911)
11. The Motor Boys Over the Ocean; or, A Marvelous Rescue in Mid-Air (1911)
12. The Motor Boys on the Wing; or, Seeking the Airship Treasure (1912)
13. The Motor Boys After a Fortune; or, The Hut on Snake Island (1912)
14. The Motor Boys on the Border; or, Sixty Nuggets of Gold (1913)
15. The Motor Boys Under the Sea; or, From Airship to Submarine (1914)
16. The Motor Boys on Road and River; or, Racing to Save a Life (1915)
17. The Motor Boys in the Army; or, Ned, Bob and Jerry as Volunteers (1918) [alternate title: Ned, Bob and Jerry as Volunteers; or, The Motor Boys in the Army]
18. The Motor Boys Bound for Home; or, Ned, Bob and Jerry on the Wrecked Troopship (1920) [alternate title: Ned, Bob and Jerry on the Wrecked Troopship; or, The Motor Boys Bound for Home]
19. The Motor Boys on Thunder Mountain; or, The Treasure Chest of Blue Rock (1924)
series 2:
1. The Motor Boys as Freshmen; or, Ned, Bob and Jerry at Boxwood Hall (1916) [alternate title: Ned, Bob and Jerry at Boxwood Hall; or, The Motor Boys as Freshmen]
2. The Motor Boys Among the Cowboys; or, Ned, Bob and Jerry on a Ranch (1917) [alternate title: Ned, Bob and Jerry on a Ranch; or, The Motor Boys Among the Cowboys]
3. [title unknown]
4. The Motor Boys on the Firing Line; or, Ned, Bob and Jerry Fighting for Uncle Sam (1919) [alternate title: Ned, Bob and Jerry Fighting for

Uncle Sam; or, The Motor Boys on the Firing Line]

802. MOTOR CYCLE [see also MOTORCYCLE CHUMS]

author: Lt. Howard Payson [pseudonym of John Henry Goldfrap]
illustrator: Charles L. Wrenn
publisher: Hurst
1. The Motor Cycle Chums Around the World (1912)
2. The Motor Cycle Chums of the Northwest Patrol (1912)
3. The Motor Cycle Chums in the Gold Fields (1912)
4. The Motor Cycle Chums' Whirlwind Tour (1913)
5. The Motor Cycle Chums South of the Equator (1914)
6. The Motor Cycle Chums Through Historic America (1915)

803. MOTOR GIRLS

author: Margaret Penrose [pseudonym of Stratemeyer Syndicate]
illustrators: G.M. Kaiser [1]; Charles Nuttall [2]; Walter S. Richards [7–9]; R. Emmett Owens [10]
publisher: Cupples & Leon
1. The Motor Girls; or, A Mystery of the Road (1910)
2. The Motor Girls on a Tour; or, Keeping a Strange Promise (1910)
3. The Motor Girls at Lookout Beach; or, In Quest of the Runaways (1911)
4. The Motor Girls Through New England; or, Held by the Gypsies (1911)
5. The Motor Girls on Cedar Lake; or, The Hermit of Fern Island (1912)
6. The Motor Girls on the Coast; or, The Waif from the Sea (1913)
7. The Motor Girls on Crystal Bay; or, The Secret of the Red Oar (1914)
8. The Motor Girls on Waters Blue; or, The Strange Cruise of the Tartar (1915)
9. The Motor Girls at Camp Surprise; or, The Cave in the Mountains (1916)
10. The Motor Girls in the Mountains; or, The Gypsy Girl's Secret (1917)

804. MOTOR MAIDS

author: Katherine Stokes
illustrator: Charles L. Wrenn
publisher: M. A. Donohue
1. The Motor Maids' School Days (1911)
2. The Motor Maids by Palm and Pine (1911)
3. The Motor Maids by Rose, Shamrock and Thistle (1912)
4. The Motor Maids in Fair Japan (1913)
5. The Motor Maids at Sunrise Camp (1914)
6. The Motor Maids Across the Continent (1917)

805. MOTOR POWER

author: Donald Grayson
publisher: David McKay
1. Bob Steele's Motorcycle; or, True to His Friends (1908)
2. Bob Steele on High Gear; or, A Prize Worth Winning (1908)
3. Bob Steele From Auto to Airship; or, A Strange Adventure in the Air (1908)
4. Bob Steele Afloat in the Clouds; or, The Boy Who Owned an Airship (1908)
5. Bob Steele's Submarine Cruise; or, Captain Nemo's Friend (1908)
6. Bob Steele in Strange Waters; or, Aboard a Strange Craft (1908)
7. Bob Steele's Motor Boat: or, The Fellow They Could Not Beat (1908)
8. Bob Steele's Winning Race; or, Fearless and True (1908)
9. Bob Steele's New Aeroplane; or, The Bird Man (1908)
10. Bob Steele's Last Flight; or, The Sale of the Comet (1908)

806. MOTOR RANGERS

author: Marvin West [pseudonym of John Henry Goldfrap]
illustrator: Charles L. Wrenn
publisher: Hurst
1. The Motor Rangers' Lost Mine (1911)
2. The Motor Rangers Through the Sierras (1911)
3. The Motor Rangers on Blue Water; or, The Secret of the Derelict (1911)
4. The Motor Rangers' Cloud Cruiser (1912)
5. The Motor Rangers' Wireless Station (1913)

6. The Motor Rangers Touring for the Trophy (1913)

807. MOTORCYCLE CHUMS [see also MOTOR CYCLE]

author: Andrew Carey Lincoln
publisher: M. A. Donohue

1. Motorcycle Chums in New England; or, The Mt. Holyoke Adventure (1912)
2. Motorcycle Chums in the Land of the Sky; or, Thrilling Adventures on the Carolina Border (1912)
3. Motorcycle Chums in Yellowstone Park; or, Lending a Helping Hand (1913)
4. Motorcycle Chums on the Sante Fe Trail; or, The key to the Indian Treasure Cave (1912) [alternate subtitle: The Key to the Treasure Box]
5. Motorcycle Chums in the Adirondacks; or, The Search for the Lost Pacemaker (1913)
6. Motorcycle Chums Stormbound; or, The Strange Adventures of a Road Chase (1914)

MOUNTAIN BOYS see PHIL BRADLEY

808. MOUNTAIN GIRL

author: Genevieve May Fox
publisher: Little, Brown

1. The Mountain Girl (1932)
2. The Mountain Girl Comes Home (1934)
3. Lona of Hollybush Creek (1935)

809. MOUNTAIN PONY

author: Henry V. Larom
publisher: Whittlesey House

1. Mountain Pony; A Story of the Wyoming Rockies (1946)
2. Mountain Pony and the Pinto Colt (1947)

810. MOVIE BOYS

author: Victor Appleton [pseudonym of Stratemeyer Syndicate]
publisher: Garden City
NOTE: All these books were originally published by Grosset and Dunlap with varying titles in The Moving Picture Boys series and the Motion Picture Chums series.

1. The Movie Boys on Call; or, Filming the Perils of a Great City (1926) [alternate title: The Moving Picture Boys; or, The Perils of a Great City Depicted]
2. The Movie Boys in the Wild West; or, Stirring Days Among the Cowboys and Indians (1926) [alternate title: The Moving Picture Boys in the West; or, Taking Scenes Among the Cowboys and Indians]
3. The Movie Boys and the Wreckers; or, Facing the Perils of the Deep (1926) [alternate title: The Moving Picture Boys on the Coast; or, Showing the Perils of the Deep]
4. The Movie Boys in the Jungle; or, Lively Times Among the Wild Beasts (1926) [alternate title: The Moving Picture Boys in the Jungle; or, Stirring Times Among the Wild Animals]
5. The Movie Boys in Earthquake Land; or, Filming Pictures Amid Strange Perils (1926) [alternate title: The Moving Picture Boys in Earthquake Land; or, Working Amid Many Perils]
6. The Movie Boys and the Flood; or, Perilous Days on the Mighty Mississippi (1926) [alternate title: The Moving Picture Boys and the Flood; or, Perilous Days on the Mississippi]
7. The Movie Boys in Peril; or, Strenuous Days Along the Panama Canal (1926) [alternate title: The Moving Picture Boys at Panama; or, Stirring Adventures Along the Great Canal]
8. The Movie Boys Under Sail; or, The Treasure of the Lost Ship (1926) [alternate title: The Moving Picture Boys Under the Sea; or, The Treasure of the Lost Ship]
9. The Movie Boys Under Fire; or, The Search for the Stolen Film (1926) [alternate title: The Moving Picture Boys on the War Front; or, The Hunt for the Stolen Army Film]
10. The Movie Boys Under Uncle Sam; or, Taking Pictures for the Army (1926) [alternate title: The Moving Picture Boys on French Battlefields; or, Taking Pictures for the U.S. Army]
11. The Movie Boys' First Showhouse; or,

Fighting for a Foothold in Fairlands (1926) [alternate title: The Motion Picture Chums' First Venture; or, Opening a Photo Playhouse in Fairlands]

12. The Movie Boys at Seaside Park; or, The Rival Photo Houses of the Boardwalk (1926) [alternate title: The Motion Picture Chums at Seaside Park; or, The Rival Photo Theatres of the Boardwalk]

13. The Movie Boys on Broadway; or, The Mystery of the Missing Cash Box (1926) [alternate title: The Motion Picture Chums on Broadway; or, the Mystery of the Missing Cash Box]

14. The Movie Boys' Outdoor Exhibition; or, The Film that Solved a Mystery (1927) [alternate title: The Motion Picture Chums' Outdoor Exhibition; or, The Film That Solved a Mystery]

811. MOVING PICTURE BOYS
[see also MOTION PICTURE CHUMS and MOVIE BOYS]

author: Victor Appleton [pseudonym of Stratemeyer Syndicate]
illustrators: Walter S. Rogers [1–8, 14, 15]; R. Emmett Owen [9, 10]; Dick Richards [11–13]
publisher: Grosset & Dunlap

1. The Moving Picture Boys; or, The Perils of a Great City Depicted (1913)
2. The Moving Picture Boys in the West; or, Taking Scenes Among the Cowboys and Indians (1913)
3. The Moving Picture Boys on the Coast; or, Showing Up the Perils of the Deep (1913)
4. The Moving Picture Boys in the Jungle; or, Stirring Times Among the Wild Animals (1913)
5. The Moving Picture Boys in Earthquake Land; or, Working Amid Many Perils (1913)
6. The Moving Picture Boys and the Flood; or, Perilous Days on the Mississippi (1914)
7. The Moving Picture Boys at Panama; or, Stirring Adventures Along the Great Canal (1915)
8. The Moving Picture Boys Under the Sea; or, The Treasure of the Lost Ship (1916)
9. The Moving Picture Boys on the War Front; or, The Hunt for the Stolen Army Film (1918)
10. The Moving Picture Boys on French Battlefields; or, Taking Pictures for the U.S. Army (1919)
11. The Moving Picture Boys' First Showhouse; or, Opening Up for Business in Fairlands (1921)
12. The Moving Picture Boys at Seaside Park; or, The Rival Photo Theatres of the Boardwalk (1921)
13. The Moving Picture Boys on Broadway; or, The Mystery of the Missing Cash Box (1921)
14. The Moving Picture Boys' Outdoor Exhibition; or, The Film That Solved a Mystery (1922)
15. The Moving Picture Boys' New Idea; or, The First Educational Photo Playhouse (1922)

812. MOVING PICTURE GIRLS

author: Laura Lee Hope [pseudonym of the Stratemeyer Syndicate]
illustrator: Walter S. Rogers
publishers: Grosset & Dunlap; Saalfield

1. The Moving Picture Girls; or, First Appearances in Photo Dramas (1914)
2. The Moving Picture Girls at Oak Farm; or, Queer Happenings While Taking Rural Plays (1914)
3. The Moving Picture Girls Snowbound; or, The Proof on the Film (1914)
4. The Moving Picture Girls Under the Palms; or, Lost in the Wilds of Florida (1914)
5. The Moving Picture Girls at Rocky Ranch; or, Great Days Among the Cowboys (1914)
6. The Moving Picture Girls at Sea; or, A Pictured Shipwreck that Became Real (1915)
7. The Moving Picture Girls in War Plays; or, The Sham Battles at Oak Farm (1916)

813. MRS. ELLIOTT'S SERIES

author: Mary Elliott
publisher: McLoughlin Brothers

1. Beauty but Skin Deep (1850)

2. The Lost Chicken (1856)
3. The Little Mimic (1864)

814. MRS. LESLIE'S BOOKS FOR LITTLE CHILDREN [alternate title: LITTLE FRANKIE]

author: Madeline Leslie
publishers: Crosby and Ainsworth; Woolworth, Ainsworth; Crosby, Nichols, Lee
1. Little Frankie and His Mother (1860)
2. Little Frankie at His Plays (1860)
3. Little Frankie and His Cousin (1860)
4. Little Frankie and His Father (1860)
5. Little Frankie on a Journey (1860)
6. Little Frankie at School (1860)

815. MRS. LESLIE'S JUVENILE SERIES

author: Madeline Leslie
publisher: Shepard, Clark & Brown
1. Jack the Chimney Sweeper; and Other Stories for Children (1859)
2. Play and Study (1858)
3. Howard and His Teacher; The Sister's Influence and Other Stories (1858)
4. Little Agnes; or, The Rich Poor and the Poor Rich (1859)
5. I'll Try; or, The Young Housekeeper (1859)
6. Art and Artlessness (1864)

MRS. LESLIE'S PEARL SERIES see PEARL

816. MRS. MEIGS

author: Elizabeth Frances Corbett
publishers: David Appleton [1]; Appleton-Century [2–5]
1. The Young Mrs. Meigs (1931)
2. A Nice Long Evening (1933)
3. Mrs. Meigs and Mr. Cunningham (1936)
4. Mr and Mrs. Meigs (1940)
5. Excuse Me, Mrs. Meigs (1943)

817. MRS. PIGGLE-WIGGLE

author: Betty MacDonald
publisher: J. B. Lippincott
1. Mrs. Piggle-Wiggle (1947)
2. Mrs. Piggle-Wiggle's Magic (1947)
3. Mrs. Piggle-Wiggle's Farm (1954)
4. Hello, Mrs. Piggle-Wiggle (1957)

818. MUNSEY'S POPULAR SERIES

author: Oliver Optic [pseudonym of William Taylor Adams]
publisher: F. A. Munsey
382. The Yankee Middy
387. Brave Old Salt
393. The Starry Flag
397. Breaking Away
405. Seek and Find
412. Freaks of Fortune
418. Make or Break
424. Down the River
430. Through by Daylight
435. Lightning Express
441. On Time
447. Switch Off
453. Brake Up
460. Bear and Forbear
523. Building Himself Up
528. Lyon Hart's Heroism
534. Louis Chiswick's Mission
540. Royal Tarr's Pluck
546. The Professor's Son
552. Striving for His Own
559. Making a Man of Himself
565. Every Inch a Boy
571. His Own Helper
577. Honest Kit Dunstable
583. The Young Pilot
589. The Cruise of the "Dandy"
595. Three Young Silver Kings
603. The Young Hermit of Lake Minnetonka
615. The Prisoners of the Cave
627. Among the Missing
634. Always in Luck

819. MURDER REVISITED

author: Hilda Frances Margaret Prescott
publisher: Macmillan
1–4. [titles unknown]
5. Dead and Not Buried (1938)

820. MUSEUM

author: Francis Rolt-Wheeler
publisher: Lothrop, Lee & Shepard
1. The Monster Hunters (1916)
2. The Polar Hunters (1917)
3. The Aztec Hunters (1918)
4. The Wreck Hunters (1922)
5. The Sahara Hunters (1923)

6. The Gem Hunters (1924)
7. Hunters of the Ocean Depths
8. The News Hunters (1926)
9. The Tusk Hunters (1927)

821. MUSKET BOYS [alternative title: REVOLUTIONARY SERIES]
author: George A. Warren
publishers: Cupples & Leon; Gold
1. The Musket Boys of Old Boston; or, The First Blow for Liberty (1909)
2. The Musket Boys Under Washington; or, The Tories of Old New York
3. The Musket Boys on the Delaware; or, A Stirring Victory at Trenton (1910)

822. MYSTERY AND ADVENTURE
author: Hugh McAlister
publisher: Saalfield
1. The Mystery at Roaring Brook Farm (1929)
2. Flaming River
3. Conqueror of the High Road
4. Stand By
5. A Viking of the Sky
6. The Flight of the Silver Ship
7. Steve Holworth
8. Sea Gold (1931)

823. MYSTERY AND ADVENTURE SERIES FOR GIRLS [see also MAXIE; BETTY GORDON; JANE ALLEN COLLEGE SERIES]
authors: Edith Bancroft [1]; Alice B. Emerson [2]; Grace May North [pseudonym of Carol Norton] [3, 4, 12]; Harriet Pyne Grove [5, 6, 8–10]; Carol Norton [7]; Elsie Bell Gardner [11]
publisher: A.L. Burt
1. Jane Allen of the Sub-Team (1917)
2. Betty Gordon at Bramble Farm; or, The Mystery of a Nobody (1920)
3. The Seven Sleuths' Club (1928)
4. Bobs, A Girl Detective (1928)
5. The Secret of Steeple Rocks (1928)
6. The Phantom Treasure (1928)
7. The Phantom Yacht (1928)
8. The Strange Likeness (1929)
9. The Mystery of the Sandalwood Boxes (1929)
10. The S.P. Mystery (1930)

11. Maxie, An Adorable Girl; or, Her Adventures in the British West Indies (1932)
12. The Phantom Town (1933)

824. MYSTERY BOYS I
author: Howard Roger Garis
illustrator: H. G. Nicholas
publisher: Milton Bradley
1. Mystery Boys in Ghost Canyon (1930)
2. Mystery Boys at Round Lake (1931)

825. MYSTERY BOYS II
author: Van Powell [pseudonym of A. Van Buren]
publishers: A. L. Burt; World Syndicate
1. The Mystery Boys and the Inca Gold (1931)
2. The Mystery Boys and Captain Kidd's Message (1931)
3. The Mystery Boys and the Secret of the Golden Sun (1931)
4. The Mystery Boys and the Chinese Jewels (1931)
5. The Mystery Boys and the Hindu Treasure (1931)

826. MYSTERY HUNTERS
author: Capwell Wyckoff
publisher: A. L. Burt
1. The Mystery Hunters at the Haunted Lodge (1934)
2. The Mystery Hunters at the Old Frontier
3. The Mystery Hunters at Lakeside Camp
4. The Mystery Hunters on Special Detail (1936)

827. MYSTERY STORIES FOR BOYS
author: Roy J. Snell
publisher: Reilly & Lee
1. Triple Spies (1922)
2. Lost in the Air
3. Panther Eye
4. The Crimson Flash
5. White Fire
6. The Black Schooner
7. The Hidden Trail
8. The Firebug
9. The Red Lure

10. Forbidden Cargoes
11. Johnny Longbow
12. The Rope of Gold
13. The Arrow of Fire
14. The Gray Ghost
15. Riddle of the Storm
16. The Galloping Ghost
17. Whispers at Dawn
18. Mystery Wings
19. Red Dynamite
20. Seal of Secrecy
21. The Shadow Passes
22. The Sign of the Green Arrow (1939)

828. NAN
author: Myra Sawyer Hamlin
publishers: Roberts [1–2]; Little, Brown [3–5]
1. Nan at Camp Chicopee; or, Nan's Summer with the Boys (1896)
2. Nan in the City; or, Nan's Winter with the Girls (1897)
3. Nan's Chicopee Children (1900)
4. Catherine's Proxy (1902)
5. Persis Putnam's Treasure; or, Nan's Girls at Camp Chicopina (1908)

829. NAN SHERWOOD
author: Annie Roe Carr [pseudonym of the Stratemeyer Syndicate]
publisher: Sully
1. Nan Sherwood at Lakeview Hall; or, The Mystery of the Haunted Boathouse (1916)
2. Nan Sherwood at Pine Camp; or, The Old Lumberman's Secret (1916)
3. Nan Sherwood's Winter Holidays; or, Rescuing the Runaways (1916)
4. Nan Sherwood at Rose Ranch; or, The Old Mexican's Treasure (1919)
5. Nan Sherwood at Palm Breach; or, Strange Adventures Among the Orange Groves (1921)
6. Nan Sherwood's Summer Holidays
7. Nan Sherwood on the Mexican Border (1937)

830. NANCY I
author: Dorita Fairlie Bruce
publisher: Oxford University Press
1. The Boarding School Girl (1925)
2. The New Girl and Nancy (1926)

3. Nancy to the Rescue (1927)
4. Nancy at St. Bride's (1933)
5. Nancy in the Sixth (1935)
6. Nancy Returns to St. Bride's (1938)
7. Nancy Calls the Tune (1944)

831. NANCY II
author: Jean Henry Large
publisher: David Appleton
1. Nancy Goes Girl Scouting (1930)
2. Nancy's Lone Girl Scouts (1930)
3. Nancy Goes Camping (1931)

832. NANCY III
author: Mildred Wasson
publisher: Harper
1. Nancy, a Story of the Younger Set (1932)
2. Miss Nancy Prentiss (1934)
3. Nancy Sails (1936)
4. Bill and Nancy (1940)

833. NANCY AND NICK
author: Olive Roberts Barton
publisher: Doran
1. Wonderful Land of Up (1918)
2. Nancy and Nick in Helter-Skelter-Land (1921)
3. Nancy and Nick in Scrub-Up-Land (1921)
4. Nancy and Nick in the Land-of-Dear-Knows-Where (1921)
5. Nancy and Nick in the Land-of-Near-By (1921)
6. Nancy and Nick in Topsy-Turvy-Land (1921)

834. NANCY BRUCE AND THE CARLSON GIRLS
author: Jennie D. Lindquist
publisher: Harper
1. The Golden Name Day (1955)
2. The Little Silver House (1959)
3. The Crystal Tree (1966)

835. NANCY DREW
author: Carolyn Keene [pseudonym of the Stratemeyer Syndicate]
publishers: Grosset & Dunlap [1–56, 61–63]; Wanderer [57–60, 64]
1. The Secret of the Old Clock (1930)
2. The Hidden Staircase (1930)

3. The Bungalow Mystery (1930)
4. The Mystery at Lilac Inn (1930)
5. The Secret at Shadow Ranch (1930)
6. The Secret of Red Gate Farm (1931)
7. The Clue in the Diary (1932)
8. Nancy's Mysterious Letter (1932)
9. The Sign of the Twisted Candles (1933)
10. The Password to Larkspur Lane (1933)
11. The Clue of the Broken Locket (1934)
12. The Message in the Hollow Oak (1935)
13. The Mystery of the Ivory Charm (1936)
14. The Whispering Statue (1937)
15. The Haunted Bridge (1937)
16. The Clue of the Tapping Heels (1939)
17. The Mystery of the Brass Bound Trunk (1940)
18. The Mystery at the Moss-Covered Mansion (1941)
19. The Quest of the Missing Map (1942)
20. The Clue in the Jewel Box (1943)
21. The Secret in the Old Attic (1944)
22. The Clue in the Crumbling Wall (1945)
23. The Mystery of the Tolling Bell (1946)
24. The Clue in the Old Album (1947)
25. The Ghost of Blackwood Hall (1948)
26. The Clue of the Leaning Chimney (1949)
27. The Secret of the Wooden Lady (1950)
28. The Clue of the Black Keys (1951)
29. The Mystery at the Ski Jump (1952)
30. The Clue of the Velvet Mask (1953)
31. The Ringmaster's Secret (1953)
32. The Scarlet Slipper Mystery (1954)
33. The Witch Tree Symbol (1955)
34. The Hidden Window Mystery (1957)
35. The Haunted Showboat (1958)
36. The Secret of the Golden Pavilion (1959)
37. The Clue in the Old Stagecoach (1960)
38. The Mystery of the Fire Dragon (1961)
39. The Clue of the Dancing Puppet (1962)
40. The Moonstone Castle Mystery (1963)
41. The Clue of the Whistling Bagpipes (1964)
42. The Phantom of Pine Hill (1965)
43. The Mystery of the 99 Steps (1966)
44. The Clue in the Crossword Cipher (1967)
45. The Spider Sapphire Mystery (1968)
46. The Invisible Intruder (1969)
47. The Mysterious Mannequin (1970)
48. The Crooked Bannister (1971)
49. The Secret of Mirror Bay (1972)
50. The Double Jinx Mystery (1973)
51. The Mystery of the Glowing Eye (1974)
52. The Secret of the Forgotten City (1975)
53. The Sky Phantom (1976)
54. The Strange Message in the Parchment (1977)
55. The Mystery of Crocodile Island (1978)
56. The Thirteenth Pearl (1979)
57. The Triple Hoax (1979)
58. The Flying Saucer Mystery (1980)
59. The Secret in the Old Lace (1980)
60. The Greek Symbol Mystery (1981)
61. The Nancy Drew Cookbook: Clues to Good Cooking (1973)
62. The Hardy Boys and Nancy Drew Meet Dracula (1978)
63. The Nancy Drew Sleuth Book: Clues to Good Sleuthing (1979)
64. Nancy Drew Book of Hidden Clues (1980)

836. NANCY LEE
author: Margaret Warde [pseudonym of Edith Kellogg Dunton]
illustrator: Pemberton Ginther
publisher: Penn Publishing
1. Nancy Lee (1912)
2. Nancy Lee's Spring Term (1913)
3. Nancy Lee's Lookout (1915)
4. Nancy Lee's Namesake (1917)

837. NANCY NAYLOR
author: Elizabeth Lansing
publisher: Thomas Y. Crowell
1. Nancy Naylor, Air Pilot (1941)
2. Nancy Naylor Flies South (1943)
3. Nancy Naylor, Flight Nurse (1944)

4. Nancy Naylor, Captain of Flight Nurses (1946)
5. Nancy Naylor, Visiting Nurse (1947)

838. NANCY PEMBROKE

author: Margaret T. Van Epps
publisher: A. L. Burt
1. Nancy Pembroke, College Maid (1930)
2. Nancy Pembroke's Vacation in Canada (1930)
3. Nancy Pembroke, Sophomore at Roxford (1930)
4. Nancy Pembroke in New Orleans (1930)
5. Nancy Pembroke, Junior (1930)
6. Nancy Pembroke in Nova Scotia (1930)
7. Nancy Pembroke, Senior (1931)

839. NAT RIDLEY RAPID FIRE DETECTIVE STORIES

author: Roy Rockwood [pseudonym of the Stratemeyer Syndicate]
publisher: Garden City
1. Guilty or Not Guilty? or, Nat Ridley's Great Track Case (1926)
2. Tracked to the West; or, Nat Ridley at the Magnet Mine (1926)
3. In the Nick of Time; or, Nat Ridley Saving a Life (1926)
4. The Crime on the Limited; or, Nat Ridley in the Follies (1926)
5. A Daring Abduction; or, Nat Ridley's Biggest Fight (1926)
6. The Stolen Nuggets of Gold; or, Nat Ridley on the Yukon (1926)
7. A Secret of the Stage; or, Nat Ridley and the Bouquet of Death (1926)
8. The Great Circus Mystery; or, Nat Ridley on a Crooked Trail (1926)
9. A Scream in the Dark; or, Nat Ridley's Crimson Clue (1926)
10. The Race Track Crooks; or, Nat Ridley's Queerest Puzzle (1926)
11. The Stolen Liberty Bonds; or, Nat Ridley's Circle of Clues (1926)
12. In the Grip of the Kidnappers; or, Nat Ridley in High Society (1926)
13. The Double Dagger; or, Nat Ridley's Mexican Trail (1926)
14. The Mountain Inn Mystery; or, Nat Ridley with the Forest Rangers (1927)
15. The Western Express Robbery; or, Nat Ridley and the Mail Thieves (1927)
16. Struck Down at Midnight; or, Nat Ridley and His Rivals (1927)
17. Detective Against Detective; or, Nat Ridley Showing His Nerve (1927)

840. NATHALIE PAGE

author: Rena I. Halsey
publisher: Lothrop, Lee & Shepard
1. Blue Robin, the Girl Pioneer (1917)
2. America's Daughter (1918)
3. The Liberty Girl (1919)

841. NAVY BOYS I

author: Halsey Davidson
publisher: George Sully
1. Navy Boys After the Submarines; or, Protecting the Giant Convoy (1918)
2. Navy Boys Chasing a Sea Raider; or, Landing a Million Dollar Prize (1919)
3. Navy Boys Behind the Big Guns; or, Sinking the German U-Boats (1919)
4. Navy Boys to the-Rescue; or, The Wireless Call for Help
5. Navy Boys at the Big Surrender; or, Rounding Up the German Fleet
6. Navy Boys on Special Service; or, Guarding the Floating Treasury (1920)

842. NAVY BOYS II

authors: James Otis [pseudonym of James Otis Kaler] [2–8]; William P. Chipman [1, 9–11]; Frederick A. Ober [12]
publisher: A. L. Burt
1. The Navy Boys in Defense of Liberty (1904)
2. The Navy Boys on Long Island Sound; A Story of the Whale Boat Navy in 1776 [alternate title: Amos Dunkel, Oarsman]
3. The Navy Boys at the Siege of Havana; The Experience of Three Boys Serving Under Israel Putnam in 1762 [alternate title: At the Siege of Havana]
4. The Navy Boys with Grant at Vicksburg; A Boy's Story of the Civil War [alternate title: With Grant at Vicksburg]
5. The Navy Boys' Cruise with Paul

Jones; A Boy's Story of a Cruise with the Great Commodore in 1776 [alternate title: A Cruise with Paul Jones]
6. The Navy Boys on Lake Ontario; The Story of Two Boys and Their Adventures in the War of 1812 [alternate title: Afoot in Freedom's Cause]
7. The Navy Boys' Cruise on the Pickering [alternate title: The Cruise of the Pickering]
8. The Navy Boys in New York Bay [alternate title: The Capture of the Laughing Mary]
9. The Navy Boys on the Track of the Enemy
10. The Navy Boys' Daring Capture; The Story of How the Navy Boys Helped to Capture the British Cutter Margaretta in 1775 (1903)
11. The Navy Boys' Cruise to the Bahamas; The Story of Two Yankee Middies with the First Cruise of an American Squadron in 1775 (1904)
12. The Navy Boys' Cruise with Columbus (1905)

NAVY BOYS III *see* **UNCLE SAM'S NAVY BOYS**

843. NED BREWSTER
author: Chauncey J. Hawkins
publisher: Little, Brown
1. Ned Brewster's Year in the Big Woods (1912)
2. Ned Brewster's Bear Hunt
3. Ned Brewster's Caribou Hunt (1914)

844. NED BUNTLINE'S OWN SERIES
author: Ned Buntline
publisher: Hilton & Co.
1. Netta Bride; or, The King of the Vultures (1864)
2. Netta Bride and the Poor of New York (1865)
3. Rose Seymour; or, The Ballet Girl's Revenge: A Tale of the New York Drama (1865)
4. Mermet Ben; or, The Astrologer King: A Story of Magic and Wonderful Illusions (1865)

5. Magdalena, the Outcast; or, The Millionaire's Daughter: A Story of Life in the Empire City (1865)
6. Agnes; or, The Beautiful Milliner

845. NEW ADVENTURE AND MYSTERY SERIES FOR BOYS
[*see also* **EAGLE LAKE**]
authors: Philip Hart [2, 3, 7, 9, 14, 15, 19]; Henry Gardner Hunting [4]; Milton Richards [pseudonym of Milo Milton Oblinger] [5]; Levi Parker Wyman [6, 13, 16, 17]; Capwell Wyckoff [8, 10–12, 18]
publisher: A. L. Burt
1. The Valdmere Mystery; or, The Atomic Ray (1929)
2. The Wreck of the Dauntless (1929)
3. The Flight of the Mystic Owls (1929)
4. Barry Dare and the Mysterious Box (1929)
5. Tom Blake's Mysterious Adventure (1929)
6. Donald Price's Victory (1930)
7. Adventures of a Patriot (1930)
8. The Secret of the Armor Room (1930)
9. The Strange Teepee (1931)
10. The Mystery at Lake Retreat (1931)
11. The Mystery of Gaither Cove (1932)
12. The North Point Cabin Mystery (1932)
13. Blind Man's Inlet (1932)
14. The Mysterious Trail (1934)
15. The Golden Lure (1934)
16. The Battalion Captain (1936)
17. The Haunted House Mystery (1936)
18. The Search for the City of Ghosts (1936)
19. The Black Skimmer; A Story of Adventure and Mystery

846. NEW DAY PRESS
author: Martha Smith
publisher: New Day Press
1. George Abraham Jefferson Thinks About Freedom (1900)

847. NEW EIGHTPENNY SERIES
author: Annette A. Salaman
publisher: Griffith & Farran
1. Aunt Annette's Stories to Ada (1879)

848. NEW SERIES OF TEMPER-ANCE STORIES FOR CHIL-DREN
author: Timothy Shay Arthur
publisher: T.S. Arthur & Sons
1–6. [titles unknown]
7. Birdie in the Home Nest (1869)

849. NEWSPAPER BOYS
author: Stephen Rudd
publisher: Gore
1. The Mystery of the Missing Eyebrows (1921)
2. The Luck of a Rainy Night
3. The Rise of Route 19
4. The White Bag's Secret
5. The Clue of the Twisted Paper
6. The Long Low Whistle
7. The Mystery of the Blue Milk
8. The Leak at Coogan's Chimney
9. The Growl of the Lost Dog
10. The Courage of Renfrew Horn
11. The Fall of the East Side Bully
12. The Scoop of the Cub Reporter

850. NIXIE BUNNY
author: Joseph C. Sindelar
illustrator: Helen Geraldine Hodge
publisher: Beckley-Cardy
1. Nixie Bunny in Manners-Land (1912)
2. Nixie Bunny in Workaday-Land
3. Nixie Bunny in Holiday-Land
4. Nixie Bunny in Faraway-Lands

851. NORMAN CARVER
author: Clarence B. Burleigh
publisher: Lothrop, Lee & Shepard
1. All Among the Loggers; or, Norman Carver's Winter in a Lumber Camp (1908)
2. With Pickpoles and Peavey; or, Two Live Boys on the East Branch Drive
3. The Young Guide; or, Two Live Boys in the Maine Woods (1910)

852. NORTH BANK
author: Ralph Henry Barbour
publisher: David Appleton
1. Third Base Benson (1921)
2. Kick Formation (1922)
3. Coxswain of the Eight (1923)

NORTH LAND *see* DICK KENT

853. NORTH POLE
author: Edwin James Houston
publisher: John C. Winston
1. The Discovery of the North Pole (1907)
2. The Search for the North Pole (1907)

854. NORTHWEST STORIES
author: Leroy Snell
publisher: Cupples & Leon
1. The Lead Disk (1934)
2. Shadow Patrol
3. The Wolf Cry
4. The Spirit of the North
5. The Challenge of the Yukon
6. The Phantom of the River (1936)

855. NURSERY RHYME
author: Sarah Catherine Martin
publisher: Donohue, Henneberry
1. Old Mother Hubbard and Her Dog (1896)

856. OAKDALE
author: Morgan Scott [pseudonym of Gilbert Patten]
publishers: Hurst; A. L. Burt
1. Ben Stone at Oakdale (1911)
2. Boys of Oakdale Academy
3. Rival Pitchers of Oakdale
4. Oakdale Boys in Camp
5. The Great Oakdale Mystery
6. New Boys at Oakdale (1913)

857. OCEAN WIRELESS BOYS
author: Wilbur Lawton [pseudonym of John H. Goldfrap]
publisher: Hurst
1. The Ocean Wireless Boys on the Atlantic (1914)
2. The Ocean Wireless Boys and the Lost Liner
3. The Ocean Wireless Boys of the Iceberg Patrol
4. The Ocean Wireless Boys and the Naval Code
5. The Ocean Wireless Boys on the Pacific
6. The Ocean Wireless Boys on Warswept Seas (1917)

858. OLD DEERFIELD
author: Mary Prudence Wells Smith
publisher: Little, Brown
1. The Boy Captive of Old Deerfield
   (1904)
2. The Boy Captive in Canada (1905)
3. Boys of the Border (1907)
4. Boys and Girls of Seventy-Seven (1909)

859. OLD GLORY
author: Edward Stratemeyer
publishers: Lee & Shepard; Lothrop, Lee
   & Shepard
1. Under Dewey at Manila; or, The War
   Fortunes of a Castaway (1898)
2. A Young Volunteer in Cuba; or, Fighting for the Single Star
3. Fighting in Cuban Waters; or, Under
   Schley on the Brooklyn
4. Under Otis in the Philippines; or, A
   Young Officer in the Tropics
5. The Campaign of the Jungle; or, Under
   Lawton Through Luzon (1900)
6. Under MacArthur in Luzon; or, Last
   Battles in the Philippines (1901)

860. OLD THATCH
author: Enid Blyton
publishers: Johnston & Bacon; Coker; W.
   & A.K. Johnston
1. Robin Hood and His Merry Men
   (1955)
2. Gulliver's Adventures in the Land of
   Lilliput (1960)
3. Aesop's Fables (1960)
4. Hiawatha, the Red Indian (1955)
5. Round the Year Stories (1950)
6. A Book of Magic (1950)
7. Animals at Home (1950)
8. The Adventures of Bobs (1950)
9. A Visit to the Zoo, and Other Stories
   (1952)
10. The Two Sillies, and Other Stories
   (1952)
11. Nature Tales (1952)
12. Jolly Tales (1952)
13. New Testament Stories (1952)
14. Old Testament Stories (1952)

861. OLIVER OPTIC BOOKS I
author: Oliver Optic [pseudonym of
   William Taylor Adams]

publisher: Hurst
1. All Aboard
2. The Boat Club
3. Brave Old Salt
4. The Do-Somethings
5. Fighting Joe
6. In School and Out
7. Little by Little
8. The Little Merchant
9. Now or Never
10. Poor and Proud
11. Proud and Lazy
12. Rich and Humble
13. The Sailor Boy
14. The Soldier Boy
15. Try Again
16. Watch and Wait
17. Work and Win
18. The Yankee Middy
19. The Young Lieutenant

862. OLIVER OPTIC BOOKS II
author: Oliver Optic [pseudonym of
   William Taylor Adams]
publisher: New York Book Co.
1. The Boat Club
2. All Aboard
3. Little by Little
4. Now or Never
5. Poor and Proud
6. Try Again
7. Fighting Joe
8. Haste and Waste
9. Hope and Have
10. In School and Out
11. Rich and Humble
12. Work and Win

863. OLIVER OPTIC SERIES I
author: Oliver Optic [pseudonym of
   William Taylor Adams]
publishers: M. A. Donohue; Hurst
1. All Aboard
2. Brave Old Salt
3. The Boat Club
4. Fighting Joe
5. Haste and Waste
6. Hope and Have
7. In School and Out
8. Little by Little
9. Now or Never
10. Outward Bound

11. Poor and Proud; or, The Fortunes of Katy Redburn: A Story for Young Folks (1912)
12. Rich and Humble
13. The Sailor Boy
14. The Soldier Boy
15. Three Millions
16. Try Again
17. Watch and Wait; or, The Young Fugitives: A Story for Young People (1864)
18. Work and Win
19. The Yankee Middy
20. The Young Lieutenant

864. OLIVER OPTIC SERIES II
author: Oliver Optic [pseudonym of William Taylor Adams]
publishers: Lee & Shepard; Lothrop, Lee & Shepard
1. The Soldier Boy
2. The Young Lieutenant
3. Fighting Joe
4. The Sailor Boy
5. The Yankee Middy
6. Brave Old Salt; or, Life on the Quarter Deck: A Story of the Great Rebellion (1894)
7. The Boat Club
8. All Aboard
9. Now or Never
10. Try Again
11. Poor and Proud; or, The Fortunes of Katy Redburn: A Story for Young Folks (1912)
12. Little by Little
13. Through by Daylight
14. Lightning Express
15. On Time
16. Switch Off
17. Brake Up
18. Bear and Forbear
19. Rich and Humble
20. In School and Out
21. Watch and Wait
22. Work and Win
23. Hope and Have
24. Haste and Waste
25. The Starry Flag
26. Breaking Away
27. Seek and Find
28. Freaks of Fortune
29. Make or Break
30. Down the River
31. A Missing Million
32. A Millionaire at Sixteen
33. A Young Knight-Errant
34. Strange Sights Abroad
35. Outward Bound
36. Shamrock and Thistle
37. Red Cross
38. Dikes and Ditches
39. Palace and Cottage
40. Down the Rhine
41. Up the Baltic
42. Northern Lands
43. Cross and Crescent
44. Sunny Shores
45. Vine and Olive
46. All Adrift
47. Going West
48. Field and Forest
49. Little Bobtail
50. Just His Luck

OLIVER OPTIC'S BOAT CLUB *see* **BOAT CLUB**

OLIVER OPTIC'S STARRY FLAG *see* **STARRY FLAG**

ONWARD AND UPWARD *see* **UPWARD AND ONWARD**

865. ONYX
author: Carolyn Wells
publisher: Franklin Bigelow
1. The Eternal Feminine (1913)
2. Girls and Gayety (1913)
3. Pleasing Prose (1913)
4. The Re-Echo Club (1913)

866. OOZE LEATHER CHRISTMAS
authors: Anne O'Hagan [2]; Bertram Lebhar [10]; John Kendrick Bangs [unknown 1]; Lee Bertrand [unknown 2]
publisher: Browne & Howell
  1. [title unknown]
  2. Christmas Roses (1914)
3–9. [titles unknown]
 10. When Santa Claus Was Lost (1914)
unknown numbers:
[1] Santa Claus and Little Billee (1914)
[2] Their Christmas (1914)

867. OPIUM
author: Lyman Frank Baum
publisher: Opium Books
1. [title unknown]
2. John Dough and the Cherub (1906)

868. ORIOLE BOOKS
author: Amy Bell Marlowe [pseudonym of the Stratemeyer Syndicate]
illustrator: Walter S. Rogers
publisher: Grosset & Dunlap
1. When Oriole Came to Harbor Light (1920)
2. When Oriole Traveled Westward (1921)
3. When Oriole Went to Boarding School (1927)
4. Oriole's Adventures: Four Complete Adventure Books for Girls in One Big Volume (1933) [includes the three listed above and The Girls of Rivercliff School (1916)]

869. OUR BOYS' PRIZE LIBRARY
author: Oliver Optic [pseudonym of William Taylor Adams]
publishers: Lee & Shepard; Charles T. Dillingham
1. Just His Luck

870. OUR FAVORITE TOY BOOKS
author: [unknown]
publisher: J.E. Potter
1. The Robber Kitten
2. The Boy Turned into a Monkey; or, How the Mischievous Youngster Was Cured

871. OUR LUCKY SERIES
authors: John Townsend Trowbridge [1, 4]; Oliver Optic [pseudonym of William Taylor Adams] [2]; Elijah Kellogg [3]
publisher: Lee & Shepard; Charles T. Dillingham
1. His Own Master (1877)
2. Just His Luck (1878)
3. Good Old Times; or, Grandfather's Struggles for a Homestead (1877)
4. Bound in Honor; or, A Harvest of Wild Oats (1877)

OUR OWN LAND *see* FOUR BOYS

872. OUR YOUNG AEROPLANE SCOUTS
author: Horace Porter [pseudonym of Horace Porter Biddle De Hart]
publisher: A. L. Burt
1. Our Young Aeroplane Scouts in France and Belgium; or, Saving the Fortunes of the Trouvilles (1915)
2. Our Young Aeroplane Scouts in Germany; or, Winning the Iron Cross (1915)
3. Our Young Aeroplane Scouts in Russia; or, Lost on the Frozen Steppes (1915)
4. Our Young Aeroplane Scouts in Turkey; or, Bringing the Light to Yusef (1915)
5. Our Young Aeroplane Scouts in England; or, Twin Stars in the London Sky Patrol (1916)
6. Our Young Aeroplane Scouts in Italy; or, Flying with the War Eagles of the Alps (1916)
7. Our Young Aeroplane Scouts at Verdun; or, Driving Armored Meteors Over Flaming Battle Fronts (1917)
8. Our Young Aeroplane Scouts in the Balkans; or, Wearing the Red Badge of Courage Among the Warring Legions (1917)
9. Our Young Aeroplane Scouts in the War Zone; or, Serving Uncle Sam in the Great Cause of the Allies (1918)
10. Our Young Aeroplane Scouts Fighting to the Finish; or, Striking Hard Over the Sea for the Stars and Stripes (1918)
11. Our Young Aeroplane Scouts at the Marne; or, Harrying the Huns From Allied Battleplanes (1919)
12. Our Young Aeroplane Scouts in at the Victory; or, Speedy High Flyers Smashing the Hindenburg Line (1919)

873. OUT OF SCHOOL
author: Elizabeth Stuart Phelps
publisher: D. Lothrop
1. The Boys of Brimstone Court (1879)

874. OUTBOARD BOYS
author: Roger Carroll Garis
publisher: A. L. Burt

1. The Outboard Boys at Mystery Island; or, Solving the Secret of Hidden Cove (1933)
2. The Outboard Boys at Shadow Lake; or, Solving the Secret of the Strange Monster (1933)
3. The Outboard Boys at Pirate Beach; or, Solving the Secret of the Houseboat (1933)
4. The Outboard Boys at Shark River; or, Solving the Secret of Mystery Tower (1934)

OUTBOARD-MOTOR BOAT see OUTBOARD BOYS

875. OUTDOOR CHUMS
author: Quincy Allen [pseudonym of the Stratemeyer Syndicate]
illustrators: H. Richard Boehm [1–5]; N.C. Richards [6]; Walter S. Rogers [7–8]
publisher: Grosset & Dunlap
1. The Outdoor Chums; or, The First Tour of the Rod, Gun and Camera Club (1911)
2. The Outdoor Chums on the Lake; or, Lively Adventures on Wildcat Island (1911)
3. The Outdoor Chums in the Forest; or, Laying the Ghost of Oak Ridge (1911)
4. The Outdoor Chums on the Gulf; or, Rescuing the Lost Balloonists (1911)
5. The Outdoor Chums After Big Game; or, Perilous Adventures in the Wilderness (1911)
6. The Outdoor Chums on a Houseboat; or, The Rivals of the Mississippi (1913)
7. The Outdoor Chums in the Big Woods; or, The Rival Hunters of Lumber Run (1915)
8. The Outdoor Chums at Cabin Point; or, The Golden Cup Mystery (1916)

876. OUTDOOR GIRLS
author: Laura Lee Hope [pseudonym of the Stratemeyer Syndicate]
illustrators: Walter S. Rogers [6–8, 10–21]; Margaret Temple Braley [22–23]; R. Emmett Owen [9]
publisher: Grosset & Dunlap
1. The Outdoor Girls of Deepdale; or, Camping and Tramping for Fun and Health (1913)
2. The Outdoor Girls at Rainbow Lake; or, The Stirring Cruise of the Motor Boat Gem (1913)
3. The Outdoor Girls in a Motor Car; or, The Haunted Mansion of Shadow Valley (1913)
4. The Outdoor Girls in a Winter Camp; or, Glorious Days on Skates and Ice Boats (1913)
5. The Outdoor Girls in Florida; or, Wintering in the Sunny South (1913)
6. The Outdoor Girls at Ocean View; or, The Box That Was Found in the Sand (1915)
7. The Outdoor Girls on Pine Island; or, A Cave and What It Contained (1916)
8. The Outdoor Girls in Army Service; or, Doing Their Bit for the Soldier Boys (1918)
9. The Outdoor Girls at the Hostess House; or, Doing Their Best for the Soldiers (1919)
10. The Outdoor Girls at Bluff Point; or, A Wreck and a Rescue (1920)
11. The Outdoor Girls at Wild Rose Lodge; or, The Hermit of Moonlight Falls (1921)
12. The Outdoor Girls in the Saddle; or, The Girl Miner of Gold Run (1922)
13. The Outdoor Girls Around the Camp-Fire; or, The Old Maid of the Mountains (1923)
14. The Outdoor Girls on Cape Cod; or, Sally Ann of Lighthouse Rock (1924)
15. The Outdoor Girls at Foaming Falls; or, Robina of Red Kennels (1925)
16. The Outdoor Girls Along the Coast; or, The Cruise of the Motor Boat Liberty (1926)
17. The Outdoor Girls at Spring Hill Farm; or, The Ghost of the Old Milk House (1927)
18. The Outdoor Girls at New Moon Ranch; or, Riding with the Cowboys (1928)
19. The Outdoor Girls on a Hike; or, The Mystery of the Deserted Airplane (1929)
20. The Outdoor Girls on a Canoe Trip;

or, The Secret of the Brown Mill (1930)
21. The Outdoor Girls at Cedar Ridge; or, The Mystery of the Old Windmill (1931)
22. The Outdoor Girls in the Air; or, Saving the Stolen Invention (1932)
23. The Outdoor Girls in Desert Valley; or Strange Happenings in a Cowboy Camp (1933)

877. OVER THERE
author: George Harvey Ralphson
publisher: M. A. Donohue
1. Over There with the Marines at Chateau Thierry (1919)
2. Over There with the Canadians at Vimy Ridge (1919)
3. Over There with the Doughboys at St. Mihiel (1919)
4. Over There with Pershing's Heroes at Cantigny (1919)
5. Over There with the Engineers at Cambrai (1920)
6. Over There with the Yanks in the Argonne Forest (1920)

878. OXFORD
author: Thomas Hughes
publisher: Homewood
1. Tom Brown at Oxford

879. OZ
authors: Lyman Frank Baum [1–14]; Ruth Plumly Thompson [15–28, 30–34, 43–44]; John R. Neill [35–37; Jack Snow [38–39]; Rachael R. Cosgrove [40]; Eloise Jarvis McGraw [42, 45]; Lauren Lynn McGraw Wagner [42, 45]; Susan Saunders [46]
publishers: Reilly & Britton [1–13; Whitman [29]; Reilly & Lee [14–28, 30–42]; International Wizard of Oz Club [43–45]; Random [46]
1. The Wonderful Wizard of Oz (1900)
2. The Marvelous Land of Oz (1904)
3. Ozma of Oz (1907)
4. Dorothy and the Wizard in Oz (1908)
5. The Road to Oz (1909)
6. The Emerald City of Oz (1910)
7. The Patchwork Girl of Oz (1913)
8. Tik-Tok of Oz (1914)

9. The Scarecrow of Oz (1915)
10. Rinkitink in Oz (1916)
11. The Lost Princess of Oz (1917)
12. The Tin Woodman of Oz (1918)
13. The Magic of Oz (1919)
14. Glinda of Oz (1920)
15. The Royal Book of Oz (1921)
16. Kabumpo in Oz (1922)
17. The Cowardly Lion of Oz (1923)
18. Grampa in Oz (1924)
19. The Lost King of Oz (1925)
20. The Hungry Tiger of Oz (1925)
21. The Gnome King of Oz (1927)
22. The Giant Horse of Oz (1928)
23. Jack Pumpkinhead of Oz (1929)
24. The Yellow Knight of Oz (1930)
25. Pirates in Oz (1931)
26. The Purple Prince of Oz (1932)
27. Ojo in Oz (1933)
28. Speedy in Oz (1934)
29. The Laughing Dragon of Oz (1935)
30. The Wishing Horse of Oz (1935)
31. Captain Salt in Oz (1936)
32. Handy Mandy in Oz (1937)
33. The Silver Princess in Oz (1938)
34. Ozoplaning with the Wizard of Oz (1939)
35. The Wonder City of Oz (1940)
36. The Scalawagons of Oz (1941)
37. Lucky Bucky in Oz (1942)
38. The Magic Mimics in Oz (1946)
39. The Shaggy Man of Oz (1949)
40. The Hidden Valley of Oz (1951)
41. The Visitors From Oz (1960)
42. Merry Go Round in Oz (1963)
43. Yankee in Oz (1972)
44. The Enchanted Island of Oz (1976)
45. The Forbidden Fountain of Oz (1980)
46. Dorothy and the Magic Belt (1985)

880. PACIFIC
author: Horatio Alger
publishers: Porter & Coates; Henry T. Coates; Loring
1. The Young Adventurer; or, Tom's Trip Across the Plains (1878)
2. The Young Miner; or, Tom Nelson in California (1879)
3. The Young Explorer; or, Among the Sierras (1880)
4. Ben's Nugget; or, A Boy's Search for Fortune (1882)

881. PADDLE YOUR OWN CANOE
author: Edward Sylvester Ellis
publisher: J.C. Winston
1. The Forest Messengers (1907)
2. The Mountain Star (1907)
3. The Queen of the Clouds (1907)

882. PAM AND PENNY
author: Rosamund Du Jardin
publisher: J. B. Lippincott
1. Double Date (1951)
2. Double Feature (1953)
3. Showboat Summer (1955)
4. Double Wedding (1959)

PAN-AMERICAN see AMERICAN BOYS I

883 PAPYRUS
author: John Tyler Wheelwright
publisher: Lamson, Wolffe, Norwood
1. A Bad Penny (1896)

PARAMOUNT see RICK AND RUDDY

884. PARENTS' LIBRARY
author: Thomas Cromwell
publisher: S. Colman
1. The Orphan Boy's Trials (1845)

885. PATRICIA
author: Marguerite Murphy
publisher: Lothrop, Lee & Shepard
1. Patricia from New York (1925)
2. Patricia and the Other Girls (1926)
3. Patricia's Problem (1927)

886. PATRIOT LAD
author: Russell Gordon Carter
publisher: Penn
1. A Patriot Lad of Old Boston (1923)
2. A Patriot Lad of Old Philadelphia
3. A Patriot Lad of Salem
4. A Patriot Lad of Trenton
5. A Patriot Lad of Cape Cod
6. A Patriot Lad of Long Island
7. A Patriot Lad of Sarasota
8. A Patriot Lad of Old Rhode Island (1930)
9. A Patriot Lad of Maine
10. A Patriot Lad of New Hampshire
11. A Patriot Lad of Connecticut
12. A Patriot Lad of Old West Point (1936)

887. PATSY CARROLL
author: Grace Gordon
publisher: Cupples & Leon
1. Patsy Carroll at Wilderness Lodge (1917)
2. Patsy Carroll Under Southern Skies (1918)
3. Patsy Carroll in the Golden West (1920)
4. Patsy Carroll in Old New England (1921)

888. PATTY
author: Carolyn Wells [pseudonym of Mrs. Hadwin Houghton]
illustrators: E.C. Caswell [11–17]; Martin Lewis [10]; Mayo Bunker [9]
publisher: Grosset & Dunlap
1. Patty Fairfield (1901)
2. Patty at Home (1904)
3. Patty in the City (1905)
4. Patty's Summer Days (1906)
5. Patty in Paris (1907)
6. Patty's Friends (1908)
7. Patty's Pleasure Trip (1909)
8. Patty's Success (1910)
9. Patty's Motor Car (1911)
10. Patty's Butterfly Days (1912)
11. Patty's Social Season (1913)
12. Patty's Suitors (1914)
13. Patty's Romance (1915)
14. Patty's Fortune (1916)
15. Patty Blossom (1917)
16. Patty-Bride (1918)
17. Patty and Azalea (1919)

889. PATTY LOU
author: Basil Miller
publisher: Zondervan
1. Patty Lou of the Golden West (1942)
2. Patty Lou and the White Gold Ranch (1943)
3. Patty Lou's Pot of Gold (1943)
4. Patty Lou in the Coast Guard (1944)
5. Patty Lou, the Flying Nurse (1945)
6. Patty Lou, the Girl Forester (1947)
7. Patty Lou, Flying Missionary (1948)
8. Patty Lou in the Wilds of Central America (1949)

9. Patty Lou Under Western Skies (1950)
10. Patty Lou Home on the Range (1951)
11. Patty Lou at Sunset Pass (1952)
12. Patty Lou Lost in the Jungle (1953)
13. Patty Lou, Range Nurse (1954)
14. Patty Lou and the Seminole Indians (1955)

890 PAUL AND PEGGY
author: Florence E. Scott
publisher: Hurst
1. Here and There with Paul and Peggy (1914)
2. Across the Continent with Paul and Peggy (1915)
3. Through the Yellowstone with Paul and Peggy (1916)

891. PEARL
author: Madeline Leslie
publisher: Ward & Drummond
1. The Pearl of Diligence; or, The Basket-Makers (1868)
2. The Pearl of Penitence; or, Charley's Sad Story (1868)

892. PEE-WEE HARRIS
author: Percy Kees Fitzhugh
illustrator: H.S. Barbour
publisher: Grosset & Dunlap
1. Pee-Wee Harris (1922)
2. Pee-Wee Harris on the Trail (1922)
3. Pee-Wee Harris in Camp (1922)
4. Pee-Wee Harris in Luck (1922)
5. Pee-Wee Harris Adrift (1922)
6. Pee-Wee Harris: F.O.B. Bridgeboro (1923)
7. Pee-Wee Harris, Fixer (1924)
8. Pee-Wee Harris, as Good as His Word (1925)
9. Pee-Wee Harris, Mayor for a Day (1926)
10. Pee-Wee Harris and the Sunken Treasure (1927)
11. Pee-Wee Harris on the Briny Deep (1928)
12. Pee-Wee Harris in Darkest Africa (1929)
13. Pee-Wee Harris Turns Detective (1930)

893. PEERLESS
author: Howard Roger Garis
publisher: J.S. Ogilvie
130. The King of Unadilla; Stories of Court Secrets Concerning His Majesty (1903)

894. PEGGY
author: Emma Bugbee
publisher: Dodd, Mead
1. Peggy Covers the News (1936)
2. Peggy Covers Washington (1937)
3. Peggy Covers London (1939)
4. Peggy Covers the Clipper (1941)
5. Peggy Goes Overseas (1945)

895. PEGGY LEE
author: Anna Andrews
publisher: Cupples
1. Peggy and Michael of the Coffee Plantation (1931)
2. Peggy Lee and the Mysterious Island (1931)
3. Peggy Lee of the Golden Thistle Plantation (1931)
4. Peggy Lee, Sophomore (1932)

896. PEGGY OWEN
author: Lucy Foster Madison
publisher: Penn
1. Peggy Owen — A Story for Girls (1908)
2. Peggy Owen, Patriot (1910)
3. Peggy Owen at Yorktown (1911)
4. Peggy Owen and Liberty (1912)

897. PEGGY STEWART
author: Gabrielle E. Jackson
publisher: Macmillan
1. Peggy Stewart (1911)
2. Peggy Stewart at Home (1912)
3. Peggy Stewart at School (1912)

898. PEMROSE LORRY
author: Isabelle Hornibrook
publisher: Little, Brown
1. Pemrose Lorry, Camp Fire Girl (1921)
2. Pemrose Lorry, Radio Amateur (1923)
3. Pemrose Lorry, Sky Sailor (1924)
4. Pemrose Lorry, Torchbearer (1926)

899. PENELOPE
author: Dorothea Castelhun

publisher: L. C. Page
1. Penelope's Problems (1922)
2. Penelope and the Golden Orchard (1924)
3. Penelope in the Golden Orchard (1925)
4. Penelope in California (1926)

900. PENNY DREADFUL
author: A. Stephen Tring
publisher: Oxford University Press
1. Penny Dreadful (1947)
2. Penny Triumphant (1953)
3. Penny Penitent (1953)
4. Penny Puzzled (1955)
5. Penny Dramatic (1956)
6. Penny in Italy (1957)
7. Penny and the Pageant (1959)
8. Penny Says Goodbye (1961)

901. PENNY MARSH
author: Dorothy Deming
publisher: Dodd, Mead
1. Penny Marsh, Public Health Nurse (1938)
2. Penny Marsh, Supervisor of Public Health Nurses (1939)
3. Penny Marsh Finds Adventure in Public Health Nursing (1940)
4. Ginger Lee, War Nurse (1942)
5. Penny Marsh and Ginger Lee, Wartime Nurses (1943)
6. Penny and Pam, Nurse and Cadet (1944)
7. Pam Wilson, Registered Nurse (1946)
8. Penny Marsh, R.N., Director of Nurses (1960)

902. PENNY NICHOLS
author: Joan Clark
publisher: Goldsmith
1. Penny Nichols and the Black Imp (1936)
2. Penny Nichols Finds a Clue (1936)
3. Penny Nichols and the Mystery of the Lost Key (1936)
4. Penny Nichols and the Knob Hill Mystery (1939)

903. PENNY PARKER
author: Mildred Wirt
publisher: Cupples & Leon
1. Clue of the Silken Ladder (1941)

2. Ghost Beyond the Gate (1943)
3. Saboteurs on the River (1943)
4. Hoofbeats on the Turnpike (1944)
5. Voice from the Cave (1944)
6. Guilt of the Brass Thieves (1945)
7. Signal in the Dark (1946)
8. Whispering Walls (1946)
9. The Cry at Midnight (1947)
10. Swamp Island (1947)
11. Behind the Green Door (1958)
12. Danger at the Drawbridge (1958)
13. Tale of the Witch Doll (1958)
14. The Vanishing Houseboat (1958)

904. THE PEOPLE'S LIBRARY
author: Frederick Marryat
publishers: Harper; Cassell; Aldine
[only the following numbers are known]
1. The Children of the New Forest (1899)
69. Mr. Midshipman Easy (1908)
71. Masterman Ready (1909)
94. Peter Simple (1909)
[# unknown]. The Little Savage (1874)

905. PERRY PIERCE MYSTERY STORIES
author: Clinton W. Locke [pseudonym of the Stratemeyer Syndicate]
illustrators: Russell H. Tandy [1–3]; C.C. Stevens [4]
publisher: Henry Altemus
1. Who Closed the Door; or, Perry Pierce and the Old Storehouse Mystery (1931)
2. Who Opened the Safe; or, Perry Pierce and the Secret Cipher Mystery (1931)
3. Who Hid the Key; or, Perry Pierce Tracing the Counterfeit Money (1932)
4. Who Took the Papers; or, Perry Pierce Gathering the Printed Clues (1934)

906. PETER AND POLLY
author: Rose Lucia
publisher: American Book
1. Peter and Polly in Summer (1912)
2. Peter and Polly in Winter (1914)
3. Peter and Polly in Spring (1915)
4. Peter and Polly in Autumn (1918)

PETER LOOMIS *see* **SYLVIA ARDEN**

907. PHIL BRADLEY
author: Silas K. Boone
publishers: New York Book Company; M.
A. Donohue
1. Phil Bradley's Mountain Boys; or, The
   Birch Bark Lodge (1914)
2. Phil Bradley at the Wheel; or, The
   Mountain Boys' Mad Auto Dash
3. Phil Bradley's Shooting Box; or, The
   Mountain Boys on Currituck Sound
4. Phil Bradley's Snowshoe Trail; or,
   The Mountain Boys in the Canadian
   Wilds
5. Phil Bradley's Winning Way (1916)
6. Phil Bradley's Big Exploit (1919)

PHIL HARDY *see* **BOUND TO WIN I**

908. PHILIPPA
author: Margarita Spalding Gerry
publisher: Harper
1. Philippa's Fortune (1921)
2. Philippa at the Chateau (1922)
3. Philippa's Experiments (1923)

909. PHILLIP HART ADVEN-
TURE [*see also* ADVENTURE
AND MYSTERY]
author: [unknown]
publisher: Saalfield
1. The Black Skimmer (1929)
2. The Golden Lure (1929)
3. The Mysterious Trail (1929)

910. PHILLIP EXETER
author: Albertus T. Dudley
publisher: Lothrop, Lee & Shepard
1. Following the Ball (1904)
2. Making the Nine
3. In the Line
4. With Mask and Mitt
5. The Great Year
6. The Yale Cup
7. A Fullback Afloat
8. The Pecks in Camp
9. One Half Miler (1913)

911. PHILLIP KENT
author: Thomas Truxton Hare
publisher: Penn
1. Phillip Kent (1914)
2. Phillip Kent in the Lower School

3. Phillip Kent in the Upper School
4. Ken of Malvern (1919)

912. PHOEBE GAY
author: Helen Dawes Brown
publisher: Houghton, Mifflin
1. Little Miss Phoebe Gay (1895)
2. Her Sixteenth Year (1901)
3. How Phoebe Found Herself (1912)

913. PIERCES
author: Loula Grace Erdman
publisher: Dodd, Mead
1. The Wild Blows Free (1952)
2. The Wide Horizon (1956)
3. The Good Land (1959)

914. PIGEON CAMP
author: Martha James
publisher: Lothrop, Lee & Shepard
1. Jimmie Suter and the Boys of Pigeon
   Camp (1906)
2. The Boys of Pigeon Camp: Their Luck
   and Fun (1907)
3. The Hero of Pigeon Camp (1907)

915. PINE CONE STORIES
author: Willis Boyd Allen
publisher: D. Lothrop
1. Pine Cones (1885)
2. Silver Rags (1886)
3. The Northern Cross; or, Randolph's
   Last Year at the Boston Latin School
   (1887)
4. Kelp; A Story of the Isles of Shoals
   (1888)
5. Cloud and Cliff; or, Summer Days at
   the White Mountains (1889)
6. Gulf and Glacier; or, The Percivals in
   Alaska (1892)

PIONEER *see* **JAMES OTIS' PIONEER**

916. PIONEER BOYS I [alternate
title: THE YOUNG PIONEERS]
[*see also* FRONTIER II]
author: Horatio Alger, Jr. [pseudonym of
the Stratemeyer Syndicate]; Harrison
Adams [pseudonym of George Rath-
bone]
illustrators: Charles Livingston Bull [1–2];

H. Richard Boehm [3]; Walter S. Rogers [4–6]; Frank T. Merrill [7–8]
publisher: L. C. Page
1. Pioneer Boys of the Ohio; or, Clearing the Wilderness (1912)
2. Pioneer Boys on the Great Lakes; or, On the Trail of the Iroquois (1912)
3. Pioneer Boys of the Mississippi; or, The Homestead in the Wilderness (1913)
4. Pioneer Boys of the Missouri; or, In the Country of the Sioux (1914)
5. Pioneer Boys of the Yellowstone; or, Lost in the Land of Wonders (1915)
6. Pioneer Boys of the Columbia; or, In the Wilderness of the Great Northwest (1916)
7. Pioneer Boys of the Colorado; or, Braving the Perils of the Grand Canyon Country (1926)
8. Pioneer Boys of Kansas; or, A Prairie Home in Buffalo Land (1928)

PIONEER BOYS II see FRONTIER II

917. PIONEER SCOUT
author: Everett Titsworth Tomlinson
publisher: Doubleday
1. Scouting with Daniel Boone (1914)
2. Scouting with Kit Carson
3. Scouting with General Funston (1917)
4. Scouting with General Pershing (1918)

918. PIPPI
author: Astrid Lindgren
publisher: Viking
1. Pippi Longstocking (1950)
2. Pippi Goes on Board (1957)
3. Pippi in the South Seas (1959)
4. Pippi on the Run (1971)
5. New Adventures of Pippi Longstocking (1988)

919. PLAY AND STUDY
author: Madeline Leslie
publisher: Lee & Shepard
1. Howard and His Teacher, the Sister's Influence and Other Stories (1858)

920. PLEASANT HOUR
authors: Anna Sewell [3]; John Habberton [4]; Lewis Carroll [5]; Robert Louis Stevenson [6]; Edward Everett Hale [8]; Charles Dickens [9]; Margaret Waters [11]
publisher: Barse & Hopkins
1. Stories of Robin Hood, and the Little Lame Prince (1900)
2. Little Red Riding-Hood and Other Stories (1899)
3. Black Beauty: the Autobiography of a Horse (1929)
4. Helen's Babies (1920)
5. Alice's Adventures in Wonderland (1919)
6. A Child's Garden of Verses (1909)
7. The Night Before Christmas and Other Christmas Poems (1900)
8. The Man Without a Country (1900)
9. A Christmas Carol
10. Cinderella; or, The Little Glass Slipper and Other Stories (1900)
11. The Little Lame Prince (1910)

921. PLEASEWELL
author: Sarah Catherine Martin
publisher: McLoughlin Brothers
1. Mother Hubbard and Her Dog (1890)
2. The 3 Little Kittens (1890)

922. PLEASURE READING
author: Edward William Dolch
publisher: Garrard
1. Bible Stories for Pleasure Reading (1950)
2. Fairy Stories for Pleasure Reading (1950)
3. [title unknown]
4. Aesop's Stories for Pleasure Reading (1951)
5. Gospel Stories for Pleasure Reading (1955)
6. Old World Stories for Pleasure Reading (1952)
7. Far East Stories for Pleasure Reading
8. Famous Stories for Pleasure Reading (1950)
9. Greek Stories for Pleasure Reading (1955)
10. Andersen Stories for Pleasure Reading (1955)
11. Robin Hood Stories for Pleasure Reading (1957)

12. Robinson Crusoe, Retold from D. Defoe

923. PLUMMER CHILDREN
author: Christine Noble Glovan
publisher: Houghton Mifflin
1. Those Plummer Children (1934)
2. Five at Ashefield (1935)
3. Judy and Chris; Further Adventures of Those Plummer Children (1936)
4. Narcissus an' de Chillun; Final Adventures of Those Plummer Children (1938)

924. POINTS WEST
author: Edith Janice Craine
publisher: A. L. Burt
1. At Uncle Fred's Ranch (1929)
2. Holidays on the Ranch (1929)
3. Libby Lon (1929)
4. Little Moon (1929)
5. Tenderfoot Ranchers (1929)
6. Wooly West (1929)

925. POLLY
author: Emma C. Dowd
publisher: Houghton
1. Polly of the Hospital Staff (1912)
2. Polly of Lady Gay Cottage (1913)
3. Doodles, the Sunshine Boy (1915)
4. Polly and the Princess (1917)
5. When Polly Was Eighteen (1921)

926. POLLY AND OLIVER
author: David Scott Daniel
publisher: Cape
1. Mission for Oliver (1953)
2. Polly and Oliver (1954)
3. Polly and Oliver at Sea (1960)
4. Polly and Oliver Besieged (1963)
5. Polly and Oliver Pursued (1964)

927. POLLY BREWSTER
author: Lilian Elizabeth Becker Roy
illustrators: H.S. Barbour [1–13]; Russell H. Tandy [14–15]
publisher: Grosset & Dunlap
1. Polly of Pebbly Pit (1922)
2. Polly in New York (1922)
3. Polly and Her Friends Abroad (1922)
4. Polly's Business Venture (1922)
5. Polly and Eleanor (1922)

6. Polly's Southern Cruise (1923)
7. Polly in South America (1924)
8. Polly in the Southwest (1925)
9. Polly in Alaska (1926)
10. Polly in the Orient (1927)
11. Polly in Egypt (1928)
12. Polly's New Friend (1929)
13. Polly and Carola (1930)
14. Polly and Carola at Ravenswood (1931)
15. Polly Learns to Fly (1932)
16. Polly Learns to Play (1932)

928. POLLY FRENCH
author: [unknown]
publisher: Whitman
1. Polly French of Whitford High
2. Polly French Takes Charge
3. The Surprising Stranger

929. POLLY PAGE
author: Izola L. Forrester
publisher: Jacobs
1. The Polly Page Yacht Club (1910)
2. The Polly Page Ranch Club (1911)
3. The Polly Page Motor Club (1913)
4. The Polly Page Camping Club (1915)

930. POLLY PENDLETON
author: Dorothy Whitehill
publishers: Barse & Hopkins [1–10]; Barse [11–12]; Grosset & Dunlap [13]
1. Polly's First Year at Boarding School (1916)
2. Polly's Summer Vacation (1917)
3. Polly's Senior Year at Boarding School (1917)
4. Polly Sees the World at War (1918)
5. Polly and Lois (1920)
6. Polly and Bob (1922)
7. Polly's Reunion (1924)
8. Polly's Polly (1925)
9. Polly at Pixie's Haunt (1926)
10. Polly's House Party (1927)
11. Polly's Polly at Boarding School (1928)
12. Joyful Adventures of Polly (1929)
13. Polly's Polly and Priscilla (1932)

931. POLLY PRENTISS
author: Elizabeth Lincoln Gould
publisher: Penn

1. Little Polly Prentiss (1902)
2. Polly Prentiss Goes to School (1912)
3. Polly Prentiss Goes A-Visiting (1913)

932. POLLYANNA
authors: Eleanor H. Porter [1–2]; Harriet
    Lumis Smith [3–6]; Elizabeth Borton
    [7–10]; Margaret Rebecca Chalmers [11]
publisher: L. C. Page
1. Pollyanna (1913)
2. Pollyanna Grows Up (1915)
3. Pollyanna of the Orange Blossoms
    (1924)
4. Pollyanna's Jewels (1925)
5. Pollyanna's Debt of Honor (1927)
6. Pollyanna's Western Adventure (1929)
7. Pollyanna in Hollywood (1931)
8. Pollyanna's Castle in Mexico (1934)
9. Pollyanna's Door to Happiness (1936)
10. Pollyanna's Golden Horseshoe (1939)
11. Pollyanna's Protegee (1944)

933. PONY RIDER BOYS
author: Frank Glines Patchin
publishers: Henry Altemus; Saalfield
1. The Pony Rider Boys in the Rockies;
    or, The Secret of the Lost Claim (1909)
2. The Pony Rider Boys in Texas; or,
    The Veiled Riddle of the Plains (1910)
3. The Pony Rider Boys in Montana; or,
    The Mystery of the Old Custer Trail
    (1910)
4. The Pony Rider Boys in the Ozarks;
    or, The Secret of Ruby Mountain
    (1910)
5. The Pony Rider Boys in the Alkali; or,
    Finding a Key to the Desert Maze
    (1910)
6. The Pony Rider Boys in New Mexico;
    or, The End of the Silver Trail (1910)
7. The Pony Rider Boys in the Grand
    Canyon; or, The Mystery of Bright
    Angel Gulch (1912)
8. The Pony Rider Boys with the Texas
    Rangers; or, On the Trail of the Bor-
    der Bandits (1920)
9. The Pony Rider Boys on the Blue
    Ridge; or, A Lucky Find in the Car-
    olina Mountains (1924)
10. The Pony Rider Boys in New Eng-
    land; or, An Exciting Quest in the
    Maine Wilderness (1924)

11. The Pony Rider Boys in Louisiana; or,
    Following the Game Trails in the
    Canebrake (1924)
12. The Pony Rider Boys in Alaska; or,
    The Gold Diggers of Taku Pass (1924)

POPPY OTT BOOKS see POPPY OTT DETECTIVE STORIES

934. POPPY OTT DETECTIVE STORIES
author: Leo Edwards [pseudonym of
    Edward Edson Lee]
illustrator: Bert Salg
publisher: Grosset & Dunlap
1. Poppy Ott and the Stuttering Parrot
    (1926)
2. Poppy Ott's Seven-League Stilts
    (1926)
3. Poppy Ott and the Galloping Snail
    (1927)
4. Poppy Ott's Pedigreed Pickles (1927)
5. Poppy Ott and the Freckled Goldfish
    (1928)
6. Poppy Ott and the Tittering Totem
    (1929)
7. Poppy Ott and the Prancing Pancake
    (1930)
8. Poppy Ott Hits the Trail (1933)
9. Poppy Ott & Co., Inferior Decorators
10. The Monkey's Paw
11. The Hidden Dwarf

935. PRESIDENTIAL ELECTION CAMPAIGN BIOGRAPHIES
author: Oliver Optic [pseudonym of
    William Taylor Adams]
publisher: University Microfilms
1. Our Standard-Bearer

936. PRINCESS
authors: Frances Margaret [1]; Helen
    Eggleston Haskell [2]
publisher: L.C. Page
1. Little Lady Margorie (1903)
2. Billy's Princess (1907)

937. PRINCESS POLLY
author: Amy Brooks
publishers: Platt & Peck [1–6]; A. L. Burt
    [7]
1. Princess Polly (1910)

2. Princess Polly's Playmates (1911)
3. Princess Polly at School (1912)
4. Princess Polly by the Sea (1913)
5. Princess Polly's Gay Winter (1914)
6. Princess Polly at Play (1915)
7. Princess Polly at Cliffmore (1925)

938. PRIVATEERS OF 1812
author: James Otis [pseudonym of James Otis Kaler]
illustrators: A.B. Shute [1]; J.W. Kennedy [2–3]; William F. Stecher [4]; J. Watson Davis [5]
publishers: D. Estes; Estes & Lauriat; W. A. Wilde; A. L. Burt
1. The Cruise of the Comet; The Story of a Privateer of 1812, Sailing from Baltimore, as Set Down by Stephen Burton (1898)
2. Captain Tom, the Privateersman of the Armed Brig Chasseur, as Set Down by Stephen Burton, of Baltimore (1899)
3. The Armed Ship America; or, When We Sailed From Salem (1900)
4. The Cruise of the Enterprise; Being a Story of the Struggle and Defeat of the French Privateering Expeditions Against the United States in 1779 (1902)
5. The Cruise of the Pickering; A Boy's Story of Privateering in 1780

939. PRUDENCE
author: Ethel Heuston
publisher: Bobbs-Merrill
1. Prudence of the Parsonage (1915)
2. Prudence Says So (1916)
3. Prudence's Daughter (1924)

940. PRUE
author: Amy Brooks
publisher: Lothrop, Lee & Shepard
1. Little Sister Prue (1908)
2. Prue at School (1909)
3. Prue's Playmates (1910)
4. Prue's Merry Times (1911)
5. Prue's Little Friends (1912)
6. Prue's Jolly Winter (1913)

941. PURPLE PENNANT
author: Ralph Henry Barbour
publisher: David Appleton

1. The Purple Pennant (1916)
2. The Secret Play (1915)
3. The Lucky Seventh (1915)

942. PUTNAM HALL
author: Arthur M. Winfield [pseudonym of the Stratemeyer Syndicate]
publishers: Mershon; Grosset & Dunlap [reissued the series in different order]
1. The Putnam Hall Cadets; or, Good Times in School and Out (1901) [reissued in 1921 as vol. 5]
2. The Putnam Hall Rivals; or, Fun and Sport Afloat and Ashore (1906) [reissued in 1921 as vol. 6]
3. The Putnam Hall Champions; or, Bound to Win Out (1908) [reissued in 1921 as vol. 4]
4. The Putnam Hall Rebellion; or, The Rival Runaways (1909) [reissued in 1921 as vol. 3]
5. The Putnam Hall Encampment; or, The Secret of the Old Mill (1910) [reissued in 1921 as vol. 2]
6. The Putnam Hall Mystery; or, The School Chums' Strange Discovery (1911) [reissued in 1921 as vol. 1]

943. QUIET HOUR
author: J. Ellis
publisher: Simpkins, Marshall, Hamilton, Kent
1. The Golden Threads of Life (1909)

944. RACER BOYS [see also FRANK AND ANDY]
author: Clarence Young [pseudonym of the Stratemeyer Syndicate]
illustrator: Walter S. Rogers
publisher: Cupples & Leon
1. The Racer Boys; or, The Mystery of the Wreck (1912) [reprinted as Frank and Andy Afloat: or, The Cave on the Island (1921)]
2. The Racer Boys at Boarding School; or, Striving for the Championship (1912) [reprinted as Frank and Andy at Boarding School; or, Rivals for Many Honors (1921)]
3. The Racer Boys to the Rescue; or, Stirring Days in a Winter Camp (1912) [alternate subtitle: Stirring Adventures

in a Winter Camp] [alternate title:
Frank and Andy in a Winter Camp; or,
The Young Hunters' Strange Discovery]
4. The Racer Boys on the Prairies; or, The
   Treasure of Golden Park (1913)
5. The Racer Boys on Guard; or, The
   Rebellion at Riverview Hall (1913)
6. The Racer Boys Forging Ahead; or,
   The Rivals of the School League (1914)

945. RADIO BOYS I

author: Allen Chapman [pseudonym of
   Edward Stratemeyer]
illustrator: Walter S. Rogers
publisher: Grosset & Dunlap
1. The Radio Boys' First Wireless; or,
   Winning the Ferberton Prize (1922)
2. The Radio Boys at Ocean Point; or,
   The Message That Saved the Ship
   (1922)
3. The Radio Boys at the Sending Station; or, Making Good in the Wireless
   (1922)
4. The Radio Boys at Mountain Pass; or,
   The Midnight Call for Assistance
   (1922)
5. The Radio Boys Trailing a Voice; or,
   Solving a Wireless Mystery (1922)
6. The Radio Boys with the Forest
   Rangers; or, The Great Fire on Spruce
   Mountain (1923)
7. The Radio Boys with the Iceberg
   Patrol; or, Making Safe the Ocean
   Lanes (1924)
8. The Radio Boys with the Flood Fighters; or Saving the City in the Valley
   (1925)
9. The Radio Boys on Signal Island; or,
   Watching for the Ships of Mystery
   (1926)
10. The Radio Boys in Gold Valley; or,
    The Mystery of the Deserted Mining
    Camp (1927)
11. The Radio Boys Aiding the Snow-
    bound; or, Starvation Days at Lumber
    Run (1928)
12. The Radio Boys on the Pacific; or,
    Shipwrecked on an Unknown Island
    (1929)
13. The Radio Boys to the Rescue; or,
    The Search for the Barmore Twins
    (1930)

946. RADIO BOYS II

author: Gerald Breckinridge
publisher: A. L. Burt
1. The Radio Boys on the Mexican Border (1922)
2. The Radio Boys on Secret Service
   Duty
3. The Radio Boys with the Revenue
   Guards (1922)
4. The Radio Boys' Search for the Inca's
   Treasure (1922)
5. The Radio Boys Rescue the Lost
   Alaska Expedition (1922)
6. The Radio Boys in Darkest Africa
   (1923)
7. The Radio Boys Seek the Lost Atlantis
   (1923)
8. The Radio Boys with the Border
   Patrol
9. The Radio Boys as Soldiers of Fortune
   (1925)
10. The Radio Boys with the Air Patrol
    (1931)

947. RADIO BOYS III

authors: Frank Honeywell [1–2]; J. W.
   Duffield [3–4]; Wayne Whipple [5]
publisher: M. A. Donohue
1. The Radio Boys in the Secret Service;
   or, Cast Away on an Iceberg (1922)
2. The Radio Boys in the Thousand
   Islands; or, The Yankee-Canadian
   Wireless Trail (1922)
3. The Radio Boys in the Flying Service;
   or, Held for Ransom by Mexican Bandits (1922)
4. The Radio Boys Under the Sea; or,
   The Hunt for Sunken Treasure
   (1923)
5. The Radio Boys' Cronies; or, Bill
   Brown's Radio (1923)

948. RADIO DETECTIVES

author: Alpheus Hyatt Verrill
publisher: David Appleton
1. The Radio Detectives (1922)
2. The Radio Detectives Under the Sea
   (1922)
3. The Radio Detectives Southward
   Bound (1922)
4. The Radio Detectives in the Jungle
   (1922)

949. RADIO GIRLS
author: Margaret Penrose [pseudonym of the Stratemeyer Syndicate]
illustrator: Thelma Gooch
publisher: Cupples & Leon
1. The Radio Girls of Roselawn; or, A Strange Message from the Air (1922)
2. The Radio Girls on the Program; or, Singing and Reciting at the Sending Station (1922)
3. The Radio Girls on Station Island; or, The Wireless from the Steam Yacht (1922)
4. The Radio Girls at Forest Lodge; or, The Strange Hut in the Swamp (1924)

950. RADIOPHONE BOYS
author: Roy Judson Snell
publisher: Reilly & Lee
1. The Desert Patrol (1923)
2. The Sea-Going Tank (1924)
3. The Flying Sub
4. Dark Treasure
5. Whispering Isles
6. The Invisible Wall (1928)

951. RAGGED DICK [see also ALGER; ALGER SERIES FOR BOYS]
author: Horatio Alger
publishers: John C. Winston; Loring; Porter & Coates; Henry T. Coates
1. Ragged Dick; or, Street Life in New York with the Bootblacks (1868)
2. Fame and Fortune; or, The Progress of Richard Hunter (1868)
3. Mark, the Match Boy; or, Richard Hunter's Ward (1869)
4. Rough and Ready; or, Life among the New York Newsboys (1869)
5. Ben, the Luggage Boy; or, Among the Wharves (1870)
6. Rufus and Rose; or, The Fortunes of Rough and Ready (1870)

952. RAGGEDY ANN AND ANDY STORIES
author: Johnny Gruelle
publishers: Volland [1–17]; Johnny Gruelle Co. [18–22]; Bobbs [23–28]
1. Raggedy Ann's Very Own Fairy Stories (1917)
2. Raggedy Ann Stories (1918)
3. Raggedy Andy Stories (1918)
4. Raggedy Ann's Friendly Fairies (1919)
5. Raggedy Ann and Andy and the Camel with the Wrinkled Knees (1924)
6. Raggedy Ann and Andy's Alphabet and Numbers (1925)
7. Raggedy Ann and Andy's Animal Friends (1925)
8. Raggedy Ann and Andy's Merry Adventures (1925)
9. Raggedy Ann and Andy's Sunny Stories (1925)
10. Raggedy Ann's Wishing Pebble (1925)
11. Raggedy Ann and the Paper Dragon (1926)
12. Raggedy Ann's Wooden Willie (1927)
13. Raggedy Ann's Magical Wishes (1928)
14. Marcella: A Raggedy Ann Story (1929)
15. Raggedy Ann in the Deep, Deep Woods (1930)
16. Raggedy Ann in Cookie Land (1931)
17. Raggedy Ann's Lucky Pennies (1932)
18. Raggedy Ann in the Magic Book (1939)
19. Raggedy Ann and the Golden Butterfly (1940)
20. Raggedy Ann and Andy and the Nice Fat Policeman (1942)
21. Raggedy Ann and Betsy Bonnet String (1943)
22. Raggedy Ann in the Snow White Castle (1946)
23. Raggedy Ann and the Golden Ring (1961)
24. Raggedy Ann and the Happy Meadow (1961)
25. Raggedy Ann and the Hobby Horse (1961)
26. Raggedy Ann and the Wonderful Witch (1961)
27. Raggedy Ann and Andy and the Kindly Rag Man (1975)
28. Raggedy Ann and Andy and Witchie Kissabye (1975)

953. RAILROAD I
author: Burton E. Stevenson
publisher: L. C. Page
1. The Young Section Hand; or, The Adventures of Allan West (1905)

2. The Young Apprentice; or, Allan West's Chum
3. The Young Train Dispatcher
4. The Young Train Master (1912)

RAILROAD II *see* **RALPH OF THE RAILROAD**

954. RALPH OF THE RAILROAD
author: Allen Chapman [pseudonym of Edward Stratemeyer]
illustrators: Clare Angell [1,5]; Charles Nuttall [4–5]; H. Richard Boehm [6]; R. Emmett Owen [7]; Walter S. Rogers [8–11]
publishers: Grosset & Dunlap; Chatterton-Peck
 1. Ralph of the Roundhouse; or, Bound to Become a Railroad Man (1906)
 2. Ralph in the Switch Tower; or, Clearing the Track (1907)
 3. Ralph on the Engine; or, The Young Fireman of the Limited Mail (1909)
 4. Ralph on the Overland Express; or, The Trials and Triumphs of a Young Engineer (1910)
 5. Ralph on the Railroad: Four Complete Adventure Books for Boys in One Big Volume (1910) [contains titles 1–4]
 6. Ralph, the Train Dispatcher; or, The Mystery of the Pay Car (1911)
 7. Ralph on the Army Train; or, The Young Railroader's Most Daring Exploit (1918)
 8. Ralph on the Midnight Flyer; or, The Wreck at Shadow Valley (1923)
 9. Ralph and the Missing Mail Pouch; or, The Stolen Government Bonds (1924)
10. Ralph on the Mountain Division; or, Fighting Both Flames and Flood (1927)
11. Ralph and the Train Wreckers; or, The Secret of the Blue Freight Cars (1928)

955. RALPH OSBORN
author: Edward L. Beach
publisher: W. A. Wilde
1. Ralph Osborn — Midshipman at Annapolis (1909)
2. Midshipman Ralph Osborn at Sea
3. Ensign Ralph Osborn

4. Lt. Ralph Osborn Aboard a Destroyer (1912)

956. RAMBLER CLUB
author: W. Crispin Sheppard
publisher: Penn
 1. The Rambler Club Afloat (1909)
 2. The Rambler Club's Winter Camp
 3. The Rambler Club in the Mountains
 4. The Rambler Club on Circle T. Ranch
 5. The Rambler Club Among the Lumberjacks
 6. The Rambler Club's Gold Mine
 7. The Rambler Club's Aeroplane
 8. The Rambler Club's Houseboat
 9. The Rambler Club's Motor Car
10. The Rambler Club's Ball Nine
11. The Rambler Club with the Northwest Mounted
12. The Rambler Club's Football Team
13. The Rambler Club's Motor Yacht
14. The Rambler Club on the Texas Border
15. The Rambler Club in Panama (1916)

957. RAMONA
author: Beverly Cleary
publishers: Morrow [1–12,14–15]; Dell Yearling [13]
 1. Henry Higgins (1950)
 2. Henry and Beezus (1952)
 3. Henry and Ribsy (1954)
 4. Beezus and Ramona (1955)
 5. Henry and the Paper Route (1957)
 6. Henry and the Clubhouse (1962)
 7. Ribsy (1964)
 8. Ramona the Pest (1968)
 9. Ramona the Brave (1975)
10. Ramona and Her Father (1977)
11. Ramona and Her Mother (1979)
12. Ramona Quimby, Age 8 (1981)
13. Cutting Up with Ramona (1983)
14. Ramona Forever (1984)
15. The Beezus and Ramona Diary (1986)
16. The Ramona Quimby Diary (1984)

958. RANCH GIRLS
author: Margaret Vandercook
publisher: Winston
1. The Ranch Girls at Rainbow Lodge (1911)

2. The Ranch Girls' Pot of Gold (1912)
3. The Ranch Girls at Boarding School (1913)
4. The Ranch Girls in Europe (1914)
5. The Ranch Girls at Home Again (1915)
6. The Ranch Girls and Their Great Adventure (1917)
7. The Ranch Girls and Their Heart's Desire (1920)
8. The Ranch Girls and the Silver Arrow (1921)
9. The Ranch Girls and the Mystery of the Three Roads (1924)

959. RANDY
author: Amy Brooks
publishers: Lee & Shepard [1–6]; Lothrop, Lee & Shepard [7–9]
1. Randy's Summer (1900)
2. Randy's Winter (1901)
3. Randy and Her Friends (1902)
4. Randy and Prue (1903)
5. Randy's Good Times (1904)
6. Randy's Luck (1905)
7. Randy's Loyalty (1906)
8. Randy's Prince (1907)

RANDY STARR *see* **SKY FLYERS**

960. RANGE AND GRANGE HUSTLERS
author: Frank Glines Patchin
publisher: Henry Altemus
1. The Range and Grange Hustlers on the Ranch; or, The Boy Shepherds of the Great Divide (1912)
2. The Range and Grange Hustlers' Greatest Round-Up; or, Pitting Their Wits Against a Packer's Combine (1912)
3. The Range and Grange Hustlers on the Plains; or, Following the Steam Plows Across the Prairies (1913)
4. The Range and Grange Hustlers at Chicago; or, The Conspiracy of the Wheat Pit (1913)

RANGE AND TRAIL *see* **BAR B series**

961. RANGER BOYS
author: Claude A. LaBelle
publisher: A. L. Burt
1. The Ranger Boys to the Rescue (1922)

2. The Ranger Boys and the Border Smugglers (1922)
3. The Ranger Boys Outwit the Timber Thieves (1922)
4. The Ranger Boys and Their Reward (1922)
5. The Ranger Boys Find the Hermit (1932)

962. RAYMOND BENSON
author: Clarence B. Burleigh
publisher: Lothrop, Lee & Shepard
1. The Camp on the Letter K; or, Two Live Boys in the Maine Woods (1906)
2. Raymond Benson at Krampton; or, Two Live Boys at Prep School
3. The Kenton Pines; or, Raymond Benson at College (1907)
4. The Smugglers of Chestnut (1907)

963. REBECCA OF SUNNY-BROOK FARM
author: Kate Douglas Smith
publisher: [unknown]
1. Rebecca of Sunnybrook Farm
2. New Chronicles of Rebecca

964. RED BRIDGE
author: Emily Clemens Pearson
publisher: National Temperance Society
1. Echo-Bank; A Temperance Tale (1867)

965. RED CROSS GIRLS
author: Margaret Vandercook
publisher: Winston
1. The Red Cross Girls in Belgium (1916)
2. The Red Cross Girls in the British Trenches (1916)
3. The Red Cross Girls on the French Firing Line (1916)
4. The Red Cross Girls with the Russian Army (1916)
5. The Red Cross Girls with the Italian Army (1917)
6. The Red Cross Girls with the Stars and Stripes (1918)
7. The Red Cross Girls Afloat with the Flag (1918)
8. The Red Cross Girls with Pershing to Victory (1919)
9. The Red Cross Girls with the U.S. Marines (1919)

10. The Red Cross Girls in the National Capitol (1920)

966. RED GILBERT
author: Russell Gordon Carter
publisher: Penn
1. Red Gilbert's Flying Circus (1924)
2. Red Gilbert's Floating Menagerie (1926)

967. RED RANDELL
author: Robert S. Bowen
publisher: Grosset & Dunlap
1. Red Randell at Pearl Harbor (1944)
2. Red Randell on Active Duty
3. Red Randell Over Tokyo
4. Red Randell at Midway
5. Red Randell on New Guinea
6. Red Randell in the Aleutians
7. Red Randell in Burma
8. Red Randell's One-Man War (1946)

968. REDFIELD'S TOY BOOKS
author: Anna Letitia Barbauld
publishers: Kiggins & Kellogg; J.S. Redfield
[missing numbers are titles unknown[
series 1:
1. Tom Thumb's Picture Alphabet, in Rhyme
2. Rhymes for the Nursery (1840)
3. Pretty Rhymes about Birds and Animals for Little Boys and Girls
4. Life on One Farm, in Amusing Rhyme
5. The Story Book, for Good Little Girls
6. The Beacon; or, Warnings to Thoughtless Boys
7. The Picture Book, with Stories in Easy Words for Little Readers
8. The Little Sketch-Book; or, Useful Objects Illustrated (1855)
9. History of Domestic Animals (1835)
10. The Museum of Birds
11. The Little Keepsake, a Poetic Gift for Children
12. The Book of the Sea, for the Instruction of Little Sailors (1835)
series 2:
1. The ABC in Verse for Young Learners (1850)
2. Riddles for the Nursery (1855)

3. Figures in Verse and Simple Rhymes, for Little Learners (1835)
5. The Christmas Dream of Little Charles (1866)
10. Pauline and Her Pets (1843)
series 3:
1. The Alphabet in Rhyme (1849)
2. The Multiplication Table in Rhyme, for Young Arithmeticians
5. The Young Arithmetician; or, The Reward of Perseverance (1859)
8. The Young Sailor; or, The Sea-Life of Tom Bowline (1835)
9. The Selfish Girl; A Tale of Truth (1840)
11. The Flower-Vase; or, Pretty Poems for Good Little Children (1858)
series 4:
3. Home Pastimes; or, Agreeable Exercises for the Mind (1850)
4. The Juvenile Sunday-Book; Containing Sketches in Prose and Verse Adapted to the Moral Improvement of the Young (1840)
5. William Seaton and the Butterfly; with a History of That Beautiful Insect (1850)
6. The Young Girl's Book of Healthful Amusements and Exercises (1840)
7. Theodore Carleton; or, Perseverance Against Ill-Fortune (1850)
8. The Aviary; or, Child's Book of Birds (1840)
9. The Jungle; or, Child's Book of Wild Animals (1840)
10. Sagacity and Fidelity of the Dog: Illustrated by Interesting Anecdotes (1840)
11. Coverings for the Head and Feet in All Ages and All Countries (1840)
12. Romance of Indian History; or, Thrilling Incidents in the Early Settlement of America (1852)

969. RENFREW
author: Laurie York Erskine
publishers: David Appleton; Grosset & Dunlap
1. Renfrew of the Royal Mounted (1922)
2. Renfrew Rides Again
3. Renfrew Rides the Sky
4. Renfrew Rides the North

5. Renfrew's Long Trail
6. Renfrew Rides the Range
7. Renfrew in the Valley of Vanished Men
8. Renfrew Flies Again (1941)

REVOLUTIONARY SERIES *see* **MUS-
KET BOYS**

970. REVOLUTIONARY WAR GIRLS
author: Amy E. Blanchard
publisher: W. A. Wilde
1. A Girl of '76 (1898)
2. A Revolutionary Maid: A Story of the Middle Period of the War for Independence (1899)
3. A Daughter of Freedom: A Story of the Latter Period of the War for Independence (1900)
4. A Heroine of 1812: A Maryland Romance (1901)
5. A Loyal Lass: A Story of the Niagara Campaign of 1814 (1902)
6. A Gentle Pioneer: Being the Story of the Early Days in the New West (1903)

971. REX COLE JR. DETECTIVE STORIES
author: Gordon Chapman
publishers: Barse; Grosset & Dunlap; Whitman
1. Rex Cole Jr. and the Crystal Clue (1931)
2. Rex Cole Jr. and the Grinning Ghost (1931)

972. REX KINGDON
author: Gordon Braddock [pseudonym of Gilbert Patten]
publishers: Hurst; A. L. Burt
1. Rex Kingdon of Ridgewood High (1914)
2. Rex Kingdon in the North Woods
3. Rex Kingdon at Walcott Hall
4. Rex Kingdon Behind the Bat
5. Rex Kingdon on Storm Island (1917)

REX LEE AIR STORIES *see* **REX LEE FLYING STORIES**

973. REX LEE FLYING STORIES
author: Thomson Burtis

publisher: Grosset & Dunlap
1. Rex Lee, Gypsy Flyer (1928)
2. Rex Lee on the Border Patrol (1928)
3. Rex Lee, Ranger of the Sky (1928)
4. Rex Lee, Sky Trailer (1929)
5. Rex Lee, Ace of the Air Mail (1929)
6. Rex Lee, Night Flyer (1929)
7. Rex Lee's Mysterious Flight (1930)
8. Rex Lee, Rough Rider of the Air (1930)
9. Rex Lee, Aerial Acrobat (1930)
10. Rex Lee, Trailing Air Bandits (1931)
11. Rex Lee, Flying Detective (1932)

974. RICK AND RUDDY
author: Howard Roger Garis
illustrators: Jown Goss [1]; W.B. King [3–5]; Milo Winter [2]
publishers: Milton Bradley; McLoughlin Bros. [reprinted series with alternate titles]
1. Rick and Ruddy; The Story of a Boy and His Dog (1920) [alternate title: The Face in the Dismal Cavern]
2. Rick and Ruddy in Camp; The Adventures of a Boy and His Dog (1921) [alternate title: The Mystery of the Brass Bound Box]
3. Rick and Ruddy Afloat; The Cruise of a Boy and His Dog (1922) [alternate title: Swept From the Storm]
4. Rick and Ruddy Out West (1923) [alternate title: The Secret of Lost River]
5. Rick and Ruddy on the Trail (1924) [alternate title: On the Showman's Trail]

975. RIDDLE CLUB
author: Alice Dale Hardy [pseudonym of the Stratemeyer Syndicate]
illustrator: Walter S. Rogers
publisher: Grosset & Dunlap
1. The Riddle Club at Home; How the Club Was Formed, What Riddles Were Asked and How the Members Solved a Mystery (1924)
2. The Riddle Club in Camp; How They Journeyed to the Lake, What Happened Around the Campfire and How a Forgotten Name Was Recalled (1924)

3. The Riddle Club Through the Holidays; The Club and Its Doings, How the Riddles Were Solved and What the Snowman Revealed (1924)
4. The Riddle Club at Sunrise Beach; How They Toured to the Shore, What Happened on the Sand and How They Solved the Mystery of Rattlesnake Island (1925)
5. The Riddle Club at Shadybrook; Why They Went There, What Happened on the Way and What Occurred During Their Absence from Home (1926)
6. The Riddle Club at Rocky Falls; How They Went Up the River, What Adventures They Had in the Woods and How They Solved the Mystery of the Deserted Hotel (1929)

976. RIVAL CAMPERS
author: Ruel Perley Smith
publisher: L. C. Page
1. The Rival Campers; or, The Adventures of Henry Burns (1905)
2. The Rival Campers Afloat; or, The Prize Yacht "Viking"
3. The Rival Campers Ashore; or, The Mystery of the Red Mill
4. The Rival Campers Among the Oyster Pirates; or, Jack Harvey's Adventures (1908) [alternate title: Jack Harvey's Adventures; or, The Rival Campers Among the Oyster Pirates]

977. RIVER MOTOR-BOAT BOYS
author: Harry Gordon [pseudonym of Edward S. Ellis]
publisher: A. L. Burt
1. The River Motor-Boat Boys on the Amazon; or, The Secret of Cloud Island (1913)
2. The River Motor-Boat Boys on the Columbia; or, The Confession of a Photograph
3. The River Motor-Boat Boys on the Mississippi; or, The Trail to the Gulf (1913)
4. The River Motor-Boat Boys on the St. Lawrence; or, The Lost Channel (1913)
5. The River Motor-Boat Boys on the Ohio; or, The Three Blue Lights (1913)

6. The River Motor-Boat Boys on the Colorado; or, The Clue in the Rocks
7. The River Motor-Boat Boys on the Yukon; or, The Lost Mine of Rainbow Bend
8. The River Motor-Boat Boys on the Rio Grande; or, In Defense of the Rambler (1915)

978. ROBIN HOOD
author: [unknown]
publisher: McLoughlin
1. Robinson Crusoe (1889)
2. Ali Baba; or, The Forty Thieves (1886)
3. Story of Robin Hood (1889)
4. Jack the Giant Killer (1889)
5. Aladdin; or, The Wonderful Lamp (1889)
6. Rip Van Winkle (1889)

979. ROBIN REDBREAST
author: Madeline Leslie
publisher: Woolworth, Ainsworth; A.S. Barnes; Crosby & Nichols
1. Little Robins Learn to Fly (1860)
2. Little Robins in the Nest (1860)
3. Little Robins' Friends (1860)
4. Little Robins in Trouble (1860)
5. Little Robins' Love One to Another (1860)
6. The Robin's Nest (1860)

ROBIN'S NEST STORIES see ROBIN REDBREAST

980. ROBINSON CRUSOE
author: [unknown]
publisher: McLoughlin Brothers
1. Robinson Crusoe (1898)
2. The Story of Robin Hood (1889)

981. ROCKET RIDERS
author: Howard Roger Garis
publisher: A. L. Burt
1. Rocket Riders Across the Ice; or, Racing Against Time (1933)
2. Rocket Riders Over the Desert; or, Seeking the Lost City (1933)
3. Rocket Riders in Stormy Seas; or, Trailing the Treasure Divers (1933)
4. Rocket Riders in the Air; or, A Chase in the Clouds (1934)

982. ROCKLANDS SCHOOL

author: Elsie Oxenham [pseudonym of Elsie Jeanette Dunkerley]
publisher: Collins
1. The Girls of Rocklands School (1929)
2. The Second Term at Rocklands (1930)
3. The Third Term at Rocklands (1931)

983. ROCKSPUR ATHLETIC

author: Gilbert Patten
publishers: Street & Smith; David McKay
1. The Rockspur Nine; A Story of Base Ball (1900) [alternate subtitle: The Greatest Baseball Story Ever Written]
2. The Rockspur Eleven; A Story of Football (1900) [alternate subtitle: A Fine Football Story for Boys]
3. The Rockspur Rivals; A Story of Winter Sports (1901) [alternate subtitle: A Story of Winter Sports for Boys]

984. ROCKY MOUNTAIN

author: Harry Castlemon [pseudonym of Charles Austin Fosdick]
publisher: Porter & Coates
1. Frank Among the Rancheros (1865)
2. Frank at Don Carlos' Rancho (1868)
3. Frank in the Mountains (1868)

985. ROD AND GUN

author: Harry Castlemon [pseudonym of Charles Austin Fosdick]
publisher: Porter & Coates
1. Don Gordon's Shooting-Box (1883)
2. The Rod and Gun Club (1883)
3. The Young Wild-Fowlers (1885)
4. The Young Game-Warden (1896)

986. ROGER PAULDING

author: Edward Latimer Beach
publisher: Penn
1. Roger Paulding, Apprentice Seaman (1911)
2. Roger Paulding, Gunner's Mate (1912)
3. Roger Paulding, Gunner
4. Roger Paulding, Ensign (1914)

987. ROLLO I [see also LUCY; JONAS'S STORIES]

author: Jacob Abbott
publishers: Phillips; Sampson & Co.; William Crosby; Crowell; Brown, Taggard & Chase; Sheldon
1. Rollo Learning to Talk
2. Rollo Learning to Read
3. Rollo at Work; or, The Way for a Boy to Learn (1865)
4. Rollo at Play
5. Rollo at School
6. Rollo's Vacation
7. Rollo's Experiments
8. Rollo's Museum
9. Rollo's Travels (1865)
10. Rollo's Correspondence
11. Rollo's Philosophy — Water
12. Rollo's Philosophy — Air
13. Rollo's Philosophy — Fire
14. Rollo's Philosophy — Sky

988. ROLLO II

author: Jacob Abbott
publisher: [unknown]
1. On the Atlantic
2. In Paris
3. In Switzerland
4. In London
5. On the Rhine
6. In Scotland
7. In Geneva
8. In Holland
9. In Naples
10. In Rome

989. ROLLO III

author: Jacob Abbott
publisher: [unknown]
1. Labor Lost: C. Elky, Preparations, A Bad Beginning, What Rollo Might Do, A New Plan, Hirup! Hirup!, An Overture
2. The Apple Gathering: A, The Garden House, Jolly, The Pet Lamb, The Meadow Russett, Insubordination, Subordination, The New Plan Tried, A Present, The Strawberry Bed, The Farmer's Story
3. The Steepletrap
4. The Halo Round the Moon
5. The Freshet: Maria and the Caravan, Small Craft, The Principles of Order, Clearing Up
6. The Two Wheelbarrows: The Two Little Wheelbarrows, Rides, The

Corporals, The Old Nails, A Conversation, Rollo Learns to Work at Last, The Corporals Again
7. Trouble on the Mountain
8. Causey Building: C. Sand Men, The Gray Garden, A Contract, Instructions, Keeping Tally, Rights Defined, Calculation
9. Rollo's Garden

990. ROSALIE DARE
author: Amy Brooks
publisher: Lothrop, Lee & Shepard
1. Rosalie Dare (1924)
2. Rosalie Dare's Test (1925)
3. What Rosalie Dare Won (1926)

991. ROSE-BUD
author Sara Crompton
publisher: James Hogg & Son
1–11. [titles unknown]
12. The Life of Robinson Crusoe in Short Words (1859)

992. ROSE CAMPBELL
author: Louisa May Alcott
publisher: Little, Brown
1. Eight Cousins (1874)
2. Rose in Bloom (1876)

993. ROSE CARNATION
authors: George Manville Fenn [1]; Evelyn Everett-Green [2]; Frances E. Crompton [3]; Amanda Minnie Douglas [4]; John Strange Winter [5]; Mary Dow Brine [6]
publisher: Henry Altemus
1. The Powder Monkey (1906)
2. Little Lady Val; A Tale of the Days of Good Queen Bess (1906)
3. Little Swan Maidens (1906)
4. What Charlie Found to Do (1906)
5. That Little French Baby (1906)
6. Mother's Little Man (1906)

994. ROSEMARY
author: Josephine Lawrence
publisher: Cupples & Leon
1. Rosemary (1922)
2. Rainbow Hill (1924)
3. Rosemary and the Princess (1927)

995. ROSS GRANT
author: John Garland
publisher: Penn
1. Ross Grant Tenderfoot (1924)
2. Ross Grant Goldhunter (1924)
3. Ross Grant on the Trail (1924)
4. Ross Grant in Miner's Camp (1924)

996. ROUGHING IT
author: Harry Castlemon [pseudonym of Charles Austin Fosdick]
publisher: Porter & Coates
1. George in Camp; or, Life on the Plains (1879)
2. George at the Wheel; or, Life in the Pilot-House (1881)
3. George at the Fort; or, Life Among the Soldiers (1882)

997. ROVER BOYS
author: Arthur M. Winfield [pseudonym of Edward Stratemeyer]
publishers: Chatterton-Peck; Whitman; Grosset & Dunlap
1. The Rover Boys at School; or, The Cadets of Putnam Hall (1899)
2. The Rover Boys on the Ocean; or, A Chase for a Fortune (1899)
3. The Rover Boys in the Jungle; or, Stirring Adventures in Africa (1899)
4. The Rover Boys Out West; or, The Search for A Lost Mine (1900)
5. The Rover Boys on the Great Lakes; or, The Secret of the Island Cave (1901)
6. The Rover Boys in the Mountains; or, A Hunt for Fame and Fortune (1902)
7. The Rover Boys on Land and Sea; or, The Crusoes of Seven Islands (1903)
8. The Rover Boys in Camp; or, The Rivals of Pine Island (1904)
9. The Rover Boys on the River; or, The Search for the Missing Houseboat (1905)
10. The Rover Boys on the Plains; or, The Mystery of Red Rock Ranch (1906)
11. The Rover Boys in Southern Waters; or, The Deserted Yacht (1907)
12. The Rover Boys on the Farm; or, Last Days at Putnam Hall (1908)
13. The Rover Boys on Treasure Isle; or,

The Strange Cruise of the Steam Yacht (1909)

14. The Rover Boys at College; or, The Right Road and the Wrong (1910)
15. The Rover Boys Down East; or, The Struggle for the Stanhope Fortune (1911)
16. The Rover Boys in the Air; or, From College Campus to the Clouds (1912)
17. The Rover Boys in New York; or, Saving Their Father's Honor (1913)
18. The Rover Boys in Alaska; or, Lost in the Fields of Ice (1914)
19. The Rover Boys in Business; or, The Search for the Missing Bonds (1915)
20. The Rover Boys on a Tour; or, Last Days at Brill College (1916)
21. The Rover Boys at Colby Hall; or, The Struggles of the Young Cadets (1917)
22. The Rover Boys on Snowshoe Island; or, The Old Lumberman's Treasure Box (1918)
23. The Rover Boys Under Canvas; or, The Mystery of the Wrecked Submarine (1919)
24. The Rover Boys on a Hunt; or, The Mysterious House in the Woods (1920)
25. The Rover Boys in the Land of Luck; or, Stirring Adventures in the Oilfields (1921)
26. The Rover Boys at Big Horn Ranch; or, The Cowboys' Double Roundup (1922)
27. The Rover Boys at Big Bear Lake; or, The Camps of the Rival Cadets (1923)
28. The Rover Boys Shipwrecked; or, A Thrilling Hunt for Pirates' Gold (1924)
29. The Rover Boys on Sunset Trail; or, The Old Miner's Mysterious Message (1925)
30. The Rover Boys Winning a Fortune; or, Strenuous Days Afloat and Ashore (1926)

998. ROY BLAKELEY
author: Percy Kees Fitzhugh
illustrators: Howard L. Hastings [1, 2]; R. Emmett Owen [8, 9]; H.S. Barbour [12, 15, 16]; Russell H. Tandy [18]; Charles Durant [17]

publisher Grosset & Dunlap
1. Roy Blakeley, His Story; Being the True Narrative of His Adventures and Those of His Troop (1920)
2. Roy Blakeley's Adventures in Camp (1920)
3. Roy Blakeley's Camp on Wheels (1920)
4. Roy Blakeley, Pathfinder (1920)
5. Roy Blakeley's Silver Fox Patrol
6. Roy Blakeley's Motor Caravan
7. Roy Blakeley, Lost, Strayed or Stolen
8. Roy Blakeley's Bee-Line Hike (1922)
9. Roy Blakeley at the Haunted Camp (1922)
10. Roy Blakeley's Funny-Bone Hike (1923)
11. Roy Blakeley's Tangled Trails
12. Roy Blakeley on the Mohawk Trail (1925)
13. Roy Blakeley's Elastic Hike
14. Roy Blakeley's Roundabout Hike
15. Roy Blakeley's Happy-Go-Lucky Hike (1928)
16. Roy Blakeley's Go-As-You-Please Hike (1929)
17. Roy Blakeley's Wild Goose Chase (1930)
18. Roy Blakeley Up in the Air (1931)

999. ROY ROGERS
author: Don Middleton
publisher: Whitman
1. Roy Rogers and the Gopher Creek Gunman (1945)
2. Roy Rogers and the Raiders of Sawtooth Ridge (1946)
3. Roy Rogers and the Rimrod Renegades (1952)

1000. ROY STOVER
author: Philip A. Barlett
publishers: Barse; Grosset & Dunlap
1. The Lakeport Bank Mystery (1929)
2. The Mystery of the Snowbound Express (1929)
3. The Cliff Island Mystery (1929)

1001. RUBY AND RUTH
author: Minnie E. Paull
publisher: Cupples & Leon
1. Ruby and Ruth

2. Ruby's Ups and Downs
3. Ruby at School
4. Ruby's Vacation

1002. RUSHTON BOYS

author: Spencer Davenport [pseudonym of the Stratemeyer Syndicate
illustrator: Walter S. Rogers
publishers: Hearst's International Library; George Sully; Whitman

1. The Rushton Boys at Rally Hall; or, Great Days in School and Out (1916)
2. The Rushton Boys in the Saddle; or, The Ghost of the Plains (1916)
3. The Rushton Boys at Treasure Cove; or, The Missing Chest of Gold (1916) [alternate subtitle: The Missing Oaken Chest]

1003. RUSS FARRELL

author: Thompson Burtis
publishers: Doubleday-Page; Doubleday-Doran

1. Russ Farrell, Airman (1924)
2. Russ Farrell, Test Pilot
3. Russ Farrell, Circus Flyer
4. Russ Farrell, Border Patrolman (1929)
5. Russ Farrell Over Mexico (1929)

1004. RUSTY

author: Frances R. Sterrett
publisher: Penn

1. Rusty of the Tall Pines (1928)
2. Rusty of the High Towers (1929)
3. Rusty of the Mountain Peaks (1930)
4. Rusty of the Meadow Lands (1931)

1005. RUTH DARROW FLYING STORIES

author: Mildred A. Wirt
publisher: Barse

1. Ruth Darrow in the Air Derby; or, Recovering the Silver Trophy (1930)
2. Ruth Darrow in the Fire Patrol; or, Capturing the Redwood Thieves (1930)
3. Ruth Darrow in Yucatan (1931)
4. Ruth Darrow and the Coast Guard (1931)

1006. RUTH FIELDING

author: Alice B. Emerson [pseudonym of the Stratemeyer Syndicate]

illustrators: Walter S. Rogers [6,8–10]; R. Emmett Owen [11–12,14,16]; Thelma Gooch [17–19]; Bess Goc Willis [23]; Ernest Townsend [24]; M.J. LeBeuthillier [27]; Russell H. Tandy [28–30]
publisher: Cupples & Leon

1. Ruth Fielding of the Red Mill; or, Jasper Parloe's Secret (1913)
2. Ruth Fielding at Briarwood Hall; or, Solving the Campus Mystery (1913)
3. Ruth Fielding at Snow Camp; or, Lost in the Backwoods (1913)
4. Ruth Fielding at Lighthouse Point; or, Nita, the Girl Castaway (1913)
5. Ruth Fielding at Silver Ranch; or, Schoolgirls Among the Cowboys (1913)
6. Ruth Fielding on Cliff Island; or, The Old Hunter's Treasure Box (1915)
7. Ruth Fielding at Sunrise Farm; or, What Became of the Ruby Orphans (1915)
8. Ruth Fielding and the Gypsies; or, The Missing Pearl Necklace (1915)
9. Ruth Fielding in Moving Pictures; or, Helping the Dormitory Fund (1916)
10. Ruth Fielding Down in Dixie; or, Great Times in the Land of Cotton (1916) [alternate subtitle: Great Days in the Land of Cotton]
11. Ruth Fielding at College; or, The Missing Examination Papers (1917)
12. Ruth Fielding in the Saddle; or, College Girls in the Land of Gold (1917)
13. Ruth Fielding in the Red Cross; or, Doing Her Best for Uncle Sam (1918)
14. Ruth Fielding at the War Front; or, The Hunt for the Lost Soldier (1918)
15. Ruth Fielding Homeward Bound; or, A Red Cross Worker's Ocean Perils (1919)
16. Ruth Fielding Down East; or, The Hermit of Beach Plum Point (1920)
17. Ruth Fielding in the Great Northwest; or, The Indian Girl Star of the Movies (1921)
18. Ruth Fielding on the St. Lawrence; or, The Queer Old Man of the Thousand Islands (1922)
19. Ruth Fielding Treasure Hunting; or, A Moving Picture That Became Real (1923)

20. Ruth Fielding in the Far North; or, The Lost Motion Picture Company (1924)
21. Ruth Fielding at Golden Pass; or, The Perils of an Artificial Avalanch (1925)
22. Ruth Fielding in Alaska; or; The Girl Miners of Snow Mountain (1926)
23. Ruth Fielding and Her Great Scenario; or, Striving for the Moving Picture Prize (1927)
24. Ruth Fielding at Cameron Hall; or, A Mysterious Disappearance (1928)
25. Ruth Fielding Clearing Her Name; or, The Rivals of Hollywood (1929)
26. Ruth Fielding in Talking Pictures; or, The Prisoners of the Tower (1930)
27. Ruth Fielding and Baby Jane (1931)
28. Ruth Fielding and Her Double (1932)
29. Ruth Fielding and Her Greatest Triumph; or, Saving Her Company from Disaster (1933)
30. Ruth Fielding and Her Crowning Victory; or, Winning Honors Abroad (1934)

1007. SADDLE BOYS
author: James Carson
illustrator: Walter S. Rogers
publisher: Cupples & Leon
1. The Saddle Boys of the Rockies; or, Lost on Thunder Mountain (1913)
2. The Saddle Boys in the Grand Canyon; or, The Hermit of the Cave (1913)
3. The Saddle Boys on the Plains; or, After a Treasure of Gold (1913)
4. The Saddle Boys at Circle Ranch; or, In at the Grand Round-Up (1913)
5. The Saddle Boys on Mexican Trails; or, In the Hands of the Enemy (1915)

1008. SAFETY FIRST
author: W.T. Nichols
publisher: Penn
1. The Safety First Club (1917)
2. The Safety First Club and the Flood (1917)
3. The Safety First Club Fights Fire (1917)

1009. SAILOR BOY
author: Oliver Optic [pseudonym of William Taylor Adams]
publisher: Lee & Shepard
1. The Yankee Middy; or, The Adventures of a Naval Officer; A Story of the Great Rebellion (1865)

SAINT LAURENCE see ST. LAWRENCE

1010. SAINT NICHOLAS
author: Richard Philip Garrold
publisher: Benziger Brothers
1. The Boys of St. Batt's; A Day-School Story (1912)

1011. SAM STEELE [see also BOY FORTUNE HUNTERS]
author: Hugh Fitzgerald [pseudonym of Lyman Frank Baum]
publisher: Reilly & Britton
1. Sam Steele's Adventures on Land and Sea (1906)
2. Sam Steele's Adventures in Panama (1907)

1012. SANDMAN STORIES
author: Abbie Phillips Walker
publisher: H. Hamilton
1. Sandman Twilight Stories (1951)
2. Sandman's 3-minute Stories (1951)
3. Sandman's Stories of Twinkle-Eyes (1951)
4. Sandman's Stories of Snowed-In Hut (1951)
5. Sandman's Stories of Drusilla Doll (1951)
6. Sandman's Might-Be-So Stories (1951)
7. The Sandman's Hour: Stories for Bedtime (1951)

1013. SANTA CLAUS
author: [unknown]
publisher: McLoughlin
1. Old Mother Hubbard and Her Dog (1889)
2. Busy Days; Stories and Pictures for the Nursery (1897)
3. Santa Claus and His Works (1889)
4. Cinderella (1889)
5. Old Dame Trot and Her Comical Cat (1891)

1014. SARA CREWE
author: Francis Hodgson-Burnett

publisher: Unwin
1. Sara Crewe; or, What Happened at Miss Minchins (1887)
2. Editha's Burglar and Sara Crewe (1888)

1015. SAY AND DO
author: Susan Warner
publisher: Robert Carter & Brothers
1. The Rapids of Niagara (1879)
2. The Little Camp of Eagle Hill (1876)
3. Sceptres and Crowns (1875)
4. Willow Brook (1874)
5. The Flag of Truce (1875)
6. Bread and Oranges (1875)

1016. SCENES DE LA VIE AMER-ICAINE
author: Oliver Optic [pseudonym of William Taylor Adams]
publisher: Gedalge Jeune
1. The Boat Club

1017. SCHONBERG-COTTA
author: Elizabeth Rundle Charles
publisher: T. Nelson & Sons
1. Chronicles of the Schonberg-Cotta Family (1868)
2. The Draytons and the Davenants; A Story of the Civil Wars (1877)
3. The Bertram Family (1882)
4. Diary of Mrs. Kitty Trevylyan; A Story of the Times of Whitefield and the Wesleys (1886)
5. Wanderings over Bible Lands and Seas (1892)
6. The Victory of the Vanquished; A Story of the First Century (1883)
7. Winifred Bertram and the World She Lived In (1884)
8–10. [titles unknown]
11. Diary of Brother Bartholomew, with Other Tales and Sketches of Christian Life in Lands and Ages (1871)

1018. SCHOOL AND CAMP
author: Edward Augustus Rand
publisher: D. Lothrop
1. Pushing Ahead; or, Big Brother Dave (1880)

1019. SCHOOL ATHLETIC
author: John Prescott Earle

publisher: Penn
1. On the School Team (1908)
2. The School Team in Camp (1909)
3. Captain of the School Team
4. School Team on the Diamond (1911)

1020. SCIENTIFIC AMERICAN BOYS
author: A. Russel Bond
publisher: Munn
1. The Scientific American Boy (1907)
2. The Scientific American Boy at School
3. With the Men Who Do Things
4. Pick, Shovel and Pluck (1914)

1021. SCOTT BURTON
author: Edward G. Cheyney
publisher: David Appleton
1. Scott Burton, Forester (1917)
2. Scott Burton on the Range
3. Scott Burton and the Timber Thieves
4. Scott Burton, Logger
5. Scott Burton's Claim (1926)

1022. SCRANTON HIGH
author: Donald Ferguson
publisher: Saalfield
1. The Chums of Scranton High; or, Hugh Morgan's Uphill Fight (1919)
2. The Chums of Scranton High Out for the Pennant; or, In the Three Town League (1919)
3. The Chums of Scranton High on the Cinder Path (1919)
4. The Chums of Scranton High at Ice Hockey (1919)

1023. SCRIBNER SERIES FOR YOUNG PEOPLE [see also HENTY and HENTY SERIES FOR BOYS]
author: Arthur Stanwood Pier
publisher: Charles Scribner's Sons
1. Boys of St. Timothy's (1904)
2. With Wolfe in Canada; or, The Winning of a Continent (1920)
3. With Lee in Virginia; A Story of the American Civil War (1900)
4. Under Drake's Flag; A Tale of the Spanish Main (1900)
5. By Pike and Dyke; A Tale of the Rise of the Dutch Republic (1923)

1024. SEA AND SHORE

authors: [as indicated below]
publisher: Street & Smith

5. Theodora; Founded on the Celebrated Drama (1888) [au: Jolen Purcell Coryell]
6. The Masked Lady; or, The Fortunes of a Dragon (1889) [au: Maturin Murray Ballou]
10. La Tosca (1889) [au: John Russell Coryell]
13. The Irish Monte Cristo; or, The Secrets of the Catacombs (1889) [au: Alexander Robertson]
14. The Fortune-Teller of New Orleans; or, The Two Lost Daughters (1889) [au: William Henry Peck]
16. Siballa the Sorceress; or, The Flower Girl of London: A Tale of the Days of Richard III (1890)
18. The Yankee Champion; or, The Tory and His League: A Revolutionary Story of Land and Sea (1890) [au: Sylvanus Cobb]
24. Buffalo Bill's Last Victory; or, Dove Eye, the Lodge Queen (1890) [au: Ned Buntline]
25. Dashing Charlie, the Texan Whirlwind [au: Ned Buntline]
28. Texas Jack, the White King of the Pawnees (1891) [au: Ned Buntline]
44. Put Asunder: A Novel (1892) [au: Charlotte M. Brame]

1025. SEA SHORE AND MOUNTAIN

authors: Hugh Conway[1]; Robert Louis Stevenson[2]
publisher: Street & Smith

1. Living or Dead (1900)
2. Kidnapped: Being Memoirs of the Adventures of David Balfour in the Year 1751

1026. SEA STORIES FOR BOYS

author: John Gabriel Rowe
publisher: [unknown]

1. Crusoe Island
2. The Island Treasure
3. The Mystery of the Derelict
4. The Lightship Pirates
5. The Secret of the Golden Idol

SEA TREASURE *see* DEEP SEA

1027. SECKATARY HAWKINS

author: ["Himself"]
publisher: Robert F. Schulkers

1. Stoner's Boy (The Mystery of the Gray Ghost) (1926)
2. Seckatary Hawkins in Cuba (The Mystery of the Cazenova Treasure)
3. The Red Runners (The Mystery of the Hypnotizing Eyes)
4. The Gray Ghost (The Return of Stoner's Boy)
5. Stormie the Dog-Stealer (The Mystery of the Baying Hounds)
6. The Knights of the Square Table (The Mystery of the Lonely House)
7. Ching Toy (The Mystery of the Magic Triangle)
8. The Chinese Coin (The Mystery of the Cave of Wonders)
9. The Yellow Y (The Mystery of the Boy with the Longbow)
10. Herman the Fiddler (The Mystery of the Three-Eyed Ape) (1930)

1028. SHELDON SIX

author: Grace M. Remick
publisher: Penn

1. The Sheldon Six — Anne (1920)
2. The Sheldon Six — Rose (1921)
3. The Sheldon Six — Connie (1923)
4. The Sheldon Six — Susan (1924)

1029. SHERBURNE

author: Amanda M. Douglas
publisher: Dodd, Mead

1. Sherburne House (1892)
2. Lyndell Sherburne (1893)
3. The Sherburne Cousins (1894)
4. A Sherburne Romance (1895)
5. The Mistress of Sherburne (1896)
6. The Children at Sherburne House (1897)
7. The Sherburne Girls (1898)
8. The Heir of Sherburne (1899)
9. A Sherburne Inheritance (1901)
10. A Sherburne Quest (1902)
11. Honor Sherburne (1904)
12. In the Sherburne Line (1907)

1030. SHILLING STORY BOOKS
author: William Henry Giles Kingston
publisher: Cassell, Petter, Galpin
1. Among the Red-Skins; or, Over the Rocky Mountains (1880)

1031. SHIP AND SHORE [see also STRATEMEYER POPULAR SERIES]
author: Edward Stratemeyer
publisher: Merriam
1. The Last Cruise of the Spitfire; or, Luke Foster's Strange Voyage (1894)
2. Reuben Stone's Discovery; or, The Young Miller of Torrent Bend (1900)
3. True to Himself; or, Roger Strong's Struggle for Place (1900)

1032. SIDNEY
author: Anna Chapin Ray
publisher: Little, Brown
1. Sidney: Her Summer on the St. Lawrence (1905)
2. Janet: Her Winter in Quebec (1906)
3. Day: Her Year in New York (1907)
4. Sidney at College (1908)
5. Janet at Odds (1909)
6. Sidney: Her Senior Year (1910)

1033. SILVER FOX FARM
author: James Otis [pseudonym of James Otis Kaler]
illustrator: Copeland
publisher: Thomas Y. Crowell
1. The Wireless Station at Silver Fox Farm (1910)
2. The Aeroplane at Silver Fox Farm (1911)
3. Building an Airship at Silver Fox Farm (1912)
4. Airship Cruising From Silver Fox Farm (1913)

1034. SILVER LAKE
author: Madeline Leslie
publishers: Henry A. Sumner; Henry A. Young
1. Truth and Trust; or, The Iron Mountain (1868)
2. Hopes and Fears; or, Broad Oaks (1868)

1035. SILVER STAR
author: Basil Miller
publisher: Zondervan
1. Kay and Kim in Wild Horse Canyon
2. Silver Star in Rainbow Valley
3. Silver Star and the Black Raider

1036. SIX GIRLS
author: Marion Ames Taggart
publisher: W. A. Wilde
1. Six Girls and Bob (1906)
2. Six Girls and the Tea Room (1907)
3. Six Girls Growing Older (1908)
4. Six Girls and the Seventh One (1909)
5. Betty Gaston, the Seventh Girl (1910)
6. Six Girls and Betty (1911)
7. Six Girls Grown Up (1912)

1037. SIX LITTLE BUNKERS
author: Laura Lee Hope [pseudonym of the Stratemeyer Syndicate]
illustrators: R. Emmett Owen [1–6]; Walter S. Rogers [7–14]
publisher: Grosset & Dunlap
1. Six Little Bunkers at Grandma Bell's (1918)
2. Six Little Bunkers at Aunt Jo's (1918)
3. Six Little Bunkers at Cousin Tom's (1918)
4. Six Little Bunkers at Grandpa Ford's (1918)
5. Six Little Bunkers at Uncle Fred's (1918)
6. Six Little Bunkers at Captain Ben's (1920)
7. Six Little Bunkers at Cowboy Jack's (1921)
8. Six Little Bunkers at Mammy June's (1922)
9. Six Little Bunkers at Farmer Joel's (1923)
10. Six Little Bunkers at Miller Ned's (1924)
11. Six Little Bunkers at Indian John's (1925)
12. Six Little Bunkers at Happy Jim's (1928)
13. Six Little Bunkers at Skipper Bob's (1930)
14. Six Little Bunkers at Lighthouse Nell's (1930)

1038. SIX TO SIXTEEN
authors: Palmer Cox [1]; Charles Dickens [2]
publisher: H.M. Caldwell
1. Dickens' Christmas Stories for Children (1902)
2–10. [titles unknown]
11. The Christmas Pudding and Other Brownie Stories (1906)

1039. SKIPPY DARE MYSTERY STORIES
author: Hugh Lloyd [pseudonym of Percy Kees Fitzhugh]
publisher: Grosset & Dunlap
1. Among the Pirates (1934)
2. Hold for Ransom (1934)
3. Prisoner in Devil's Bay (1934)

1040. SKY BUDDIES [see also AIR-PLANE BOYS]
author: Edith Janice Craine
publisher: [unknown]
1. With the Revolutionists in Bolivia (1931)
2. Flying to Amy-Ran Fastness
3. At Platinum River

1041. SKY DETECTIVE STORIES
author: Ambrose Newcomb
publisher: Gold
1. Eagles of the Sky; or, With Jack Ralston Along the Airways (1930)
2. The Sky Detectives; or, How Jack Ralston Got His Man
3. Sky Pilot's Great Chase; or, Jack Ralston's Dead Stick Landing
4. Wings Over the Rockies; or, Jack Ralston's New Cloud Chaser
5. Trackers of the Fog Pack; or, Jack Ralston Flying Blind
6. Flying the Coast Skyway; or, Jack Ralston's Swift Patrol (1931)

1042. SKY FLYERS [alternate title: RANDY STARR]
author: Eugene Martin
illustrator: Howard L. Hastings
publisher: Henry Altemus
1. Randy Starr After an Air Prize; or, The Sky Flyers in a Dash Down the States (1931)

2. Randy Starr Above Stormy Seas; or, The Sky Flyers on a Perilous Journey (1931)
3. Randy Starr Leading the Air Circus; or, The Sky Flyers in a Daring Stunt (1932)
4. Randy Starr Tracing the Air Spy; or, The Sky Flyers Seeking the Stolen Plane (1933)

1043. SKY PILOT [see also AIR-PLANE GIRL]
author: Harrison Bardwell [pseudonym of Edith Janice Craine]
publisher: World Syndicate
1. The Mystery of Seal Islands (1931)
2. The Mystery Ship (1931)

1044. SKY SCOUTS [see also AIR MYSTERY]
author: Van Powell [pseudonym of A. Van Buren Powell]
publisher: A. L. Burt
1. The Mystery Crash (1932)
2. The Haunted Hanger (1932)
3. The Vanishing Air Liner (1932)
4. The Ghost of Mystery Airport (1932)

1045. SLEEPY-TIME-TALES [see also TUCK-ME-IN-TALES]
author: Arthur Scott Bailey
illustrators: Harry L. Smith [1,3–11]; Joseph B. Guzie [2]
publisher: Grosset & Dunlap
1. The Tale of Fatty Coon (1915)
2. The Tale of Tommy Fox (1915)
3. The Tale of Frisky Squirrel (1915)
4. The Tale of Jimmy Rabbit (1916)
5. The Tale of Paddy Muskrat (1916)
6. The Tale of Peter Mink (1916)
7. The Tale of Sandy Chipmunk (1916)
8. The Tale of Ferdinand Frog (1918)
9. The Tale of Bobby Bobolink (1920)
10. The Tale of Grandfather Mole (1920)
11. The Tale of Grumpy Weasel (1920)

1046. SLIM TYLER AIR STORIES
author: Richard H. Stone [pseudonym of the Stratemeyer Syndicate]
publisher: Cupples & Leon
1. Sky Riders of the Atlantic; or, Slim Tyler's First Trip in the Clouds (1930)

2. Lost Over Greenland; or, Slim Tyler's Search for Dave Boyd (1930)
3. An Air Cargo of Gold; or, Slim Tyler, Special Bank Messenger (1930)
4. Adrift Over Hudson Bay; or, Slim Tyler in the Land of Ice (1931)
5. An Airplane Mystery; or, Slim Tyler on the Trail (1931)
6. Secret Sky Express; or, Slim Tyler Saving a Fortune (1932)

1047. SLUMBER-TOWN TALES
author: Arthur Scott Bailey
publisher: Grosset & Dunlap
1. The Tale of Grunty Pig (1921)
2. The Tale of Miss Kitty Cat (1921)
3. The Tale of Pony Twinkleheels (1921)
4. The Tale of Mistah Mule (1923)

1048. SMILING POOL
author: Thornton Waldo Burgess
publisher: Aeonian
1. Jerry Muskrat at Home (1926)
2. Longlegs the Heron (1927)

SMITH BOYS see THOSE SMITH BOYS

1049. SNIPP, SNAPP, SNURR
author: Lindman
publisher: A. Whitman
1. Snipp, Snapp, Snurr and the Red Shoes (1932)
2. Snipp, Snapp, Snurr and the Gingerbread (1932)
3. Snipp, Snapp, Snurr and the Buttered Bread (1934)
4. Snipp, Snapp, Snurr and the Magic Horse (1935)
5. Snipp, Snapp, Snurr and the Yellow Sled (1936)
6. Snipp, Snapp, Snurr and the Big Surprise (1937)
7. Snipp, Snapp, Snurr and the Big Farm (1946)
8. Snipp, Snapp, Snurr Learn to Swim (1954)
9. Snipp, Snapp, Snurr and the Reindeer (1957)
10. Snipp, Snapp, Snurr and the Seven Dogs (1959)

1050. SNOW BIRD
author: [unknown]
publisher: D. Lothrop
1. Santa Claus' Ride; Jolly Jingles and Stories (1895)
2. Doll's Tea Party; Merry Play Time (1895)
3. Ralph's Ulster; and Other Stories (1880)

1051. SOLDIER BOY
author: Oliver Optic [pseudonym of William Taylor Adams]
publisher: Lee & Shepard
1–2. [titles unknown]
3. Fighting Joe; or, The Fortunes of a Staff Officer; A Story of the Great Rebellion (1866)

1052. SOLDIERS OF FORTUNE
author: [unknown]
publisher: Lothrop, Lee & Shepard
1. On to Peking; or, Old Glory in China (1900)
2. Under the Mikado's Flay; or, Young Soldier's of Fortune
3. At the Fall of Port Arthur; or, A Young American in the Japanese Navy
4. With Togo for Japan; or, Three Young Americans On Land and Sea (1906)

1053. SORAK JUNGLE SERIES
author: Harvey D. Richards
publisher: Cupples & Leon
1. Sorak of the Malay Jungle; or, How Two Young Americans Face Death and Win a Friend (1933)
2. Sorak and the Clouded Tiger; or, How the Terrible Ruler of the North Is Hunted and Destroyed
3. Sorak and the Sultan's Ankus; or, How a Perilous Journey Leads to a Kingdom of Giants
4. Sorak and the Tree-Men; or, How Sorak and His Friends Escape Their Captors (1935)

1054. SPACE ADVENTURE
authors: Jack Coggins [1, 3]; Philip Briggs [2]; Patrick Moore [4, 6]; Hereward Ohlson [5]
publisher: Lutterworth

1. Rockets, Jets, Guided Missiles and Space Ships (1953)
2. The Silent Planet; A Story of Two Boys and a Daring Rescue from Outer Space (1957)
3. By Space Ship to the Moon (1953)
4. Wheel in Space; The Amazing Story of How a Satellite Was Built in Spite of Treachery and Danger (1956)
5. Thunderbolt and the Rebel Planet; The Captain of the Spaceways Leads an Expedition to the Strange World of Pluvius (1954)
6. Destination Luna; The Thrilling Story of a Boy's Adventurous Trip to the Moon (1955)

1055. SPARKLING GEMS FOR YOUTH
author: Madeline Leslie
publisher: Andrew F. Graves
1. Gem of Uprightness; or, Dick and Oliver (1872)

1056. SPECTACLES
author: Sarah West Lander
publisher: John R. Anderson
1. Spectacles for Young Eyes: Boston (1862)
2. Spectacles for Young Eyes: St. Petersburg (1864)
3. Spectacles for Young Eyes: Pekin (1868)
4. Spectacles for Young Eyes: Moscow (1863)
5. Spectacles for Young Eyes: Zurich (1864)
6. Spectacles for Young Eyes: Berlin (1865)
7. Spectacles for Young Eyes: Rome (1865)
8. Spectacles for Young Eyes: New York (1868)

1057. SPEEDWELL BOYS
author: Roy Rockwood [pseudonym of the Stratemeyer Syndicate]
illustrator: Walter S. Rogers
publisher: Cupples & Leon
1. The Speedwell Boys on Motorcycles; or, The Mystery of a Great Conflagration (1913)
2. The Speedwell Boys and Their Racing Auto; or, A Run for the Golden Cup (1913)
3. The Speedwell Boys and Their Power Launch; or, To The Rescue of the Castaways (1913)
4. The Speedwell Boys in a Submarine; or, The Treasure of Rocky Cove (1913)
5. The Speedwell Boys and Their Ice Racer; or, Lost in the Great Blizzard (1915)

1058. SPORT STORIES
author: Harold M. Sherman
publisher: Grosset & Dunlap
1. Batter Up
2. Double Play
3. Bases Full
4. Hit by Pitcher
5. Safe
6. Hit and Run
7. Mayfield's Fighting Five
8. Shoot the Ball
9. Flashing Steel
10. Flying Heels
11. Slashing Sticks
12. Number 44

1059. SPORTS
author: Walter Camp
publisher: David Appleton
1. The Substitute (1908)
2. Jack Hall at Yale
3. Danny the Freshman
4. Old Ryerson
5. Danny Fists
6. Captain Danny (1915)

SPORTSMAN'S CLUB see FRANK NELSON

1060. SPRINGDALE
author: Dorita Fairlie Bruce
publisher: Oxford University Press
1. The Captain of Springdale (1932)
2. The New House at Springdale (1934)
3. The Prefects at Springdale (1938)

1061. SPY
author: Anne Emery
publisher: Rand
1. A Spy in Old Philadelphia (1958)
2. A Spy in Old New Orleans (1960)

3. A Spy in Old Detroit (1963)
4. A Spy in Old West Point (1965)

1062. SQUARE DOLLAR BOYS
author: Harrie Irving Hancock
publisher: Henry Altemus
1. The Square Dollar Boys Wake Up; or, Fighting the Trolley Franchise Steal (1912)
2. The Square Dollar Boys Smash the Ring; or, In the Lists Against the Crooked Land Deal (1912)
3. The Square Dollar Boys' Still Hunt; or, Breaking a Twentieth Century Mississippi Bubble (1912)

1063. ST. DUNSTAN
author: Warren L. Eldred
publisher: Lothrop, Lee & Shepard
1. The Crimson Ramblers (1909)
2. Camp St. Dunstan
3. The Boys of Brookfield Academy
4. The Lookout Island Campers
5. The Oak Street Boys' Club
6. St. Dunstan Boy Scouts
7. Classroom and Campus (1912)

1064. ST. LAWRENCE
author: Everett T. Tomlinson
publisher: Lothrop, Lee & Shepard
1. Camping on the St. Lawrence; or, On the Trail of the Early Discoverers (1899)
2. The House-Boat on the St. Lawrence; or, Following the Frontenac
3. Cruising in the St. Lawrence; or, A Summer Vacation in Historic Waters (1902)

1065. ST. MARY'S
author: William Heyliger
publisher: David Appleton
1. Bartley, Freshman Pitcher (1911)
2. Bucking the Line
3. Captain of the Nine
4. Strike Three
5. Off Side
6. Against Odds (1915)

1066. ST. NICHOLAS SERIES FOR BOYS AND GIRLS
authors: Oliver Optic [pseudonym of William Taylor Adams] [1]; William Dalton [2]
publisher: International Book Co.
1. Nature's Young Noblemen (1890)
2. The Tiger Prince; or, Adventures in the Wilds of Abyssinia (1870)

1067. STANDARD SERIES OF TEMPERANCE TALES
author: Mary Dwinell Chellis
publisher: Henry A. Sumner
1. Bill Drock's Investment (1881)
2. Mark Dunning's Enemy (1881)

1068. STAR
author: Susan Warner
publisher: Frederick Warne
1–12. [titles unknown]
    13. Say and Seal (1870)
unknown numbers:
    1. Ellen Montgomery's Bookshelf (1890)
    2. The Golden Ladder; Stories Illustrative of the Eight Beatitudes (1887)

1069. STAR ISLAND
author: Marjory Hall
publisher: Funk
1. Star Island (1953)
2. Star Island Again (1955)
3. Three Stars for Star Island (1958)

1070. STARRY FLAG
author: Oliver Optic [pseudonym of William Taylor Adams]
publisher: Lee & Shepard
1. The Starry Flag; or, The Young Fisherman of Cape Ann (1867)
2. Freaks of Fortune; or, Half Round the World (1868)
3. Seek and Find; A Story for Boys (1875)
4. Seek and Find; or, The Adventures of a Smart Boy (1867)
5. Make or Break; or, The Rich Man's Daughter (1868)
6. Down the River; or, Buck Bradford and His Tyrants (1868)

1071. STARS AND STRIPES
author: Frank Cobb
publisher: Saalfield

1. The Potter Boys in the Front Line Trenches (1919)
2. The Potter Boys Under Old Glory (1918)
3. [title unknown]
4. Hunting Down the Spy (1916)

STERLING BOY SCOUTS *see* BOY SCOUTS XVIII

1072. STEVE KNIGHT FLYING STORIES
author: Ted Copp
publisher: Grosset & Dunlap
1. The Mystery of Devil's Hand (1941)
2. The Bridge of Bombers
3. The Phantom Fleet (1942)

STORIES ABOUT CAMP FIRE GIRLS *see* CAMPFIRE GIRLS XII

1073. STORIES FOR SUMMER DAYS AND WINTER NIGHTS
author: [unknown]
publisher: Groombridge & Sons
series 1:
1. [title unknown]
2. Ally's Birth-Day (1867)
3. [title unknown]
4. Right Is Right (1867)
5. The Crusaders (1867)
6–7. [titles unknown]
8. The Fairy-Craft of Nature (1867)
9. Little Tim and His Friend the Cobbler (1879)
10. The Children and the Sage (1856)
11. [title unknown]
12. David Allen; A Village Tale (1879) [number unknown]: Carl Thorn's Revenge (1849)
series 2:
1. [title unknown]
2. Madelaine Tube and Her Blind Brother; A Christmas Story for Young People (1867)
3. [title unknown]
4. The Boy and the Brook (1867)
5–11. [titles unknown]
12. Louis Duval; A Tale of the French Revolution (1867)
13. The Foundling of the Wreck (1867)

14–16. [titles unknown]
17. Home at the Haven; A Tale (1867)
18–19. [titles unknown]
20. The King and the Bondmen (1867)

1074. STORIES OF AMERICAN HISTORY
author: James Otis [pseudonym of James Otis Kaler]
illustrators: Geroge Foster Barnes; J. Steeple Davis; Frank T. Merrill
publishers: D. Estes; Estes & Lauriat
1. The Boys of 1745 at the Capture of Louisbourg (1895)
2. The Island Refuge; Casco Bay in 1676 (1895)
3. Neal, the Miller, a Son of Liberty (1895)
4. Under the Liberty Tree; A Story of the "Boston Massacre" (1896)
5. The Boys of Fort Schuyler (1897)
6. The Signal Boys of '75; A Tale of Boston During the Siege (1897)
7. The Boys of '98 (1898)
8. When Israel Putnam Served the King (1898)
9. Off Santiago with Sampson (1899)
10. When Dewey Came to Manila; or, Among the Filipinos (1899)
11. The Boston Boys of 1775; or, When We Besieged Boston (1900)
12. Defending the Island; A Story of Bar Harbor in 1758 (1904)

1075. STORY TREE
author: Abby Morton Diaz
publisher: D. Lothrop
1. Mercy Jane; Little Stories for Little Folks (1880)
2. Brave Little Goose-Girl; Little Stories for Little Folks (1880)

1076. STRATEMEYER POPULAR SERIES [see also SHIP AND SHORE]
author: Edward Stratemeyer
1. Richard Dare's Venture; or, Striking out for Himself (1899)
2. Reuben Stone's Discovery; or, The Young Miller of Torrent Bend (1900)
3. True to Himself; or, Roger Strong's Struggle for Place (1900)

4. To Alaska for Gold; or, The Fortune Hunters of the Yukon (1899)
5. Joe the Surveyor; or, The Value of a Lost Claim (1903)
6. Larry the Wanderer; or, The Rise of a Nobody (1904)

1077. SUBMARINE BOYS
author: Victor G. Durham
publishers: Henry Altemus; Saalfield
1. The Submarine Boys on Duty; or, Life on a Diving Torpedo Boat (1909)
2. The Submarine Boys' Trial Trip; or, "Making Good" as Young Experts (1909)
3. The Submarine Boys and the Middies; or, The Prize Detail at Annapolis (1909)
4. The Submarine Boys and the Spies; or, Dodging the Sharks of the Deep (1910)
5. The Submarine Boys' Lightning Cruise; or, The Young Kings of the Deep
6. The Submarine Boys for the Flag; or, Deeding Their Lives to Uncle Sam
7. The Submarine Boys and the Smugglers; or, Breaking Up the New Jersey Custom Frauds
8. The Submarine Boys' Secret Mission; or, Beating an Ambassador's Game (1912)

1078. SUE BARTON
author: Helen Dore Boylston
publisher: Little, Brown
1. Sue Barton, Student Nurse (1936)
2. Sue Barton, Senior Nurse (1937)
3. Sue Barton, Visiting Nurse (1938)
4. Sue Barton, Rural Nurse (1939)
5. Sue Barton, Superintendent of Nurses (1940)
6. Sue Barton, Neighborhood Nurse (1949)
7. Sue Barton, Staff Nurse (1952)

1079. SUGAR CREEK GANG
author: Paul Hutchens
publisher: William B. Eerdmans
1. The Sugar Creek Gang; A Story for Boys (1940)
2. The Haunted House at Sugar Creek (1949)

3. The Green Tent Mystery at Sugar Creek (1950)

1080. SUNBEAM [see also TRAP TO CATCH A SUNBEAM]
author: [unknown]
publisher: International Art Publishing Co.
5. Realities of Irish Life (1882)
19. Puss in Boots (1880)
23. Visit to the Farm (1880)
[# unknown]. The Dream Chintz (1850)

1081. SUNBEAM STORIES
authors: Constance Woodhead [1–2]; Colleen Jenkins [3–6]
publisher: Warne
1. The Little Goose-Girl (1952)
2. King Midas; or, The Golden Touch (1952)
3. The Sleeping Beauty (1952)
4. Hansel and Gretal (1952)
5. The Brave Tin Soldier (1952)
6. Beauty and Beast (1952)

1082. SUNNY BOY
author: Ramy Allison White [pseudonym of the Stratemeyer Syndicate]
illustrators: Charles L. Wrenn [1–3]; Howard L. Hastings [4–9]; John M. Foster [10–13]
publishers: Barse & Hopkins [1–10]; Barse & Company [11–13]; Grosset & Dunlap [14]
1. Sunny Boy in the Country (1920)
2. Sunny Boy at the Seashore (1920)
3. Sunny Boy in the Big City (1920)
4. Sunny Boy in School and Out (1921)
5. Sunny Boy and His Playmates (1922)
6. Sunny Boy and His Games (1923)
7. Sunny Boy in the Far West (1924)
8. Sunny Boy on the Ocean (1925)
9. Sunny Boy with the Circus (1926)
10. Sunny Boy and His Big Dog (1927)
11. Sunny Boy in the Snow (1929)
12. Sunny Boy at Willow Farm (1929)
13. Sunny Boy and His Cave (1930)
14. Sunny Boy at Rainbow Lake (1931)

1083. SUNNY HOUR
authors: Anna Burham [2]; Nellie Blessing Eyster [6]

publisher: McLoughlin Brothers
1. By the Sea Shore (1880)
2. With My Pets (1887)
3. Busy Days (1880)
4. Among the Flowers (1880)
5. Tom Harding and His Friends (1869)
6. Two Little Girls: and Other Stories (1899)

1084. SUNSHINE
authors: Madeline Leslie [4]; Evelyn Charles Vivian [5]
publishers: McLoughlin Brothers; A.F. Graves
1. The Silly Hare (1893)
2. The Three Bears (1893)
3. Cock Robin (1893)
4. Tony and His Harp (1870)
5. Robin Hood

1085. SUPERIOR LIBRARY
author: Oliver Optic [pseudonym of William Taylor Adams]
publisher: Superior Printing Co.
1. Outward Bound

1086. SUSAN
author: Cyrus T. Brady
publisher: Moffat, Yard
1. The Blue Ocean's Daughter (1907)
2. The Adventures of Lady Susan (1908)

1087. SUSANNAH
author: Muriel Denison
publisher: Dodd, Mead
1. Susannah, a Little Girl with the Mounties (1936)
2. Susannah of the Yukon (1938)
3. Susannah at Boarding School (1938)
4. Susannah Rides Again (1940)

1088. SUSIE SUNSHINE
author: [unknown]
publisher: McLoughlin Brothers
1. [title unknown]
2. Three Little Kittens; and, Mr. Fox (1899)

1089. SWEETHEART
author: Oliver Optic [pseudonym of William Taylor Adams]
publisher: George Munro's Sons

120. All Aboard; or, Life on the Lake (1898)

1090. SYLVIA ARDEN
author: Margaret Piper Chalmers
publisher: L. C. Page
1. Sylvia's Experiment; or, The Story of an Unrelated Family (1914)
2. Sylvia of the Hill Top (1916)
3. Sylvia Arden Decides (1917)
4. Wild Wings; a Romance of Youth (1921)
5. Peter's Best Seller (1923)
6. Babbie (1925)

1091. T. HAVILAND HICKS
author: Raymond Elderdice
publisher: David Appleton
1. T. Haviland Hicks, Freshman (1915)
2. T. Haviland Hicks, Sophomore
3. T. Haviland Hicks, Junior
4. T. Haviland Hicks, Senior (1916)

1092. TABITHA
author: Ruth Alberta Brown
publisher: Saalfield
1. Tabitha at Ivy Hall (1911
2. Tabitha's Glory (1912)
3. Tabitha's Vacation (1913)

1093. TABLEAUX DE LA VIE AMERICAINE
author: Oliver Optic [pseudonym of William Taylor Adams]
publisher: Gedalge Jeune
1. Try Again

1094. TAHARA
author: Harold M. Sherman
publishers: Barse & Hopkins; Gold
1. Tahara, Boy Mystic of India (1933)
2. Tahara Among African Tribes (1933)
3. Tahara, Boy King of the Desert (1933)
4. Tahara in the Land of Yucatan (1933)

1095. TAIT
author: Everett T. Tomlinson
publisher: Barse & Hopkins
1. The Pennant (1912)
2. Carl Hall of Tait
3. Captain Dan Richards
4. Jack Stone of Tait School (1917)

TALES OF THE ADMIRAL'S GRAND-
DAUGHTER *see* ADMIRAL'S
GRANDDAUGHTER

1096. TAMMY
author: Elizabeth Baker
publisher: Houghton
1. Tammy Camps Out (1958)
2. Tammy Climbs Pyramid Mountain
   (1962)
3. Tammy Goes Canoeing (1966)
4. Tammy Camps in the Rocky Mountains (1970)

1097. TED AND NINA
author: Marguerite de Angeli
publisher: Doubleday
1. Ted and Nina Go to the Grocery Store
   (1935)
2. Ted and Nina Have a Happy Rainy
   Day (1936)

1098. TED JONES
author: Frank Glines Patchin
publisher: Henry Altemus
1. Ted Jones, Fortune Hunter; or, The
   Adventures of the Luckless Three in
   Pearl Fishing (1928) [alternate subtitle:
   Perilous Adventures with a Chinese
   Pearl Trader]
2. Ted Jones at Desperation Island; or,
   The Affair with the Yellow Coral Prince
   (1928)
3. Ted Jones' Weeks of Terror; or, The
   Luckless Three's Revolt Against the
   Sandalwood Sharpers (1928)
4. Ted Jones Under Sealed Orders; or,
   The Mysterious Treasure Trail to the
   Red Lagoon (1928)

1099. TED MARSH
author: Elmer Sherwood [pseudonym of
   Samuel Leuwenkrohn]
publisher: Whitman
1. Ted Marsh, the Boy Scout
2. Ted Marsh on an Important Mission
3. Ted Marsh, the Young Volunteer
4. Ted Marsh and the Enemy
5. Ted Marsh and His Friend Steve
6. Ted Marsh and His Great Adventure

1100. TED SCOTT FLYING STO-RIES
author: Franklin W. Dixon [pseudonym of
   the Stratemeyer Syndicate]
illustrators: Walter S. Rogers [1–14];
   Clemens Gretter [15–18]; I.B. Hazelton
   [19–20]
publisher: Grosset & Dunlap
1. Over the Ocean to Paris; or, Ted
   Scott's Daring Long-Distance Flight
   (1927)
2. Rescued in the Clouds; or, Ted Scott,
   Hero of the Air (1927)
3. Over the Rockies with the Air Mail;
   or, Ted Scott Lost in the Wilderness
   (1927)
4. First Stop Honolulu; or, Ted Scott
   Over the Pacific (1927)
5. Search for the Lost Flyers; or, Ted
   Scott Over the West Indies (1928)
6. South of the Rio Grande; or, Ted
   Scott on a Secret Mission (1928)
7. Across the Pacific; or, Ted Scott's Hop
   to Australia (1928)
8. Lone Eagle of the Border; or, Ted Scott
   and the Diamond Smugglers (1929)
9. Flying Against Time; or, Ted Scott
   Breaking the Ocean to Ocean Record
   (1929)
10. Over the Jungle Trails; or, Ted Scott
    and the Missing Explorers (1929)
11. Lost at the South Pole; or, Ted Scott
    in Blizzard Land (1930)
12. Through the Air to Alaska; or, Ted
    Scott's Search in Nugget Valley (1930)
13. Flying to the Rescue; or, Ted Scott
    and the Big Dirigible (1930)
14. Danger Trails of the Sky; or, Ted
    Scott's Great Mountain Climb (1931)
15. Following the Sun Shadow; or, Ted
    Scott and the Great Eclipse (1932)
16. Battling the Wind; or, Ted Scott Fly-
    ing Around Cape Horn (1933)
17. Brushing the Mountain Top; or, Aid-
    ing the Lost Traveler (1934)
18. Castaways of the Stratosphere; or, Ted
    Scott Hunting the Vanquished Bal-
    loonist (1935)
19. Hunting the Sky Spies; or, Testing the
    Invisible Plane (1941)
20. The Pursuit Patrol; or, Chasing the
    Platinum Pirates (1943)

1101. TEDDY I
author: Anna Chapin Ray
publisher: Little, Brown
1. Teddy: Her Book (1898)
2. Phoebe: Her Profession (1900)
3. Teddy: Her Daughter (1901)
4. Nathalie's Chum (1902)
5. Ursula's Freshman (1903)
6. Nathalie's Sister (1904)

1102. TEDDY II
author: Howard Roger Garis
publishers: Cupples & Leon; Books Inc.
1. Teddy and the Mystery Dog (1936)
2. Teddy and the Mystery Monkey (1936)
3. Teddy and the Mystery Cat (1937)
4. Teddy and the Mystery Parrot (1938)
5. Teddy and the Mystery Pony (1939)
6. Teddy and the Mystery Deer (1940)
7. Teddy and the Mystery Goat (1941)

1103. TEENIE WEENIES
author: William Donahey
publisher: Reilly and Lee
1. The Adventures of the Teenie Weenies (1920)
2. Down the River with the Teenie Weenies (1921)
3. The Teenie Weenies Under the Rose Bush (1922)
4. The Teenie Weenies in the Wildwood (1923)

1104. TEXAN
author: Joseph A. Altsheler
publisher: David Appleton
1. The Texan Star (1912)
2. The Texan Scouts
3. The Texan Triumph (1913)

1105. THOSE SMITH BOYS
author: Howard Roger Garis
publisher: M. A. Donohue
1. Those Smith Boys; or, The Mystery of the Thumbless Man (1910)
2. Those Smith Boys on the Diamond; or, Nip and Tuck for Victory (1912)

1106. THREE GAYS
author: Ethel C. Brown
publisher: Penn
1. The Three Gays (1915)
2. The Three Gays at Merryton (1916)
3. The Three Gays in Maine (1917)
4. The Three Gays at the Old Farm (1918)

1107. THREE LITTLE TRIPPERTROTS
author: Howard Roger Garis
publisher: Graham and Matlack
1. Three Little Trippertrots; How They Ran Away, and How They Got Back Again (1912)
2. Three Little Trippertrots on Their Travels; The Wonderful Things They Saw and the Wonderful Things They Did (1912)

1108. THREE LITTLE WOMEN
author: Gabrielle E. Jackson
publisher: Winston
1. Three Little Women (1908)
2. Three Little Women at Work (1909)
3. Three Little Women's Success (1910)
4. Three Little Women as Wives (1914)

1109. THREE VASSAR GIRLS
author: Elizabeth Williams Champney
publishers: D. Estes; Estes & Lauriat
1. Three Vassar Girls in Switzerland (1890)
2. Three Vassar Girls in the Holy Land (1892)

1110. THRILLING ADVENTURE
author: Harriet Pyne Grove
publisher: Saalfield
1. The Mystery of the Sandalwood Boxes (1929)

1111. TIM MURPHY
author: Graham M. Dean
publisher: Gold
1. Daring Wings
2. Sky Trail
3. Circle 4 Patrol

1112. TIPPY PARRISH
author: Janet Lambert
publisher: Dutton
1. Miss Tippy (1948)
2. Little Miss Atlas (1949)
3. Miss America (1951)
4. Don't Cry, Little Girl (1952)

5. Rainbow After Rain (1953)
6. Welcome Home, Mrs. Jordan (1953)
7. A Song in Their Hearts (1956)

1113. TOBEY AND MIDGE HEYDON
author: Rosamund Du Jardin
publisher: J. B. Lippincott
1. Practically Seventeen (1949)
2. Class Ring (1951)
3. Boy Trouble (1953)
4. The Real Thing (1956)
5. Wedding in the Family (1958)
6. One of the Crowd (1961)

1114. TOD HALE
author: Ralph Henry Barbour
publishers: Dodd, Mead; Grosset & Dunlap
1. Tod Hale with the Crew (1926)
2. Tod Hale at Camp (1927)
3. Tod Hale on the Scrub (1928)
4. Tod Hale on the Nine (1928)

1115. TOLD IN THE NURSERY
author: [unknown]
publisher: [unknown]
1. Three Little Kittens and Other Stories (1889)

1116. TOLD TO THE CHILDREN
authors: Maria Edgeworth [1–2]; Amy Steedman [3]; Loney Chisholm [4]
publishers: T.C. & E.C. Jack; E.P. Dutton
1. Simple Susan (1910)
2. Stories of Robin Hood (1950)
3. Nursery Tales (1908)
4. Nursery Rhymes (1908)

1117. TOM BROWN I
author: Thomas Hughes
publishers: M. A. Donohue's, Henneberry
1. Tom Brown's School Days (1870)
2. Tom Brown at Oxford (1859)

1118. TOM BROWN II
author: Emily Baker
publisher: George Routledge & Sons
1. Harry Winthrope's School Days; A Tale of Old Blundell's School (1907)

1119. TOM CARDIFF
author: Howard Roger Garis
illustrator: W.B. King
publisher: Milton Bradley
1. Tom Cardiff's Circus (1926)
2. Tom Cardiff in the Big Top (1927)

1120. TOM FAIRFIELD
author: Allen Chapman [pseudonym of Edward Stratemeyer]
illustrators: Louis Wisa [1–4]; Walter S. Rogers [5]
publisher: Cupples & Leon
1. Tom Fairfield's School Days; or, The Chums of Elmwood Hall (1913)
2. Tom Fairfield at Sea; or, The Wreck of the Silver Star (1913)
3. Tom Fairfield in Camp; or, The Secret of the Old Mill (1913)
4. Tom Fairfield's Pluck and Luck; or, Working to Clear His Name (1913)
5. Tom Fairfield's Hunting Trip; or, Lost in the Wilderness (1915)

1121. TOM SLADE [see also various BOY SCOUT]
author: Percy Kees Fitzhugh
illustrators: Howard L. Hastings; Walter S. Rogers; R. Emmett Owen; Thomas Clarity
publisher: Grosset & Dunlap
1. Tom Slade, Boy Scout (1915)
2. Tom Slade at Temple Camp (1917)
3. Tom Slade on the River (1917)
4. Tom Slade with the Colors (1918)
5. Tom Slade on a Transport (1918)
6. Tom Slade with the Boys Over There (1918)
7. Tom Slade, Motorcycle Dispatch-Rider (1918)
8. Tom Slade with the Flying Corps; A Campfire Tale (1919)
9. Tom Slade at Black Lake
10. Tom Slade on Mystery Trail (1921)
11. Tom Slade's Double Dare (1922)
12. Tom Slade on Overlook Mountain (1923)
13. Tom Slade Picks a Winner
14. Tom Slade at Bear Mountain (1925)
15. Tom Slade: Forest Ranger (1926)
16. Tom Slade in the North Woods (1927)
17. Tom Slade at Shadow Isle (1928)

18. Tom Slade in the Haunted Cavern (1929)
19. Tom Slade, Parachute Jumper

1122. TOM STRONG
author: Alfred Bishop Mason
publisher: Holt
1. Tom Strong, Washington's Scout (1911)
2. Tom Strong, Boy Captain
3. Tom Strong, Junior
4. Tom Strong, Third
5. Tom Strong, Lincoln's Scout (1919)

1123. TOM SWIFT [see also TOM SWIFT JR. ADVENTURES]
author: Victor Appleton [pseudonym of the Stratemeyer Syndicate]
illustrators: R. Mencl [1–5]; H. Richard Boehm [6–16]; Walter S. Rogers [17–20,24–34]; Nat Falk [35–38]; H.R. White [40]
publishers: Grosset & Dunlap; Whitman
1. Tom Swift and His Motor-Cycle; or, Fun and Adventure on the Road (1910)
2. Tom Swift and His Motor-Boat; or, The Rivals of Lake Carlopa (1910)
3. Tom Swift and His Airship; or, The Stirring Cruise of the Red Cloud (1910)
4. Tom Swift and His Submarine Boat; or, Under the Ocean for Sunken Treasure (1910)
5. Tom Swift and His Electric Runabout; or, The Speediest Car on the Road (1910)
6. Tom Swift and His Wireless Message; or, The Castaways of Earthquake Island (1911)
7. Tom Swift Among the Diamond Makers; or, The Secret of Phantom Mountain (1911)
8. Tom Swift in the Caves of Ice; or, The Wreck of the Airship (1911)
9. Tom Swift and His Sky Racer; or, The Quickest Flight on Record (1911)
10. Tom Swift and His Electric Rifle; or, Daring Adventures in Elephant Land (1911)
11. Tom Swift in the City of Gold; or, Marvelous Adventures Underground (1912)
12. Tom Swift and His Air Glider; or, Seeking the Platinum Treasure (1912)
13. Tom Swift in Captivity; or, A Daring Escape by Airship (1912)
14. Tom Swift and His Wizard Camera; or, Thrilling Adventures While Taking Moving Pictures (1912) [alternate subtitle: The Perils of Moving Picture Taking]
15. Tom Swift and His Great Searchlight; or, On the Border for Uncle Sam (1912)
16. Tom Swift and His Giant Canon; or, The Longest Shots on Record (1913)
17. Tom Swift and His Photo Telephone; or, The Picture That Saved a Fortune (1914)
18. Tom Swift and His Aerial Warship; or, The Naval Terror of the Seas (1915)
19. Tom Swift and His Big Tunnel; or, The Hidden City of the Andes (1916)
20. Tom Swift in the Land of Wonders; or, The Underground Search for the Idol of Gold (1917)
21. Tom Swift and His War Tank; or, Doing His Bit for Uncle Sam (1918) [alternate subtitle: Doing His Best for Uncle Sam]
22. Tom Swift and His Air Scout; or, Uncle Sam's Mastery of the Sky (1919)
23. Tom Swift and His Undersea Search; or, The Treasure on the Floor of the Atlantic (1920)
24. Tom Swift Among the Fire Fighters; or, Battling with Flames From the Air (1921)
25. Tom Swift and His Electric Locomotive; or, Two Miles a Minute on the Rails (1922)
26. Tom Swift and His Flying Boat; or, The Castaways of the Giant Iceberg (1923)
27. Tom Swift and His Great Oil Gusher; or, The Treasure of Goby Farm (1924)
28. Tom Swift and His Chest of Secrets; or, Tracing the Stolen Inventions (1925)
29. Tom Swift and His Airline Express; or, From Ocean to Ocean by Daylight (1926)
30. Tom Swift Circling the Globe; or, The Daring Cruise of the Air Monarch (1927)

31. Tom Swift and His Talking Pictures; or, The Greatest Invention on Record (1928)
32. Tom Swift and His House on Wheels; or, A Trip to the Mountain of Mystery (1929)
33. Tom Swift and His Big Dirigible; or, Adventures of the Forest of Fire (1930)
34. Tom Swift and His Sky Train; or, Overland Through the Clouds (1931)
35. Tom Swift and His Giant Magnet; or, Bringing Up the Lost Submarine (1932)
36. Tom Swift and His Television Detector; or, Trailing the Secret Plotters (1933)
37. Tom Swift and His Ocean Airport; or, Foiling the Haargolanders (1934)
38. Tom Swift and His Planet Stone; or, Discovering the Secret of Another World (1935)
39. Tom Swift and His Giant Telescope (1939)
40. Tom Swift and His Magnetic Silencer (1941)

1124. TOM SWIFT JR. ADVEN-TURES [see also TOM SWIFT]

author: Victor Appleton II [pseudonym]
publisher: Grosset & Dunlap
1. Tom Swift and His Jetmarine (1954)
2. Tom Swift and His Rocket Ship (1954)
3. Tom Swift and His Giant Robot (1954)
4. Tom Swift and His Atomic Earth Blaster (1954)
5. Tom Swift and His Outpost in Space (1955)
6. Tom Swift and His Diving Seacopter (1956)
7. Tom Swift on the Phantom Satellite (1956)
8. Tom Swift and His Ultrasonic Cycloplane (1957)
9. Tom Swift and His Deep-Sea Hydrodome (1958)
10. Tom Swift in the Race to the Moon (1958)
11. Tom Swift and His Space Solartron (1958)
12. Tom Swift and His Spectromarine Selector (1960)

13. Tom Swift and His Triphibian Atomicar (1962)
14. Tom Swift in the Caves of Nuclear Fire
15. Tom Swift and His Flying Lab
16. Tom Swift and His Electronic Retroscope
17. Tom Swift and the Cosmic Astronauts

1125. TOMMY TIPTOP

author: Raymond Stone [pseudonym of the Stratemeyer Syndicate]
illustrators: R. Mencl [5]; R. Emmett Owen [6]
publishers: Graham & Matlack [1–5]; C. E. Graham Co. [6]
1. Tommy Tiptop and His Baseball Nine; or, The Boys of Riverdale and Their Good Times (1912)
2. Tommy Tiptop and His Football Eleven; or, A Great Victory and How It Was Won (1912)
3. Tommy Tiptop and His Winter Sports; or, Jolly Times on the Ice and in Camp (1912)
4. Tommy Tiptop and His Boat Club; or, The Young Hunters of Hemlock Island (1914)
5. Tommy Tiptop and His Boy Scouts; or, The Doings of the Silver Fox Patrol (1915)
6. Tommy Tiptop and His Great Show; or, Raising Some Money That Was Needed (1917)

1126. TOP NOTCH DETECTIVE STORIES

author: William Hall
publisher: Cupples & Leon
1. Show Vengence; or, The Mystery of Pete Shine (1934)
2. Green Fire; or, The Mystery of the Indian Diamond (1934)
3. Hidden Danger; or, The Secret of the Bank Vault (1934)

1127. TOYLAND I

author: Mary Herrick Bird
publisher: Edward Stern
1. How the Indian Suit Ran Away (1908)

1128. TOYLAND II
author: Josephine Lawrence
publisher: Barse
1. The Unhappy Paper Doll (1928)
2. [title unknown]
3. The Dollville Railroad (1928)

1129. TRAIL BLAZERS
authors: Edward L. Sabin [1–6, 10–14];
    H.C. Forbes-Lindsey [7–8]; Charles
    Fletcher Allen [9]
illustrators: Charles H. Stephens; Lyle
    Justis; Will Thomson
publisher: J. B. Lippincott
1. With Carson and Fremont (1912)
2. On the Plains with Custer (1913)
3. Buffalo Bill and the Overland Trail
4. Gold Seekers of '49
5. With Sam Houston in Texas (1916)
6. Opening the West with Lewis and
    Clark (1917)
7. Captain John Smith
8. Daniel Boone, Backwoodsman
9. David Crockett, Scout
10. Lost with Lieutenant Pike (1919)
11. Into Mexico with General Scott
    (1920)
12. With George Washington into the
    West (1924)
13. In the Ranks of Old Hickory (1927)
14. Klondike Pardners (1929)

**1130. TRAILER STORIES FOR
    GIRLS**
author: Mildred A. Wirt
publisher: Cupples & Leon
1. The Crimson Cruiser (1937)
2. The Runaway Caravan (1937)
3. Timbered Treasure (1937)
4. The Phantom Trailer (1938)

**1131. TRAP TO CATCH A SUN-
    BEAM [see also SUNBEAM]**
author: Mrs. Henry S. Mackarness
publisher: J. Miller
1. Old Joliffe: Not a Goblin Story (1880)
2. The Cloud with the Silver Lining and
    Other Stories (1880)
3. The Dream Chintz (1881)

1132. TRIANGULAR LEAGUE
author: Albertus T. Dudley

publisher: Lothrop, Lee & Shepard
1. The School Four (1909)
2. At the Home Plate
3. Unofficial Prefect (1916)

1133. TRIGGER BERG
author: Leo Edwards [pseudonym of
    Edward Edson Lee]
illustrator: Bert Salg
publisher: Grosset & Dunlap
1. Trigger Berg and the Treasure Tree
    (1930)
2. Trigger Berg and His 700 Mouse Traps
    (1930)
3. Trigger Berg and the Sacred Pig (1931)
4. Trigger Berg and the Cockeyed Ghost
    (1933)

1134. TRIPLETS
author: Bertha B. Moore
publisher: Eerdmans
1. The Baers' Christmas (1938)
2. The Three Baers (1938)
3. The Triplets in Business (1939)
4. The Triplets Go South (1940)
5. The Triplets Over J.O.Y. (1941)
6. The Triplets Go Places (1942)
7. The Triplets Sign Up (1943)
8. The Triplets Become Good Neighbors
    (1945)
9. The Triplets Receive a Reward (1946)
10. The Triplets Have an Adventure
    (1947)
11. The Triplets Make a Discovery
    (1948)
12. The Triplets Fly High (1950)
13. The Triplets Go to Camp (1952)
14. The Triplets Take Over (1953)
15. The Triplets Try Television (1954)

1135. TRIXIE BELDEN
authors: Julie Campbell [1–6]; Kathryn
    Kenny [7–19]
publisher: Whitman
1. Trixie Belden and the Secret of the
    Mansion (1948)
2. Trixie Belden and the Red Trailer Mys-
    tery (1950)
3. Trixie Belden and the Gatehouse Mys-
    tery (1951)
4. Trixie Belden and the Mysterious Visi-
    tor (1954)

5. Trixie Belden and the Mystery Off Glen Road (1956)
6. Trixie Belden and the Mystery in Arizona (1958)
7. Trixie Belden and the Black Jacket Mystery (1960)
8. Trixie Belden and the Mysterious Code (1961)
9. Trixie Belden and the Happy Valley Mystery (1961)
10. Trixie Belden and the Marshland Mystery (1962)
11. Trixie Belden and the Mystery at Bob-White Cave (1963)
12. Trixie Belden and the Mystery of the Blinking Eye (1963)
13. Trixie Belden and the Mystery on Cobbett's Island (1963)
14. Trixie Belden and the Mystery of the Emeralds (1964)
15. Trixie Belden and the Mystery on the Mississippi (1965)
16. Trixie Belden and the Mystery of the Missing Heiress (1965)
17. Trixie Belden and the Mystery of the Uninvited Guest
18. Trixie Belden and the Mystery of the Phantom Grasshopper
19. Trixie Belden and the Secret of the Unseen Treasure

1136. TRUDY AND TIMOTHY
author: Bertha Currier Porter
publisher: Penn
1. Trudy and Timothy (1917)
2. Trudy and Timothy Out-of-Doors (1919)
3. Trudy and Timothy and the Trees (1920)
4. Trudy and Timothy, Foresters (1922)

1137. TRUE ADVENTURE
author: William Edgar Geil
publisher: Doubleday, Page & Co.
1. Adventures in the African Jungle Hunting Pygmies (1917)

1138. TRUE BLUE; STIRRING STORIES OF NAVAL ACADEMY LIFE
author: Clarke Fitch [pseudonym of Upton Sinclair]

publisher: Street & Smith
1. Clif Faraday's Honor; or, A Pledge to the Enemy (1898)
2. Clif Faraday in Command; or, The Fight of His Life (1899)
3. Clif, The Naval Cadet; or, Exciting Days at Annapolis (1903)

1139. TUCK-ME-IN-TALES [see also SLEEPY-TIME-TALES]
author: Arthur Scott Bailey
illustrator: Harry L. Smith
publisher: Grosset & Dunlap
1. The Tale of Old Mr. Crow (1917)
2. The Tale of Solomon Owl (1917)
3. The Tale of Jasper Jay (1917)
4. The Tale of Rusty Wren (1917)
5. The Tale of Jolly Robin (1917)
6. The Tale of Betsy Butterfly (1918)
7. The Tale of Buster Bumblebee (1918)
8. The Tale of Daddy Longlegs (1918)
9. The Tale of Freddie Firefly (1918)
10. The Tale of Kiddie Katydid (1918)
11. The Tale of Chirpy Cricket (1920)
12. The Tale of Mrs. Ladybug (1921)
13. The Tale of Old Dog Spot (1921)
14. The Tale of the Muley Cow (1921)
15. The Tale of Reddy Woodpecker (1922)
16. The Tale of Grandma Goose (1923)

1140. TUCKER TWINS
author: Nell Speed
publisher: Hurst
1. At Boarding School with the Tucker Twins (1915)
2. Vacation with the Tucker Twins (1916)
3. Back at School with the Tucker Twins (1917)
4. Tripping with the Tucker Twins (1919)
5. A House Party with the Tucker Twins (1921)
6. In New York with the Tucker Twins (1924)

1141. TUFFY BEAN
author: Leo Edwards [pseudonym of Edward Edson Lee]
illustrator: Bert Salg
publisher: Grosset & Dunlap
1. Tuffy Bean's Puppy Days (1931)
2. Tuffy Bean's One-Ring Circus (1931)

3. Tuffy Bean at Funny-Bone Farm
   (1931)
4. Tuffy Bean and the Lost Fortune
   (1932)
5. Tuffy Bean's Hunting Days (1933)

1142. TWILIGHT

author: [unknown]
publishers: Cupples & Leon; Harper
1. Robinson Crusoe (1900)
2. Puss in Boots (1900)
3. Little King Daffodil (1900)
4. The Water Babies; A Fairy Tale for a
   Land Boy (1925)
5. Pinocchio; The Adventures of a Puppet
   (1925)
6. Last Fairy Tales (1884)
7. Laboulaye's Fairy Book; Fairy Tales of
   all Nations (1925)

1143. TWILIGHT ANIMAL

author: George Ethelbert Walsh
publishers: John C. Winston; R.F. Fenno
1–2. [titles unknown]
3. Bumper the White Rabbit and His
   Friends (1922)
4. Bumper the White Rabbit and His
   Enemies (1917)
5–10. [titles unknown]
11. Washer the Raccoon (1918)
[#'s unknown]:
1. Bobby Gray Squirrel (1922)
2. White Tail the Deer (1917)
3. White Tail the Deer's Adventures
   (1922)
4. Buster the Big Brown Bear (1917)

1144. TWILIGHT STORIES FOR LITTLE FOLK

author: Flo Lancaster
publisher: J.A. McCann
1. [title unknown]
2. The Pigmy Pirates (1920)

1145. TWINS

author: Dorothy Whitehill
publisher: Barse & Hopkins
1. Janet, a Twin (1920)
2. Phyllis, a Twin (1920)
3. The Twins in the South (1920)
4. The Twins in the West (1920)
5. The Twins' Summer Vacation (1920)

1146. TWINS OF THE WORLD

author: Lucy Fitch Perkins
publisher: Houghton
1. The Dutch Twins (1911)
2. The Japanese Twins (1912)
3. The Irish Twins (1913)
4. The Eskimo Twins (1914)
5. The Mexican Twins (1915)
6. The Cave Twins (1916)
7. The Belgian Twins (1917)
8. The French Twins (1918)
9. The Spartan Twins (1918)
10. The Scotch Twins (1919)
11. The Italian Twins (1920)
12. The Puritan Twins (1921)
13. The Swiss Twins (1922)
14. The Filipino Twins (1923)
15. The Colonial Twins of Virginia
    (1924)
16. The American Twins of 1812 (1925)
17. The American Twins of the Revolu-
    tion (1926)
18. The Pioneer Twins (1927)
19. The Farm Twins (1928)
20. Kit and Kat; More Adventures of the
    Dutch Twins (1929)
21. The Indian Twins (1930)
22. The Pickaninny Twins (1931)
23. The Norwegian Twins (1933)
24. The Spanish Twins (1934)
25. The Chinese Twins (1935)

1147. TWO AMERICAN BOYS

author: Sherman Crockett
publisher: Hurst
1. Two American Boys with the Allied
   Armies (1915)
2. Two American Boys in the French War
   Trenches
3. Two American Boys with the Dard-
   enelles Battle Fleet
4. Two American Boys Aboard a Sub-
   mersible
5. Two American Boys with Pershing in
   France (1918)

1148. TWO LITTLE FRIENDS

author: Margaret Sidney [pseudonym of
   Harriet Mulford Stone Lothrop]
illustrator: Hermann Heyer
publisher: Lothrop, Lee & Shepard
1. Two Little Friends in Norway (1906)

1149. TWO LITTLE WOMEN

author: Carolyn Wells [pseudonym of
   Mrs. Hadwin Houghton]
illustrator: E.C. Caswell
publisher: Dodd, Mead
1. Two Little Women (1915)
2. Two Little Women and Treasure House
   (1916)
3. Two Little Women on a Holiday (1917)

TWO LIVE BOYS *see* **RAYMOND
   BENSON**

1150. TWO WILD CHERRIES

author: Howard Roger Garis
illustrator: John M. Foster
publishers: Milton Bradley; McLoughlin
   Brothers
1. Two Wild Cherries; or, How Dick and
   Janet Lost Something (1924)
2. Two Wild Cherries in the Country; or,
   How Dick and Janet Saved the Mill
   (1924)
3. Two Wild Cherries in the Woods; or,
   How Dick and Janet Caught the Bear
   (1924)
4. Two Wild Cherries at the Seashore
   (1925)

1151. U.S. MIDSHIPMAN

author: Yates Stirling
publisher: Penn
1. A U.S. Midshipman Afloat
2. A U.S. Midshipman in China
3. A U.S. Midshipman in the Philippines
4. A U.S. Midshipman in Japan
5. A U.S. Midshipman in the South Seas

1152. U.S. SERVICE

author: Francis Rolt-Wheeler
publisher: Lothrop, Lee & Shepard
1. The Boy with the U.S. Survey (1909)
2. The Boy with the U.S. Foresters (1910)
3. The Boy with the U.S. Census (1911)
4. The Boy with the U.S. Fisheries
5. The Boy with the U.S. Indians (1913)
6. The Boy with the U.S. Explorers
   (1914)
7. The Boy with the U.S. Life-Savers
8. The Boy with the U.S. Mail
9. The Boy with the U.S. Weather Men
10. The Boy with the U.S. Trappers

11. The Boy with the U.S. Inventors
12. The Boy with the U.S. Secret Service
13. The Boy with the U.S. Miners
14. The Boy with the U.S. Diplomats
15. The Boy with the U.S. Radio
16. The Boy with the American Red
   Cross
17. The Boy with the U.S. Marines
18. The Boy with the U.S. Naturalists
19. The Boy with the U.S. Navy (1927)

1153. UNCLE DICK'S SERIES

author: Sarah Catherine Martin
publisher: McLoughlin Brothers
1. Old Mother Hubbard (1879)
2. Nursery Rhymes (1889)
3. Little Red Riding Hood (1860)
4. Baby (1879)
5. Jack the Giant Killer (1870)
6. My Mother (1899)
7. Our Pets (1889)

1154. UNCLE FRANK'S SERIES

author: [unknown]
publisher: McLoughlin Brothers
1. Death of Cock Robin (1899)
2. Grandma's Tales (1864)
3. Funny Alphabet (1864)
4. The History of Goody Two Shoes
   (1865)
5. Story of Simple Simon (1869)
6. The History of Jack Spratt and His
   Cat (1899)
7. Whittington and His Cat (1879)
8. Lord Bateman (1861)
9. House that Jack Built (1861)
10. Jack Spratt (1889)
11. The History of Jackey Jingle and
   Sukey Single (1865)

1155. UNCLE SAM'S ARMY BOYS

author: Andrew S. Burley
publisher: M. A. Donohue
1. Uncle Sam's Army Boys on the Rhine;
   or, Bob Hamilton in the Argonne
   Death Trap (1919)
2. Uncle Sam's Army Boys in Italy; or,
   Bob Hamilton Under Fire in the Piave
   District
3. Uncle Sam's Army Boys in Khaki; or,
   Bob Hamilton and the Munition Plant
   Plot

4. Uncle Sam's Army Boys with Old
Glory; or, Bob Hamilton Along Pershing's Trail (1920)

**1156. UNCLE SAM'S BIG PIC-
TURE**
author: Paul Pryor [pseudonym]
publisher: McLoughlin Brothers
1. Pocahontas; or, The Indian Maiden
(1873)
2. The Life of General Putnam (1873)

1157. UNCLE SAM'S BOYS [alter-
nate title: BOYS OF THE ARMY]
[see also ARMY]
author: Harrie Irving Hancock
publisher: Henry Altemus
1. Uncle Sam's Boys in the Ranks; or Two
Recruits in the United States Army
(1910)
2. Uncle Sam's Boys on Field Duty; or,
Winning Corporal's Chevrons (1911)
3. Uncle Sam's Boys as Sergeants; or,
Handling Their First Real Commands
(1911)
4. Uncle Sam's Boys on Their Mettle; or,
A Chance to Win Officers' Commissions (1911)
5. Uncle Sam's Boys in the Philippines;
or, Following the Flag Against the
Moros (1912)
6. Uncle Sam's Boys as Lieutenants; or,
Serving Old Glory as Line Officers
(1919)
7. Uncle Sam's Boys with Pershing's
Troops at the Front; or Dick Prescott at
Grips with the Boche (1919)
8. Uncle Sam's Boys Smash the Germans;
or, Winding Up the Great War (1919)

1158. UNCLE SAM'S NAVY BOYS
[alternate title: NAVY BOYS]
author: Jasper Martin
publisher: M. A. Donohue
1. Uncle Sam's Navy Boys with the Submarine Chasers; or, On Patrol Duty in
the North Sea (1919)
2. Uncle Sam's Navy Boys Afloat; or, The
Raid Along the Atlantic Seaboard
3. Uncle Sam's Navy Boys in Action; or,
Running Down Enemy Commerce
Destroyers

4. Uncle Sam's Navy Boys with the
Marines; or, Standing Like a Rock at
Chateau Thierry (1920)

1159. UNCLE TOBY'S SERIES
author: [unknown]
publisher: McLoughlin Brothers
1. Dick Whittington and His Cat (1879)
2. Naughty Puppies (1886)
3. Dame Duck's Lecture (1886)
4. Dog Trusty (1886)
5. Tommy Tatters (1889)
6. Little Totty (1886)

1160. UNCLE WIGGILY [see also
BEDTIME STORIES]
author: Howard Roger Garis
publishers: A.L. Burt; Platt & Munk;
Whitman; Charles E. Graham; American Crayon Co.
1. Uncle Wiggily's Adventures (1912)
2. Uncle Wiggily's Automobile (1913)
3. Uncle Wiggily's Fortune (1913)
4. Uncle Wiggily's Travels (1913)
5. Uncle Wiggily's Fortune (1913)
6. Uncle Wiggily's Journey (1914)
7. Uncle Wiggily Longears (1915)
8. Uncle Wiggily at the Seashore (1915)
9. Uncle Wiggily's Airship (1915)
10. Uncle Wiggily and Mother Goose
(1916)
11. Uncle Wiggily in the Country (1916)
12. Uncle Wiggily in the Woods (1917)
13. Uncle Wiggily's Arabian Nights (1917)
14. Uncle Wiggily on the Farm (1918)
15. Uncle Wiggily's Story Book (1918)
16. Uncle Wiggily and Alice in Wonderland (1918)
17. Uncle Wiggily and Alice in Wonderland (1918)
18. Uncle Wiggily's Apple Roast; or, How
Nurse Jane's Pin Cushion Fooled the
Skuddlemagoon (1919)
19. Uncle Wiggily's Hallowe'en Party
(1919)
20. How He Helped Jack Frost (1919)
21. Uncle Wiggily's Auto Sled; or, How
Mr. Hedgehog Helped Him Get Up
the Slippery Hill (1920) with: How
Uncle Wiggily Made a Snow Pudding;
with: What Happened in the Snow
Fort

65. Uncle Wiggily's Empty Watch (1927)
66. Uncle Wiggily and the Beaver Boys (1927)
67. Uncle Wiggily's Fishing Trip; or, The Good Luck He Had with the Clothes Hook (1927) with: How the Pip and Skee Were Struck by the Chestnut Burrs; with: The Good Time at the Marshmallow Roast
68. Uncle Wiggily and the Turkey Gobler; or, The Battle of Cranberry Hill (1927)
69. Uncle Wiggily's Water Spout (1927)
70. Uncle Wiggily's Puzzle Book (1928)
71. Uncle Wiggily and the Sea Urchin (1929)
72. Uncle Wiggily's Blow-Up Surprise (1929)
73. Uncle Wiggily's Make Believe Tarts (1929)
74. Uncle Wiggily's Ice Boat (1929)
75. Uncle Wiggily's Water Spout; or, What Came of an April Shower (1929)
76. Uncle Wiggily and His Friend Jack Frost (1929)
77. Uncle Wiggily's Rolling Hoop (1929)
78. Uncle Wiggily's Wash Tub Ship (1929)
79. Uncle Wiggily's Snow Fort (1929)
80. Uncle Wiggily's Bungalow (1930)
81. Uncle Wiggily's Icicle Spear; or, The Battle with the Two Bad Chaps (1931) with: Uncle Wiggily Captures the Skee; with: Uncle Wiggily's Trick Skating
82. Uncle Wiggily's Blunder Pup; or, Uncle Wiggily Sees Some Dog Tricks (1933)
83. Uncle Wiggily and the Snowball Eggs (1933)
84. Uncle Wiggily's Christmas Tennis Racket (1933)
85. Uncle Wiggily and His Friends (1939)
86. Uncle Wiggily's Story Book (1939)
87. Uncle Wiggily and the Snow Plow (1939)
88. Uncle Wiggily and the Pepperment (1939)
89. Uncle Wiggily Learns to Dance (1939)
90. Uncle Wiggily and the Apple Dumpling (1939)

91. Uncle Wiggily and the Red Spots (1939)
92. Uncle Wiggily and the Sleds (1939)
93. Uncle Wiggily and the Canoe (1939)
94. Uncle Wiggily and the Barber (1939)
95. Uncle Wiggily and the Sleds (1939)
96. Uncle Wiggily and His Friends (1939)
97. Uncle Wiggily's Travels (1939)
98. Uncle Wiggily and the Pirates; or, How the Enemy Craft of Private Fox Was Sunk (1940) with: How the Bobcat Nearly Spoiled a Nutting Party; with: Uncle Wiggily and Nurse Jane Gather Mayflowers
99. Uncle Wiggily on Roller Skates; or, What Happened When the Skillery Scallery Alligator Gave Chase (1940)
100. Uncle Wiggily in the Country (1940)
101. Uncle Wiggily and the Littletails (1942)
102. Uncle Wiggily's Fortune (1942)
103. Uncle Wiggily and the Cowbird: Read the Stories: Color the Pictures (1943)
104. Uncle Wiggily Starts Off (1943)
105. Uncle Wiggily and the Troublesome Boys (1943)
106. Uncle Wiggily and the Red Monkey (1943)
107. Uncle Wiggily and Granddaddy Longlegs (1943)
108. Uncle Wiggily and the Paper Boat (1943)
109. Uncle Wiggily and the Black Cricket (1943)
110. Uncle Wiggily and the Milkman (1943)
111. Uncle Wiggily Helps Jimmy: 12 Stories (1946)
112. Uncle Wiggily's Happy Days (1947)
113. Uncle Wiggily's Happy Days (1947)

UNITED STATES NAVAL SERIES *see* **RALPH OSBORN]**

1161. UP AND DOING [*see also* **FAIRVIEW BOYS**]
author: Frederick Gordon [pseudonym of the Stratemeyer Syndicate]
publisher: Graham & Matlack

1. The Young Crusoes of Pine Island; or,
   The Wreck of the Puff (1912)
2. Sammy Brown's Treasure Hunt; or,
   Lost in the Mountains (1912)
3. Bob Bouncer's Schooldays; or, The
   Doings of a Real, Live Everyday Boy
   (1912)

1162. UPWARD AND ONWARD

author: Oliver Optic [pseudonym of
William Taylor Adams]
publisher: Lee & Shepard
1. Field and Forest; or, The Fortunes of a
   Farmer (1871)
2. Plane and Plank; or, The Mishaps of a
   Mechanic (1870)
3. Desk and Debit; or, The Catastrophes
   of a Clerk (1871)
4. Cringle and Cross-Tree; or, The Sea
   Swashes of a Sailor (1872)
5. Bivouac and Battle; or, The Struggles
   of a Soldier (1871)
6. Sea and Shore; or, The Tramp of a
   Traveller (1872)

1163. VALENTINE'S BOOK TOYS DOLLY SERIES

author: [unknown]
publisher: Valentine & Sons
1. Black Sambo (1900)

1164. VARSITY [see also FIRESIDE HENTY; HENTY]

author: George Alfred Henty
publisher: W.B. Conkey
1. Facing Death; or, The Hero of the
   Vaughan Pit: A Tale of the Coal Mines
   (1900)

1165. VASSAR

authors: Dinah Maria Mulock [1]; Annie
Emma Armstrong Challice [2]; L.T.
Meade [3]
publisher: W.L. Allison
1. The Adventures of a Brownie as Told
   to My Child (1900)
2. Three Bright Girls; A Story of Chance
   and Mischance (1899)
3. Deb and the Duchess; A Story for Boys
   and Girls (1890)

1166. VASSAR SERIES FOR GIRLS [see also SCHONBERG-COTTA]

authors: Mrs. Molesworth [21]; Elizabeth
Rundle Charles [22]; Juliana Horatia
Gatty Ewing [23]
publisher: Donohue Brothers
1–20. [titles unknown]
  21. Robin Redbreast; a Story for Girls
      (1897)
  22. Chronicles of the Schonberg-Cotta
      Family (1900)
  23. Six to Sixteen; A Story for Girls
      (1899)

1167. VENTURE BOYS

author: Howard Roger Garis
illustrator: Perc E. Cowen
publisher: Harper and Brothers
1. The Venture Boys Afloat; or, The
   Wreck of the Fausta (1917)
2. The Venture Boys in Camp; or, The
   Mystery of Kettle Hill (1918)

1168. VICKI BARR FLIGHT STEWARDESS

authors: Helen Wells [1–4,9–14]; Julie
Tatham [5–8]
publisher: Grosset & Dunlap
1. Silver Wings for Vicki (1947)
2. Vicki Finds the Answer (1947)
3. The Hidden Valley Mystery (1948)
4. The Secret of Magnolia Manor (1949)
5. The Clue of the Broken Blossom
   (1950)
6. Behind the White Veil (1951)
7. The Mystery at Hartwood House
   (1952)
8. Peril Over the Airport (1953)
9. The Mystery of the Vanishing Lady
   (1954)
10. The Search for the Missing Twin
    (1957)
11. The Ghost at the Waterfall (1960)
12. The Clue of the Gold Coin (1961)
13. The Mystery of Flight 908 (1962)
14. The Mystery of the Brass Idol (1964)

1169. VICTOR

author: Ednah Dow Littlehale Cheney
publisher: Educational Trading Companies
1. Jenny of the Lighthouse (1877)

1170. VICTORY
author: Robina F. Hardy
publisher: T. Nelson & Sons
1. Phemie's Fortune (1893)
2. The Story of a Coral Necklace (1889)

1171. VICTORY ALGER
author: Horatio Alger, Jr. [pseudonym]
publisher: M.A. Donohue
1. Adrift in New York
2. Andy Grant's Pluck
3. Driven from Home
4. In a New World
5. Jed, the Poorhouse Boy
6. Luke Walton
7. Risen from the Ranks
8. Shifting for Himself
9. Sink or Swim
10. Store Boy
11. Tony, the Tramp
12. Young Explorer
13. Harry Vane; or, In a New World (1920)

VICTORY BOY SCOUTS *see* HICK-
   ORY RIDGE BOY SCOUTS

1172. VIRGINIA
author: Helen Sherman Griffith
publisher: Penn
1. Oh, Virginia! (1920)
2. No, Virginia! (1922)
3. Now, Virginia! (1923)
4. Why, Virginia! (1924)
5. Yes, Virginia! (1928)
6. Hail, Virginia! (1930)

1173. VIRGINIA DAVIS
author: Grace May North [pseudonym of
   Carol Norton]
publisher: A.L. Burt
1. Virginia of V.M. Ranch (1924)
2. Virginia at Vine Haven (1924)
3. Virginia's Adventure Club (1924)
4. Virginia's Ranch Neighbors (1924)
5. Virginia's Romance (1924)

1174. WALNUT GROVE
authors: D.S. Erickson [1]; Mary Atkins
   [2]
publishers: Henry A. Sumner; H.A.
   Young
1. Good Measure (1880)

2. Little Pea-Nut Merchant; or, Harvard's
   Aspirations (1869)
3. Carl Bartlett; or, What Can I Do
   (1869)

1175. WAR
author: Harry Castlemon [pseudonym of
   Charles Austin Fosdick]
illustrator: George G. White
publisher: Porter & Coates
1. True to His Colors (1889)
2. Rodney, the Partisan (1890)
3. Marcy, the Blockade-Runner (1891)
4. Marcy, the Refugee (1892)
5. Rodney, the Overseer (1892)
6. Sailor Jack, the Trader (1893)

WAR ADVENTURE *see* DAVE DAW-
   SON

1176. WAR FOR THE UNION
author: Everett Titsworth Tomlinson
publisher: Lothrop, Lee & Shepard
1. For the Stars and Stripes (1909)
2. The Young Blockaders (1910)

1177. WAR OF 1812
author: Everett Titsworth Tomlinson
publisher: Lothrop, Lee & Shepard
1. The Search for Andrew Field (1895)
2. The Boy Soldiers of 1812
3. The Boy Officers of 1812
4. Tecumseh's Young Braves
5. Guarding the Border
6. The Boys with Old Hickory
7. The Boy Sailors of 1812 (1900)

**1178. WAR OF THE REVOLU-
   TION**
author: Everett Titsworth Tomlinson
publishers: W. A. Wilde; Grosset & Dunlap
1. Three Colonial Boys (1895)
2. Three Young Continentals
3. Washington's Young Aides
4. Two Young Patriots
5. In the Camp of Cornwallis (1902)

1179. WARD HILL
author: Everett Titsworth Tomlinson
publishers: Rowland; Gold
1. Ward Hill at Weston (1897)

2. Ward Hill the Senior
3. Ward Hill at College
4. Ward Hill the Teacher (1909)

WARNE'S STAR *see* **STAR**

1180. WARNE'S THEN AND NOW JUVENILE SERIES
author: [unknown]
publisher: Frederick Warne
1. Cock Robin and Other Nursery Tales (1865)
2. Tom Thumb and Other Nursery Tales (1865)
3. Valentine and Orson; and Other Tales (1880)

1181. WAY TO WIN
author: Robina F. Hardy
publisher: T. Nelson & Sons
1. The Launch of the Victory (1891)
2. Frieda's First Lesson (1887)
3. The Ghost of Greythorn Manor (1887)

1182. WEBSTER
author: Frank V. Webster
publisher: Cupples & Leon
1. Only a Farm Boy; or, Dan Hardy's Rise in Life (1909)
2. Tom, the Telephone Boy; or, The Mystery of a Message
3. The Boy From the Ranch; or, Roy Bradner's City Experiences
4. The Young Treasure Hunter; or, Fred Stanley's Trip to Alaska
5. Bob, the Castaway; or, The Wreck of the Eagle
6. The Young Firemen of Lakeville; or, Herbert Dare's Pluck
7. The News Boy Partners; or, Who Was Dick Box
8. The Boy Pilot of the Lakes; or, Nat Morton's Perils
9. Two Boy Gold Miners; or, Lost in the Mountains
10. Jack, the Runaway; or, On the Road with the Circus
11. Comrades of the Saddle; or, The Young Rough Riders of the Plains
12. The Boys of Bellwood School; or, Frank Jordan's Triumph
13. Bob Chester's Grit; or, From Ranch to Riches
14. Airship Andy; or, The Luck of a Brave Boy
15. The High School Rivals; or, Fred Markham's Struggles
16. Darry, the Lifesaver; or, The Heroes of the Coast
17. Dick, the Bank Boy; or, A Missing Fortune
18. Ben Hardy's Flying Machine; or, Making a Record for Himself
19. The Boys of the Wireless; or, A Stirring Rescue from the Deep
20. Harry Watson's High School; or, The Rivals of Riverton
21. The Boy Scouts of Lennox; or, The Hike Over Big Bear Mountain
22. Tom Taylor at West Point; or, The Old Army Officer's Secret
23. Cowboy Dave; or, The Round-Up at Rolling River
24. The Boys of the Battleship; or, For the Honor of Uncle Sam
25. Jack of the Pony Express; or, The Young Rider of the Mountain Trails

1183. WEE WINKLES
author: Gabrielle E. Jackson
publisher: Harper
1. Wee Winkles and Wideaway (1905)
2. Wee Winkles and Snowball (1906)
3. Wee Winkles and Her Friends (1907)
4. Wee Winkles at the Mountains (1908)

1184. WELCOME FRIEND
author: Oliver Optic [pseudonym of William Taylor Adams]
publisher: Street & Smith
1-2. [titles unknown]
3. Three Young Silver Kings; or, At Fortune's Call (1887)
4. Making a Man of Himself; or, Right Makes Might (1884)

1185. WELLWORTH COLLEGE
author: Leslie W. Quirk
publisher: L-B
1. Fourth Down (1913)
2. The Freshman Eight
3. The Third Strike
4. Ice-Boat Number One (1916)

1186. WENDY BRENT

author: Dorothy Deming
publishers: Mead [1]; Dodd, Mead [2–4]
1. The Curious Calamity in Ward 8 (1954)
2. The Strange Disappearance From Ward 2 (1956)
3. The Mysterious Discovery in Ward K (1959)
4. The Baffling Affair in the County Hospital (1962)

1187. WEST POINT I

author: Frederick Garrison [pseudonym of Upton Sinclair]
publisher: David McKay
1. Off for West Point
2. A Cadet's Honor
3. On Guard
4. The West Point Treasure
5. The West Point Rivals

1188. WEST POINT II

author: Harrie Irving Hancock
publisher: Henry Altemus
1. Dick Prescott's First Year at West Point; or, Two Chums in the Cadet Gray (1910)
2. Dick Prescott's Second Year at West Point; or, Finding the Glory of the Soldier's Life (1911)
3. Dick Prescott's Third Year at West Point; or, Standing Firm for Flag and Honor (1911)
4. Dick Prescott's Fourth Year at West Point; or, Ready to Drop the Gray for Shoulder Straps (1911) [alternate subtitle: Dropping the Gray for Shoulder Straps]

1189. WEST POINT III

author: Paul B. Malone
publisher: Penn
1. Winning His Way at West Point (1904)
2. A Plebe at West Point
3. A West Point Yearling
4. A West Point Cadet
5. A West Point Lieutenant (1911)

1190. WESTERN STAR

author: Ned Buntline
publisher: J.S. Ogilvie

1. Buffalo Bill and His Adventures in the West (1886)

1191. WESTY MARTIN [*see also* various BOY SCOUT series]

author: Percy Kees Fitzhugh
illustrators: Howard L. Hastings [5–7]; Richard A. Holberg [3]; Machtey [8]
publisher: Grosset & Dunlap
1. Westy Martin (1924)
2. Westy Martin in the Yellowstone (1924)
3. Westy Martin in the Rockies (1925)
4. Westy Martin on the Santa Fe Trail
5. Westy Martin on the Old Indian Trail (1928)
6. Westy Martin in the Land of the Purple Sage (1929)
7. Westy Martin on the Mississippi (1930)
8. Westy Martin in the Sierras (1931)

1192. WHISPERING PINES

author: Elijah Kellogg
publisher: Lee & Shepard
1. The Sophomores of Radcliffe; or, James Trafton and His Bosum Friends (1871)
2. Winning His Spurs; or, Henry Morton's First Trial (1873)

1193. WHITE RIBBON BOYS

author: Raymond Sperry, Jr. [pseudonym of Howard Roger Garis]
publisher: Cupples & Leon
1. White Ribbon Boys of Chester; or, The Old Tavern Keeper's Secret (1916)
2. White Ribbon Boys at Long Shore; or, The Rescue of Dan Bates (1916)

1194. WIDE AWAKE GIRLS

author: Katherine Ruth Ellis
publisher: Little
1. The Wide Awake Girls (1908)
2. The Wide Awake Girls at Winsted (1909)
3. The Wide Awake Girls at College (1910)

1195. WILD ADVENTURE

author: Edward Sylvester Ellis
publishers: F.F. Lovell; International Book Co.

1. On the Trail of Geronimo; or, In the Apache Country (1889)
2. The White Mustang; or, A Tale of the Lone Star State (1889)
3. The Land of Mystery (1889)

1196. WILLIE WINKIE
author: [unknown]
publisher: McLoughlin Brothers
1. Lucy and Dickey, and Other Tales (1870)

1197. WINDERMERE
authors: [listed after titles]
publisher: Rand McNally
1. The Life and Adventures of Robinson Crusoe (1916) [Daniel Defoe]
2. Robin Hood (1928) [Edith Heath]
3. Grimm's Fairy Tales (1913) [Jacob Grimm]
4. Treasure Island (1915) [Robert Louis Stevenson]
5. The Adventures of Remi (1925) [Hector Malot]
6. Tanglewood Tales (1913) [Nathaniel Hawthorne]
7. King Arthur and His Knights; A Noble and Joyous History (1924) Thomas Mallory]
8. Fairy Tales by the Brothers Grimm (1913) [Jacob Grimm]
9. Gulliver's Travels (1912) [Jonathan Swift]
10. Fairy Tales (1936) [Hans Christian Anderson]
11. Tales of India (1935) [Rudyard Kipling]
12. Heidi: A Story for Children and Those Who Love Children (1921) [Johanna Spyri]
13. Hans Brinker; or, The Silver Skates (1936) [Mary Mapes Dodge]
14. Twenty Thousand Leagues under the Sea (1922) [Jules Verne]
15. Ivanhoe: A Romance (1918) [Walter Scott]
16. The Swiss Family Robinson; or, Adventures on a Desert Island (1916) [Johann David Wyss]
17. Kidnapped; Being Memoirs of the Adventures of David Balfour in the Year 1751 (1938) [Robert Louis Stevenson]
18. A Wonder-Book for Girls and Boys (1913) [Nathaniel Hawthorne]
19. Alice's Adventures in Wonderland and Through the Looking-Glass (1916) [Lewis Carroll]

1198. WINNER
author: Everett Titsworth Tomlinson
publisher: American Baptist Publication Society; Gold
1. The Winner (1903)
2. Winning His W
3. Winning His Degree (1905)

1199. WINONA
author: Margaret Widdemer
publisher: J. B. Lippincott
1. Winona of the Camp Fire (1915)
2. Winona of Camp Karonya (1917)
3. Winona's War Farm (1918)
4. Winona's Way: A Story of Reconstruction (1919)
5. Winona On Her Own (1922)
6. Winona's Dreams Come True (1923)

1200. WINTER SUNSHINE
author: Margaret Sidney [pseudonym of Harriet Mulford Stone Lothrop]
publisher: D. Lothrop
1. Tressy's Christmas (1880)
2. One Cent (1880)

1201. WINWOOD CLIFF
author: Daniel Wise
publisher: Lee & Shepard
1. Ben Blinker; or, Maggie's Golden Motto, and What it Did for Her Brother (1877)
2. [title unknown]
3. Roderick Ashcourt; A Story Showing How a Manly Boy and a Noble Girl Bravely Battled with Great Troubles (1880)

1202. WISHING-STONE
author: Thornton W. Burgess
publisher: Little, Brown
1. Tommy and the Wishing-Stone
2. Tommy's Wishes Come True
3. Tommy's Change of Heart

1203. WONDER ISLAND BOYS
author: Roger T. Finlay
publisher: New York Book Co.
1. The Castaways (1914)
2. Exploring the Island
3. The Mysteries of the Caverns
4. The Tribesmen
5. The Capture and the Pursuit
6. The Conquest of the Savages
7. Adventures on Strange Islands
8. Treasures of the Islands (1915)

1204. WONDER-STORY
author: [unknown]
publisher: McLoughlin Brothers
1. Jack the Giant Killer (1889)
2. Story of Robin Hood (1889)

1205. WOODBINE
author: Madeline Leslie
publisher: Andrew F. Graves
1. Live and Learn (1868)
2. [title unknown]
3. The Governor's Pardon; or, The Bridge
   of Sighs (1868)
4. Walter and Frank; or, The Apthorp
   Farm (1869)

1206. WOODCRAFT
author: Lilian Elizabeth Becker Roy
illustrators: Walter S. Rogers; H.S. Barbour
publishers: George H. Doran; Grosset &
   Dunlap
1. The Woodcraft Girls at Camp (1916)
2. The Little Woodcrafter's Book (1917)
3. The Woodcraft Girls in the City
   (1918)
4. The Woodcraft Boys at Sunset Island
   (1919)
5. The Little Woodcrafters' Fun on the
   Farm (1928)
6. The Woodcraft Boys in the Rockies
   (1928)
7. The Woodcraft Girls Camping in
   Maine (1928)

WOODCRAFT BOYS see WOOD-
   CRAFT

WOODCRAFT GIRLS see WOOD-
   CRAFT

1207. WOODLAWN
author: Madeline Leslie
publishers: Woolworth, Ainsworth; A.S.
   Barnes; Henry A. Young
1. Bertie's Home; or, The Way to be
   Happy (1868)
2. Bertie and the Painters; or, The Way to
   be Happy (1868)
3. [title unknown]
4. Bertie and the Plumbers; or, The Way
   to be Happy (1868)
5. [title unknown]
6. Bertie and the Gardeners; or, The Way
   to be Happy (1868)

1208. WOODRANGER
author: George Waldo Browne
publisher: L. C. Page
1. The Woodranger (1899)
2. The Young Gunbearer
3. The Hero of the Hills
4. With Roger's Rangers (1906)

1209. WORKING UPWARD
author: Edward Stratemeyer
publishers: Allison; Lee & Shepard
1. The Young Auctioneer (1897)
2. Bound to Be an Electrician (1897)
3. Shorthand Tom, the Reporter (1897)
4. Fighting for His Own (1897)

1210. WORLD ADVENTURE
authors: Osa Johnson [1]; John Harrison
   [2]; Charles Miller [4]; Jean Creasey
   [5]; Gilbert Clarence Klingel [6];
   Howard Hill [7]; Attilio Gatti [8];
   Charles D. Brower [9]; Hassoldt Davis
   [10]; Charles McKew Parr [11]
publisher: R. Hale
1. Jungle Friends (1941)
2. Dusty's Adventure, and Other Stories
   (1959)
3. Life among the Cannibals (1958)
4. Adventure in a London Fog, and Other
   Stories (1959)
5. Round the World in 465 Days
   (1958)
6. Wonders of Inagua, Which Is the
   Name of a Very Lonely and Nearly
   Forgotten Island (1959)
7. Wild Adventure (1959)
8. Jungle Killers (1958)

9. King of the Arctic; A Lifetime of Adventure in the Far North (1958)
10. Nepal, Land of Mystery (1959)
11. So Noble a Captain; The Life and Voyages of Ferdinand Magellan (1958)

1211. WORLD OF ADVENTURE

author: Joseph Berg Esenwein
illustrator: H.G. Nicholas
publisher: McLoughlin Brothers
1. Calling All Boys (1937)
2. Sport and Adventure (1937)
3. Real Stories for Real Girls (1937)

1212. WORLD WAR

author: Joseph Alexander Altsheler
publisher: David Appleton
1. The Guns of Europe (1915)
2. The Hosts of the Air (1915)
3. The Forest of Swords (1915)

1213. WORLD'S WAR

author: James Fiske
publisher: Saalfield
1. Fighting in the Clouds for France
2. Facing the German Foe
3. On Board the Mine-Laying Cruiser
4. Under Fire for Servia
5. With the Belgians to the Front
6. In Russian Trenches
7. At the Fall of Warsaw
8. Fighting in the Alps
9. Shelled by an Unseen Foe
10. With the Heroes of the Marne

1214. WRIGHT AMERICAN FICTION

author: Oliver Optic [pseudonym of William Taylor Adams]
publisher: Research Publications
1. Hatchie, the Guardian Slave
2. In Doors and Out
3. The Way of the World
4. Living Too Fast

1215. WYNDHAM

author: Ralph Henry Barbour
publisher: David Appleton
1. Bases Full (1923)
2. The Fighting Scrub (1924)
3. Hold 'Em Wyndham (1925)

1216. X BAR X BOYS

author: James Cody Ferris [pseudonym of the Stratemeyer Syndicate]
illustrators: Walter S. Rogers [1–10]; J. Clemens Gretter [11–15]; Paul Laune [16–21]
publisher: Grosset & Dunlap
1. The X Bar X Boys on the Ranch (1926)
2. The X Bar X Boys in Thunder Canyon (1926)
3. The X Bar X Boys on Whirlpool River (1926)
4. The X Bar X Boys on Big Bison Trail (1927)
5. The X Bar X Boys at the Round-Up (1927)
6. The X Bar X Boys at Nugget Camp (1928)
7. The X Bar X Boys at Rustlers' Gap (1929)
8. The X Bar X Boys at Grizzly Pass (1929)
9. The X Bar X Boys Lost in the Rockies (1930)
10. The X Bar X Boys Riding for Life (1931)
11. The X Bar X Boys in Smoky Valley (1932)
12. The X Bar X Boys at Copperhead Gulch (1933)
13. The X Bar X Boys Branding the Wild Herd (1934)
14. The X Bar X Boys at the Strange Rodeo (1935)
15. The X Bar X Boys with the Secret Rangers (1936)
16. The X Bar X Boys Hunting the Prize Mustangs (1937)
17. The X Bar X Boys at Triangle Mine (1938)
18. The X Bar X Boys and the Sagebrush Mystery (1939)
19. The X Bar X Boys in the Haunted Gully (1940)
20. The X Bar X Boys Seeking the Lost Troopers (1941)
21. The X Bar X Boys Following the Stampede (1942)

1217. Y.M.C.A BOYS

author: Brooks Henderley [pseudonym of the Stratemeyer Syndicate]

illustrators: Walter S. Rogers [1]; R. Emmett Owen [2–3]
publisher: Cupples & Leon
1. The Y.M.C.A. Boys of Cliffwood; or, The Struggle for the Holwell Prize (1916)
2. The Y.M.C.A Boys on Bass Island; or, The Mystery of Russabaga Camp (1916)
3. The Y.M.C.A. Boys at Football; or, Lively Doings On and Off the Gridiron (1917)

1218. YACHT CLUB
author: Oliver Optic [pseudonym of William Taylor Adams]
illustrator: John Andrew
publisher: Lee & Shepard
1. Little Bobtail; or, The Wreck of the Penobscot (1872)
2. The Yacht Club; or, The Young Boat-Builder (1873)
3. Money-Maker; or, The Victory of the Basilisk (1873)
4. The Coming Wave; or, The Hidden Treasure of High Rock (1874)
5. The Dorcas Club; or, Our Girls Afloat (1874)
6. Ocean-Born; or, The Cruise of the Clubs (1875)

1219. YANK BROWN
author: David Stone
publisher: Barse & Hopkins
1. Yank Brown, Halfback (1921)
2. Yank Brown, Forward
3. Yank Brown, Cross Country Runner
4. Yank Brown, Miler
5. Yank Brown, Pitcher
6. Yank Brown, Honor Man (1925)

1220. YANKEE FLYER
author: Al Avery [pseudonym of R.G. Montgomery]
publisher: Grosset & Dunlap
1. A Yankee Flyer with the R.A.F. (1941)
2. A Yankee Flyer in the Far East
3. A Yankee Flyer in Normandy
4. A Yankee Flyer in North Africa
5. A Yankee Flyer in Italy
6. A Yankee Flyer Over Berlin
7. A Yankee Flyer in the South Pacific
8. A Yankee Flyer on a Rescue Mission

9. A Yankee Flyer Under Sealed Orders (1946)

1221. YANKEE GIRL
author: Alice Turner Curtis
publisher: Penn
1. A Yankee Girl at Fort Sumter (1920)
2. A Yankee Girl at Bull Run (1921)
3. A Yankee Girl at Shiloh (1922)
4. A Yankee Girl at Antietam (1923)
5. A Yankee Girl at Gettysburg (1924)
6. A Yankee Girl at Vicksburg (1926)
7. A Yankee Girl at Hampton Roads (1927)
8. A Yankee Girl at Lookout Mountain (1928)
9. A Yankee Girl at the Battle of the Wilderness (1929)
10. A Yankee Girl at Richmond (1930)

1222. YARDLEY HALL
author: Ralph Henry Barbour
publisher: David Appleton
1. Fourth Down (1908)
2. Forward Pass (1909)
3. Double Play (1909)
4. Winning His Y (1910)
5. Guarding the Goal (1910)
6. For Yardley (1911)
7. Around the End (1913)
8. Changed Signals (1913)

1223. YOUNG AMERICA
author: Dorothy Brooks
publisher: Educational Publishing
1. Stories of the Red Children (1923)

1224. YOUNG AMERICA ABROAD
author: Oliver Optic [pseudonym of William Taylor Adams]
publisher: Lee & Shepard
series 1:
1. Outward Bound; or, Young America Afloat: A Story of Travel and Adventure (1866)
2. Shamrock and Thistle; or, Young America in Ireland and Scotland: A Story of Travel and Adventure (1867)
3. Red Cross; or, Young America in England and Wales: A Story of Travel and Adventure (1895)

4. Dikes and Ditches; or, Young America in Holland and Belgium: A Story of Travel and Adventure (1868)
5. Palace and Cottage; or, Young America in France and Switzerland: A Story of Travel and Adventure (1896)
6. Down the Rhine; or, Young America in Germany: A Story of Travel and Adventure (1869)

series 2:
1. Up the Baltic; or Young America in Norway, Sweden and Denmark: A Story of Travel and Adventure (1871)
2. Northern Lands; or, Young America in Russia and Prussia: A Story of Travel and Adventure (1874)
3. Vine and Olive; or, Young America in Spain and Portugal: A Story of Travel and Adventure (1876)
4. Sunny Shores; or, Young America in Italy and Austria: A Story of Travel and Adventure (1874)
5. Cross and Crescent; or, Young America in Turkey and Greece: A Story of travel and Adventure (1876)
6. Isles of the Sea; or, Young America Homeward Bound: A Story of Travel and Adventure (1905)

YOUNG AMERICA AFLOAT *see* **LOG CABIN**

1225. YOUNG AMERICA LIBRARY FOR BOYS

author: Oliver Optic [pseudonym of William Taylor Adams]
publisher: Hurst
1. The Little Merchant
2. Watch and Wait
3. The Young Lieutenant
4. In School and Out
5. Little by Little
6. Rich and Humble
7. Brave Old Salt
8. Fighting Joe
9. The Yankee Middy
10. Work and Win

1226. YOUNG CONTINENTALS

author: John Thomas McIntyre
publisher: Penn

1. The Young Continentals at Lexington (1909)
2. The Young Continentals at Bunker Hill
3. The Young Continentals at Trenton
4. The Young Continentals at Monmouth (1912)

1227. YOUNG CRUSADERS

author: George P. Atwater
publisher: Little, Brown
1. The Young Crusaders
2. The Young Crusaders at Washington

1228. YOUNG EAGLES

author: Harris Patton
publisher: Gold
1. Young Eagles (1932)
2. Riding Down (1932)

1229. YOUNG ENGINEERS

author: Harrie Irving Hancock
publishers: Henry Altemus; Saalfield
1. The Young Engineers in Colorado; or, At Railroad Building in Earnest (1912)
2. The Young Engineers in Arizona; or, Laying Tracks on the Man-Killer Quicksand (1912)
3. The Young Engineers in Nevada; or, Seeking Fortune on the Turn of a Pick
4. The Young Engineers in Mexico; or, Fighting the Mine Swindlers (1913)
5. The Young Engineers on the Gulf; or, The Mystery of the Million Dollar Break-Water (1920)

1230. YOUNG FARMER

author: George B. Hill
publisher: Penn
1. The Young Farmer (1913)
2. The Young Farmer at College (1914)

1231. YOUNG FOLKS

author: [unknown]
publisher: D. Lothrop
1. The Life and Adventures of Robinson Crusoe (1884)
2. Puss in Boots (1888)
3. Will Phillips; or, Ups and Downs in Christian Boy-Life (1873)

1232. YOUNG HEROES
authors: Ernest L. Thurston (1); Capwell Wyckoff (3)
publisher: Saalfield
1. The Young Boss of Camp Eighteen
2. Tongues of Flame
3. Mystery Hunters on Special Detail

1233. YOUNG HUNTERS
author: Ralph Bonehill [pseudonym of the Stratemeyer Syndicate]
publishers: W. L. Allison; Donohue Bros.
1. Gun and Sled; or, The Young Hunters of Snowtop Island (1900)
2. Young Hunters in Porto [sic.] Rico; or, The Search for a Lost Treasure (1900)

1234. YOUNG KENTUCKIANS
author: Byron Archibald Dunn
publisher: McClurg
1. General Nelson's Scout (1898)
2. On General Thomas' Staff
3. Battling for Atlanta
4. From Atlanta to the Sea
5. Raiding with Morgan (1903)

1235. YOUNG MINERALIST
author: Edwin J. Houston
publisher: Griffith & Rowland
1. A Chip off the Old Block; or, At the Bottom of the Ladder
2. The Land of Drought; or, Across the Great American Desert
3. The Jaws of Death; or, In and Around the Canyons of Colorado

1236. YOUNG MISSOURIANS
author: Byron Archibald Dunn
publisher: McClurg
1. With Lyon in Missouri (1910)
2. The Scout of Pea Ridge
3. The Courier of the Ozarks
4. Storming Vicksburg
5. The Last Raid (1914)

1237. YOUNG PATRIOTS
authors: James Otis [pseudonym of James Otis Kaler] [1–8]; William Pendleton Chipman [9]
illustrators: J. Watson Davis [1–4,6–7]; G.G. White [5]
publisher: A. L. Burt

1. Corporal 'Lige's Recruit; A Story of Crown Point and Ticonderoga (1898)
2. Cruise with Paul Jones; A Story of Naval Warfare in 1778 (1898)
3. Morgan, the Jersey Spy; A Story of the Siege of Yorktown in 1781 (1898)
4. Sarah Dillard's Ride; A Story of the Carolinas in 1780 (1898)
5. Traitor's Escape; A Story of the Attempt to Seize Benedict Arnold After He Had Fled to New York (1898)
6. Tory Plot; A Story of the Attempt to Kill General Washington in 1776 (1899)
7. With the Swamp Fox; A Story of General Marion's Young Spies (1899)
8. On the Kentucky Frontier; A Story of the Fighting Pioneers of the West (1900)
9. The Young Minuteman; A Story of the Capture of General Prescott in 1777 (1899)

YOUNG PIONEERS see PIONEER BOYS I

1238. YOUNG PURITANS
author: Mary Prudence Wells Smith
publishers: Roberts [1–2]; Little, Brown [3–4]
1. The Young Puritans of Old Hadley (1897)
2. The Young Puritans in King Philip's War (1898)
3. The Young Puritans in Captivity (1899)
4. The Young and Old Puritans of Hatfield (1900)

1239. YOUNG REPORTER [*see also* **LARRY DEXTER and GREAT NEWSPAPER**]
author: Howard Roger Garis
publishers: Grosset & Dunlap; George Sully
1. Larry Dexter and the Stolen Boy; or, A Young Reporter on the Lakes (1912)
2. The Young Reporter at the Battle Front; or, A Young War Correspondent's Double Mission (1915) [alternative title: Larry Dexter in Belgium]
3. The Young Reporter at the Big Flood;

or, The Peril's of News Gathering (1907)
4. Larry Dexter's Great Search; or, The Hunt for the Missing Millionaire (1909)
5. Larry Dexter and the Bank Mystery; or, A Young Reporter in Wall Street (1912)

1240. YOUNG SPORTSMAN

author: Ralph Bonehill [pseudonym of the Stratemeyer Syndicate]
publisher: M. A. Donohue
1. The Young Oarsmen of Lakeview; or, The Mystery of Hermit Island (1900)
2. Leo, the Circus Boy; or, Life Under the Great White Canvas (1900)
3. Rival Cyclists; or, Fun and Adventures on the Wheel (1900)

1241. YOUNG TRAILERS

author: Joseph Alexander Altsheler
publisher: David Appleton
1. The Young Trailers (1907)
2. The Forest Runners
3. The Keepers of the Trail

4. The Eyes of the Woods; A Story of the Ancient Wilderness (1917)
5. The Free Rangers
6. The Rifleman of the Ohio
7. The Scouts of the Valley; A Story of Wyoming and the Chemung (1911)
8. The Border Watch (1917)

1242. YOUNG VIRGINIANS [see also various BOY SCOUT series]

author: Byron Archibald Dunn
illustrator: J. Allen St. John
publisher: A. C. McClurg
1. The Boy Scouts of the Shenandoah (1916)
2. With the Army of the Potomac
3. Scouting for Sheridan (1918)

1243. ZERO CLUB

author: Ralph Bonehill
publishers: David McKay; Street & Smith
1. The Tour of the Zero Club; or, Adventures Amid Ice and Snow (1894)
2. The Tour of the Zero Club; or, For Fame and Fortune (1902)

AUTHOR INDEX

References are to bold entry numbers

Abbott, Jacob 644, 735, 987, 988, 989
Adams, Eustace 16
Adams, Harrison *see* Rathborne, George
Adams, William Taylor 6, 24, 28, 37, 59, 61, 105, 107, 138, 145, 146, 147, 148, 156, 157, 221, 224, 229, 231, 261, 411, 427, 428, 443, 444, 496, 497, 519, 530, 549, 563, 567, 590, 594, 663, 672, 673, 677, 722, 731, 737, 738, 771, 818, 861, 862, 863, 864, 869, 871, 935, 1009, 1016, 1051, 1066, 1070, 1085, 1089, 1093, 1162, 1184, 1214, 1218, 1224, 1225
Aimwell, Walter 14
Akers, Floyd *see* Baum, Lyman Frank
Alcott, Louisa May 718, 992
Alden, William Livingstone 565
Aldridge, Janet 770
Alger, Edwin 173
Alger, Horatio 24, 268, 730, 880
Alger, Horatio, Jr. 25, 916, 1171
Allen, Charles Fletcher 1129
Allen, Quincy 875
Allen, Willis Boyd 915
Altsheler, Joseph Alexander 318, 481, 547, 1104, 1212, 1241
Ames, Franklin T. 414
Ames, Marion 382
Amsbary, Mary Anne 623
Anderson, Hans Christian 1197
Andrews, Anna 895
Anthony, Lotta Rowe 55
Appleton, Victor 387, 797, 810, 811, 1123

Appleton, Victor, II 1124
Armstrong, Jack 606
Arnold, Henry Harley 85, 128
Arthur, Timothy Shay 848
Arundel, Louis 799
Ashmun, Margaret 602
Atkins, Mary 527, 1174
Atwater, George P. 1227
Avery, A. 16
Avery, Al *see* Montgomery, R.G.

Bacon, Edward 251
Bacskai, Lotta 515
Bailey, Arthur Scott 348, 1045, 1047, 1139
Bailey, Bernadine 304, 305
Bailey, Carolyn Sherwin 216, 217, 218, 309, 462, 466, 658, 710
Baird, Jean K. 575
Baker, Elizabeth 1096
Baker, Emerson 24
Baker, Emily 1118
Baker, Etta Anthony 420
Baker, Willard F. 160, 188
Ballou, Maturin Murray 1024
Bancroft, Edith 617, 823
Bangs, John Kendrick 866
Banner, R. 232
Barbauld, Anna Letitia 968
Barbour, Ralph Henry 9, 57, 121, 298, 299, 341, 412, 439, 461, 478, 513, 535, 580, 582, 584, 852, 941, 1114, 1215, 1222
Bardwell, Harrison *see* Craine, Edith Janice
Barlett, Philip A. 1000
Barnes, Elmer Tracey 796, 798
Barnum, Vance 474, 640
Barton, George 102
Barton, Olive Roberts 833
Bates, Esther 748

Bates, Gordon *see* Chase, Josephine
Baum, Lyman Frank 70, 183, 358, 458, 646, 717, 763, 787, 867, 879, 1011
Baxter, Betty 98
Beach, Charles Amory 20
Beach, Edward Latimer 50, 955, 986
Begie, Harold 319
Benham, Walter 103
Benson, Elliott 275
Berry, Erick 667
Bertrand, Lee 866
Best, Herbert 667
Bird, Mary Herrick 1127
Bishop, Austin 164
Blackford, Charles Minor 667
Blaine, John 189
Blanchard, Amy Ella 366, 470, 970
Blank, Clair 10, 118
Blyton, Enid 860
Bond, A. Russel 1020
Bonehill, Ralph 185, 186, 451, 487, 664, 779, 1233, 1240, 1243
Bonesteel, Mary Greene 104
Bonner, Richard 187
Bontemps, Arna Wendell 667
Boone, Silas K. 907
Borton, Elizabeth 691, 932
Bowen, Robert Sidney 361, 967
Boylston, Helen Dore 289, 1078
Braddock, Gordon *see* Patten, Gilbert
Braden, James Andrew 81, 230, 235, 600
Brady, Cyrus Townsend 383, 1086
Brainerd, Edna S. 345
Brainerd, Norman 447
Brame, Charlotte M. 1024

ILLUSTRATOR INDEX

References are to bold entry numbers; illustrator names are unknown for many series

TITLE INDEX

References are to bold entry numbers